ELITE STUDENT EDITION

5 STEPS TO A 5

AP Physics C
2024

ELITE STUDENT EDITION

5 STEPS TO A >5™

AP Physics C
2024

Greg Jacobs

Mc Graw Hill

New York   Chicago   San Francisco   Athens   London   Madrid
Mexico City   Milan   New Delhi   Singapore   Sydney   Toronto

1 2 3 4 5 6 7 8 9   LHS   28 27 26 25 24 23
1 2 3 4 5 6 7 8 9   LHS   28 27 26 25 24 23 (Elite Student Edition)

ISBN   978-1-265-34788-8
MHID   1-265-34788-3

e-ISBN   978-1-265-34879-3
e-MHID   1-265-34879-0

ISBN   978-1-265-34918-9 (Elite Student Edition)
MHID   1-265-34918-5

e-ISBN   978-1-265-35062-8 (Elite Student Edition)
e-MHID   1-265-35062-0

McGraw Hill, the McGraw Hill logo, 5 Steps to a 5, and related trade dress are trademarks or registered trademarks of McGraw Hill and/or its affiliates in the United States and other countries and may not be used without written permission. All other trademarks are the property of their respective owners. McGraw Hill is not associated with any product or vendor mentioned in this book.

AP, Advanced Placement Program, and College Board are registered trademarks of the College Board, which was not involved in the production of, and does not endorse, this product.

The series editor was Grace Freedson, and the project editor was Del Franz. Series design by Jane Tenenbaum.

McGraw Hill products are available at special quantity discounts to use as premiums and sales promotions or for use in corporate training programs. To contact a representative, please visit the Contact Us pages at www.mhprofessional.com.

McGraw Hill is committed to making our products accessible to all learners. To learn more about the available support and accommodations we offer, please contact us at accessibility@mheducation.com. We also participate in the Access Text Network (www.accesstext.org), and ATN members may submit requests through ATN.

CONTENTS

STEP 4

Review the Knowledge You Need to Score High

STEP 5   Build Your Test-Taking Confidence

ELITE STUDENT EDITION

5 Minutes to a 5

Appendixes

ACKNOWLEDGMENTS

I extend my thanks to Grace Freedson, who was the driving force behind this book's publication, and especially to Don Reis, who was not only a superb editor but also an unwavering source of support. I also appreciate Ruth Mills's awesome work on the second edition and Bev Weiler and Clara Wente's careful and thorough editing of the questions and example problems for the 2010–2011 edition.

Thank you to Chat Hull and Jessica Broaddus, veterans of my 2002 Physics B class, who provided the idea for two free-response questions.

My 2004 students at Woodberry Forest School were extremely helpful in the development of this book. It was they who served as guinea pigs, reading chapters for clarity and correctness, making suggestions, and finding mistakes. They are Andrew Burns, Jordan Crittenden, David Fulton, Henry Holderness, Michael Ledwith, Johnny Phillips, Rob Sellers, and Chris Straka from Physics C; Wes Abcouwer, Wyatt Bone, Matt Brown, David Goodson, Bret Holbrook, Mike Johnson, Rich Lane, Jake Miller, Jake Reeder, Charles Shackelford, Beau Thomas, David Badham, Marks Brewbaker, Charlton deSaussure, Palmer Heenan, Wilson Kieffer, Brian McCormick, Eli Montague, Christian Rizzuti, Pierre Rodriguez, and Frazier Stowers from Physics B; and Andy Juc, Jamie Taliaferro, Nathan Toms, Matt Laughridge, Jamie Gardiner, Graham Gardiner, Robbie Battle, William Crosscup, Jonas Park, Billy Butler, Bryan May, Fletcher Fortune, and Stuart Coleman from the general physics class. Although Josh and I bear responsibility for all errors in the text, the folks mentioned above deserve credit for minimizing our mistakes.

The idea for the Four-Minute Drill came originally from Keen Johnson Babbage, my seventh-grade social studies teacher. I've borrowed the idea from him for over two decades of teaching AP. Thank you!

The faculty and administration at Woodberry, in particular Jim Reid, the science department chairman, deserve mention. They have been so supportive of me professionally.

Additional thanks go to members of my 2009 AP physics classes who helped edit the practice tests: Min SuKim, Cannon Allen, Collins MacDonald, Luke Garrison, Chris Cirenza, and Landon Biggs. And to later students: Michael Bauer, Vinh Hoang, and Evan Sun.

Most important, I'd like to thank Shari and Milo Cebu for putting up with me during all of my writing projects.

ABOUT THE AUTHOR

GREG JACOBS teaches AP Physics C, AP Physics 1, and conceptual physics at Woodberry Forest School, the nation's premier boarding school for boys. He is a reader and consultant for the College Board—this means he grades the AP Physics exams, and he runs professional development seminars for other AP teachers. Greg is president of the USAYPT, a nonprofit organization promoting physics research at the high school level. Greg was honored as an AP Teacher of the Year by the Siemens Foundation. Outside the classroom, Greg has coached baseball, football, and debate. He umpires high school baseball. He is the lead broadcaster for Woodberry football, baseball, soccer, and basketball. Greg writes a physics teaching blog available at **www.jacobsphysics.blogspot.com**.

INTRODUCTION: THE FIVE-STEP PROGRAM

Welcome!

I know that preparing for the Advanced Placement (AP) Physics exam can seem like a daunting task. There's a lot of material to learn, and some of it can be rather challenging. But I also know that preparing for the AP exam is much easier—and much more enjoyable—if you do it with a friendly guide. So let me introduce myself; my name is Greg, and I'll be your friendly guide for this journey.

Why This Book?

To understand what makes this book unique, you should first know a little bit about who I am. I have taught all versions of AP Physics over the past two decades, helping more than 90% of my Physics C students garner 5s on the exam. I am also an AP Physics question leader—which means I set the rubrics for the AP exams and supervise their scoring.

I know, from my own experiences and from talking with countless other students and teachers, what you *don't* need in a review book. You don't need to be overwhelmed with unimportant, technical details; you don't need to read confusing explanations of arcane topics; you don't need to be bored with a dull text.

Instead, what I think you do need—and what this book provides—are the following:

- A text that's written in clear, simple language.
- A thorough review of every topic you need to know for the AP exam.
- Practice test questions that are exactly in the style and format of the actual AP exams.

Organization of the Book: The Five-Step Program

You will be taking a lengthy, comprehensive exam this May. You want to be well prepared enough that the exam takes on the feel of a command performance, not a trial by fire. Following the Five-Step program is the best way to structure your preparation.

Step 1: Set Up Your Study Program

Physics does not lend itself well to cramming. Success on the AP exam is invariably the result of diligent practice over the course of months, not the result of an all-nighter on the eve of exam day. Step 1 gives you the background and structure you need before you even start exam preparation.

Step 2: Determine Your Test Readiness

I have included a diagnostic test, of course, broken down by topic. But more important to your preparation are the *fundamentals quizzes* in Chapter 4. These quizzes, a unique feature of the *5 Steps to a 5* program, are different from test-style problems.

A problem on the AP exam usually requires considerable problem solving or critical thinking skills. Rare is the AP question that asks about straightforward facts that you can memorize—you'll get maybe one of those on an entire 35-question multiple-choice test. Rather than asking you to spit out facts, the AP exam asks you to use the facts you know to reason deeply about a physical situation. But if you don't know the fundamental facts, you certainly won't be able to reason deeply about anything!

Thus, a good place to start your test preparation is by quizzing yourself. Find out what fundamental facts you know, and which you need to know. The *5 Steps* fundamentals quizzes will diagnose your areas of strength and weakness. Once you can answer every question on a fundamentals quiz quickly and accurately, you are ready for deeper questions that will challenge you on the AP exam.

Step 3: Develop Strategies for Success

Yes, yes, I know you've been listening to general test-taking advice for most of your life. Yet, I have *physics-specific* advice for you. An AP physics test requires a dramatically different approach than does a state standards test or an SAT.

I start you with the secret weapon in attacking an AP test: memorizing equations. I explain *why* you should memorize, then I suggest some ways to make the learning process smoother. Next, I move on to discuss the major types of questions you'll see on the AP exam, and how to approach each with confidence.

Finally, I present you with drills on some of the most common physics situations tested on the AP exams. These exercises will allow you to conquer any fear or uncertainty you may have about your skills.

Step 4: Review the Knowledge You Need to Score High

This is a comprehensive review of all the topics on the AP exam. Now, you've probably been in an AP Physics class all year; you've likely read[1] your textbook. This review is meant to be just that—*review*, in a readable format, and focused exclusively on the AP exam.

These review chapters are appropriate both for quick skimming, to remind yourself of salient points, and for in-depth study, working through each practice problem. I do not go into nearly as much detail as a standard textbook; but the advantage of this lack of detail is that you can focus only on those issues germane to the AP Physics exams.

Step 5: Build Your Test-Taking Confidence

Here are your full-length practice tests. Unlike other practice tests you may take, this one comes with thorough explanations. One of the most important elements in learning physics is making, and then learning from, mistakes. I don't just tell you what you got wrong; I explain why your answer is wrong, and how to do the problem correctly. It's okay to make a mistake here, because if you do, you won't make that same mistake again on that Monday in mid-May.

[1] Or at least tried to read.

The Graphics Used in This Book

To emphasize particular skills and strategies, I use several icons throughout this book. An icon in the margin will alert you that you should pay particular attention to the accompanying text. I use these three icons:

1. This icon points out a very important concept or fact that you should not pass over.

2. This icon calls your attention to a problem-solving strategy that you may want to try.

3. This icon indicates a tip that you might find useful.

Boldfaced words indicate terms that are included in the glossary at the end of the book. Boldface is also used to indicate the answer to a sample problem discussed in the test.

ELITE STUDENT EDITION

5 STEPS TO A 5™

AP Physics C
2024

STEP 1

Set Up Your
Study Program

CHAPTER 1

How to Approach Your AP Physics Course

IN THIS CHAPTER

Summary: Recognize the difference between truly understanding physics and just doing well in your physics class.

Key Ideas

✪ Focus on increasing your knowledge of physics, not on pleasing your teacher.
✪ Don't spend more than 10 minutes at one time on a problem without getting anywhere—come back to it later if you don't get it.
✪ Form a study group; your classmates can help you learn physics better.
✪ If you don't understand something, ask your teacher for help.
✪ Don't cram; although you can memorize equations, the skills you need to solve physics problems can't be learned overnight.

Before we even dive into the nitty-gritty of the AP Physics exam, it's important for you to know that the AP exam is an *authentic* physics test. What this means is that it's not possible to "game" this test—in order to do well, *you must know your physics*. Therefore, the purpose of this book is twofold:

(1) to teach you the ways in which the AP exam tests your physics knowledge, and
(2) to give you a review of the physics topics that will be tested—and to give you some hints on how to approach these topics.

Everyone who takes the AP exam has just completed an AP Physics course. **Recognize that your physics course is the place to start your exam preparation!** Whether or not you are satisfied with the quality of your course or your teacher, the best way to start preparing for the exam is by doing careful, attentive work in class all year long.

Okay, for many readers, we're preaching to the choir. You don't want to hear about your physics class; you want the specifics about the AP exam. If that's the case, go ahead and turn to Chapter 2, and get started on your exam-specific preparation. But we think that you can get even more out of your physics class than you think you can. Read these pieces of time-tested advice, follow them, and we promise you'll feel more comfortable about your class *and* about the AP exam.

Ignore Your Grade

This must be the most ridiculous statement you've ever read. But it may also be the most important of these suggestions. Never ask yourself or your teacher "Can I have more points on this assignment?" or "Is this going to be on the test?" You'll worry so much about giving the teacher merely what she or he wants that you won't learn physics in the way that's best for you. Whether your score is perfect or near zero, ask, "Did I really understand all aspects of these problems?"

Remember, the AP exam tests your physics knowledge. If you understand physics thoroughly, you will have no trouble at all on the AP test. But, while you may be able to argue yourself a better grade in your physics *class,* even if your comprehension is poor, the AP readers are not so easily moved.

If you take this advice—if you really, truly ignore your grade and focus on physics— your grade will come out in the wash. You'll find that you got a very good grade after all, because you understood the subject so well. But you *won't care,* because you're not worried about your grade!

Don't Bang Your Head Against a Brick Wall

Our meaning here is figurative, although there are literal benefits also. Never spend more than 10 minutes or so staring at a problem without getting somewhere. If you honestly have no idea what to do at some stage of a problem, STOP. Put the problem away. Physics has a way of becoming clearer after you take a break.

On the same note, if you're stuck on some algebra, don't spend forever trying to find what you know is a trivial mistake, say a missing negative sign or some such thing. Put the problem away, come back in an hour, and start from scratch. This will save you time in the long run.

And finally, if you've put forth a real effort, you've come back to the problem many times and you still can't get it: relax. Ask the teacher for the solution, and allow yourself to be enlightened. You will not get a perfect score on every problem. But you don't care about your grade, remember?

Work with Other People

When you put a difficult problem aside for a while, it always helps to discuss the problem with others. Form study groups. Have a buddy in class with whom you are consistently comparing solutions.

Although you may be able to do all your work in every other class without help, we have never met a student who is capable of solving every physics problem on his or her own.

It is not shameful to ask for help. Nor is it dishonest to seek assistance—as long as you're not copying, or allowing a friend to carry you through the course. Group study is permitted and encouraged in virtually every physics class around the globe.

Ask Questions When Appropriate

We know your physics teacher may seem mean or unapproachable, but in reality, physics teachers do want to help you understand their subject. If you don't understand something, don't be afraid to ask. Chances are that the rest of the class has the same question. If your question is too basic or requires too much class time to answer, the teacher will tell you so.

Sometimes the teacher will not answer you directly, but will give you a hint, something to think about so that you might guide yourself to your own answer. Don't interpret this as a refusal to answer your question. You must learn to think for yourself, and your teacher is helping you develop the analytical skills you need for success in physics.

Keep an Even Temper

A football team should not give up because they allow an early field goal. Similarly, you should not get upset at poor performance on a test or problem set. No one expects you to be perfect. Learn from your mistakes, and move on—it's too long a school year to let a single physics assignment affect your emotional state.

On the same note, however, a football team should not celebrate victory because it scores a first-quarter touchdown. You might have done well on this test, but there's the rest of a nine-month course to go. Congratulate yourself, then concentrate on the next assignment.

Don't Cram

Yes, we know that you got an "A" on your history final because, after you slept through class all semester, you studied for 15 straight hours the day before the test and learned everything. And, yes, we know you are willing to do the same thing this year for physics. We warn you, both from our and from others' experience: *it won't work*. Physics is not about memorization and regurgitation. Sure, there are some equations you need to memorize. But problem-solving skills cannot be learned overnight.

Furthermore, physics is cumulative. The topics you discuss in December rely on the principles you learned in September. If you don't understand basic vector analysis and free-body diagrams, how can you understand the relationship between an electric field (which is a vector quantity) and an electric force, or the multitude of other vector quantities that you will eventually study?

So, the answer is to keep up with the course. Spend some time on physics every night, even if that time is only a couple of minutes, even if you have no assignment due the next day. Spread your "cram time" over the entire semester.

Never Forget, Physics Is "Phun"

The purpose of all these problems, these equations, and these exams is to gain knowledge about physics—a deeper understanding of how the natural world works. Don't be so caught up in the grind of your coursework that you fail to say "Wow!" occasionally. Some of the things you're learning are truly amazing. Physics gives insight into some of humankind's most critical discoveries, our most powerful inventions, and our most fundamental technologies. Enjoy yourself. You have an opportunity to emerge from your physics course with wonderful and useful knowledge, and unparalleled intellectual insight. Do it.

CHAPTER 2

What You Need to Know About the AP Physics C Exams

IN THIS CHAPTER

Summary: Learn what topics are tested, how the test is scored, and basic test-taking information.

Key Ideas

✪ Most colleges will award credit for a score of 4 or 5, some for a 3.
✪ Multiple-choice questions account for half of your final score.
✪ There is no penalty for guessing on the multiple-choice questions. You should answer every question.
✪ Free-response questions account for half of your final score.
✪ Your composite score on the two test sections is converted to a score on the 1-to-5 scale.

Background Information

The AP Physics exam was first offered by the College Board in 1954. Since then, the number of students taking the test has grown rapidly. In 2015, more than 90,000 students took at least one of the AP Physics C exams, and those numbers go up every year.

Some Frequently Asked Questions About the AP Physics C Exams

Why Should I Take an AP Physics Exam?

Many of you take the AP Physics exam because you are seeking college credit. A score of 3 or above makes you qualified for credit from most colleges and universities. This means you are one or two courses closer to graduation before you even start college!

Therefore, one compelling reason to take the AP exam is economic. How much does a college course cost, even at a relatively inexpensive school? You're talking several thousand dollars. If you can save those thousands of dollars by paying less than a hundred dollars now, why not do so?

Your odds of earning college credit are good. In recent years, more than 80% of all students have scored 3 or higher on Physics C – mechanics, and over 70% of all students have scored 3 or higher on Physics C – E&M. But even if you do not score high enough to earn credit, the background you've gained will make it easier for you to pass the equivalent college course. And, the fact that you elected to attempt these courses tells admissions committees that you are serious about learning advanced physics.

You'll hear a whole lot of misinformation about AP credit policies. Don't believe anything a friend (or even an adult) tells you; instead, find out for yourself. A good way to learn about the AP credit policy of the school you're interested in is to look it up on the College Board's official Web site, at http://collegesearch.collegeboard.com/apcreditpolicy/index.jsp. Even better, contact the registrar's office or the physics department chair at the college directly.

What Are the Different AP Physics Courses?

You can take various AP Physics courses. They differ in both the range of topics covered and the level at which those topics are tested. Here's the rundown:

Physics 1 and Physics 2 (Algebra Based)

Physics 1 is intended to simulate the first semester of the standard algebra-based college physics course. It covers classical mechanics, waves, and circuits. Physics 2 is intended to simulate the second semester of the college course, covering electromagnetism, thermodynamics, fluids, and atomic physics. Although they mimic semester courses in college, each of these is a full-year high school course.

When the College Board says "algebra based," they mean it—not only is no calculus necessary, but no mathematics beyond definitions of the basic trig functions are required. Most of the Physics 1 and 2 exams require verbal, not mathematical, responses.

Physics 1 in particular is ideal for ALL college-bound high school students. For those who intend to major in math or the heavy-duty sciences, Physics 1 and Physics 2 serve as perfect introductions to college-level work. For those who want nothing to do with physics after high school, Physics 1 and Physics 2 are terrific terminal courses—you get exposure to many facets of physics at a rigorous yet understandable level.

Physics C

These courses are ONLY for those who have already taken a solid introductory physics course and are considering a career in math or science. Some schools teach Physics C as a follow-up to Physics 1, but as long as you've had a rigorous introduction to the subject, that introduction does not have to be at the AP level.

Physics C is two separate courses: (1) Newtonian Mechanics and (2) Electricity and Magnetism. Of course, the Physics 1 and 2 courses cover these topics as well. However, the C courses go into greater depth and detail. The problems are more involved, and they demand a higher level of conceptual understanding. You can take either or both 90-minute Physics C exams.

The C courses require some calculus. Although much of the material can be handled without it, you should be taking a good calculus course concurrently.

Is Physics C Better Than Physics 1/2? Should I Take More Than One Exam?

If you're doing well in AP Physics 1—that is, if you're likely to earn a 4 or a 5 on the AP Physics 1 exam—you are equally likely to earn a qualifying score on the AP Physics C Mechanics exam with little or no extra preparation. Yes, even if you have never taken calculus. Our recommendation would be, take AP Physics 1, because that's what your class prepared you for, that's the one you're likely to get a higher score on, and that's the harder exam anyway. Then in the spring, look through this book and try some of the Mechanics practice test questions. If you can get about half of the questions right, you'll probably earn a qualifying score—so pay the extra fee and do the late signup.

We strongly recommend taking only the exam that your high school AP course prepared you for. Physics C is not considered "better" than Physics 1 in the eyes of colleges and scholarship committees; they are different courses with different intended audiences. It is far better to do well on the exam that your class prepared you for than to do poorly on multiple exams.

I Heard the AP Physics C Exams are Changing. Is That true?

The College Board has released a draft course and exam description for a slightly different set of exams in the future. But that "future" is not May 2024. This year's exams will be exactly the same as the last two decades' worth of exams.

What Is the Format of the Exam?

Table 2.1 summarizes the format of the AP Physics C exams.

Table 2.1   AP Physics C exams

AP Physics C – Mechanics

SECTION	NUMBER OF QUESTIONS	TIME LIMIT
I. Multiple-Choice Questions	35	45 minutes
II. Free-Response Questions	3	45 minutes

AP Physics C – Electricity and Magnetism

SECTION	NUMBER OF QUESTIONS	TIME LIMIT
I. Multiple-Choice Questions	35	45 minutes
II. Free-Response Questions	3	45 minutes

Who Writes the AP Physics Exam?

Development of each AP exam is a multiyear effort that involves many education and testing professionals and students. At the heart of the effort is the AP Physics Development Committee, a group of college and high-school physics teachers who are typically asked to serve for three years. The committee and other physics teachers create a large pool of multiple-choice questions. With the help of the testing experts at Educational Testing Service (ETS), these questions are then pre-tested with college students for accuracy, appropriateness, clarity, and assurance that there is only one possible answer. The results of this pre-testing allow each question to be categorized by degree of difficulty. After several more months of development and refinement, Section I of the exam is ready to be administered.

The free-response questions that make up Section II go through a similar process of creation, modification, pre-testing, and final refinement so that the questions cover the necessary areas of material and are at an appropriate level of difficulty and clarity. The committee also makes a great effort to construct a free-response exam that will allow for clear and equitable grading by the AP readers.

At the conclusion of each AP reading and scoring of exams, the exam itself and the results are thoroughly evaluated by the committee and by ETS. In this way, the College Board can use the results to make suggestions for course development in high schools and to plan future exams.

What Topics Appear on the Exam?

The College Board, after consulting with physics teachers at all levels, develops a curriculum that covers material that college professors expect to cover in their first-year classes. Based on this outline of topics, the multiple-choice exams are written such that those topics are covered in proportion to their importance to the expected understanding of the student.

Confused? Suppose that faculty consultants agree that, say, atomic and nuclear physics is important to the physics curriculum, maybe to the tune of 10%. If 10% of the curriculum is devoted to atomic and nuclear physics, then you can expect roughly 10% of the exam will address atomic and nuclear physics. This includes both the multiple-choice and the free-response sections—so a topic that is not tested in the free-response section will have *extra* multiple-choice questions to make up the difference.

The following are the general outlines for the AP Physics curriculum and exams. Remember this is just a guide, and each year the exam differs slightly in the percentages.

AP PHYSICS C, MECHANICS

A.	Kinematics	18%
B.	Newton's Laws	20%
C.	Work, Energy, Power	14%
D.	Linear Momentum	12%
E.	Rotational Motion	18%
F.	Oscillations and Gravitation	18%

AP PHYSICS C, ELECTRICITY AND MAGNETISM

A.	Electrostatics	30%
B.	Conductors, Capacitors, Dielectrics	14%
C.	Electric Circuits	20%
D.	Magnetic Fields	20%
E.	Electromagnetism	16%

What Types of Questions Are Asked on the Exam?

The multiple-choice questions tend to focus either on your understanding of concepts or on your mastery of equations and their meaning. Here's an example of a "concept" multiple-choice question.

Which of the following is an expression of conservation of charge?

(A) Kirchoff's loop rule
(B) Kirchoff's junction rule
(C) Ohm's law
(D) Snell's law
(E) Kinetic theory of gases

The answer is **B**. Kirchoff's junction rule states that whatever charge comes in must come out. If you don't remember Kirchoff's junction rule, turn to Chapter 19, Circuits.

And here's an example of an "equation" multiple-choice question.

If the separation between plates in a parallel-plate capacitor is tripled, what happens to the capacitance?

(A) It is reduced by a factor of 9.
(B) It is reduced by a factor of 3.
(C) It remains the same.
(D) It increases by a factor of 3.
(E) It increases by a factor of 9.

The answer is **B**. For this kind of question, you either remember the equation for the capacitance of a parallel-plate capacitor, $C = \dfrac{\varepsilon_0 A}{d}$, or you don't. For help, turn to Chapter 6, Memorizing Equations in the Shower.

You are given a sheet that contains a bunch of physical constants (like the mass of a proton), SI units, and trigonometric values (like "tan 45° = 1"). All in all, this sheet is pretty useless—you'll probably only refer to it during the course of the test if you need to look up an obscure constant. That doesn't happen as often as you might think.

The free-response questions take 15 minutes apiece to answer, and they test both your understanding of concepts and your mastery of equations. Some of the free-response questions ask you to design or interpret the results of an experimental setup; others are more theoretical. Luckily, in addition to the constant sheet, you will also get a sheet that contains every equation you will ever need. You still need to have your equations memorized! It is not useful to hunt through the equation sheet trying to find the one you need, any more than it's a useful writing strategy to hunt randomly through the dictionary trying to find an appropriate word.

We talk in much more detail about both the multiple-choice and the free-response sections of the test later, in Step 5, so don't worry if this is all a bit overwhelming now.

Who Grades Our Free-Response Questions?

Every June, a group of physics teachers gathers for a week to assign grades to test takers' hard work. Each of these readers spends a day or so getting trained on only one question. Because each reader becomes an expert on that question, and because each exam book is anonymous, this process provides for consistent and unbiased scoring of that question.

During a typical day of grading, a random sample of each reader's scores is selected and cross-checked by experienced "table leaders" to ensure that consistency is maintained throughout the day and the week. Each reader's scores on a given question are also statistically analyzed to make sure scores are not given that are significantly higher or lower than the mean scores given by other readers of that question.

Will Our Exam Remain Anonymous?

You can be absolutely sure that your exam will remain anonymous. Even if your high school teacher happens to randomly read your booklet, there is virtually no way he or she will know that exam is yours.* To the reader, each student is a number, and to the computer, each student is a bar code.

What about that permission box on the back? The College Board uses some exams to help train high school teachers so that they can help the next generation of physics students to avoid common mistakes. If you check this box, you simply give permission to use your exam in this way. Even if you give permission, your anonymity is maintained.

How Is Our Final Grade Determined, and What Does It Mean?

Each section counts for 50% of the exam. The total composite score is thus a weighted sum of the multiple-choice and free-response sections. In the end, when all of the numbers have been crunched, the chief faculty consultant converts the range of composite scores to the five-point scale of the AP grades.

This conversion is not a true curve; it's not that there's some target percentage of 5s to give out. This means you're not compcting against other test takers. Rather, the five-point scale is adjusted each year to reflect the same standards as in previous years. The goal is that students who earn 5s this year are just as strong as those who earned 5s in 2016 and 2017.

Although these values change dramatically from year to year depending on the statistics of each exam, it generally takes about 65% of the available points to earn a 5; it takes about 50% of the points to earn a 4; and it takes about 35% of the points to earn a 3. We've used similar percentages in the tables at the end of the practice exams in this book to give you a rough example of a conversion. When you complete the practice exams, you can use this to give yourself a hypothetical grade.

Point is, you are NOT expected to get classroom-style scores of 90% for an A. The exam is intended to differentiate between levels of students, and the exam tests far more than pure recall, so 70% is a very strong score, not a weak score.

You should receive your AP grade in early July.

How Do I Register and How Much Does It Cost?

Beginning with the 2020 exams, registration for AP exams must be completed by mid-November.* You do not have to be enrolled in an officially titled AP Physics course to register for the exam.

In 2020, the fee for taking the exam is $94—that's $94 each for Physics C – Mechanics and Physics C – Electricity & Magnetism. Students who demonstrate financial need may receive a reduction—you can find out more from your school's AP coordinator or the College Board Web site.

What If I'm Not Sure in November Whether I Want to Take the Exam?

Sign up anyway.

If you're in an official AP class, the College Board has provided all sorts of excellent resources that your teacher can share with you, including personal progress checks that can be used throughout the year and a bank of extra questions written by the

---

*Well, unless you write something like, "Hi, please kick Mr. Kirby in the butt for me. Thank you! Sincerely, George."

*For those who are taking a second-semester-only class, the registration deadline is in March. Be careful about how your school labels their courses. If they clearly label Mechanics as the first semester course and E&M as the second semester, then you must sign up for Mechanics by November, but you can wait until March for E&M. BUT! If they label Physics C as a single year-long course, then you must sign up for both exams in November. Of course, I'd say, just sign up for both exams in November regardless. Then there can't be any confusion.

development committee. Between these resources and this book, you will not encounter any surprises on the exam.

The College Board has done considerable research at pilot schools to determine whether requiring registration in November has an effect on student performance. They found out that it does—a dramatic effect. Students who committed in November to taking the exam outperformed those who didn't commit until March by an enormous margin.

I'm sure some wiseacres will say, "But I just know I'm gonna fail." That's called defeatism, and you shouldn't tolerate that from yourself. If you were to tell your softball coach, "Hey, I'm going to strike out at the plate, let grounders go through my legs, and drop all the fly balls hit to me," would the coach let you play? More likely, he or she would kick you off the team! When you pretend that you can't do anything in physics, you do yourself a tremendous disservice.

When in doubt regarding registration procedures, the best source of information is the College Board's Web site, collegeboard.org.

What If Our School Only Offers Physics 1/2 and Not AP Physics C, or Vice Versa? Or, What If Our School Doesn't Offer AP Physics at All?

Ideally, you should enroll in the AP class for the exam you wish to take. But not every school offers exactly what you want to take.

If your school offers one exam or the other, you are much better off taking the exam for which your teacher prepared you. Sure, if you are an excellent Physics 1 student, you can probably pass the Physics C exam with some extra preparation; but if you're a top Physics 1 student, why not just earn your 5 on the 1 exam rather than take a chance at merely passing the C exam? Or, if you've been preparing for Physics C, you might think you have a better chance for success on the "easier" 1 exam. But the 1 exam tests different topics and is in a completely different style than Physics C. Additionally, everyone who's had exposure to both exams agrees that Physics 1 is harder than physics C. So you're still most likely better off on the exam your class taught toward.

If your school doesn't offer either AP course, then you should look at the content outline and talk to your teacher. Chances are, you will want to take the P1 exam, and chances are you will have to do a good bit of independent work to learn the topics that your class didn't discuss. But, if you are a diligent student in a rigorous course, you will probably be able to do fine.

What Should I Bring to the Exam?

On exam day, we suggest bringing the following items:

- Several pencils and an eraser that doesn't leave smudges
- Black or blue pens for the free-response section*
- A ruler or straightedge
- A watch so that you can monitor your time (You never know if the exam room will have a clock on the wall.)
- Your school code

---

*Yes, I said pens. Your rule of thumb should be to do graphs in pencil and everything else in pen. If you screw up, cross out your work and start over. Then if you change your mind about what you crossed out, just circle it and say, "Hey, reader, please grade this! I didn't mean to cross it out!"

- Your photo identification and Social Security number
- Tissues
- A calculator
- Your quiet confidence that you are prepared (Please don't study the morning before the exam—that won't do you any good. Stop the studying the night before, and relax. Good luck.)

CHAPTER 3

How to Plan Your Time

IN THIS CHAPTER

Summary: What to study for the Physics C exam, plus three schedules to help you plan.

Key Ideas

✪ Focus your attention and study time on those topics that are most likely to increase your score.

✪ Study the topics that you're afraid will appear, and relax about those that you're best at.

✪ Don't study so widely that you don't get good at some specific type of problem.

The AP Physics exam is held on a Monday afternoon in mid-May. You may think that you just started your exam preparation today, when you opened this book . . . but, in reality, you have been getting ready for the AP test all year. The AP exam is an authentic test of your physics knowledge and skills. Your AP Physics *class* presumably is set up to teach those skills. So, don't give your class short shrift. Diligent attention to your class lectures, demonstrations, and assignments can only save you preparation time in the long run.

Of course, you may not be satisfied with the quantity or quality of your in-class instruction. And even if your class is the best in the country, you will still need a reminder of what you covered way back at the beginning of the year. That's where this book, and extracurricular AP exam preparation, are useful.

What Should I Study?

You will hear plenty of poorly thought-out advice about how to deal with the vast amounts of material on the AP Physics exams, especially if you are taking both Mechanics and E&M.

Fact is, in the month or two before the exam, you do not have enough time to re-teach yourself the entire course. So, you ask a presumed expert, "What should I study?"

Bad Answer Number 1: *"Everything."*

This logic says, every topic listed in the AP course description is guaranteed to show up somewhere on the exam, whether in the free-response or the multiple-choice sections. So, you must study everything. That's ridiculous, I say to my students. You've been studying "everything" all year. You need to focus your last-month study on those topics that are most likely to increase your score.

Bad Answer Number 2: *"Let me use my crystal ball to tell you exactly what types of problems will show up on this year's free-response exam. Study these."*

I know teachers who think they're oracles . . . "An RC circuit was on last year's test, so it won't be on this year's. And, we haven't seen point charges for two straight years, so we'll definitely see one this year."[1] Suffice it to say that a teacher who is not on the test development committee has no possible way of divining which specific types of problems will appear on the exam, any more than a college basketball "expert" can say with confidence which teams will make the final four. And, even if you *did* know which topics would be covered on the free-response section, all of the other topics must appear on the multiple-choice section! So don't choose your study strategy based on an oracle's word.

Good Answer: *"Do a cost-benefit analysis"*

You know how much time you have left. Use that limited time to study the topics that are most likely to increase your score. The trick is identifying those topics. Start with honest, hyperbole-free answers to two questions, in the following manner.

Imagine that the AP Physics Genie[2] has granted you two boons. You may choose one type of problem that *will* be tested on the free-response exam, and you may choose one type of problem that will *not* appear on the free response. Now, answer:

1. What topic or problem type do you ask the genie to put on the exam?
2. What topic or problem type do you forbid the genie to put on the exam?

If you are extremely comfortable, say, solving kinematics and projectile problems, why would you spend any time on those? It won't hurt to give yourself a quick reminder of fundamental concepts, but in-depth study of what you know well is a waste of valuable time. On the other hand, if you're *un*comfortable with, say, energy-position diagrams, then spend a couple of evenings learning how to deal with them. Study the topics you're afraid will appear; relax about those you're best at.

This is an important point—don't study so broadly that you don't get good at some specific type of problem. Use Chapter 8's drill exercises, or the end-of-chapter examples in this book, or some similar handout from your teacher, or a subset of your textbook's end-of-chapter problems to keep practicing until you actually are *hoping* to see certain types of problems on your test. That's far more useful than just skimming around.

---

[1] A moment's thought will find some inconsistency in the above logic.

[2] . . . who is not a real person . . .

For the mechanics exam, focus your preparation on Chapter 16, Rotational Motion. For the E&M exam, understand how to use Gauss's law and the time-varying circuits: RC, RL, and LC.

Though there are other subtopics that are unique to Physics C, extra preparation on these topics will probably benefit you the most, because they are (a) far enough removed from first-year material that they truly require extra work and (b) understandable with a reasonable amount of supplemental study.

Have a Plan for the Exam

When it comes to the last few days before the exam, think about your mental approach. You can do very well on the exam even if you have difficulty with a few of the topics. But, know ahead of time which topics you are weak on. If you have trouble, say, with electric fields, plan on skipping electric fields multiple-choice questions so as to concentrate on those that you'll have more success on. Don't fret about this decision—just make it ahead of time, and follow your plan. On the free-response test, though, be sure to approach every problem. Sure, it's okay to decide that you will not waste time on electric fields due to point charges. But if you read the entire problem, you might find that parts (d) and (e) are simple $F = qE$ questions, or ask about some aspect of electricity that you understand just fine.

Understand Physics First, Then AP Physics C

Be sure you understand physics before preparing specifically for the AP Physics C exams.

I've taught Physics C with great success for many years. But, not just anyone can sign up for my Physics C class. I only take students who have completed Physics 1, and for good reason. The C course is very deep. It requires that you have not just an idea about, but a true *mastery* of, Physics 1- and 2-level material.

Now, your first physics course might not have formally been labeled "Advanced Placement." Any rigorous introductory class is sufficient preparation for Physics C. Nevertheless, before you even begin to discuss a calculus-based approach to problem-solving, you MUST have a solid conceptual understanding of physics at the introductory level.

My advice to my Physics C students has always been to know the basics. An average difficulty Physics C question is equivalent to an above-average (and more calculational) Physics 1 or 2 question. Someone who knows physics cold at the 1/2 level could do quite well on the Physics C exam.

Therefore, you start your preparation by answering the following with brutal honesty: "Could I solve *any* Physics 1 level mechanics, or Physics 2 E&M, problem? Would I recognize the appropriate equations, relationships, and definitions instantly, without wrinkling my forehead for more than a few seconds?"

If the answer is "no," then the most efficient way to improve your Physics C performance is to learn the fundamentals. Use your algebra-based physics textbook or *5 Steps to a 5: AP Physics 1*. There's no substitute for a thorough knowledge of basic physics principles. Don't worry about calculus concepts, don't worry about the special Physics C–specific material, just work until you have the material down at the introductory level. Even if this is the only exam preparation you have time for, you will be far better served by shoring up your fundamentals than by grasping at more difficult concepts.

Once you are rock-solid on your algebra-based physics, then it's time to think about the advanced topics on the C exam.

A Word About Calculus

Yes, Physics C is "calculus-based" physics. And yes, you will be asked to evaluate a few integrals and/or derivatives here and there. But it is vitally important that you understand that Physics C is *not* a math course. The development committee is not trying to find out whether you know how to evaluate $\int \sin x \cdot dx$. Rather, they are looking to see whether you understand how to apply calculus concepts to physics problems. What do we mean by calculus concepts? Two things.

1. Recognizing When a Calculus Approach Is Necessary

In algebra-based physics you learned that the work done by a force is equal to that force times parallel displacement. You will use that relationship in Physics C, too. However, in Physics C, you must recognize the limitations of that relationship: you can only multiply force times parallel displacement *when the force is constant*. If the force is changing, you must use calculus concepts, knowing that work is the integral of force with respect to distance.

Physics 1–style situations, in which calculus is not necessary, *will* appear on the Physics C exam. Your challenge is to recognize when a quantity is changing in such a way that calculus must be used.

2. Understanding the Conceptual and Graphical Meanings of Integrals and Derivatives

On a graph, an integral is the area under the graph; a derivative is the slope of a graph at a given point. Consider a problem in which you're asked to find the work done by a non-constant force. If you're given a graph of that force vs. position, then all you've got to do is find the area under the graph—*no integration necessary*.

You should have an idea of the meaning of a derivative or integral, even without evaluating it, or without graphing the function in question. This isn't as hard as it looks! Consider the following multiple-choice problem:

A box is pushed across a frictionless table a distance of 9 m. The horizontal force pushing the box obeys the function $F(x) = 50(5 - \sqrt{x})$, where F is in newtons and x is in meters. How much work is done by the pushing force?

(A) 2500 J
(B) 1350 N
(C) 900 J
(D) 250 J
(E) 90 J

"Whoa," you say. "This is a hard calculus problem, especially without a calculator." Your first instinct is to take the integral $\int_{0}^{9} 50(5 - \sqrt{x})dx$. That becomes hard toot sweet. No chance you can get that done in the minute or so you have on a multiple-choice problem. So, what to do?

You know in your bones that if this force were constant, then all you'd have to do is multiply the force by 9 m. This force is not constant. But, we can approximate an *average* force from the function, can't we? Sure . . . the initial force is $50(5 - 0) = 250$ N. The force at the end of the push is $50(5 - \sqrt{9}) = 100$ N. So, the average force is somewhere in between 100 N and 250 N.[3] Guess that this average force is between 150 N and 200 N. That gives work done between (150 N)(9 m) and (200 N)(9 m), or between 1350 N and 1800 N. Only choice B fits.

Note that ANY kind of estimate of the average force would still get you close to the correct answer. This is a classic calculus *concepts* question . . . it's not about evaluating the integral, it's about understanding the meaning of work.

What Specific Calculus Methods Do I Have to Know?

You will be expected to evaluate straightforward integrals and derivatives. Remember, this is not a math test—the exam is not trying to test your math skills but rather your ability to apply calculus to physical situations. This means the actual integrals and derivatives will not be from the most difficult questions on your AP Calculus BC test!

You should know:

- Derivatives and integrals of polynomial functions
- Derivatives and integrals of sin x and cos x—but we've never seen questions that require trigonometric identities on the exam
- Derivatives and integrals with ln x or e^x
- Derivatives using the chain rule
- Integration with u-substitution

If you need a review of these topics, take a look at your calculus book or at *5 Steps to a 5: AP Calculus AB*.

Two other mathematical techniques are necessary on the Physics C exam:

- Basic first- and second-order differential equations
- Integrals involving linear density

These topics are covered briefly in this book.

Three Different Study Schedules

MONTH	PLAN A: FULL SCHOOL YEAR	PLAN B: ONE SEMESTER	PLAN C: 6 WEEKS
September–October	Chapters 1–5	——	——
November	Chapters 9–10, Chapter 6	——	——
December	Chapters 11–13	——	——
January	Chapters 14–15	Chapters 2–6	——
February	Chapters 16–17	Chapters 9–13	——
March	Chapters 18–19	Chapters 14–17	——
April	Chapter 20, Chapters 7–8	Chapters 18–20	Skim Chapters 9–18, Chapter 6
May	Review everything; Practice Exams	Chapters 7–8; Review everything; Practice Exams	Skim Chapters 19–20, Chapters 7–8; Practice Exams

---

[3]Not *exactly* in between, because this function is not linear. However, you'll see that any approximation of the average force will do here.

Plan A: You Have a Full School Year to Prepare

Although its primary purpose is to prepare you for the AP Physics exam you will take in May, this book can enrich your study of physics, your analytical skills, and your problem-solving abilities.

SEPTEMBER–OCTOBER (Check off the activities as you complete them.)
— Determine the study mode (A, B, or C) that applies to you.
— Carefully read Steps 1 and 2 of this book.
— Work through the diagnostic exam.
— Get on the Web and take a look at the AP Web site(s).
— Skim Step 4. (Reviewing the topics covered in this section will be part of your year-long preparation.)
— Buy a few color highlighters.
— Flip through the entire book. Break the book in. Write in it. Highlight it.
— Get a clear picture of what your own school's AP Physics curriculum is.
— Begin to use this book as a resource to supplement the classroom learning.

NOVEMBER (The first 10 weeks have elapsed.)
— Read and study Chapter 9, A Bit About Vectors.
— Read and study Chapter 10, Free-Body Diagrams and Equilibrium.
— Read Chapter 6, Memorizing Equations in the Shower.

DECEMBER
— Read and study Chapter 11, Kinematics.
— Read and study Chapter 12, Newton's Second Law, $F_{net} = ma$.
— Read and study Chapter 13, Momentum.
— Review Chapters 9–10.

JANUARY (20 weeks have elapsed.)
— Read and study Chapter 14, Energy Conservation.
— Read and study Chapter 15, Gravitation and Circular Motion.
— Review Chapters 9–13.

FEBRUARY
— Read and study Chapter 16, Rotational Motion (for Physics C students only).
— Read and study Chapter 17, Simple Harmonic Motion.
— Review Chapters 9–15.

MARCH (30 weeks have now elapsed.)
— Read and study Chapter 18, Electrostatics.
— Read and study Chapter 19, Circuits.
— Review Chapters 9–20.

APRIL
— Read and study Chapter 20, Magnetism.
— Review Chapters 9–19.
— Read Chapters 7–8 carefully!

MAY (first 2 weeks) (THIS IS IT!)
— Review Chapters 9–20—all the material!!!
— Take the Practice Exams, and score yourself.
— Get a good night's sleep before the exam. Fall asleep knowing that you are well prepared.

GOOD LUCK ON THE TEST.

Plan B: You Have One Semester to Prepare

Working under the assumption that you've completed one semester of your physics course, the following calendar will use those skills you've been practicing to prepare you for the May exam.

JANUARY–FEBRUARY
— Carefully read Steps 1 and 2 of this book.
— Work through the diagnostic exam.
— Read and study Chapter 9, A Bit About Vectors.
— Read and study Chapter 10, Free-Body Diagrams and Equilibrium.
— Read and study Chapter 11, Kinematics.
— Read and study Chapter 12, Newton's Second Law, $F_{net} = ma$.
— Read and study Chapter 13, Momentum.
— Read Chapter 6, Memorizing Equations in the Shower.

MARCH (10 weeks to go.)
— Read and study Chapter 14, Energy Conservation.
— Read and study Chapter 15, Gravitation and Circular Motion.
— Read and study Chapter 16, Rotational Motion.

— Read and study Chapter 17, Simple Harmonic Motion.
— Review Chapters 9–13.

APRIL
— Read and study Chapter 18, Electrostatics.
— Read and study Chapter 19, Circuits.
— Read and study Chapter 20, Magnetism.
— Review Chapters 9–17.

MAY (first 2 weeks) (THIS IS IT!)
— Review Chapters 9–20—all the material!!!
— Read Chapters 7–8 carefully!
— Take the Practice Exams and score yourself.
— Get a good night's sleep before the exam. Fall asleep knowing that you are well prepared.

GOOD LUCK ON THE TEST.

Plan C: You Have Six Weeks to Prepare

At this point, we assume that you have been building your physics knowledge base for more than six months (if you're a Physics C student, you've probably been studying physics for more than a year). You will, therefore, use this book primarily as a specific guide to the AP Physics exam. Given the time constraints, now is not the time to try to expand your AP Physics knowledge. Rather, you should focus on and refine what you already do know.

APRIL 1–15
— Skim Steps 1 and 2 of this book.
— Skim Chapters 9–13.
— Skim and highlight the Glossary at the end of the book.
— Read Chapter 6, and work on memorizing equations.

APRIL 16–MAY 1
— Skim Chapters 14–18.
— Continue to work on memorizing equations.

MAY (first 2 weeks) (THIS IS IT!)
— Skim Chapters 19–20.
— Carefully go over the Rapid Review sections of Chapters 10–20.
— Read Chapter 7.
— Take the Practice Exams and score yourself.
— Get a good night's sleep before the exam. Fall asleep knowing that you are well prepared.

GOOD LUCK ON THE TEST.

STEP 2

Determine Your Test Readiness

CHAPTER 4

Fundamentals Quizzes

IN THIS CHAPTER

Summary: To test your readiness for the exam, take these short quizzes on these two fundamental topics of AP Physics.

Key Ideas
✪ Find out what you know—and what you don't know—about mechanics.
✪ Find out what you know—and what you don't know—about electricity and magnetism.
✪ Focus your exam preparation time only on the areas you don't already know well.

These short quizzes may be helpful if you're looking for some additional review of the most fundamental topics in AP Physics. If you can get all these right, you are READY for the exam!
   The answers are printed at the end of this chapter.

Mechanics Quiz

1. What is the mass of a block with weight 100 N?

2. Give the equations for two types of potential energy, identifying each.

3. When an object of mass m is on an incline of angle θ, one must break the weight of the object into components parallel and perpendicular to the incline.
    i.   What is the component of the weight parallel to the incline?_____
    ii. What is the component of the weight perpendicular to the incline?_____

4. Write two expressions for work, including the definition of work and the work-energy principle.

5. Quickly identify as a vector or a scalar:

   _____ acceleration   _____ force   _____ momentum
   _____ velocity   _____ speed   _____ displacement
   _____ work   _____ mass   _____ kinetic energy

6. Name at least four things that can NEVER go on a free-body diagram.

7. Write two expressions for impulse. What are the units of impulse?

8. In what kind of collision is momentum conserved? In what kind of collision is kinetic energy conserved?

9. What is the mass of a block with weight W?

10. A ball is thrown straight up. At the peak of its flight, what is the ball's acceleration? Be sure to give both magnitude and direction.

11. A mass experiences a force vector with components 30 N to the right, 40 N down. Explain how to determine the magnitude and direction (angle) of the force vector.

12. Write the definition of the coefficient of friction, μ. What are the units of μ?

13. How do you find acceleration from a velocity-time graph?

14. How do you find displacement from a velocity-time graph?

15. How do you find velocity from a position-time graph?

16. An object has a positive acceleration. Explain *briefly* how to determine whether the object is speeding up, slowing down, or moving with constant speed.

17. Given the velocity of an object, how do you tell which direction that object is moving?

18. When is the gravitational force on an object mg? When is the gravitational force Gm_1m_2/r^2?

19. What is the direction of the net force on an object that moves in a circle at constant speed?

20. Under what conditions is the equation $x - x_0 = v_0 t + \frac{1}{2}at^2$ valid? Give a specific situation in which this equation might seem to be valid, but is NOT.

Electricity and Magnetism Quiz

1. Given the charge of a particle and the electric field experienced by that particle, give the equation to determine the electric force acting on the particle.

2. Given the charge of a particle and the magnetic field experienced by that particle, give the equation to determine the magnetic force acting on the particle.

3. What are the units of magnetic flux? What are the units of EMF?

4. A wire carries a current to the left, as shown below. What is the direction and magnitude of the magnetic field produced by the wire at point P?

5. When is the equation kQ/r^2 valid? What is this an equation for?

6. The electric field at point P is 100 N/C; the field at point Q, 1 meter away from point P, is 200 N/C. A point charge of $+1$ C is placed at point P. What is the magnitude of the electric force experienced by this charge?

7. Can a current be induced in a wire if the flux through the wire is zero? Explain.

8. True or false: In a uniform electric field pointing to the right, a negatively charged particle will move to the left. If true, justify with an equation; if false, explain the flaw in reasoning.

9. Which is a vector and which is a scalar: electric field and electric potential?

10. Fill in the blank with either "parallel" or "series":

    a. Voltage across resistors in _____ must be the same for each.
    b. Current through resistors in _____ must be the same for each.
    c. Voltage across capacitors in _____ must be the same for each.
    d. Charge stored on capacitors in _____ must be the same for each.

11. A uniform electric field acts to the right. In which direction will each of these particles accelerate?

    a. proton
    b. positron (same mass as electron, but opposite charge)
    c. neutron
    d. anti-proton (same mass as proton, but opposite charge)

12. A uniform magnetic field acts to the right. In which direction will each of these particles accelerate, assuming they enter the field moving toward the top of the page?

    a. proton
    b. positron (same mass as electron, but opposite charge)
    c. neutron
    d. anti-proton (same mass as proton, but opposite charge)

13. How do you find the potential energy of an electric charge?

Answers to Mechanics Quiz

1. Weight is mg. So, mass is weight divided by g, which would be 100 N/(10 N/kg) = 10 kg.

2. PE = mgh, gravitational potential energy;
   PE = $\frac{1}{2}kx^2$, potential energy of a spring.

3. i. $mg \sin\theta$ is parallel to the incline.
    ii. $mg \cos\theta$ is perpendicular to the incline.

4. The definition of work is work = force times parallel displacement. The work-energy principle states that net work = change in kinetic energy.

5. vectors: acceleration, force, momentum, velocity, displacement

scalars: speed, work, mass, kinetic energy

6. Only forces acting on an object and that have a single, specific source can go on free-body diagrams. Some of the things that cannot go on a free-body diagram but that students often put there by mistake:

motion	mass	acceleration	*ma*
centripetal force	velocity	inertia	

7. Impulse is force times time interval, and also change in momentum. Impulse has units either of newton·seconds or kilogram·meters/second.

8. Momentum is conserved in *all* collisions. Kinetic energy is conserved only in elastic collisions.

9. Using the reasoning from question #1, if weight is *mg*, then $m = W/g$.

10. The acceleration of a projectile is *always g*; i.e., 10 m/s², downward. Even though the velocity is instantaneously zero, the velocity is still changing, so the acceleration is *not* zero. (By the way, the answer "−10 m/s²" is wrong unless you have clearly and specifically defined the down direction as negative for this problem.)

11. The magnitude of the resultant force is found by placing the component vectors tip-to-tail. This gives a right triangle, so the magnitude is given by the Pythagorean theorem, 50 N. The angle of the resultant force is found by taking the inverse tangent of the vertical component over the horizontal component, $\tan^{-1}(40/30)$. This gives the angle measured from the horizontal.

12.
$$\mu = \frac{F_f}{F_n}$$

friction force divided by normal force. μ has no units.

13. Acceleration is the slope of a velocity-time graph.

14. Displacement is the area under a velocity-time graph (i.e., the area between the graph and the horizontal axis).

15. Velocity is the slope of a position-time graph. If the position-time graph is curved, then instantaneous velocity is the slope of the tangent line to the graph.

16. Because acceleration is not zero, the object *cannot* be moving with constant speed. If the signs of acceleration and velocity are the same (here, if velocity is positive), the object is speeding up. If the signs of acceleration and velocity are different (here, if velocity is negative), the object is slowing down.

17. An object *always* moves in the direction indicated by the velocity.

18. Near the surface of a planet, *mg* gives the gravitational force. Newton's law of gravitation, Gm_1m_2/r^2, is valid everywhere in the universe. (It turns out that *g* can be found by calculating $GM_{\text{planet}}/R_{\text{planet}}^2$, where R_{planet} is the planet's radius.)

19. An object in uniform circular motion experiences a *centripetal,* meaning "center seeking," force. This force must be directed to the center of the circle.

20. This and all three kinematics equations are valid only when acceleration is constant. So, for example, this equation can NOT be used to find the distance travelled by a mass attached to a spring. The spring force changes as the mass moves; thus, the acceleration of the mass is changing, and kinematics equations are not valid. (On a problem where kinematics equations aren't valid, conservation of energy usually is what you need.)

Answers to Electricity and Magnetism Quiz

1. $F = qE$.

2. $F = qvB \sin \theta$.

3. Magnetic flux is BA, so the units are tesla·meters^2 (or, alternatively, webers). EMF is a voltage, so the units are volts.

4. Point your right thumb in the direction of the current, i.e., to the left. Your fingers point in the direction of the magnetic field. This field wraps around the wire, pointing into the page above the wire and out of the page below the wire. Since point P is below the wire, the field points out of the page.

5. This equation is only valid when a point charge produces an electric field. (Careful—if you just said "point charge," you're not entirely correct. If a point charge experiences an electric field produced by something else, this equation is irrelevant.) It is an equation for the electric field produced by the point charge.

6. Do *not* use $E = kQ/r^2$ here because the electric field is known. So, the source of the electric field is irrelevant—just use $F = qE$ to find that the force on the charge is (1 C)(100 N/C) = 100 N. (The charge is placed at point P, so anything happening at point Q is irrelevant.)

7. Yes! Induced EMF depends on the *change* in flux. So, imagine that the flux is changing rapidly from one direction to the other. For a brief moment, flux will be zero; but flux is still changing at that moment. (And, of course, the induced current will be the EMF divided by the resistance of the wire.)

8. False. The negative particle will be *forced* to the left. But the particle could have entered the field while moving to the right . . . in that case, the particle would continue moving to the right, but would slow down.

9. Electric field is a vector, so fields produced in different directions can cancel. Electric potential is a scalar, so direction is irrelevant.

10. Voltage across resistors in parallel must be the same for each.
Current through resistors in series must be the same for each.
Voltage across capacitors in parallel must be the same for each.
Charge stored on capacitors in series must be the same for each.

11. The positively charged proton will accelerate with the field, to the right.
The positively charged positron will accelerate with the field, to the right.
The uncharged neutron will not accelerate.
The negatively charged anti-proton will accelerate against the field, to the left.

12. Use the right-hand rule for each:
The positively charged proton will accelerate into the page.
The positively charged positron will accelerate into the page.
The uncharged neutron will not accelerate.
The negatively charged anti-proton will accelerate out of the page.

13. If you know the electric potential experienced by the charge, $PE = qV$.

What Do I Know, and What Don't I Know?

I'll bet you didn't get every question on both of these fundamentals quizzes correct. That's okay. The whole point of these quizzes is for you to determine where to focus your study.

It's a common mistake to "study" by doing 20 problems on a topic on which you are already comfortable. But that's not studying . . . that's a waste of time. You don't need to drill yourself on topics you already understand! It's also probably a mistake to attack what for you is the toughest concept in physics right before the exam. Virtually every student has that one chapter they just don't get, however hard they try. That's okay.

The fundamentals quizzes that you just took can tell you exactly what you should and should not study. Did you give correct answers with full confidence in the correctness of your response? In that case, you're done with that topic. No more work is necessary. The place to focus your efforts is on the topics where either you gave wrong answers that you thought were right, or right answers that you weren't really sure about.

Now, take the diagnostic test. Once you've used the fundamentals quizzes and diagnostic test to identify the specific content areas you want to work on, proceed to the review in Chapters 9–20. Read a chapter, work through the examples in the chapter, and attempt some of the problems at the end of the chapter. Then come back to these fundamentals quizzes. When you respond to every question confidently, you are ready.

CHAPTER 5

Take a Diagnostic Test

IN THIS CHAPTER

Summary: Assess your strengths and weaknesses by answering some sample questions and then reading the answers and explanations, so you'll know where to focus your efforts when preparing for the exam.

› Diagnostic Test

Kinematics

1. Which of the following must be true of an object that is slowing down?

   (A) Its acceleration must be negative.
   (B) Its velocity must be smaller than its acceleration.
   (C) It must experience more than one force.
   (D) Its acceleration and its velocity must be in opposite directions.
   (E) Its velocity must be negative.

2. A baseball is thrown straight up. It reaches a peak height of 15 m, measured from the ground, in a time of 1.7 s. Treating "up" as the positive direction, what is the acceleration of the ball when it reaches its peak height?

   (A) 0 m/s^2
   (B) +8.8 m/s^2
   (C) −8.8 m/s^2
   (D) +9.8 m/s^2
   (E) −9.8 m/s^2

Newton's laws

3. What is the vertical component of $\mathbf{F}_1$ in the above diagram?

   (A) ½$\mathbf{F}_1$
   (B) $\mathbf{F}_1$
   (C) $\mathbf{F}_1 \cos \theta$
   (D) $\mathbf{F}_1 \sin \theta$
   (E) $\mathbf{F}_1 \tan \theta$

4. The box pictured above moves at constant speed to the left. Which of the following is correct?

   (A) The situation is impossible. Because more forces act right, the block must move to the right.
   (B) $T_3 > T_1 + T_2$
   (C) $T_3 < T_1 + T_2$
   (D) $T_3 = T_1 + T_2$
   (E) A relationship among the three tensions cannot be determined from the information given.

The following diagram relates to Questions 5 and 6.

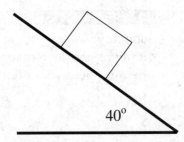

A block of mass m is sliding up a frictionless incline, as shown above. The block's initial velocity is 3 m/s up the plane.

5. What is the component of the weight parallel to the plane?

   (A) mg
   (B) $mg \cos 40°$
   (C) $mg \sin 40°$
   (D) $g \sin 40°$
   (E) $g \cos 40°$

6. What is the acceleration of the mass?

   (A) 3 m/s^2, up the plane
   (B) $mg \sin 40°$, up the plane
   (C) $mg \sin 40°$, down the plane
   (D) $g \sin 40°$, up the plane
   (E) $g \sin 40°$, down the plane

GO ON TO THE NEXT PAGE

Work/Energy

7. Which of the following is a scalar?

   (A) velocity
   (B) acceleration
   (C) displacement
   (D) kinetic energy
   (E) force

8. A 500-g block on a flat tabletop slides 2.0 m to the right. If the coefficient of friction between the block and the table is 0.1, how much work is done on the block by the table?

   (A) 0.5 J
   (B) 1.0 J
   (C) 0 J
   (D) 100 J
   (E) 50 J

9. A block has 1500 J of potential energy and 700 J of kinetic energy. Ten seconds later, the block has 100 J of potential energy and 900 J of kinetic energy. Friction is the only external force acting on the block. How much work was done on this block by friction?

   (A) 600 J
   (B) 200 J
   (C) 1400 J
   (D) 1200 J
   (E) 120 J

Momentum

10. Two identical small balls are moving with the same speed toward a brick wall. After colliding with the wall, ball 1 sticks to the wall while ball 2 bounces off the wall, moving with almost the same speed that it had initially. Which ball experiences greater impulse?

    (A) ball 1
    (B) ball 2
    (C) Both experience the same impulse.
    (D) The answer cannot be determined unless we know the time of collision.
    (E) The answer cannot be determined unless we know the force each ball exerts on the wall.

11. Ball A moves to the right with a speed of 5.0 m/s; Ball B moves to the left with a speed of 2.0 m/s. Both balls have a mass of 1.0 kg. What is the total momentum of the system consisting only of balls A and B?

    (A) 7.0 N·s to the right
    (B) 3.0 N·s to the right
    (C) zero
    (D) 7.0 N·s to the left
    (E) 3.0 N·s to the left

12. Momentum of an isolated system always remains constant. However, in a collision between two balls, a ball's momentum might change from, say, +1 kg m/s to −1 kg m/s. How can this be correct?

    (A) It is *not* correct. Momentum conservation means that the momentum of an object must remain the same.
    (B) A force outside the two-ball system must have acted.
    (C) Friction is responsible for the change in momentum.
    (D) Although one ball's momentum changed, the momentum of *both* balls in total remained the same.
    (E) Momentum is conserved because the magnitude of the ball's momentum remained the same.

Circular motion

13. Which of the following must be true of an object in uniform circular motion?

    (A) Its velocity must be constant.
    (B) Its acceleration and its velocity must be in opposite directions.
    (C) Its acceleration and its velocity must be perpendicular to each other.
    (D) It must experience a force away from the center of the circle.
    (E) Its acceleration must be negative.

Harmonic motion

14. A mass on a spring has a frequency of 2.5 Hz and an amplitude of 0.05 m. What is the period of the oscillations?

    (A) 0.4 s
    (B) 0.2 s
    (C) 8 s
    (D) 20 s
    (E) 50 s

GO ON TO THE NEXT PAGE

15. A mass *m* oscillates on a horizontal spring of constant *k* with no damping. The amplitude of the oscillation is *A*. What is the potential energy of the mass at its maximum displacement?

(A) zero
(B) *mgh*
(C) *kA*
(D) ½*mv²*
(E) ½*kA²*

Rotational motion

16. A ball of mass *m* is spinning about a diameter. If it were instead to make twice as many rotations per second, what would happen to the ball's rotational inertia and its angular momentum?

Moment of inertia	Angular momentum
(A) remains the same	quadruples
(B) doubles	remains the same
(C) doubles	quadruples
(D) doubles	doubles
(E) remains the same	doubles

Gravitation

17. A satellite orbits the moon far from its surface in a circle of radius *r*. If a second satellite has a greater speed, yet still needs to maintain a circular orbit around the moon, how should the second satellite orbit?

(A) with a radius *r*
(B) with a radius greater than *r*
(C) with a radius less than *r*
(D) Only an eccentric elliptical orbit can be maintained with a larger speed.
(E) No orbit at all can be maintained with a larger speed.

Electrostatics

18. Which of the following statements about electric potential is correct?

(A) A proton experiences a force from a region of low potential to a region of high potential.
(B) The potential of a negatively charged conductor must be negative.
(C) If the electric field is zero at point *P*, then the electric potential at *P* must also be zero.
(D) If the electric potential is zero at point *P*, then the electric field at *P* must also be zero.
(E) The electric potential with respect to earth ground can be less than zero at all points on an isolated wire conductor.

19. A uniform electric field points to the right, as shown above. A test charge can be placed at one of three points as shown in the above diagram. At which point does the test charge experience the greatest force?

(A) point *A*
(B) point *B*
(C) point *C*
(D) The charge experiences the greatest force at two of these three points.
(E) The charge experiences the same force at all three points.

20. An electron in an electric field is suspended above the Earth's surface. Which of the following diagrams correctly shows the forces acting on this electron?

GO ON TO THE NEXT PAGE

Circuits

21. Which of the following will increase the capacitance of a parallel plate capacitor?

(A) increasing the charge stored on the plates
(B) decreasing the charge stored on the plates
(C) increasing the separation between the plates
(D) decreasing the separation between the plates
(E) decreasing the area of the plates

22. A 10-V battery is connected to two parallel 10-Ω resistors, as shown above. What is the current through and voltage across each resistor?

	Current	Voltage
(A)	1 A	5 V
(B)	1 A	10 V
(C)	0.5 A	5 V
(D)	2 A	10 V
(E)	2 A	5 V

Magnetic fields and force

23. A positive point charge enters a uniform rightward magnetic field with a velocity v, as diagramed above. What is the direction of the magnetic force on the charge?

(A) in the same direction as v
(B) to the right
(C) to the left
(D) out of the page
(E) into the page

24. A long wire carries a current I toward the top of the page. What is the direction of the magnetic field produced by this wire to the left of the wire?

(A) into the page
(B) out of the page
(C) toward the bottom of the page
(D) toward the top of the page
(E) to the right

Electromagnetism

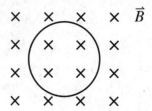

25. A circular loop of wire in the plane of the page is placed in a magnetic field pointing into the page, as shown above. Which of the following will NOT induce a current in the loop?

(A) moving the wire to the right in the plane of the page
(B) increasing the area of the loop
(C) increasing the strength of the magnetic field
(D) rotating the wire about a diameter
(E) turning the magnetic field off

END OF DIAGNOSTIC TEST

› Answers and Explanations

1. **D**—Choices A and E don't make sense because the direction of an object's acceleration or velocity is essentially arbitrary—when solving a problem, you can usually pick the "positive" direction based on convenience. So neither value *must* be negative. We can rule out choice B because we know that a fast moving object can slow down very gradually. And there's no reason why you need multiple forces to make an object slow down, so that gets rid of choice C.

2. **E**—When an object is thrown in the absence of air resistance near the surface of the Earth, its acceleration in the vertical direction is always g, the acceleration due to gravity, which has a magnitude of 9.8 m/s^2. The acceleration due to gravity is directed down, toward the Earth. So the ball's acceleration is −9.8 m/s^2.

3. **D**—The vertical component of a vector is the magnitude of the vector times the sine of the angle measured to the horizontal; in this case, $\mathbf{F}_1 \sin \theta$.

4. **D**—Something that moves in a straight line at constant speed is in equilibrium. So, the sum of left forces has to equal the sum of right forces.

5. **C**—On an incline, the weight vector parallel to the plane goes with the sine of the plane's angle. $g \sin 40°$ is an acceleration, not a weight.

6. **E**—Because the weight is the only force acting parallel to the plane, $mg \sin 40° = ma$, so $a = g \sin 40°$. This acceleration is down the plane, in the direction of the net force. Yes, the block is moving up the plane, but the block is slowing down, and so the acceleration must be in the opposite direction from the velocity.

7. **D**—All forms of energy are scalar quantities: potential energy, kinetic energy, work, internal energy of a gas. Energy doesn't have direction.

8. **B**—Work is force times parallel displacement. The force acting here is the force of friction, and the displacement is 2.0 m parallel to the force of friction. The friction force is equal to the coefficient of friction (0.10) times the normal force. The normal force in this case is equal to the block's weight of 5 N (because no other vertical forces act). Combining all these equations, the work done is (2.0 m) (0.1)(5 N) = 1.0 J.

9. **D**—Look at the total energy of the block, which is equal to the potential energy plus the kinetic energy. Initially, the total energy was 2200 J. At the end, the total energy was 1000 J. What happened to the extra 1200 J? Because friction was the only external force acting, friction must have done 1200 J of work.

10. **B**—Impulse is equal to the change in an object's momentum. Ball 1 changes its momentum from something to zero. But ball 2 changes its momentum from something to zero, and *then* to something in the other direction. That's a bigger momentum change than if the ball had just stopped. (If we had been asked to find the force on the ball, then we'd need the time of collision, but the impulse can be found without reference to force or time.)

11. **B**—Momentum is a *vector*, meaning direction is important. Call the rightward direction positive. Ball A has +5 kg·m/s of momentum; ball B has −2 kg·m/s of momentum. Adding these together, we get a total of +3 kg·m/s. This answer is equivalent to 3 N·s to the right. (The units kg·m/s and N·s are identical.)

12. **D**—The law of conservation of momentum requires that *all* objects involved in a collision be taken into account. An object can lose momentum, as long as that momentum is picked up by some other object.

13. **C**—"Uniform" circular motion means that an object's *speed* must be constant. But *velocity* includes direction, and the direction of travel changes continually. The velocity of the object is always along the circle, but the acceleration is centripetal; i.e., center-seeking. The direction toward the center of the circle is perpendicular to the path of the object everywhere.

14. **A**—Period is equal to 1/frequency, regardless of the amplitude of harmonic motion.

15. E—The maximum displacement is the amplitude. Energy of a spring is $\frac{1}{2}kx^2$. So, at $x = A$, the energy is $\frac{1}{2}kA^2$.

16. E—An object's rotational inertia can be thought of as a rotational equivalent of mass; rotational inertia, like mass, is a property of an object and the axis about which it rotates. Rotational inertia does not depend on the speed of rotation. Angular momentum, equal to rotational inertia times angular velocity, *does* depend on the speed of rotation. Because the rotation rate doubled, so did angular momentum.

17. C—In an orbit, gravity provides a centripetal force. So, $GmM/r^2 = mv^2/r$. Solving for v,

$$v = \sqrt{\frac{GM}{r}}$$

where M is the mass of the moon. If the speed gets bigger, then the radius of orbit (in the denominator) must get smaller to compensate.

18. E—Most of these statements drive at the fundamental principle that the value of an electric potential can be set to anything; it is only the *difference* in electric potential between two points that has a physical usefulness. Usually potential is set to zero either at the ground or, for isolated point charges, a very long distance away from the charges. But potential can, in fact, be set to zero anywhere, meaning that the potential could easily be less than zero everywhere on a wire. (And a proton, a positive charge, is forced from high to low potential, not the other way around.)

19. E—This is a *uniform* electric field. The force on a charge in an electric field is given by $F = qE$. Therefore, as long as the electric field is the same at all three points, the force on the charge is the same as well.

20. C—Only forces can go on free-body diagrams, and the electric field is not itself a force. The force *provided by* an electric field is qE; the weight of the electron is mg.

21. D—Capacitance is a property of the structure of the capacitor. Changing the charge on (or the voltage across) a capacitor does not change the capacitance. The capacitance of a parallel-plate capacitor is given by the equation

$$C = \frac{\varepsilon_0 A}{d}$$

Decreasing d, the distance between the plates, will increase the capacitance.

22. B—These resistors are in parallel with the battery; thus, they *both* must take the voltage of the battery, 10 V. The total current in the circuit is 2.0 A, but that current splits between the two resistors, leaving 1.0 A through each. This can also be determined by a direct application of Ohm's law—because we know both the voltage and resistance for each resistor, divide V/R to get the current.

23. E—Use the right-hand rule for the force on a charged particle in a magnetic field: point your right hand in the direction of the velocity, curl your fingers toward the magnetic field, and your thumb points into the page. The charge is positive, so your thumb points in the direction of the force.

24. B—This question uses the right-hand rule for the magnetic field produced by a current-carrying wire. Point your thumb in the direction of the current; your fingers wrap around the wire in the direction of the magnetic field. To the wire's left, your fingers point out of the page.

25. A—Only a changing magnetic flux induces a current. Flux is given by $BA\cos\theta$, where B is the magnetic field, and A is the area of the loop of wire. Obviously, then, choices B, C, and E change the flux and induce a current. Choice D produces a flux by changing θ, the angle at which the field penetrates the loop of wire. In choice A, no current is induced because the field doesn't change and always points straight through the loop.

Interpretation: How Ready Are You?

Now that you have finished the diagnostic exam and checked your answers, it is time to try to figure out what it all means. First, remember that getting only about 60% of the answers correct will give you a 5 on the AP exam; about 30–40% correct is the criterion for a qualifying score of 3. You're not supposed to get 90% correct! So relax and evaluate your performance dispassionately.

Next, see if there are any particular areas in which you struggled. For example, were there any questions that caused you to think something such as, "I learned this . . . *when?!?*" or "What the heck is *this?!?*" If so, put a little star next to the chapter that contains the material in which this occurred. You may want to spend a bit more time on that chapter during your review for this exam. It is quite possible that you *never* learned some of the material in this book. Not every class is able to cover all the same information.

In general, try to interpret your performance on this test in a productive manner. If you did well, that's terrific . . . but don't get overconfident now. There's still a lot of material to review before you take the Practice Exams in Step 5—let alone the real AP exam. If you don't feel good about your performance, now is the time to turn things around. You have a great opportunity here—time to prepare for the real exam, a helpful review book, and a sense of what topics you need to work on most—so use it to its fullest. Good luck!

STEP **3**

Develop Strategies for Success

Memorizing Equations in the Shower

IN THIS CHAPTER

Summary: Learn how to memorize all the equations you absolutely need to know to ace the AP Physics exam.

Key Ideas

✪ Learn why memorizing equations is so critical.
✪ Learn equations by using them: practice solving problems without looking up the equations you need.
✪ Use mnemonic devices to help you remember.
✪ Practice speed: see how many equations you can say in four minutes.
✪ Use visual reminders: put a copy of the equation sheet somewhere you'll see it often.

Can You Ace This Quiz?

<u>Instructions:</u> We'll give you a prompt, you tell us the equation. Once you've finished, check your answers with the key at the end of this chapter.

1. Coefficient of friction in terms of F_f
2. Momentum
3. Two equations for impulse
4. Two equations for mechanical power
5. Two equations for work
6. Period of a mass on a spring
7. Three kinematics equations for constant acceleration
8. Centripetal acceleration
9. Kinetic energy
10. Gravitational force of one planet on another
11. Ohm's Law
12. Power in a circuit
13. Magnetic force on a charge
14. Magnetic force on a wire
15. Electric force on a charge
16. Electric potential energy
17. Magnetic field around a long, straight, current-carrying wire
18. Time constant for an RC circuit
19. Resistance of a wire in terms of its dimensions
20. Electric field due to a point charge

So, How Did You Do?

Grade yourself according to this scale.

20 right	Excellent
0–19 right	Start studying

You may think we're joking about our grading system, but we're completely serious. Knowing your equations is absolutely imperative. Even if you missed one question on the quiz, you need to study your equations. Right now! A student who is ready to take the AP exam is one who can ace an "equations quiz" without even thinking about it. How ready are you?

Equations Are Crucial

It's easy to make an argument against memorizing equations. For starters, you're given all the equations you need on the exam. And besides, you can miss a whole bunch of questions on the test and still get a 5.

But equations are the nuts and bolts of physics. They're the fundamentals. They should be the foundation on which your understanding of physics is built. Not knowing an equation—even one—shows that your knowledge of physics is incomplete. And every question on the AP exam assumes *complete* knowledge of physics.

Now you get equation sheets on the multiple choice section, too.

What About the Free-Response Section?

The free-response questions test your ability to solve complex, multistep problems. They also test your understanding of equations. You need to figure out which equations to use when and how. The makers of the test are being nice by giving you the equation sheet—they're reminding you of all the equations you already know in case you cannot think of that certain equation that you *know* would be just perfect to solve a certain problem. But the sheet is intended to be nothing more than a reminder. It will not tell you when to use an equation or which equation would be best in solving a particular problem. You have to know that. And you will know that only if you have intimate knowledge of every equation.

Exam tip from an AP Physics veteran:

Don't use the equation sheet to "hunt and peck." The sheet can remind you of subtle things; for example, does the magnetic field due to a wire have an r or an r^2 in the denominator? But if you don't have the general idea that the magnetic field depends on current and gets weaker farther away from a wire, then you won't recognize

$$B = \frac{\mu_0 I}{2\pi r}$$

even if you go hunting for it.

—*Wyatt, college freshman in engineering*

Some Examples

We mentioned in Step 2 that some questions on the AP exam are designed solely to test your knowledge of equations. If you know your equations, you will get the question right. Here's an example.

A pendulum of length L swings with a period of 3 s. If the pendulum's length is increased to $2L$, what will its new period be?

(A) $3/\sqrt{2}$ s

(D) 6 s

(B) 3 s

(E) 12 s

(C) $3\sqrt{2}$ s

The answer is (C). The equation for a pendulum's period is

$$T = 2\pi\sqrt{\frac{L}{g}}$$

since L is in the numerator and under the square root, multiplying L by 2 multiplies the period by $\sqrt{2}$.

Of course, the multiple-choice section will not be the only part of the exam that tests your knowledge of equations. Often, a part of a free-response question will also test your ability to use an equation. For example, check out this problem.

Four charges $+Q$ are arranged in a square of side length l.

(a) What is the magnitude of the electric field due to just one of these charges at the center of the square?

Yes, later in the problem you'll be asked to add vectors to find E due to a bunch of charges. But you can still score some easy points here if you simply remember that old standby, $E = \left(\dfrac{1}{4\pi\varepsilon_0}\right)\dfrac{Q}{r^2}$.

Memorizing equations will earn you points. It's that simple.

Treat Equations Like Vocabulary

Think about how you would memorize a vocabulary word: for example, "boondoggle." There are several ways to memorize this word. The first way is to say the word out loud and then spell it: "Boondoggle: B-O-O-N-D-O-G-G-L-E." The second way is to say the word and then say its definition: "Boondoggle: An unproductive or impractical project, often involving graft." If you were to use the first method of memorizing our word, you would become a great speller, but you would have no clue what "boondoggle" means. As long as you are not preparing for a spelling bee, it seems that the second method is the better one.

This judgment may appear obvious. Who ever learned vocabulary by spelling it? The fact is, this is the method most people use when studying equations.

Let's take a simple equation, $v_f = v_o + at$. An average physics student will memorize this equation by saying it aloud several times, and that's it. All this student has done is "spelled" the equation.

But you're not average.[1] Instead, you look at the equation as a whole, pronouncing it like a sentence: "*V f* equals *v* naught plus *at*." You then memorize what it means and when to use it: "This equation relates initial velocity with final velocity. It is valid only when acceleration is constant." If you are really motivated, you will also try to develop some intuitive sense of why the equation works. "Of course," you say, "this makes perfect sense! Acceleration is just the change in velocity divided by the time interval. If acceleration is multiplied by the time interval, then all that's left is the change in velocity

$$\frac{\Delta v}{\Delta t} \cdot \Delta t = \Delta v$$

So the final velocity of an object equals its initial velocity plus the change in velocity."

The first step in memorizing equations, then, is to learn them as if you were studying for a vocabulary test, and not as if you were studying for a spelling bee.

Helpful Tips

Memorizing equations takes a lot of time, so you cannot plan on studying your equations the night before the AP exam. If you want to really know your equations like the back of your hand, you will have to spend months practicing. But it's really not that bad. Here are four tips to help you out.

> **Tip 1:** Learn through use. Practice solving homework problems without looking up equations.

Just as with vocabulary words, you will only learn physics equations if you use them on a regular basis. The more you use your equations, the more comfortable you will be with them, and that comfort level will help you on the AP test.

The reason you should try solving homework problems without looking up equations is that this will alert you to trouble spots. When you can look at an equations sheet, it's easy to fool yourself into a false sense of confidence: "Oh, yeah, I *knew* that spring potential energy is ½kx^2." But when you don't have an equations sheet to look at, you realize that either you know an equation or you don't. So if you solve homework problems without looking up equations, you'll quickly figure out which ones you know and which you don't; and then you can focus your studying on those equations that need more review.

> **Tip 2:** Use mnemonic devices.

Use whatever tricks necessary to learn an equation. For example, it is often hard to remember that the period of a pendulum is

$$T = 2\pi \sqrt{\frac{L}{g}}$$

---

[1] In fact, just because you bought this book, we think that you're way better than average. "Stupendous" comes to mind. "Extraordinary. Gullible." Er . . . uh . . . cross that third one out.

and *not*

$$T = 2\pi \sqrt{\frac{g}{L}}$$

So make up some trick, like "The terms go in backward alphabetical order: **T**wo-pi **r**oot *L* over *g*." Be creative.

> **Tip 3:** The Four-Minute Drill.

Practice speed. Say the equations as fast as you can, then say them faster. Start at the top of the AP equations sheet[2] and work your way down. Have someone quiz you. Let that person give you a lead, like "Period of a pendulum," and you respond "Two-pi root *L* over *g*." See how many equations you can rattle off in four minutes. We call it the Four-Minute Drill.

This is much more fun with a group; for example, try to persuade your teacher to lead the class in a four-minute drill. Not only will you get out of four minutes of lecture, but you may also be able to bargain with your teacher: "Sir, if we can rattle off 50 equations in the Four-Minute Drill, will you exempt us from doing tonight's problems?"[3]

> **Tip 4:** Put a copy of the equations sheet somewhere visible.

See how the equations sheet looks next to your bathroom mirror. Or in your shower (laminated, of course). Or taped to your door. Or hung from your ceiling. You'd be surprised how much sparkle it can add to your décor. You'd also be surprised how easy it will be to memorize equations if you are constantly looking at the equations sheet.

So what are you waiting for? Start memorizing!

---

[2]We've included a copy of this sheet at the end of the book, along with a sheet of prompts to guide you through a four-minute drill.

[3]"No."

› Answer Key to Practice Quiz

1. $\mu = \dfrac{F_f}{F_n}$

2. $p = mv$

3. $I = \Delta p$ and $I = F\Delta t$

4. $P = Fv$ and $P = \dfrac{W}{t}$

5. $W = Fd$ and $W_{net} = \Delta KE$

6. $T = 2\pi\sqrt{\dfrac{m}{k}}$

7. $\begin{cases} v_f = v_o + at \\ x - x_0 = v_0 t + \frac{1}{2}at^2 \\ v_f^2 = v_0^2 + 2a(x - x_0) \end{cases}$

8. $a_c = \dfrac{v^2}{r}$

9. $KE = \frac{1}{2}mv^2$

10. $F = \dfrac{Gm_1 m_2}{r^2}$

11. $V = IR$

12. $P = IV$

13. $F = qvB \sin\theta$

14. $F = ILB \sin\theta$

15. $F = qE$

16. $U = qV$

17. $B = \dfrac{\mu_0 I}{2\pi r}$

18. $\tau = RC$

19. $R = \dfrac{\rho L}{A}$

20. $E = \dfrac{kQ}{r^2}$

CHAPTER 7

How to Approach Each Question Type

IN THIS CHAPTER

Summary: Become familiar with the three types of questions on the exam: multiple-choice, free-response, and lab questions. Pace yourself, and know when to skip a question.

Key Ideas

✪ You don't need a calculator to figure out multiple-choice questions, even though you are allowed a calculator.

✪ There are five categories of multiple-choice questions. Two of these involve numbers: easy calculations and order-of-magnitude estimates. The other three don't involve numbers at all: proportional reasoning questions, concept questions, and questions asking for the direct solution with variables only.

✪ Free-response questions test your understanding of physics, not obscure theories or technical terms.

✪ You can get partial credit on free-response questions.

✪ Each free-response section will contain at least one question that involves experiment design and analysis—in other words, a lab question.

✪ Check out our six steps to answering lab questions successfully.

How to Approach the Multiple-Choice Section

The AP exam is very, very straightforward. There are no trick questions, no unreasonably difficult problems, no math beyond the clearly articulated scope of the course. The multiple-choice questions test your physics knowledge in a variety of ways—a glance through the practice exam in this book, as well as reading through this section, can give you a sense of the types of questions asked.

Until 2015, calculators and the equation sheet were not provided during the multiple-choice section. Now, though, you can use calculators and equation sheets on the whole exam.

Important point: *The content and style of questions did not change, even though the calculator policy did.*

The point is, you do not need to use a calculator on the multiple-choice section. No multiple-choice question requires significant number crunching. More importantly, though, understand that

> Physics is NOT about numbers.

Yes, you must use numbers occasionally. Yet you must understand that the number you get in answer to a question is always subordinate to what that number represents.

Many misconceptions about physics start in math class. There, your teacher shows you how to do a type of problem, then you do several variations of that same problem for homework. The answer to one of these problems might be 30,000,000, another 16.5. It doesn't matter . . . in fact, the book (or your teacher) probably made up random numbers to go into the problem to begin with. The "problem" consists of manipulating these random numbers a certain way to get a certain answer.

In physics, though, *every number has meaning.* Your answer will not be 30,000,000; the answer may be 30,000,000 electron-volts, or 30,000,000 seconds, but not just 30,000,000. If you don't see the difference, you're missing the fundamental point of physics.

We use numbers to represent REAL goings on in nature. 30,000,000 eV (or, 30 MeV) is an energy; this could represent the energy of a particle in a multibillion-dollar accelerator, but it's much too small to be the energy of a ball dropped off of a building. 30,000,000 seconds is a time; not a few hours or a few centuries, but about one year. These two "30,000,000" responses mean entirely different things. If you simply give a number as an answer, you're doing a math problem. It is only when you can explain the meaning of any result that you may truly claim to understand physics.

So How Do I Deal with All the Numbers on the Test?

You see, in virtually all cases the test authors still assume that you have no calculator. Thus, a large majority of the multiple-choice questions involve *no numbers at all!* And those questions that do use numbers will never require more than the simplest manipulations. Here is a question you will **never** see on the AP test:

What is the magnitude of the magnetic field a distance of 1.5 m away from a long, straight wire that carries 2.3 A of current?

(A) 3.066×10^{-6} T
(B) 3.166×10^{-6} T
(C) 3.102×10^{-6} T
(D) 2.995×10^{-6} T
(E) 3.109×10^{-6} T

Yes, we know you might have seen this type of problem in class. But it will *not* be on the AP exam. Why not? Plugging numbers into a calculator is not a skill being tested by this examination. (You should have recognized that the equation necessary to solve this problem is $B = \dfrac{\mu_0 I}{2\pi r}$ though.) We hope you see that, without a calculator, it is pointless to try to get a precise numerical answer to this kind of question.

Fine . . . Then What Kinds of Questions *Will* Be Asked on the Multiple-Choice Section?

Fair enough. We break down the kinds of questions into five categories. First, the categories of questions that involve numbers:

1. easy calculations
2. order of magnitude estimates

Most questions, though, do NOT involve numbers at all. These are:

3. proportional reasoning
4. concept questions, subdivided into
   a. "Why?" questions, and
   b. diagram questions
5. direct solution with variables

Okay, let's take a look at a sample of each of these.

Easy Calculations

These test your knowledge of formulas.

A ball is dropped from a 45-m-high platform. Neglecting air resistance, how much time will it take for this ball to hit the ground?

(A) 1.0 s
(B) 2.0 s
(C) 3.0 s
(D) 4.0 s
(E) 5.0 s

You should remember the kinematics equation: $x - x_0 = v_0 t + \frac{1}{2}at^2$. Here the initial velocity is zero because the ball was "dropped." The distance involved is 45 meters, and the acceleration is caused by gravity, 10 m/s². The solution must be found without a calculator, but notice how easy they have made the numbers:

$$45 \text{ m} = 0t + \frac{1}{2}(10 \text{ m/s}^2) \cdot t^2$$

$$90 = 10t^2$$

$$9 = t^2$$

$$t = 3.0 \text{ s}$$

Everything here can be done easily without a calculator, especially if you remember to use 10 m/s² for g. No problem!

Order of Magnitude Estimates

These test your understanding of the size of things, measurements, or just numbers.

Which of the following best approximates the gravitational force experienced by a high school student due to the student sitting in an adjacent seat?

(A) 10^1 N
(B) 10^{-8} N
(C) 10^{-18} N
(D) 10^{-28} N
(E) 10^{-38} N

Wow, at first you have no idea. But let's start by looking at the answer choices. Notice how widely the choices are separated. The second choice is a hundred millionth of a newton; the third choice is a billionth of a billionth of a newton. Clearly no kind of precise calculation is necessary here.

The answer can be calculated with Newton's law of gravitation $G\dfrac{m_1 m_2}{r^2}$. You complain:

"They didn't give me any information to plug in. It's hopeless!" Certainly not. The important thing to remember is that you have very little need for precision here. This is a rough estimate! *Just plug in a power of 10 for each variable.* Watch:

1. G: The table of information says that the constant G is 6.67×10^{-11} N·m²/kg². So we just use 10^{-11} in standard units.
2. m_1, m_2: It doesn't say whether this is Olympic gymnast Shawn Johnson (41 kg) or football offensive lineman John Urschel (137 kg). What do I do? Just use 10^1 or 10^2 kg. If you're really concerned, you can make one 10^1 kg and one 10^2 kg. It won't matter.
3. r: The distance between desks in any classroom will be more than a few tens of centimeters, but less than a few tens of meters. Call it 10^0 meters and be done with it.

Okay, we're ready for our quick calculation:

$$F = G\frac{m_1 m_2}{r^2} = (10^{-11})(10^1)(10^2)/(10^0)^2 = 10^{-8} \text{ N}$$

(You remember that to multiply powers of 10, just add the exponents; to divide, subtract the exponents.)

You still object, "But when I use my calculator and plug in more precise values, I get 3.67×10^{-7} N. Or, if I use both masses as Shawn Johnson's, I get 1.1×10^{-7} N." Look at the choices again; the second answer choice is still the best answer. We got that without a calculator—and a lot quicker, too.

Proportional Reasoning

These also test your knowledge of how to use equations, except that you don't have to plug in numerical values to solve them.

Planet X is twice as massive as Earth, but its radius is only half of Earth's radius. What is the acceleration due to gravity on Planet X in terms of g, the acceleration due to gravity on Earth?

(A) $\frac{1}{4} g$
(B) $\frac{1}{2} g$
(C) g
(D) $4g$
(E) $8g$

First we need to know what equation to use. We know that the force that a planet exerts on a small mass m_1 near its surface is

$$F = \frac{GM_{\text{planet}} m_1}{R_{\text{planet}}^2}$$

Using Newton's second law ($F_{\text{net}} = ma$), we know that the acceleration of the small mass is simply

$$a = \frac{GM_{\text{planet}}}{R_{\text{planet}}^2}$$

One method of solution would be to plug in the actual mass and radius of the new planet. But no fair, you say, the mass of the Earth isn't given on the constants sheet. How do I find the mass of the planet?

You don't!

Use proportional reasoning skills instead, so:

"The mass of the planet is twice that of the Earth. Since mass is in the numerator of the equation for acceleration, doubling the mass of the planet must double the acceleration.

"Okay, but the radius of this planet is also different. Radius is in the denominator, so a smaller radius means a bigger acceleration. The radius of the new planet is half of the radius of the Earth. Therefore, the acceleration must be doubled. Almost there . . . because the radius is SQUARED in the denominator, the acceleration must be doubled AGAIN.

"So what is my final answer? The mass causes acceleration to double. The radius causes the acceleration to double, and then to double again. So the total acceleration is multiplied by a factor of 8. The acceleration on this planet is 8 g."

In the much more concise language of algebra, your reasoning might look like this:

$$a = \frac{2}{\left(\frac{1}{2}\right)^2} g = 8g$$

What if the answer choices had been like this?

(A) 2.5 m/s^2
(B) 4.9 m/s^2
(C) 9.8 m/s^2
(D) 19.6 m/s^2
(E) 78.4 m/s^2

Is the problem any different? (Answer: no.)

Concept Questions: "WHY?"

Many multiple-choice questions involve no calculations and no formulas. These test your understanding of vocabulary and explanations for physical phenomena.

Two identical train cars move toward each other, each with the same speed as the other. When the train cars collide, they stick together and remain at rest. Which of the following fundamental physics principles can best be used to explain why the attached cars cannot move after the collision?

(A) Conservation of mechanical energy
(B) Conservation of linear momentum
(C) Conservation of angular momentum
(D) Conservation of mass
(E) Conservation of rotational energy

The direct answer to this question is B: conservation of linear momentum applies to all collisions. The cars had equal momentum in opposite directions, so the net momentum before collision was zero; thus, the cars may not have any momentum after collision. Kinetic energy is a scalar, having no direction, and so kinetic energy of two moving objects cannot cancel to zero. Mechanical energy was not conserved, because kinetic energy was lost in the collision.

But even if you have a hesitation about the difference between momentum and kinetic energy conservation, you can still get close to the right answer by eliminating obvious "stupidicisms." Look at E: perhaps you recognize that there's no such thing as "conservation of rotational energy." Or likely you see right away that conservation of mass, while a legitimate concept, is usually relevant in a chemical process or fluid dynamics and can have little bearing on the speed of train cars in a collision.

Concept Questions: Diagrams

These ask you a simple question based (obviously) on a diagram.

A particle experiences a potential energy U as a function of position x as shown in the diagram above. At which position is the particle in a state of unstable equilibrium?

(A) A
(B) B
(C) C
(D) D
(E) E

For these, you either know what to do with the diagram or you don't. Here you, of course, remember that equilibrium is represented on an energy-position diagram by a horizontal slope and that unstable equilibrium requires the energy-position diagram to be at a maximum. Thus, the answer is C.

Three Things You Can Do with a Graph

You could see so, so many graphs on the AP exam. . . . It's often difficult to remember which graph means what. But if you know your equations, you can usually figure out how to interpret any graph you are faced with. Why? Because there are pretty much ONLY three things you can do with a graph:

1. Take the slope.
2. Find the area under the graph.
3. Read off an axis.

For example, an AP Physics C exam question described an experiment in which a solenoid was stretched to vary the number of turns per length, n. At constant current, the magnetic field inside was plotted as a function of n; the question asked for an experimental value of the permeability of free space μ_0. Chances are that you've never done this experiment and that you've never seen this particular graph. But you do remember your

equations: the magnetic field of a solenoid is $B = \mu_0 nI$. Solving for μ_0, $\mu_0 = \left(\dfrac{B}{n}\right)\left(\dfrac{1}{I}\right)$.

The slope of this graph is $\left(\dfrac{B}{n}\right)$. Therefore, μ_0 must be the **slope** of the graph divided by

the current in the solenoid.

Similarly, imagine a graph of force vs. time on a question that asks for impulse. Since impulse is equal to force times time interval ($\Delta p = F\Delta t$), then impulse must be the **area** under the graph.

Finally, if you're totally clueless about what to do with a graph, just try taking a slope or an area, and see what happens! You might experience a revelation.

Other diagram questions might ask you to:

- use the right-hand rule to determine the direction of a magnetic force on a particle
- identify the direction of an electric or magnetic field
- analyze the properties of a circuit
- recognize the correct free-body diagram of an object
- interpret motion graphs

Many other diagram questions are possible. Try making one yourself—pick your favorite diagram from your textbook, and ask a question about it. Chances are, you have just written an AP multiple-choice question.

Direct Solution with Variables

Because the AP test writers can't ask you to do any kind of difficult number crunching on the multiple-choice section, often they will ask you to do your problem-solving using variables only.

A pendulum of length L is drawn back to position P, as shown in the above diagram, and released from rest. The linear distance from P to the lowest point in the pendulum's swing is d; the vertical distance from P to the lowest point in the swing is h. What is the maximum speed of this pendulum in terms of the above variables and fundamental constants?

(A) $\sqrt{2gL}$

(B) $\sqrt{2gd}$

(C) $\sqrt{2gh}$

(D) $\sqrt{\dfrac{2gd}{L}}$

(E) $\sqrt{\dfrac{2gh}{L}}$

"Ugh . . . too many letters!" you say. We disagree. Solving this problem is no different than solving the same problem with numbers given. In fact, if the variables bother you, try solving with made-up numbers first:

> Let's say the height h is 5 meters, and the mass of the bob is 2 kg . . . well, we use conservation of energy. Energy at the top of the swing is all potential, all mgh. So that's $2 \times 10 \times 5 = 100$ J of potential energy.
>
> At the bottom, all this energy is kinetic. So 100 J $= \frac{1}{2}mv^2$. Solving, $v = 10$ m/s.
>
> Now how did we get that? We set $mgh = \frac{1}{2}mv^2$, and solved for v. The masses cancelled, so $v =$ square root of $2gh$. Lo and behold, that's an answer choice!

When Should You Skip a Question?

Never. There is no penalty for guessing, so guess away!

Some Final Advice on Multiple-Choice Questions

- Know your pace. Take the practice exams under test conditions (45 minutes for 35 questions, or some fraction thereof). Are you getting to all the questions? If not, you are going to need to decide your strengths and weaknesses. Know before the exam which types of problems you want to attempt first. Then, when you take your exam, FOLLOW YOUR PLAN!
- The multiple-choice questions do not necessarily start easy and get harder, as do SAT questions. So if you suspect from your practice that you may be pressed for time, know that problems on your strong topics may be scattered throughout the exam. Problem 35 might be easier for you than problem 5, so look at the whole test.

- Speaking of time, the AP test authors know the time limit of the exam—you must average a minute and a half per question in order to answer everything. So they are not going to write a question that really takes three or four minutes to solve! You must always look for the approach to a problem that will let you solve quickly. If your approach won't get you to a solution in less than two minutes, then either look for another approach or move on.
- One other alternative if you don't see a reasonable direct approach to a problem: look at the answer choices. Some might not make any sense; for example, you can eliminate any choice for a speed that is faster than light, or a couple of answer choices to concept questions might contain obvious errors. Guess from the remaining choices, and move on.
- Correct your practice exam. For any mistakes, write out an explanation of the correct answer and why you got it wrong. Pledge to yourself that you will never make the same mistake twice.

How to Approach the Free-Response Section

The best thing about the free-response section of the AP exam is this: you've been preparing for it *all year long!* "Really?" you ask. "I don't remember spending much time preparing for it."

But think about the homework problems you've been doing throughout the year. Every week, you probably answer a set of questions, each of which might take a few steps to solve, and we bet that your teacher always reminds you to show your work. This sounds like the AP free-response section to us!

The key to doing well on the free-response section is to realize that, first and foremost, these problems test your *understanding* of physics. The purpose is not to see how good your algebra skills are, how many fancy-sounding technical terms you know, or how many obscure theories you can regurgitate. So all we're going to do in this section is give you a few suggestions about how, when you work through a free-response question, you can communicate to the AP readers that you understand the concepts being tested. If you can effectively communicate your understanding of physics, you will get a good score.

What Do the Readers Look For?

Before grading a single student's exam, the high school and college physics teachers who are responsible for scoring the AP free-response section make a "rubric" for each question. A rubric is a grading guide; it specifies exactly what needs to be included for an answer to receive full credit, and it explains how partial credit should be awarded.

For example, consider part of a free-response question:

A student pulls a 1.0-kg block across a table to the right, applying a force of 8.0 N. The coefficient of kinetic friction between the block and the table is 0.20. Assume the block is at rest when it begins its motion.

(a) Determine the force of friction experienced by the block.
(b) Calculate the speed of the block after 1.5 s.

Let's look just at part (b). What do you think the AP readers are looking for in a correct answer? Well, we know that the AP free-response section tests your understanding of physics. So the readers probably want to see that you know how to evaluate the forces acting on an object and how to relate those forces to the object's motion.

In fact, if part (b) were worth 4 points, the readers might award 1 point for each of these elements of your answer:

1. Applying Newton's second law, $F_{net} = ma$, to find the block's acceleration.
2. Recognizing that the net force is not 8.0 N, but rather is the force of the student minus the force of friction [which was found in (a)], 8.0 N − 2.0 N = 6.0 N.
3. Using a correct kinematics equation with correct substitutions to find the final velocity of the block; i.e., $v_f = v_o + at$, where $v_o = 0$ and $a = 6.0$ N/1.0 kg = 6.0 m/s^2.
4. Obtaining a correct answer with correct units, 9.0 m/s.

Now, we're not suggesting that you try to guess how the AP readers will award points for every problem. Rather, we want you to see that the AP readers care much more about your understanding of physics than your ability to punch numbers into your calculator. Therefore, *you* should care much more about demonstrating your understanding of physics than about getting the right final answer.

Partial Credit

Returning to part (b) from the example problem, it's obvious that you can get lots of partial credit even if you make a mistake or two. For example:

- If you forgot to include friction, and just set the student's force equal to *ma* and solved, you could still get 2 out of 4 points.

- If you solved part (a) wrong but still got a reasonable answer, say 4.5 N for the force of friction, and plugged that in correctly here, you would still get either 3 or 4 points in part (b)! Usually the rubrics are designed not to penalize you twice for a wrong answer. So if you get part of a problem wrong, but your answer is consistent with your previous work, you'll usually get full or close to full credit.

- That said, if you had come up with a 1000 N force of friction, which is clearly unreasonable, you probably will not get credit for a wrong but consistent answer, unless you indicate the ridiculousness of the situation. You'll still get probably 2 points, though, for the correct application of principles!

- If you got the right answer using a shortcut—say, doing the calculation of the net force in your head—you would not earn full credit but you would at least get the correct answer point. However, if you did the calculation *wrong* in your head, then you would not get any credit—AP readers can read what's written on the test, but they're not allowed to read your mind. Moral of the story: communicate with the readers so you are sure to get all the partial credit you deserve.

- Notice how generous the partial credit is. You can easily get 2 or 3 points without getting the right answer and 50–75% is in the 4–5 range when the AP test is scored!

You should also be aware of some things that will NOT get you partial credit:

- You will not get partial credit if you write multiple answers to a single question. If AP readers see that you've written two answers, they will grade the one that's wrong. In other words, you will lose points if you write more than one answer to a question, even if one of the answers you write is correct.

- You will not get partial credit by including unnecessary information. There's no way to get extra credit on a question, and if you write something that's wrong, you could lose points. Answer the question fully, then stop.

The Tools You Can Use

You can use a calculator. Most calculators are acceptable—the acceptable calculator list is the same as for the SAT or the AP calculus exam. The obvious forbidden calculators are those with a keyboard, cell phones used as a calculator, or those calculators that make noise or print their answers onto paper.[1] You also cannot share a calculator with anyone during the exam.

The real question, though, is whether a calculator will really help you. The short answer is "Yes": you will be asked questions on the exam that require you to do messy calculations (for example, you might need to divide a number by π, or multiply something by the universal gravitation constant). The longer answer, though, is "Yes, but it won't help very much." To see what we mean, look back at the hypothetical grading rubric for part (b) of the example problem we discussed earlier. Two of the four possible points are awarded for using the right equations, one point is awarded for finding the magnitude of a force using basic arithmetic, and the last point is awarded for solving a relatively simple equation. So you would get half-credit if you did no math at all, and you would get full credit just by doing some very elementary math. You probably wouldn't need to touch your calculator!

So definitely bring a calculator to the exam, but don't expect that you'll be punching away at it constantly.

The other tool you can use on the free-response section is the equations sheet. You will be given a copy of this sheet in your exam booklet. It's a handy reference because it lists all the equations that you're expected to know for the exam.

However, the equations sheet can also be dangerous. Too often, students interpret the equations sheet as an invitation to stop thinking: "Hey, they tell me everything I need to know, so I can just plug-and-chug through the rest of the exam!" Nothing could be further from the truth.

First of all, you've already *memorized* the equations on the sheet. It might be reassuring to look up an equation during the AP exam, just to make sure that you've remembered it correctly. And maybe you've forgotten a particular equation, but seeing it on the sheet will jog your memory. This is exactly what the equations sheet is for, and in this sense, it's pretty nice to have around. But beware of the following:

- Don't look up an equation unless you know *exactly* what you're looking for. It might sound obvious, but if you don't know what you're looking for, you won't find it.
- Don't go fishing. If part of a free-response question asks you to find an object's momentum, and you're not sure how to do that, don't just rush to the equations sheet and search for every equation with a "P" in it.

Math and the Physics C Exam

Physics C students often worry about the math they're expected to know for the AP exam, because some of the material covered in the Physics C curriculum involves pretty complicated calculus. Maxwell's equations, for example, involve concepts that are well beyond the scope of most high school calculus classes.

---

[1]Does anyone actually use printing calculators anymore?

Whether or not you are carrying an A in your AP Calculus course is irrelevant. Most importantly, you must have a strong understanding of the physical meaning behind the mathematics. The problems that might seem to involve calculus—those that use an integral or derivative equation from the equations sheet—can often be approached with algebraic methods. Remember, an integral is just the area under a graph; a derivative is just the slope of a graph. If you have to, set up an integral and don't solve it. Or explain in words what your answer should look like. Also, note that many of the equations that appear on the equations sheet as calculus expressions rarely or never need calculus. For instance, Gauss's law has a nasty integral in it, but when used correctly, Gauss's law rarely requires any calculus. Whatever you do, it is *not* worth the time and frustration to focus exclusively on the tough calculus—this isn't a math exam, and the point distribution in the rubrics reflects this fact.

Other Advice About the Free-Response Section

- Always show your work. If you use the correct equation to solve a problem but you plug in the wrong numbers, you will probably get partial credit, but if you just write down an incorrect answer, you will definitely get no partial credit.

- If you don't know precisely how to solve a problem, simply explain your thinking process to the grader. If a problem asks you to find the centripetal acceleration of a satellite orbiting a planet, for example, and you don't know what equations to use, you might write something like this: "The centripetal force points toward the center of the satellite's orbit, and this force is due to gravity. If I knew the centripetal force, I could then calculate the centripetal acceleration using Newton's second law." This answer might earn you several points, even though you didn't do a single calculation.

- However, don't write a book. Keep your answers succinct.

- Let's say that part (b) of a question requires you to use a value calculated in part (a). You didn't know how to solve part (a), but you know how to solve part (b). What should you do? We can suggest two options. First, make up a reasonable answer for part (a), and then use that answer for part (b). Or, set some variable equal to the answer from part (a) (write a note saying something like, "Let v be the velocity found in part (a)"). Then, solve part (b) in terms of that variable. Both of these methods should allow you to get partial or even full credit on part (b).

- If you make a mistake, cross it out. If your work is messy, circle your answer so that it's easy to find. Basically, make sure the AP readers know what you want them to grade and what you want them to ignore.

- If you're stuck on a free-response question, try another one. Question #3 might be easier for you than question #1. Get the easy points first, and then only try to get the harder points if you have time left over.

- Always use units where appropriate.

- It may be helpful to include a drawing or a graph in your answer to a question, but make sure to label your drawings or graphs so that they're easy to understand.

- No free-response question should take you more than about 15 minutes to solve. They're not designed to be outrageously difficult, so if your answer to a free-response problem is outrageously complicated, you should look for a new way to solve the problem, or just skip it and move on.

Lab Questions

It is all well and good to be able to solve problems and calculate quantities using the principles and equations you've learned. However, the true test of any physics theory is whether or not it WORKS.

The AP development committee is sending a message to students that laboratory work is an important aspect of physics. To truly understand physics, you must be able to design and analyze experiments. Thus, *each free-response section will contain at least one question that involves experiment design and analysis.*

Here's an example:

In the laboratory, you are given a metal block, about the size of a brick. You are also given a 2.0-m-long wooden plank with a pulley attached to one end. Your goal is to determine experimentally the coefficient of kinetic friction, μ_k, between the metal block and the wooden plank.

(a) Draw a labeled diagram showing how the plank, the metal block, and the additional equipment you selected will be used to measure μ_k.
(b) Briefly outline the procedure you will use, being explicit about what measurements you need to make and how these measurements will be used to determine μ_k.

To answer a lab question, just follow these steps:

1. **Follow the directions.**
   Sounds simple, doesn't it? When the test says, "Draw a diagram," it means they want you to draw a diagram. And when it says, "Label your diagram," it means they want you to label your diagram. You will likely earn points just for these simple steps.

Exam tip from an AP Physics veteran:
On the 1999 AP test, I forgot to label point *B* on a diagram, even though I obviously knew where point *B* was. This little mistake cost me several points!

—*Zack, engineer*

---

2. **Use as few words as possible.**
   Answer the question, then stop. You can lose credit for an incorrect statement, even if the other 15 statements in your answer are correct. The best idea is to keep it simple.

3. **There is no single correct answer.**
   Most of the lab questions are open-ended. There might be four or more different correct approaches. So don't try to "give them the answer they're looking for." Just do something that seems to make sense—you might well be right!

4. **Don't assume you have to use all the stuff they give you.**
   It might sound fun to use a force probe while determining the time constant of an RC circuit, but really! A force probe!?!

5. **Don't over-think the question.**
   They're normally not too complicated. Remember, you're supposed to take only 15 minutes to write your answer. You're not exactly designing a subatomic particle accelerator.

6. **Don't state the obvious.**
   You may assume that basic lab protocols will be followed. So there's no need to tell the reader that you recorded your data carefully, nor do you need to remind the reader to wear safety goggles.

Now Put It All Together

Here are two possible answers to the sample question. Look how explicit we were about what quantities are measured, how each quantity is measured, and how μ_k is determined. We aren't *artistes*, so our diagram doesn't look so good. But for the AP exam, we believe in substance over style. All the necessary components are there, and that's all that matters.

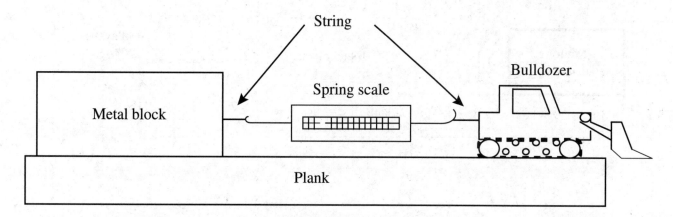

Answer #1

In the laboratory, you are given a metal block, about the size of a brick. You are also given a 2.0-m-long wooden plank with a pulley attached to one end. Your goal is to determine experimentally the coefficient of kinetic friction, μ_k, between the metal block and the wooden plank.

(a) Draw a labeled diagram showing how the plank, the metal block, and the additional equipment you selected will be used to measure μ_k.

(b) Briefly outline the procedure you will use, being explicit about what measurements you need to make and how these measurements will be used to determine μ_k.

Use the balance to determine the mass, m, of the metal block. The weight of the block is mg. Attach the spring scale to the bulldozer; attach the other end of the spring scale to the metal block with string. Allow the bulldozer to pull the block at constant speed.

The block is in equilibrium. So, the reading of the spring scale while the block is moving is the friction force on the block; the normal force on the block is equal to its weight. The coefficient of kinetic friction is equal to the spring scale reading divided by the block's weight.

Answer #2

In the laboratory, you are given a metal block, about the size of a brick. You are also given a 2.0-m-long wooden plank with a pulley attached to one end. Your goal is to determine experimentally the coefficient of kinetic friction, μ_k, between the metal block and the wooden plank.

(a) Draw a labeled diagram showing how the plank, the metal block, and the additional equipment you selected will be used to measure μ_k.

(b) Briefly outline the procedure you will use, being explicit about what measurements you need to make and how these measurements will be used to determine μ_k.

Determine the mass, m, of the block with the balance. The weight of the block is mg. Attach a string to the block and pass the string over the pulley. Hang masses from the other end of the string, changing the amount of mass until the block can move across the plank at constant speed. Use the motion detector to verify that the speed of the block is as close to constant as possible.

The block is in equilibrium. So, the weight of the hanging masses is equal to the friction force on the block; the normal force on the block is equal to its weight. The coefficient of kinetic friction is thus equal to the weight of the hanging masses divided by the block's weight.

CHAPTER 8

Extra Drill on Difficult but Frequently Tested Topics

IN THIS CHAPTER

Summary: Drills in five types of problems that you should spend extra time reviewing, with step-by-step solutions.

Key Ideas
✪ Tension problems
✪ Electric and magnetic fields problems
✪ Inclined plane problems
✪ Motion graph problems
✪ Simple circuits problems

Practice problems and tests cannot possibly cover every situation that you may be asked to understand in physics. However, some categories of topics come up again and again, so much so that they might be worth some extra review. And that's exactly what this chapter is for—to give you a focused, intensive review of a few of the most essential physics topics.

We call them "drills" for a reason. They are designed to be skill-building exercises, and as such, they stress repetition and technique. Working through these exercises might remind you of playing scales if you're a musician or of running laps around the field if you're an athlete. Not much fun, maybe a little tedious, but very helpful in the long run.

The questions in each drill are all solved essentially the same way. *Don't* just do one problem after the other . . . rather, do a couple, check to see that your answers are right,[1] and then, half an hour or a few days later, do a few more, just to remind yourself of the techniques involved.

---

[1]For numerical answers, it's okay if you're off by a significant figure or so.

Tension

How to Do It

Use the following steps to solve these kinds of problems: (1) Draw a free-body diagram for each block; (2) resolve vectors into their components; (3) write Newton's second law for each block, being careful to stick to your choice of positive direction; and (4) solve the simultaneous equations for whatever the problem asks for.

The Drill

In the diagrams below, assume all pulleys and ropes are massless, and use the following variable definitions.

$$F = 10 \text{ N}$$
$$M = 1.0 \text{ kg}$$
$$\mu = 0.2$$

Find the tension in each rope and the acceleration of the set of masses.
(For a greater challenge, solve in terms of F, M, and μ instead of plugging in values.)

1. Frictionless

2. Frictionless

3. Frictionless

4. Coefficient of Friction μ

5.

6.

7. Frictionless

8. Frictionless

9. Frictionless

10. Coefficient of Friction μ

11. Coefficient of Friction μ

12. Frictionless

13. Frictionless

14. Coefficient of Friction μ

› The Answers
(Step-by-Step Solutions to #2 and #5 Are on the Next Page.)

1. $a = 10$ m/s^2

2. $a = 3.3$ m/s^2
$T = 3.3$ N

3. $a = 1.7$ m/s^2
$T_1 = 1.7$ N
$T_2 = 5.1$ N

4. $a = 1.3$ m/s^2
$T = 3.3$ N

5. $a = 3.3$ m/s^2
$T = 13$ N

6. $a = 7.1$ m/s^2
$T_1 = 17$ N
$T_2 = 11$ N

7. $a = 3.3$ m/s^2
$T = 6.6$ N

8. $a = 6.7$ m/s^2
$T_1 = 13$ N
$T_2 = 10$ N

9. $a = 1.7$ m/s^2
$T_1 = 5.1$ N
$T_2 = 8.3$ N

10. $a = 6.0$ m/s^2
$T = 8.0$ N

11. $a = 8.0$ m/s^2
$T_1 = 10$ N
$T_2 = 4.0$ N

12. $a = 5.0$ m/s^2
$T = 15$ N

13. $a = 3.3$ m/s^2
$T_1 = 13$ N
$T_2 = 20$ N

14. $a = 0.22$ m/s^2
$T_1 = 20$ N
$T_2 = 29$ N

Step-by-Step Solution to #2:

Step 1: Free-body diagrams:

No components are necessary, so on to *Step 3:* write Newton's second law for each block, calling the rightward direction positive:

$$T - 0 = ma.$$
$$F - T = (2m)a.$$

Step 4: Solve algebraically. It's easiest to add these equations together, because the tensions cancel:

$$F = (3m)a, \text{ so } a = F/3m = (10 \text{ N})/3(1 \text{ kg}) = 3.3 \text{ m/s}^2.$$

To get the tension, just plug back into $T - 0 = ma$ to find $T = F/3 = 3.3$ N.

Step-by-Step Solution to #5:

Step 1: Free-body diagrams:

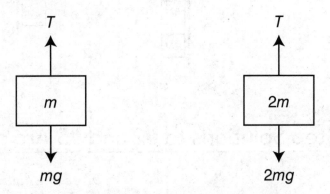

No components are necessary, so on to *Step 3:* write Newton's second law for each block, calling clockwise rotation of the pulley positive:

$$(2m)g - T = (2m)a.$$
$$T - mg = ma.$$

Step 4: Solve algebraically. It's easiest to add these equations together, because the tensions cancel:

$$mg = (3m)a, \text{ so } a = g/3 = 3.3 \text{ m/s}^2.$$

To get the tension, just plug back into $T - mg = ma$: $T = m(a + g) = (4/3)mg = 13$ N.

Electric and Magnetic Fields

How to Do It

The force of an electric field is $F = qE$, and the direction of the force is in the direction of the field for a positive charge. The force of a magnetic field is $F = qvB \sin\theta$, and the direction of the force is given by the right-hand rule.

The Drill

The magnetic field above has magnitude 3.0 T. For each of the following particles placed in the field, find (a) the force exerted by the magnetic field on the particle, and (b) the acceleration of the particle. Be sure to give magnitude *and direction* in each case.

1. an e- at rest
2. an e- moving ↑ at 2 m/s
3. an e- moving ← at 2 m/s
4. a proton moving ⊙ at 2 m/s
5. an e- moving up and to the right, at an angle of 30° to the horizontal, at 2 m/s
6. an e- moving up and to the left, at an angle of 30° to the horizontal, at 2 m/s
7. a positron moving up and to the right, at an angle of 30° to the horizontal, at 2 m/s
8. an e- moving → at 2 m/s
9. a proton moving ⊗ at 2 m/s

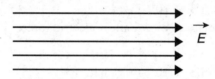

The electric field above has magnitude 3.0 N/C. For each of the following particles placed in the field, find (a) the force exerted by the electric field on the particle, and (b) the acceleration of the particle. Be sure to give magnitude *and direction* in each case.

10. an e- at rest
11. a proton at rest
12. a positron at rest
13. an e- moving ↑ at 2 m/s
14. an e- moving → at 2 m/s
15. a proton moving ⊙ at 2 m/s
16. an e- moving ← at 2 m/s
17. a positron moving up and to the right, at an angle of 30° to the horizontal, at 2 m/s

› The Answers
(Step-by-Step Solutions to #2 and #10 Are on the Next Pages.)

1. No force or acceleration, $v = 0$.

2. $F = 9.6 \times 10^{-19}$ N, out of the page.
   $a = 1.1 \times 10^{12}$ m/s², out of the page.

3. No force or acceleration, $\sin \theta = 0$.

4. $F = 9.6 \times 10^{-19}$ N, toward the top of the page.
   $a = 5.6 \times 10^{8}$ m/s², toward the top of the page.

5. $F = 4.8 \times 10^{-19}$ N, out of the page.
   $a = 5.3 \times 10^{11}$ m/s², out of the page.

6. $F = 4.8 \times 10^{-19}$ N, out of the page.
   $a = 5.3 \times 10^{11}$ m/s², out of the page.

7. $F = 4.8 \times 10^{-19}$ N, into the page.
   $a = 5.3 \times 10^{11}$ m/s², into the page.

8. No force or acceleration, $\sin \theta = 0$.

9. $F = 9.6 \times 10^{-19}$ N, toward the bottom of the page.
   $a = 5.6 \times 10^{8}$ m/s², toward the bottom of the page.

10. $F = 4.8 \times 10^{-19}$ N, left.
    $a = 5.3 \times 10^{11}$ m/s², left.

11. $F = 4.8 \times 10^{-19}$ N, right.
    $a = 2.8 \times 10^{8}$ m/s², right.

12. $F = 4.8 \times 10^{-19}$ N, right.
    $a = 5.3 \times 10^{11}$ m/s², right.

13. $F = 4.8 \times 10^{-19}$ N, left.
    $a = 5.3 \times 10^{11}$ m/s², left.
    Velocity does not affect electric force.

14. $F = 4.8 \times 10^{-19}$ N, left.
    $a = 5.3 \times 10^{11}$ m/s², left.

15. $F = 4.8 \times 10^{-19}$ N, right.
    $a = 2.8 \times 10^{8}$ m/s², right.

16. $F = 4.8 \times 10^{-19}$ N, left.
    $a = 5.3 \times 10^{11}$ m/s², left.

17. $F = 4.8 \times 10^{-19}$ N, right.
    $a = 5.3 \times 10^{11}$ m/s², right.

Step-by-Step Solution to #2:

(a) The magnetic force on a charge is given by $F = qvB \sin \theta$. Since the velocity is perpendicular to the magnetic field, $\theta = 90°$, and $\sin \theta = 1$. The charge q is the amount of charge on an electron, 1.6×10^{-19} C. v is the electron's speed, 2 m/s. B is the magnetic field, 3 T.

$$F = (1.6 \times 10^{-19} \text{ C})(2 \text{ m/s})(3 \text{ T})(1) = 9.6 \times 10^{-19} \text{ N}$$

The direction is given by the right-hand rule. Point your fingers in the direction of the electron's velocity, toward the top of the page; curl your fingers in the direction of the magnetic field, to the right; your thumb points into the page. Since the electron has a negative charge, the force points opposite your thumb, or out of the page.

(b) Even though we're dealing with a magnetic force, we can still use Newton's second law. Since the magnetic force is the only force acting, just set this force equal to *ma* and solve. The direction of the acceleration must be in the same direction as the net force.

$$9.6 \times 10^{-19} \text{ N} = (9.1 \times 10^{-31} \text{ kg})a$$
$$a = 1.1 \times 10^{12} \text{ m/s}^2, \text{ out of the page}$$

Step-by-Step Solution to #10:

(a) The electric force on a charge is given by $F = qE$. The charge q is the amount of charge on an electron, 1.6×10^{-19} C. E is the electric field, 3 N/C.

$$F = (1.6 \times 10^{-19} \text{ C})(3 \text{ N/C}) = 4.8 \times 10^{-19} \text{ N}$$

Because the electron has a negative charge, the force is opposite the electric field, or right.

(b) Even though we're dealing with an electric force, we can still use Newton's second law. Since the electric force is the only force acting, just set this force equal to ma and solve. The direction of the acceleration must be in the same direction as the net force.

$$4.8 \times 10^{-19} \text{ N} = (9.1 \times 10^{-31} \text{ kg})a$$
$$a = 2.8 \times 10^8 \text{ m/s}^2, \text{ left}$$

Inclined Planes

How to Do It

Use the following steps to solve these kinds of problems: 1) Draw a free-body diagram for the object (the normal force is perpendicular to the plane; the friction force acts along the plane, opposite the velocity); 2) break vectors into components, where the parallel component of weight is $mg(\sin \theta)$; 3) write Newton's second law for parallel and perpendicular components; and 4) solve the equations for whatever the problem asks for.

Don't forget, the normal force is NOT equal to mg when a block is on an incline!

The Drill

Directions: For each of the following situations, determine:

(a) the acceleration of the block down the plane
(b) the time for the block to slide to the bottom of the plane

In each case, assume a frictionless plane unless otherwise stated; assume the block is released from rest unless otherwise stated.

1.

20 m

40°

2.

$h = 10$ m

20 m

3.

$F_f = 10$ N

m

20 m

40°

$m = 10$ kg

4.

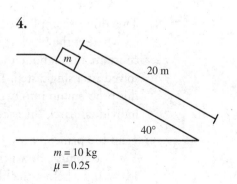

m

20 m

40°

$m = 10$ kg
$\mu = 0.25$

5.

6.

7.

8.

Careful—this one's tricky.

❯ The Answers
(A Step-by-Step Solution to #1 Is on the Next Page.)

1. $a = 6.3$ m/s², down the plane.
   $t = 2.5$ s

2. $a = 4.9$ m/s², down the plane.
   $t = 2.9$ s

3. $a = 5.2$ m/s², down the plane.
   $t = 2.8$ s

4. $a = 4.4$ m/s², down the plane.
   $t = 3.0$ s

5. Here the angle of the plane is 27° by trigonometry, and the distance along the plane is 22 m.
   $a = 4.4$ m/s², down the plane.
   $t = 3.2$ s

6. $a = 6.3$ m/s², down the plane.
   $t = 1.8$ s

7. $a = 6.3$ m/s², down the plane.
   $t = 3.5$ s

8. This one is complicated. Since the direction of the friction force changes depending on whether the block is sliding up or down the plane, the block's acceleration is NOT constant throughout the whole problem. So, unlike problem #7, this one can't be solved in a single step. Instead, in order to use kinematics equations, you must break this problem up into two parts: up the plane and down the plane. During each of these individual parts, the acceleration is constant, so the kinematics equations are valid.

   • up the plane:
   $a = 6.8$ m/s², down the plane.
   $t = 0.4$ s before the block turns around to come down the plane.

- down the plane:

  $a = 1.5$ m/s², down the plane.

  $t = 5.2$ s to reach bottom.

So, a total of $t = 5.6$ s for the block to go up and back down.

Step-by-Step Solution to #1:

Step 1: Free-body diagram:

Step 2: Break vectors into components. Because we have an incline, we use inclined axes, one parallel and one perpendicular to the incline:

Step 3: Write Newton's second law for each axis. The acceleration is entirely directed parallel to the plane, so perpendicular acceleration can be written as zero:

$$mg \sin \theta - 0 = ma.$$
$$F_N - mg \cos \theta = 0.$$

Step 4: Solve algebraically for a. This can be done without reference to the second equation. (In problems with friction, use $F_f = \mu F_N$ to relate the two equations.)

$$a = g \sin \theta = 6.3 \text{ m/s}^2$$

To find the time, plug into a kinematics chart:

$$v_o = 0$$
$$v_f = \text{unknown}$$
$$\Delta x = 20 \text{ m}$$
$$a = 6.3 \text{ m/s}^2$$
$$t = \text{???}$$

Solve for t using the second star equation for kinematics (**): $\Delta x = v_o t + \frac{1}{2}at^2$, where v_o is zero;

$$t = \sqrt{\frac{2\Delta x}{a}} = \sqrt{\frac{2(20\text{ m})}{6.3\text{ m/s}^2}} = 2.5\text{ s}$$

Motion Graphs

How to Do It

For a position–time graph, the slope is the velocity. For a velocity–time graph, the slope is the acceleration, and the area under the graph is the displacement.

The Drill

Use the graph to determine something about the object's speed. Then play "Physics *Taboo*": suggest what object might reasonably perform this motion and explain in words how the object moves. Use everyday language. In your explanation, you may *not* use any words from the list below:

velocity
acceleration
positive
negative
increase
decrease
object
constant

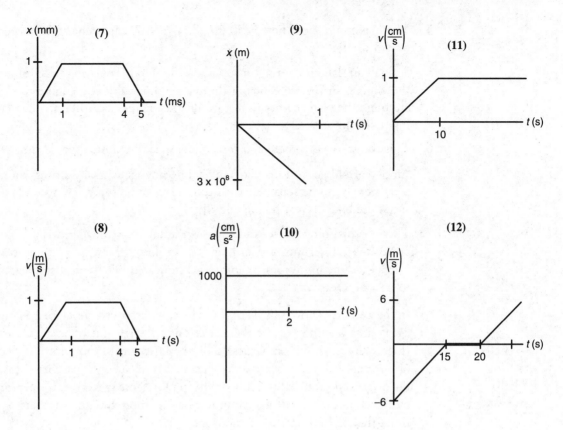

› The Answers

Note that our descriptions of the moving objects reflect our own imaginations. You might have come up with some very different descriptions, and that's fine . . . provided that your answers are conceptually the same as ours.

1. The average speed over the first 5 s is 10 m/s, or about 22 mph. So:

   Someone rolls a bowling ball along a smooth road. When the graph starts, the bowling ball is moving along pretty fast, but the ball encounters a long hill. So, the ball slows down, coming to rest after 5 s. Then, the ball comes back down the hill, speeding up the whole way.

2. This motion only lasts 1 s, and the maximum speed involved is about 5 mph. So:

   A biker has been cruising up a hill. When the graph starts, the biker is barely moving at jogging speed. Within half a second, and after traveling only a meter up the hill, the bike turns around, speeding up as it goes back down the hill.

3. The maximum speed of this thing is 30 cm/s, or about a foot per second. So:

   A toy racecar is moving slowly along its track. The track goes up a short hill that's about a foot long. After 2 s, the car has just barely reached the top of the hill, and is perched there momentarily; then, the car crests the hill and speeds up as it goes down the other side.

4. The steady speed over 200 s (a bit over 3 minutes) is 0.25 m/s, or 25 cm/s, or about a foot per second.

   A cockroach crawls steadily along the school's running track, searching for food. The cockroach starts near the 50-yard line of the football field; around 3 minutes later, the cockroach reaches the goal line and, having found nothing of interest, turns around and crawls at the same speed back toward his starting point.

5. The maximum speed here is 50 m/s, or over 100 mph, changing speed dramatically in only 5 or 10 s. So:

   A small airplane is coming in for a landing. Upon touching the ground, the pilot puts the engines in reverse, slowing the plane. But wait! The engine throttle is stuck! So, although the plane comes to rest in 5 s, the engines are still on. The plane starts speeding up backwards! Oops . . .

6. This thing covers 5 meters in 3 seconds, speeding up the whole time.

   An 8-year-old gets on his dad's bike. The boy is not really strong enough to work the pedals easily, so he starts off with difficulty. But, after a few seconds he's managed to speed the bike up to a reasonable clip.

7. Though this thing moves quickly—while moving, the speed is 1 m/s—the total distance covered is 1 mm forward, and 1 mm back; the whole process takes 5 ms, which is less than the minimum time interval indicated by a typical stopwatch. So we'll have to be a bit creative:

   In the *Discworld* novels by Terry Pratchett, wizards have developed a computer in which living ants in tubes, rather than electrons in wires and transistors, carry information. (Electricity has not been harnessed on the Discworld.) In performing a calculation, one of these ants moves forward a distance of 1 mm, stays in place for 3 ms, and returns to the original position. If this ant's motion represents two typical "operations" performed by the computer, then this computer has an approximate processing speed of 400 Hz times the total number of ants inside.

8. Though this graph *looks* like #7, this one is a velocity–time graph, and so indicates completely different motion.

   A small child pretends he is a bulldozer. Making a "brm-brm-brm" noise with his lips, he speeds up from rest to a slow walk. He walks for three more seconds, then slows back down to rest. He moved forward the entire time, traveling a total distance (found from the area under the graph) of 4 m.

9. This stuff moves 300 million meters in 1 s at a constant speed. There's only one possibility here: electromagnetic waves in a vacuum.

   Light (or electromagnetic radiation of any frequency) is emitted from the surface of the moon. In 1 s, the light has covered about half the distance to Earth.

10. Be careful about axis labels: this is an *acceleration*–time graph. Something is accelerating at 1000 cm/s² for a few seconds. 1000 cm/s² = 10 m/s², about Earth's gravitational acceleration. Using kinematics, we calculate that if we drop something from rest near Earth, after 4 s the thing has dropped 80 m.

    One way to simulate the effects of zero gravity is to drop an experiment from the top of a high tower. Then, because everything that was dropped is speeding up at the same rate, the effect is just as if the experiment were done in the Space Shuttle—at least until everything hits the ground. In this case, an experiment is dropped from a 250-ft tower, hitting the ground with a speed close to 90 mph.

11. One cm/s is ridiculously slow. Let's use the world of slimy animals:

    A snail wakes up from his nap and decides to find some food. He speeds himself up from rest to his top speed in 10 s. During this time, he's covered 5 cm, or about the length of your pinkie finger. He continues to slide along at a steady 1 cm/s, which means that a minute later he's gone no farther than a couple of feet. Let's hope that food is close.

12. This one looks a bit like those up-and-down-a-hill graphs, but with an important difference—this time the thing stops not just for an instant, but for five whole seconds, before continuing back toward the starting point.

A bicyclist coasts to the top of a shallow hill, slowing down from cruising speed (~15 mph) to rest in 15 s. At the top, she pauses briefly to turn her bike around; then, she releases the brake and speeds up as she goes back down the hill.

Simple Circuits

How to Do It

Think "series" and "parallel." The current through series resistors is the same, and the voltage across series resistors adds to the total voltage. The current through parallel resistors adds to the total current, and the voltage across parallel resistors is the same.

The Drill

For each circuit drawn below, find the current through and voltage across each resistor.
    Note: Assume each resistance and voltage value is precise to two significant figures.

1.

5.

2.

3.

6.

7.

4.

› The Answers
(A Step-by-Step Solution to #2 Is on the Next Page.)

1.

V	I	R
12 V	0.40 A	30 Ω
12 V	0.60 A	20 Ω
12 V	1.2 A	10 Ω
12 V	2.2 A	5.5 Ω

2.

V	I	R
3.2 V	1.6 mA	2 kΩ
6.8 V	0.9 mA	8 kΩ
6.8 V	0.7 mA	10 kΩ
10 V	1.6 mA	6.4 kΩ

(Remember, a kΩ is 1000 Ω, and a mA is 10^{-3} A.)

3.

V	I	R
2.5 V	0.051 A	50 Ω
2.1 V	0.021 A	100 Ω
2.1 V	0.030 A	70 Ω
4.6 V	0.051 A	91 Ω

4.

V	I	R
5.2 V	4.3 mA	1.2 kΩ
5.2 V	3.7 mA	1.4 kΩ
6.8 V	4.2 mA	1.6 kΩ
6.8 V	3.8 mA	1.8 kΩ
12 V	8.0 mA	1.5 kΩ

5.

V	I	R
3.4 V	0.034 A	100 Ω
6.8 V	0.034 A	200 Ω
10 V	0.025 A	400 Ω
10 V	0.059 A	170 Ω

6.

V	I	R
1.8 V	0.90 A	2.0 Ω
0.7 V	0.13 A	5.0 Ω
0.8 V	0.13 A	6.0 Ω
10.3 V	1.03 A	10.0 Ω
12.0 V	1.03 A	11.7 Ω

7.

V	I	R
3 V	0.15 A	20 Ω
10 V	0.10 A	100 Ω
10 V	0.05 A	200 Ω
2 V	0.15 A	13 Ω
15 V	0.15 A	100 Ω

Step-by-Step Solution to #2:

Start by simplifying the combinations of resistors. The 8 kΩ and 10 kΩ resistors are in parallel. Their equivalent resistance is given by

$$\frac{1}{R_{eq}} = \frac{1}{8\text{ k}\Omega} + \frac{1}{10\text{ k}\Omega}$$

which gives $R_{eq} = 4.4$ kΩ.

Next, simplify these series resistors to their equivalent resistance of 6.4 kΩ.

The total resistance of the entire circuit is 6.4 kΩ (i.e., 6400 Ω). Because we know the total voltage of the entire circuit to be 10 V, we can use Ohm's law to get the total current

$$I_{total} = \frac{V_{total}}{R_{total}} = \frac{10\text{ V}}{6400\ \Omega} = 0.0016\text{ A}$$

(more commonly written as 1.6 mA).

Now look at the previous diagram. The same current of 1.6 mA must go out of the battery, into the 2 kΩ resistor, and into the 4.4 kΩ resistor. The voltage across each resistor can thus be determined by $V = (1.6\text{ mA})R$ for each resistor, giving 3.2 V across the 2 kΩ resistor and 6.8 V across the 4.4 kΩ resistor.

The 2 kΩ resistor is on the chart. However, the 4.4 kΩ resistor is the equivalent of two parallel resistors. Because voltage is the same for resistors in parallel, there are 6.8 V across *each* of the two parallel resistors in the original diagram. Fill that in the chart, and use Ohm's law to find the current through each:

$$I_{8k} = 6.8\text{ V}/8000\ \Omega = 0.9\text{ mA}$$
$$I_{10k} = 6.8\text{ V}/10{,}000\ \Omega = 0.7\text{ mA}$$

STEP 4

Review the Knowledge You Need to Score High

CHAPTER 9

Kinematics

IN THIS CHAPTER

Summary: The entire goal of motion analysis is to describe, calculate, and predict where an object is, how fast it's moving, and how much its speed is changing. In this chapter, you'll review two separate approaches to make these predictions and descriptions: graphs and algebra.

Key Ideas

✪ The cart's **position** (x) tells where the cart is on a track.

✪ The cart's **speed** (v) tells how fast the cart is moving.[1]

✪ **Acceleration** (a) tells how much the object's speed changes in one second. When an object speeds up, its acceleration is in the direction of its motion; when an object slows down, its acceleration is opposite the direction of its motion.

✪ **Displacement** (Δx) tells how far the object ends up away from its starting point, regardless of any motion in between starting and ending positions.

✪ The graphical analysis of motion includes **position-time graphs** and **velocity-time graphs**. On a position-time graph, the slope is the object's speed, and the object's position is read from the vertical axis. For velocity-time graphs, the speed is read from the vertical axis, and the slope is the object's acceleration.

---

[1]Strictly speaking, speed is the magnitude—the amount—of the velocity vector. Velocity tells how fast something moves, as well as in which direction it moves. I tend to use "speed" and "velocity" interchangeably, especially in this unit; the distinction between the two is not important here.

- ✪ The **five principal motion variables** are:
  v_0 initial velocity
  v_f final velocity
  Δx displacement
  a acceleration
  t time
- ✪ In any case of accelerated motion, when three of the five principal motion variables are known, the remaining variables can be solved for using the kinematic equations.
- ✪ **Free fall** means no forces other than the object's weight are acting on the object.
- ✪ A **projectile** is an object in free fall, but it isn't falling in a straight vertical line. To approach a projectile problem, make two motion charts: one for vertical motion and one for horizontal motion.

Relevant Equations

The constant-acceleration kinematics equations,

$$v_f = v_0 + at$$

$$\Delta x = v_0 t + \tfrac{1}{2}at^2$$

$$v_f^2 = v_0^2 + 2a\Delta x$$

The equilibrium problems we saw in the last chapter all had something in common: there was no acceleration. Sure, an object can move at a constant velocity and still be in equilibrium, but as soon as an object's velocity changes, you need a new set of tricks to analyze the situation. This is where kinematics comes in.

Introduction to Motion in a Straight Line

Pretty much all motion problems can be demonstrated with a cart on a track, like in the diagram above. The motion detector can read the location of the cart up to 50 times each second. This detector can make graphs of position or velocity versus time.

The entire goal of motion analysis is to describe, calculate, and predict where the cart is, how fast it's moving, and how much its speed is changing. You'll use two separate approaches to make these predictions and descriptions: graphs and algebra.

Graphical Analysis of Motion

Before you start any analysis, tell yourself which kind of graph you're looking at. The most common mistake in studying motion graphs is to interpret a velocity-time graph as a position-time graph, or vice versa.

Position-Time Graphs

Example 1: The preceding position-time graph represents the cart on the track. The motion detector is located at position $x = 0$; the positive direction is to the left.

An AP exam question could ask all sorts of questions about this cart. How should they be approached? Use these facts, and reason from them.

FACT: In a position-time graph, the object's position is read from the vertical axis.

Look at the vertical axis in Example 1. At the beginning of the motion, the cart is located 40 cm to the left of the detector.[2] After 2 s, the cart is located 10 cm left of the detector. Therefore, in the first 2 s of its motion, the cart moved 30 cm to the right.

FACT: In a position-time graph, the object's speed is the slope of the graph. The steeper the slope, the faster the object moves. If the slope is a front slash (/), the movement is in the positive direction; if the slope is a backslash (\), the movement is in the negative direction.

Wait a second. How can I tell the slope of a curved graph? Take the slope of a target line. If I want to know how fast the object is moving after 2 seconds of motion, I take the slope drawn in the following figure.

---

[2]Why not 40 cm to the right of the detector? Because the position value is +40 cm and the positive direction is left.

Mathematically, this means you divide (change in *y*-value)/(change in *x*-value) to get a speed that's a bit more than 6 cm/s.

You'll often be asked to describe the motion of the cart in words and to justify your answer. When you describe motion, use normal language that your grandparents would understand. Avoid technical terms like "acceleration" and "negative." Instead, say "slowing down" or "moving to the right." Justify your answer with direct reference to the facts in this chapter.

Referring back to Example 1, because the slope was steeper at earlier times and shallower at later times, the cart must be slowing down. The car is moving to the right the whole time, because the slope is always a backslash.

Velocity-Time Graphs

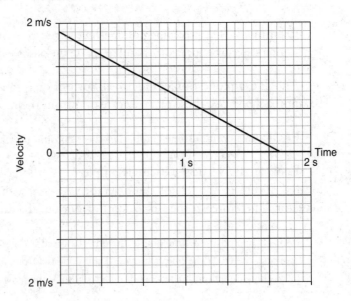

Example 2: The preceding velocity-time graph represents a different cart on the track. The positive direction is to the left.

FACT: In a velocity-time graph, the object's speed is read from the vertical axis. The direction of motion is indicated by the sign on the vertical axis.

In Example 2, at the beginning of the motion, the vertical axis reads 1.8 m/s. This means that initially, the cart was moving 1.8 m/s to the left. After 1 second, the cart was moving about 0.8 m/s. A bit less than 2 seconds into the motion, the vertical axis reads zero, so the cart stopped.

FACT: In a velocity-time graph, the object's acceleration is the slope of the graph.

You could do the rise/run calculation to find the amount of the acceleration, or you could use the definition of acceleration to see that the object lost 1 m/s of speed in 1 second, making the acceleration 1 m/s per second.[3] The cart in Example 2 was slowing down and

---

[3]Textbooks and problems on the AP exam will write this as 1 m/s². Well, that's silly—what the heck is a "second squared," anyway? When you see that notation, read it as "meters per second per second." I suggest you always write the units of acceleration as "m/s per second." Then you'll be far less likely to make "The Mistake."

moving to the left. When an object slows down, its acceleration is opposite the direction of its motion; this cart has an acceleration to the right.

The Mistake

Acceleration is **not** the same thing as speed or velocity. Speed says how fast something moves; acceleration says how quickly speed changes. Acceleration doesn't say anything about which way something is moving, unless you know whether the thing is speeding up or is slowing down.

Someone who says, "This car has an acceleration of 4 m/s per second, so it is moving at about a jogging pace," has made "The Mistake." The car is speeding up or slowing down by 4 m/s every second; the car could well be an Indy 500 racecar traveling 94 m/s right now, but only 90 m/s a second later.

Someone who says "The cart in Figure 2 has a negative acceleration, so it is moving to the right" has made "The Mistake." An acceleration to the right means either speeding up and moving right, or slowing down and moving left. While the cart's acceleration is negative—after all, the slope of the line is a backslash—the car was slowing down, making the velocity's direction opposite the acceleration's direction. The acceleration is right, and the velocity is left.

It takes a lot of practice to avoid "The Mistake." Just continually remind yourself of the meaning of acceleration (how much an object's speed changes in one second), and you'll get there.

FACT: The object's displacement is given by the area between the graph and the horizontal axis. The location of the object can't be determined from a velocity-time graph; only how far the object ended up from its starting point can be determined.

To find how far the cart in Example 2 moved, take the area of the triangle in the graph,[4] giving about 1.6 m. Since the cart's velocity as read from the vertical axis was positive that whole time, and the positive direction is left, the cart ended up 1.6 m left of where it started. But exactly where it started, no one knows.

Algebraic Analysis of Motion

Example 3: A model rocket is launched straight upward with an initial speed of 50 m/s. It speeds up with a constant upward acceleration of 2.0 m/s per second until its engines stop at an altitude of 150 m.

Sometimes you'll be asked to analyze motion from a description and not a graph. Start your analysis by defining a positive direction and clearly stating the start and the end of the motion you're considering. For example, take the upward direction as positive,[5] and consider from the launch to when the engines stop.

Next, *make a chart* giving the values of the five principal motion variables. Include a plus or minus sign on every one (except time—a negative time value means you're in a Star Trek–style movie). If a variable isn't given in the problem, leave that variable blank.

---

[4]The area of a triangle is (1/2) base × height.

[5]Could I have called the downward direction positive? Sure. Then signs of displacement, velocity, and acceleration would all be switched.

The Five Principal Motion Variables for Your Chart

v_0 initial velocity
v_f final velocity
Δx displacement
a acceleration
t time

For Example 3, the chart looks like this:

v_0	+50 m/s
v_f	
Δx	+150 m
a	+2.0 m/s per second
t	

The acceleration is positive because the rocket was speeding up; therefore, acceleration is in the same direction as the motion, which was upward. Upward was defined as the positive direction here.

FACT: In any case of accelerated motion when three of the five principal motion variables are known, the remaining variables can be solved for using the kinematic equations.

In Example 3, we know three of the five motion variables; therefore, we can find the others, and the physics is *done*.

Whoa there. Um, how is the physics "done"? Don't we have to plug the numbers into the kinematic equations, which incidentally you haven't mentioned yet?

While you will often be asked, say, to calculate how much time the engines run for, you'll just as often be asked something that doesn't involve calculation. For example, "Is it possible to determine the running time of the engines?" Or, "When the engines have run for half of their total run time, is the rocket at a height greater than, less than, or equal to 75 m?"[6]

More to the point, actually doing the math here is, well, a *math* skill, not a physics skill. As long as your answers are reasonable—a model rocket will likely burn for a few seconds, not a few thousand seconds—the exam is likely to award close to full, or sometimes even full, credit for a correct chart and for recognizing the correct equation to use.

FACT: To calculate the missing values in a motion chart, use the three kinematic equations listed as follows. Choose whichever equation works mathematically. Never solve a quadratic equation. If the math becomes overly complicated, try solving for a different missing variable first.

Kinematic Equations

1. $v_f = v_0 + at$

2. $\Delta x = v_0 t + \dfrac{1}{2}at$

3. $v_f^2 = v_0^2 + 2a\Delta.$

---

[6]The answer is *less than* 75 m. The rocket is speeding up throughout the time when the engines burn. In the second half of the burn time, the rocket is (on average) moving faster, and so it covers more distance.

Continuing with Example 3, we can use equation (3) to solve for the final velocity of the rocket[7]; this is about 56 m/s.[8] Then we can use equation (1) to get the time before the engines shut off, which is 3 seconds. If you had tried to use equation (2) to solve for time, you would have gotten a quadratic; that's why I said to use equation (3) and then (1).

Objects in Free Fall

FACT: When an object is in free fall, its acceleration is 10 m/s per second[9] toward the ground.

"Free fall" means no forces other than the object's weight are acting on the object.

Let's do more with the rocket in Example 3. When the engines stop, the rocket is moving upward at 56 m/s. The rocket doesn't just stop on a dime. It keeps moving upward, but it slows down, losing 10 m/s of speed every second.

Try making a chart for the motion from when the engines stop to when the rocket reaches the peak of its flight. We'll keep the positive direction as upward.

v_0 +56 m/s

v_f 0 (The peak of flight is when the object stops to turn around.)

Δx

a −10 m/s per second (There is negative acceleration because free-fall acceleration is always *down*.)

t

Three of the five variables are known so the physics is *done*.

Now, be careful that you keep grounded in what's physically happening, not in the algebra. For example, you might be asked for the maximum height that the rocket in Example 3 reaches.

Good job recognizing that you need equation (3) to solve for Δx. Dropping the units during the calculation, that gives $0^2 = 56^2 + 2(-10)(\Delta x)$. Solving with a calculator you get about 160 m for Δx.

Wait a second! Think what the 160 m answer means—that's the distance the rocket goes between when the engines stop and when the rocket reaches its highest height. That's not the height above the ground, just the additional height after the engines stop! The actual maximum height is this 160 m, plus the 150 m that the rocket gained with its engines on, for a total of 310 m.

Projectile Motion

A *projectile* is defined as an object in free fall. But this object doesn't have to be moving in a straight line. What if the object were launched at an angle? Then you treat the horizontal and vertical components of its motion separately.

Example 4: A ball is shot out of a cannon pointed at an angle of 30° above the horizontal. The ball's initial speed is 25 m/s. The ball lands on ground that is level with the cannon.

FACT: A projectile has no horizontal acceleration and so moves at constant speed horizontally.

A projectile is in free fall, so its vertical acceleration is 10 m/s per second downward.

---

[7]This calculation requires a calculator, of course: $v_f^2 = (50 \text{ m/s})^2 + 2(2 \text{ m/s per second})(150 \text{ m})$.

[8]Not 55.67764363 m/s. Don't make me ask your chemistry teacher to talk to you about significant figures again. Just use two or three figures on all values, and we'll all be happy.

[9]No, stop it with the 9.8 m/s per second. The College Board is very clear that you can and should use a free-fall acceleration of 10 m/s per second.

To approach a projectile problem, make *two* motion charts: one for vertical motion and one for horizontal motion.

FACT: To find the vertical component of a velocity at an angle, multiply the speed by the sine of the angle. To find the horizontal component of a velocity at an angle, multiply the speed by the cosine of the angle. This always works, as long as the angle is measured from the horizontal.

Here are the two charts for the ball's motion in Example 4. Consider up and right to be the positive directions. Let's consider the motion while the ball is in free fall—that means, starting right after the ball was shot, and ending right before the ball hits the ground. Note that the initial vertical velocity is $(25 \text{ m/s})(\sin 30°) = 13 \text{ m/s}$. The initial horizontal velocity is $(25 \text{ m/s})(\cos 30°) = 22 \text{ m/s}$. You needed to use your calculator to get these values.

Vertical	**Horizontal**
$v_0 + 22 \text{ m/s}$	$v_0 + 13 \text{ m/s}$
v_f	v_f
Δx^0	Δx
$a -10 \text{ m/s per second}$	a^0
t	t

Two entries here are tricky. Remember that displacement only means the distance traveled start to end, regardless of what happens in between. Well, this ball landed on "level ground." That means that the ball ends up at the same vertical height from which it was shot; it didn't end up any higher or lower than it started. Thus, vertical displacement is zero.

Second, the final vertical velocity is unknown, not zero. Sure, once the ball hits the ground it stops; but then it's not in free fall anymore. The "final" velocity here is the velocity in the instant before the ball hits the ground.

FACT: The horizontal and vertical motion charts for a projectile must use the same value for time.

The vertical chart is completely solvable, because three of the five variables are identified. Once the time of flight is calculated from the vertical chart, that time can be plugged into the horizontal chart, and *voila*, we have three of five horizontal variables identified; the chart can be completed.

What If Acceleration Isn't Constant?

A typical Physics C kinematics question asks you to use calculus to find position, velocity, or acceleration functions. Then you can solve a motion problem even if acceleration is not constant. The way to remember what to do is, first and foremost, to understand graphical kinematics as discussed in the section below. Then, we know that the slope of a graph is related to the *derivative* of a function; the area under a graph is related to the *integral* of a function. Therefore:

- To find velocity from a position function, take the derivative with respect to time: $v = \dfrac{dx}{dt}$

- To find acceleration from a velocity function, also take the time derivative: $a = \dfrac{dv}{dt}$

- To find position from a velocity function, take the integral with respect to time: $x = \int v\,dt$

- To find velocity from an acceleration function, take the time integral: $v = \int a\,dt$

Most of the time, even on the Physics C exam, you'll be able just to use the constant acceleration kinematics equations to solve a kinematics problem. Reserve your use of calculus for those problems that explicitly include an unusual function for position, velocity, or acceleration.

Air Resistance and the First-Order Differential Equation

The force of air resistance is usually negligible in kinematics problems. You probably don't believe me, though. After all, unless you're on the moon, or unless your teacher is using a vacuum chamber for demonstrations, air is all around us. And if I dropped a piece of paper simultaneously and from the same height as a lead weight, the weight would hit the ground first—and by a huge margin. Certainly. Obviously.

Why don't you try it? But be sure you *crinkle up the paper first* and drop it from about waist height. Notice how the lead weight hits the ground WAY before . . .

Oops.

The weight and the paper hit the ground essentially at the same time. If the weight did hit first, the difference wasn't anything you could reliably time or even be sure enough to gamble on.

Conclusion: As long as we're not throwing objects out of our car on the freeway, air resistance is not important in kinematics.

The most common questions asked:

> **When *is* air resistance important? And how should it be dealt with?**
> Air resistance should only be considered when the problem explicitly says so. Usually, a problem will suggest that the force of air acts opposite to an object's velocity, and is equal to a constant times the velocity: $F_{air} = bv$.[10]

1. **Find the terminal speed.** Terminal speed means that, after a long time, the object's speed becomes constant. To find that terminal speed, do an equilibrium problem: Free body, set up forces equal down forces, and left forces equal right forces. If something's falling straight down with no other forces, usually you'll get $bv = mg$. Then solve for v. That's the terminal speed.

2. **Sketch a graph of the speed of the object as a function of time.** Perhaps the problem will say the object was dropped from rest, or give an initial velocity. Well, you can plot that point at time $t = 0$. Then you can find the terminal velocity using the method above—the terminal speed is the constant velocity after a long time. Plot a horizontal line for the terminal velocity near the right-hand side of the t-axis.

   In between the initial velocity and the terminal velocity, just know that the velocity function will look like an exponential function, changing rapidly at first, and changing less rapidly as time goes on. Sketch a curve in between the point and the line you drew. Done.

---

[10]Occasionally you might see a different form, $F_{air} = bv^2$. In this case, you might be asked about the terminal speed, but you will NOT have to solve a differential equation.

3. **Describe the motion in words, including what's happening to the acceleration and/or the velocity.** Be sure to use a free-body diagram, and to separate the motion if necessary into parts when the object is moving up, and moving down. When the speed is zero, the force of air resistance is zero. This doesn't mean no acceleration, of course. When the speed is not zero, use a free body to figure out the amount and direction of the net force. Remind yourself of the basics of kinematics—the net force is the direction of acceleration. If the acceleration is in the direction of motion, the object speeds up; if the acceleration is opposite motion, the object slows down.

4. **Solve a differential equation to find an expression for the velocity as a function of time.** Again, start with a free-body diagram, and write $F_{net} = ma$. Now, though, you'll need to do some calculus: acceleration $a = \dfrac{dv}{dt}$. Perhaps your Newton's second law equation might say something like $mg - bv = ma$.

   Okay, solve for a and write the calculus expression for a: $\dfrac{dv}{dt} = g - \dfrac{b}{m}v$. This type of equation is called a differential equation, where a derivative of a function is proportional to the function itself. Specifically, since the *first* derivative is involved, this is called a "first-order" differential equation.

   Your calculus class may well have taught you how to solve this equation by a technique known as separation of variables: put all the v terms on one side, the t terms on the other, and integrate. If you know how to do that, great; if not, it's complex enough not in any way to be worth learning in order to possibly—*possibly*—earn yourself one or two points. Everyone, though, should be able to recognize and write the answer using the knowledge that **the solution to a first-order differential equation will involve an exponential function.** You can use facts about the initial velocity and the terminal velocity to write this function without an algorithmic solution.

   Imagine that a ball was dropped from rest in the presence of air resistance $F_{air} = bv$. Writing the second law gives you the equation shown above. What's the solution? Well, the initial velocity is zero; the terminal velocity can be found by setting acceleration to zero, meaning $v_{term} = \dfrac{mg}{b}$. The answer will *always* be something like $v(t) = Ae^{-kt}$ or $v(t) = A(1 - e^{-kt})$. Start by figuring out which: does the speed start large, and get small? If so, use the first expression. Or, does the speed start small, and get larger? If so, use the second expression. In this case, the speed starts from zero and ends up faster. So we use $v(t) = A(1 - e^{-kt})$. Generally, the k term is going to be whatever's multiplying the v in the original equation. In this case, then, $k = b/m$.

   Now, look at the initial and final conditions to find the value of A. At time $t = 0$, $v = 0$; that works no matter the value of A, because $e^0 = 1$. But after a long time, we know the terminal velocity is mg/b. And in the equation, e^{-kt} goes to zero for large t. Meaning: after a long time, the velocity function equals A. This A must be the terminal velocity!

   So our final equation looks like: $v(t) = \dfrac{mg}{b}\left(1 - e^{-\frac{b}{m}t}\right)$.

〉 Practice Problems

Multiple Choice:

1. A firework is shot straight up in the air with an initial speed of 50 m/s. What is the maximum height it reaches?

   (A) 12.5 m
   (B) 25 m
   (C) 125 m
   (D) 250 m
   (E) 1250 m

2. On a strange, airless planet, a ball is thrown downward from a height of 17 m. The ball initially travels at 15 m/s. If the ball hits the ground in 1 s, what is this planet's gravitational acceleration?

   (A) 2 m/s^2
   (B) 4 m/s^2
   (C) 6 m/s^2
   (D) 8 m/s^2
   (E) 10 m/s^2

3. An object moves such that its position is given by the function $x(t) = 3t^2 - 4t + 1$. The units of t are seconds, and the units of x are meters. After 6 s, how fast and in what direction is this object moving?

   (A) 32 m/s in the original direction of motion
   (B) 16 m/s in the original direction of motion
   (C) 0 m/s
   (D) 16 m/s opposite the original direction of motion
   (E) 32 m/s opposite the original direction of motion

Free Response:

4. An airplane attempts to drop a bomb on a target. When the bomb is released, the plane is flying upward at an angle of 30° above the horizontal at a speed of 200 m/s, as shown below. At the point of release, the plane's altitude is 2.0 km. The bomb hits the target.

   (a) Determine the magnitude and direction of the vertical component of the bomb's velocity at the point of release.
   (b) Determine the magnitude and direction of the horizontal component of the bomb's velocity at the point when the bomb contacts the target.
   (c) Determine how much time it takes for the bomb to hit the target after it is released.
   (d) At the point of release, what angle below the horizontal does the pilot have to look in order to see the target?

› Solutions to Practice Problems

1. Call "up" the positive direction, and set up a chart. We know that $v_f = 0$ because, at its maximum height, the firework stops for an instant.

v_0	+50 m/s
v_f	0
Δx	?
a	-10 m/s^2
t	?

Solve for Δx using equation: $v_f^2 = v_0^2 + 2a(\Delta x)$. The answer is (C) 125 m, or about skyscraper height.

2. Call "down" positive, and set up a chart:

v_0	+15 m/s
v_f	?
Δx	+17 m
a	?
t	1 s

Plug straight into ($\Delta x = v_0 t + \frac{1}{2}at^2$) and you have the answer. This is NOT a quadratic, because this time t is a known quantity. The answer is (B) 4 m/s^2, less than half of Earth's gravitational field, but close to Mars's gravitational field.

3. First find the velocity function by taking the derivative of the position function: $v(t) = 6t - 4$. Now plug in $t = 6$ to get the velocity after 6 s; you get 32 m/s. Note that this velocity is positive. Was the object originally moving in the positive direction? Plug in $t = 0$ to the velocity formula to find out . . . you find the initial velocity to be -4 m/s, so the object was originally moving in the negative direction, and has reversed direction after 6 s. The answer is (E).

4. (a) Because the angle 30° is measured to the horizontal, the magnitude of the vertical component of the velocity vector is just (200 m/s) (sin 30°), which is 100 m/s. The direction is "up," because the plane is flying up.

(b) The horizontal velocity of a projectile is constant. Thus, the horizontal velocity when the bomb hits the target is the same as the horizontal velocity at release, or (200 m/s)(cos 30°) = 170 m/s, to the right.

(c) Let's call "up" the positive direction. We can solve this projectile motion problem by our table method.

Horizontal			Vertical		
v_0	+170 m/s		v_0	+100 m/s	
v_f	+170 m/s		v_f	?	
Δx	?		Δx	-2000 m	
a	0		a	-10 m/s^2	
t	?		t	?	

Don't forget to convert to meters, and be careful about directions in the vertical chart.

The horizontal chart cannot be solved for time; however, the vertical chart can. Though you could use the quadratic formula or your fancy calculator to solve $x - x_0 = v_0 t + \frac{1}{2}at^2$, it's much easier to start with, $v_f^2 = v_0^2 + 2a$ $(x - x_0)$, to find that v_f vertically is -220 m/s (this velocity must have a negative sign because the bomb is moving down when it hits the ground). Then, plug in to ($v_f = v_0 + at$) to find that the bomb took 32 s to hit the ground.

(d) Start by finding how far the bomb went horizontally. Because horizontal velocity is constant, we can say distance = velocity × time. Plugging in values from the table, distance = (170 m/s)(32 s) = 5400 m. Okay, now look at a triangle:

By geometry, tan $\theta = 2000$ m/5400 m. The pilot has to look down at an angle of 20° below the horizontal; since he was already flying 30° above horizontal, he has to look 20° + 30° = 50° below his line of sight.

› Rapid Review

- In a position-time graph, the object's position is read from the vertical axis.

- In a position-time graph, the object's speed is the slope of the graph. The steeper the slope, the faster the object moves. If the slope is a front slash (/), the movement is in the positive direction; if the slope is a backslash (\), the movement is in the negative direction.

- In a velocity-time graph, the object's speed is read from the vertical axis. The direction of motion is indicated by the sign on the vertical axis.

- In a velocity-time graph, the object's acceleration is the slope of the graph.

- In a velocity-time graph, the object's displacement is given by the area between the graph and the horizontal axis. The location of the object can't be determined from a velocity-time graph; only how far it ended up from its starting point can be determined.

- In any case of accelerated motion when three of the five principal motion variables are known, the remaining variables can be solved for using the kinematic equations.

- To calculate the missing values in a motion chart, use the three kinematic equations listed below. Choose whichever equation works mathematically.

  (1) $v_f = v_0 + at$

  (2) $\Delta x = v_0 t + \frac{1}{2}at^2$

  (3) $v_f^2 = v_0^2 + 2a\Delta x$

- When an object is in free fall, its acceleration is 10 m/s per second toward the ground. "Free fall" means no forces other than the object's weight are acting on the object.

- A projectile has no horizontal acceleration, and so it moves at constant speed horizontally. A projectile is in free fall, so its vertical acceleration is 10 m/s per second downward.

- To find the vertical component of a velocity at an angle, multiply the speed by the sine of the angle. To find the horizontal component of a velocity at an angle, multiply the speed by the cosine of the angle. This always works, as long as the angle is measured from the horizontal.

- The horizontal and vertical motion charts for a projectile must use the same value for time.

CHAPTER 10

Forces and Newton's Laws

IN THIS CHAPTER

Summary: A force is a push or a pull applied by one object on another object. This chapter describes the construction and use of free-body diagrams, which are key to approaching problems involving forces.

Definitions

- ✪ A **force** is a push or a pull applied by one object and experienced by another object.
- ✪ The **net force** on an object is the single force that could replace all the individual forces acting on an object and produce the same effect. Forces acting in the same direction add together to determine the net force; forces acting in opposite directions subtract to determine the net force.
- ✪ **Weight** is the force of a planet on an object near that planet.
- ✪ The **force of friction** is the force of a surface on an object. The friction force acts parallel to the surface. **Kinetic friction** is the friction force when something is moving along the surface and acts opposite the direction of motion. **Static friction** is the friction force between two surfaces that aren't moving relative to one another.
- ✪ The **normal force** is also the force of a surface on an object. The normal force acts perpendicular to the surface.
- ✪ The **coefficient of friction** is a number that tells how sticky two surfaces are.
- ✪ **Newton's third law** says that the force of Object A on Object B is equal in amount and opposite in direction to the force of Object B on Object A.
- ✪ **Newton's second law** states that an object's acceleration is the net force it experiences divided by its mass, and is in the direction of the net force.

Describing Forces: Free-Body Diagrams

A force is a push or a pull applied by one object and experienced by another object. A force in the laboratory is often measured by a spring scale, as in the preceding picture. In AP Physics C we have to understand two aspects of forces. First, we have to describe the application of the force: What are the objects involved, and how much force is applied and in which direction? Next, we have to connect the net force acting on an object to that object's change in velocity.

Start with correct language: an object can "experience" a force, but an object cannot "have" a force. Don't let yourself say, "Ball A has a bigger force than Ball B"—that means nothing. "The net force on Ball A is bigger than on Ball B" is fine, as is "The Earth pulls harder on Ball A than on Ball B."

The canonical method of describing forces acting on an object is to draw a free-body diagram. A free-body diagram should include two elements:

(1) A labeled arrow representing each force, with each arrow beginning on the object and pointing in the direction in which the force acts
(2) A list of all the forces acting on the object, indicating the object applying the force and the object experiencing the force

On the AP exam you'll be asked something like, "Draw and label the forces (not components) that act on the car as it slows down." This means "Draw a free-body diagram."

FACT: Only gravitational and electromagnetic forces can act on an object without contact.[1]

Example 1: A car moving to the right on the freeway applies the brakes and skids to a stop.

Pretty much always start with the force of the Earth on the object, which is commonly known as its weight. Don't call this force "gravity"—that's an ambiguous term. Weight acts downward and doesn't require any contact with the Earth in order to exist.[2] Draw a downward arrow on the dot, label it "weight," and in the list write "Weight: force of Earth on the car."[3]

---

[1]In AP Physics C, anyway.
[2]Chapter 14, on gravitation, explains more about how to find the weight of an object in a gravitational field.
[3]Why not call it "force of gravity on the car?" Well, because all forces must be exerted by an *object* on another object. Since when is "gravity" an object? ☺

Any other forces must be a result of contact with the car. What's the car touching? It's touching just the ground. Since the car is touching the ground, the ground exerts a normal force perpendicular to the surface. Draw an upward arrow on the dot, label it something like "F_n," and in the list write "F_n: The force of the ground on the car."[4]

Since the car is sliding along the ground, the ground exerts a force of (kinetic) friction. By definition, kinetic friction must always act in the opposite direction of motion—the car skids right along the ground; the friction force acts to the left. Draw a leftward arrow on the dot, label it "F_f," and in the list write "F_f: The force of the ground on the car."[5]

The car is not in contact with anything else, so we're done.

F_n: Force of ground on car
F_f: Force of ground on car
Weight: Force of Earth on car

Whoa there! The car is moving to the right, so what about the force of its motion?

There's no such thing as the "force of motion." All forces must be exerted by an identifiable object; and all nongravitational and non-electromagnetic forces must be a result of contact. The car is not in contact with anything that pushes the car forward.

Then how is the car moving to the right?

It just is. It is critically important to focus *only* on the problem as stated. Questions about what happened before the problem started are irrelevant. Perhaps at first the car was pushed by the engine, or pulled by a team of donkeys, to start it moving; perhaps it had been in motion since the beginning of time. It doesn't matter. All that matters is that when we tune in to the action, the car is moving right and slowing down.

If the car had been pulled by a team of donkeys to start it moving, wouldn't we put the force of the donkeys on the car on the free-body diagram?

No, because the free-body diagram includes only forces that act *now*, not forces that acted earlier, or forces that will act in the future. If donkeys pulled the car, the force of the donkeys would appear on the free-body while the donkeys were actually pulling. After they let go and the car is slowing down, the donkeys might as well have never existed.

While it's important to learn how to draw a free-body diagram, it's just as important to learn how to *stop* drawing a free-body diagram. Don't make up forces. Unless you can clearly identify the source of the force, don't include the force.

---

[4]It makes no difference what you label the arrow, as long as you define the label in a list. You want to call it N instead of F_n? Be my guest.

[5]Yes, both the friction force and the normal force are properly listed as the force of the ground on the car.

Exam Tip from an AP Physics Veteran
If you see a problem involving forces, try drawing a free-body diagram for each object in the problem, or for a system including multiple objects. A free-body diagram will always be useful, even if you're not explicitly asked to make one.

Determining the Net Force

To determine the net force on an object, treat each direction separately. Add forces that point in the same direction; subtract forces that point in opposite directions. Or, if you know the acceleration in a direction, use $F_{net} = ma$.

FACT: When an object moves along a surface, the acceleration in a direction perpendicular to that surface must be zero. Therefore, the net force perpendicular to the surface is also zero.

In Example 1, the net force horizontally is equal to the force of friction, because that's the only force acting in the horizontal direction—there's no other force to add or subtract. Vertically, the net force is equal to the normal force minus the weight. But since the car is moving along the surface, the vertical acceleration and the vertical net force on the car are zero.

We can conclude, then, that the normal force on the car is equal to the car's weight. This isn't a general fact, though—a normal force is *not* always equal to an object's weight. If more vertical forces are acting, or if the surface is changing speed vertically (as in an elevator), the normal force can be different from the weight.

FACT: The kinetic friction force is equal to the coefficient of kinetic friction times the normal force.

$$F_f = \mu_k F_n$$

A good AP question might describe a second car, identical in mass and initial speed to the car in Example 1, but on a wet freeway. The question might ask you to explain why this second car skids to a stop over a longer distance.

The coefficient of friction is a property of the surfaces in contact. Here, since a wet road is less "sticky" than a dry road, the coefficient of friction has decreased. But since the second car is identical to the first, its weight and thus the normal force of the surface on the car is the same as before. Therefore, by the equation $F_f = \mu F_n$, the new car experiences a smaller force of friction.

With a smaller net force on the second car, its acceleration is also smaller by $F_{net} = ma$. Then the distance traveled during the skid depends on the car's acceleration by the kinematics equation (3), $v_f^2 = v_0^2 + 2a\Delta x$. Take the final speed v_f to zero and solve for Δx to see that acceleration a is in the denominator of the equation. Thus, a smaller acceleration means a larger distance to stop.

Static and Kinetic Friction

You may have learned that the coefficient of friction takes two forms: **static** and **kinetic** friction. Use the coefficient of static friction if something is stationary, and the coefficient of kinetic friction if the object is moving. The equation for the force of friction is essentially the same in either case: $F_f = \mu F_N$.

The only strange part about static friction is that the coefficient of static friction is a *maximum* value. Think about this for a moment—if a book just sits on a table, it doesn't need any friction to stay in place. But that book won't slide if you apply a very small horizontal pushing force to it, so static friction can act on the book. To find the maximum coefficient of static friction, find out how much horizontal pushing force will just barely cause the book to move; then use $F_f = \mu F_N$.

Exam tip from an AP Physics veteran:

Newton's second law works for *all* kinds of forces, not just tensions, friction, and such. Often what looks like a complicated problem with electricity or magnetism is really just an $F_{net} = ma$ problem, but the forces might be electric or magnetic in nature.

—Jonas, high school senior

Newton's Third Law

FACT: The force of Object A on Object B is equal in amount and opposite in direction to the force of Object B on Object A. These two forces, which act on different objects, are called Newton's third law companion forces.[6]

In Example 1, then, what's the Newton's third law companion force to the normal force? It's tempting to say, "Oh, the weight." After all, the weight is equal to the normal force and is opposite in direction to the normal force. But that's wrong.

To find the companion force, look at the description of the force in the free-body diagram, and reverse the objects applying and experiencing the force. The normal force is the force of the ground on the car, and that acts upward. Therefore, the third law companion force is the force of the car on the ground, acting downward.

Forces at Angles

FACT: If the net force has both a vertical and a horizontal component, use the Pythagorean theorem to determine the magnitude of the net force, and use the tangent function to determine the direction of the net force.

In most AP problems, though, the net force will be zero in one or both directions. In Example 1, the magnitude of the net force is equal to only the magnitude of the friction force, because the vertical forces must subtract to zero.

If this were an AP problem, chances are it would ask about the connection between the net force and the change in the object's speed. We'll revisit this example later.

A force at an angle is drawn on a free-body diagram just like any other force. But when you're ready to do any analysis on the free-body diagram, start by breaking the angled force into components.

---

[6]Or, sometimes, this is called a Newton's third law force pair.

Example 2: A pair of fuzzy dice is hanging by a string from your rearview mirror, as shown in the preceding figure. You speed up from a stoplight. During the acceleration, the dice do not move vertically; the string makes an angle of $\theta = 22°$ with the vertical. The dice have mass 0.10 kg.

No matter what this problem ends up asking, you'll want to draw a free-body diagram. What forces act on the dice? Certainly the weight of the dice (the force of the Earth on the dice) acts downward. No electrical forces exist, so all other forces must be contact forces. The only object actually in contact with the dice is the string. The string pulls up on the dice at an angle, as shown in the picture. I labeled the force of the string on the dice "T," which stands for "tension"—which means the force of a string.

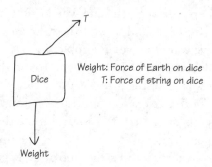

What about the force of the car on the dice?

What about it? The car is not in contact with the dice; the string is. It's the string, not the car, applying the force to the dice.

Determining the Net Force

It's likely that you'd be asked to determine the net force on these dice. But the tension acts both up *and* to the right. How do you deal with the vertical and horizontal forces, then?

FACT: When a force acts at an angle θ measured from the horizontal:

- The vertical component of that force is equal to the amount of the force itself times $\sin \theta$.
- The horizontal component of that force is equal to the amount of the force itself times $\cos \theta$.

Before you do any further work to find the net force, break all individual forces into horizontal and vertical components as best as you can. Here, the weight is already vertical. The tension becomes two separate components: $T\sin 68°$ goes in the vertical direction, and $T\cos 68°$ goes in the horizontal direction. Now you're ready to answer any possible problem.

Exam Tip from an AP Physics Veteran

Do *not* put force components on the same diagram as the force itself. You won't earn full credit. First, draw all forces at whatever angle is appropriate. Then, on a *separate diagram*, redraw the forces with the angled forces broken into components.

FACT: The acceleration of an object is F_{net}/m. This is the same thing as saying

$$\boxed{F_{net} = ma}$$

Whoa. I get that the net force is the horizontal Tcos68°, and that I can write that Tcos68° = (0.1 kg)(a). But the problem didn't give me an acceleration, it didn't give the tension—I'm stuck to solve for anything. The College Board screwed this problem up, right?

It's vanishingly unlikely that the problem is unsolvable as posed. You obviously can't ask questions of the College Board during the AP exam. So if you're absolutely sure the exam is screwed up, you can just state where you think the problem is unclear, make up the information you need, and do your best. Chances are, though, that you need to find a creative alternative way to solve the problem.

Look at the problem statement: It said that the dice have a mass of 0.10 kg. This means that the weight of the dice is 1.0 N.[7] Since the dice are moving only in a horizontal direction, vertical acceleration (and the vertical net force on the dice) must be zero. Forces in opposite directions subtract to determine the net force. Here, that means that the up force must equal the down force of 1.0 N. The up force is $T\sin 68°$, which equals 1.0 N. Plug in from your calculator that the sine of 68 degrees is 0.93, and then solve to find the tension is 1.1 N.

Now deal with the horizontal direction. The horizontal net force is $T\cos 68°$, which is (1.1 N)(0.37) = 0.41 N. Since there's no vertical net force, 0.41 N to the right is the entire net force. And then $a = F_{net}/m$, so acceleration is 0.41 N/0.10 kg = 4.1 m/s per second. That's pretty much everything there is to calculate.

The Mistake

It's tempting to use this equation in all sorts of circumstances. For example, I'm sitting in a chair. Since I'm near the Earth, the force of the Earth on me is equal to my weight of 930 N. I know my mass is 93 kg. Use $a = F_{net}/m$. My acceleration must be 930 N/93 kg, or 10 m/s per second.

Um, no. I'm sitting in a chair. My speed isn't changing, so my acceleration is zero. The value of 10 m/s per second of acceleration means I'm in free fall. What went wrong?

I experience more forces than just the force of the Earth, of course. The chair is pushing up on me. Since I know that my acceleration is zero, the chair pushes up on me with 930 N of force. Now the up force and the down force on me subtract to zero. Phew.

Only the *net* force equals mass times acceleration. Never set a force equal to *ma* unless it's the net force.

What Else Could You Be Asked?

The AP exam doesn't like to ask for calculations. So what else could be asked relating to Example 2?

---

[7]On the Earth, 1 kg of mass weighs 10 N. This fact is discussed in more detail in Chapter 14, Gravitation.

Here's one thought: If the dice were to instead hang from a bigger angle than 22° from the vertical, would the tension go up, go down, or stay the same?

The best way to answer this type of question is to make the calculation, and then explain what part of the calculation leads to the correct answer.

Make up a bigger angle: call it 60° from the vertical. (Or choose any number; just make a significant difference in the new situation. Don't choose 23°.) Start back from the beginning: The dice still have a 0.10-kg mass, and the weight of the dice is still 1.0 N. The vertical acceleration is still zero, which means we can set the up force equal to the down force. But now the up force has changed, from $T \sin 68°$ to $T \sin 30°$.[8] Now we set $T \sin 30°$ equal to 1.0 N, giving a tension of 2.0 N.

The answer, then, is that the tension increases. The weight remains the same and the vertical component of tension must stay the same, but since to calculate tension we end up dividing the 1.0-N weight by the sine of the angle from the horizontal, a smaller angle from the horizontal gives a bigger tension.

Exam Tip from an AP Physics Veteran
If you are asked whether something increases, decreases, or stays the same, you might want to start by making a calculation to see numerically what happens to the answer. Be sure to explain *why* the calculation came out the way it did.

Inclined Planes

Treat objects on inclines the same as any other objects. Draw a free-body diagram, break angled forces into components, and use $a = F_{net}/m$ in each direction. The only major difference is that you don't use horizontal and vertical components for the forces. Instead, you look separately at the forces parallel to the incline and at the forces perpendicular to the incline.

Any normal force will be perpendicular to the incline, and so won't have to be broken into components as long as the object is moving up or down the incline. Any friction force will be parallel to the incline and so won't have to be broken into components. It's the weight—the force of the Earth—that will be broken into components.

FACT: On an incline of angle θ (measured from the horizontal), break the weight into components:

- The component of the weight that is parallel to the incline is equal to the weight times $\sin \theta$.
- The component of the weight that is perpendicular to the incline is equal to the weight times $\cos \theta$.

Example problems and extra drills on this frequently tested topic are available in Chapter 17.

---

[8]Remember, we had to measure from the horizontal according to the fact on the previous page.

Multiple Objects

When two masses are connected over a pulley, it's often easiest to start by considering both objects as a single system. Draw the free-body diagram for the entire system, and use $a = F_{net}/m$ to find the acceleration of the system. Then, if you need to find the tension in the connecting rope, or if you need to talk about just one of the two connected objects, draw a new free-body diagram just for that object.

FACT: One rope has just one tension.[9]

An alternative approach is to start by drawing two separate free-body diagrams, one for each object. Write $F_{net} = ma$ for each object separately. Then, recognizing that the tension is the same in each equation, solve algebraically for the acceleration and tension.

This Chapter Was Not as Easy as You Thought

Be careful with this chapter. Most Physics C students say, "Oh, come on, this stuff is easy . . . let's move on to something challenging." Okay, you're right—if you're at the level you need to be for Physics C, basic Newton's second law problems need to be easy for you. What you must remember from this and the equilibrium chapter is the **absolute necessity** of free-body diagrams.

No matter how easy or hard an F_{net} problem may seem, you must start the problem with a free-body diagram. Points are awarded for the free-body diagram, and that diagram will ensure that you don't make minor mistakes on the rest of the problem. My own Physics C students frequently mess up on what should be straightforward problems when they try to take shortcuts. If you draw the FBD and follow the four-step problem-solving procedure, it's hard to go wrong. Even professional physicists use free-body diagrams. You must, too.

› Practice Problems

Multiple Choice:

1. A 2.0-kg cart is given a shove up a long, smooth 30° incline. If the cart is traveling 8.0 m/s after the shove, how much time elapses until the cart returns to its initial position?

   (A) 1.6 s
   (B) 3.2 s
   (C) 4.0 s
   (D) 6.0 s
   (E) 8.0 s

2. A car slides up a frictionless inclined plane. How does the normal force of the incline on the car compare with the weight of the car?

   (A) The normal force must be equal to the car's weight.
   (B) The normal force must be less than the car's weight.
   (C) The normal force must be greater than the car's weight.
   (D) The normal force must be zero.
   (E) The normal force could have any value relative to the car's weight.

3. In the diagram above, a 1.0-kg cart and a 2.0-kg cart are connected by a rope. The spring scale reads 10 N. What is the tension in the rope connecting the two carts? Neglect any friction.

   (A) 30 N
   (B) 10 N
   (C) 6.7 N
   (D) 5.0 N
   (E) 3.3 N

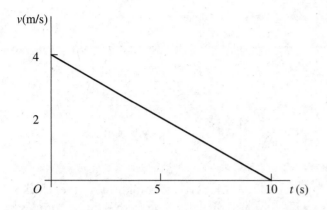

4. The velocity–time graph above represents the motion of a 5-kg box. The only force applied to this box is a person pushing. Assuming that the box is moving to the right, what is the magnitude and direction of the force applied by the person pushing?

(A) 2.0 N, right
(B) 2.0 N, left
(C) 0.4 N, right
(D) 0.4 N, left
(E) 12.5 N, left

5. A 50-g meterstick is to be suspended by a single string. A 100-g ball hangs from the left-hand edge of the meterstick. Where should the string be attached so that the meterstick hangs in equilibrium?

(A) at the left-hand edge
(B) 40 cm from left-hand edge
(C) 30 cm from right-hand edge
(D) 17 cm from left-hand edge
(E) at the midpoint of the meterstick

Free Response:

6. A 2-kg block and a 5-kg block are connected as shown above. The coefficient of friction between the 5-kg block and the flat surface is $\mu = 0.2$.

(a) Calculate the magnitude of the acceleration of the 5-kg block.
(b) Calculate the tension in the rope connecting the two blocks.

7. Bert, Ernie, and Oscar are discussing the gas mileage of cars. Specifically, they are wondering whether a car gets better mileage on a city street or on a freeway. All agree (correctly) that the gas mileage of a car depends on the force that is produced by the car's engine—the car gets fewer miles per gallon if the engine must produce more force. Whose explanation is completely correct?

Bert says: Gas mileage is better on the freeway. In town the car is always speeding up and slowing down because of the traffic lights, so because $F_{net} = ma$ and acceleration is large, the engine must produce a lot of force. However, on the freeway, the car moves with constant velocity, and acceleration is zero. So the engine produces no force, allowing for better gas mileage.

Ernie says: Gas mileage is better in town. In town, the speed of the car is slower than the speed on the freeway. Acceleration is velocity divided by time, so the acceleration in town is smaller. Because $F_{net} = ma$, then, the force of the engine is smaller in town giving better gas mileage.

Oscar says: Gas mileage is better on the freeway. The force of the engine only has to be enough to equal the force of air resistance—the engine doesn't have to accelerate the car because the car maintains a constant speed. Whereas in town, the force of the engine must often be greater than the force of friction and air resistance in order to let the car speed up.

› Solutions to Practice Problems

1. **B**—"Smooth" usually means "ignore friction." So the only force acting along the plane is a component of gravity, $mg(\sin 30°)$. The F_{net} equation becomes $mg(\sin 30°) - 0 = ma$. The mass cancels, leaving the acceleration as 5 m/s². What's left is a kinematics problem. Set up a chart, calling the direction down the plane as positive:

v_0	−8.0/s
v_f	?
$x - x_0$	0 (cart comes back to starting point)
a	+5.0 m/s²
t	??? what we're looking for

Use $(\Delta x = v_0 t + \frac{1}{2}at^2)$ to find that the time is 3.2 s.

2. **B**—The normal force exerted on an object on an inclined plane equals $mg(\cos \theta)$, where θ is the angle of the incline. If θ is greater than 0, then $\cos \theta$ is less than 1, so the normal force is less than the object's weight.

3. **E**—Consider the forces acting on each block separately. On the 1.0-kg block, only the tension acts, so $T = (1.0 \text{ kg})a$. On the 2.0-kg block, the tension acts left, but the 10 N force acts right, so $10 \text{ N} - T = (2.0 \text{ kg})a$. Add these equations together (noting that the tension in the rope is the same in both equations), getting $10 \text{ N} = (3.0 \text{ kg})a$; acceleration is 3.3 m/s². To finish, $T = (1.0 \text{ kg})a$, so tension is 3.3 N.

4. **B**— The acceleration is given by the slope of the v–t graph, which has magnitude 0.4 m/s². $F_{net} = ma$, so $5 \text{ kg} \times 0.4 \text{ m/s}^2 = 2.0 \text{ N}$. This force is to the left because acceleration is negative (the slope is negative), and negative was defined as left.

5. **D**—This is a torque problem, and the fulcrum is wherever the meterstick is attached to the string. We know that the meterstick's center of mass is at the 50-cm mark, so we can draw the following picture.

Because the stick is in equilibrium, the clockwise torques equal the counterclockwise torques: $(1 \text{ N})(x) = (0.5 \text{ N})(50 - x)$. So x = something in the neighborhood of $25/1.5 \sim 17$ cm. This answer is less than 50 cm, and is closer to the edge with the heavy mass, so it makes sense.

6. The setup is the same as in the chapter's example problem, except this time there is a force of friction acting to the left on the 5-kg block. Because this block is in equilibrium vertically, the normal force is equal to the block's weight, 50 N. The friction force is μF_N, or 10 N.

   Calling the down-and-right direction positive, we can write two equations, one for each block:

   $$(2 \text{ kg})g - T = (2 \text{ kg})a.$$
   $$T - F_f = (5 \text{ kg})a.$$

   (a) To solve for acceleration, just add the two equations together. The tensions cancel. We find the acceleration to be 1.4 m/s².
   (b) Plug back into either equation to find the final answer, that the tension is 17 N. This is more than the 14 N we found for the frictionless situation, and so makes sense. We expect that it will take more force in the rope to overcome friction on the table.

7. Although Bert is right that acceleration is zero on the freeway, this means that the NET force is zero; the engine still must produce a force to counteract air resistance. This is what Oscar says, so his answer is correct. Ernie's answer is way off—acceleration is not velocity/time, acceleration is a CHANGE in velocity over time.

› Rapid Review

- Only gravitational and electrical forces can act on an object without contact (in AP Physics 1).

- When an object moves along a surface, the acceleration in a direction perpendicular to that surface must be zero. Therefore, the net force perpendicular to the surface is also zero.

- The friction force is equal to the coefficient of friction times the normal force, $F_f = \mu F_n$.

- The force of Object A on Object B is equal in amount and opposite in direction to the force of Object B on Object A. These two forces, which act on different objects, are called Newton's third law companion forces.

- If the net force has both a vertical and a horizontal component, use the Pythagorean theorem to determine the magnitude of the net force, and use the tangent function to determine the direction of the net force.

- When a force acts at an angle θ measured from the horizontal:

  - The vertical component of that force is equal to the amount of the force itself times $\sin \theta$.

  - The horizontal component of that force is equal to the amount of the force itself times $\cos \theta$.

- The acceleration of an object is F_{net}/m (which is the same thing as saying $F_{net} = ma$).

- On an incline of angle θ (measured from the horizontal), break the weight into components:

  - The component of the weight that is parallel to the incline is equal to the weight times $\sin \theta$.

  - The component of the weight that is perpendicular to the incline is equal to the weight times $\cos \theta$.

- One rope has just one tension. (Unless it's attached to a massive pulley—but that's a rare exception.)

CHAPTER 11

Momentum

IN THIS CHAPTER

Summary: The impulse–momentum relationship can explain how force acts in a collision. Momentum is conserved in all collisions, allowing a prediction of objects' speeds before and after a collision.

Key Ideas

✪ Impulse can be expressed both as force times a time interval, *and* as a change in momentum.

✪ The total momentum of a set of objects before a collision is equal to the total momentum of a set of objects after a collision.

✪ Momentum is a vector, so leftward momentum can "cancel out" rightward momentum.

Relevant Equations

The definition of momentum:

$$p = mv$$

The impulse–momentum theorem:

$$\Delta p = F\Delta t$$

Location of the center of mass:

$$Mx_{cm} = m_1 x_1 + m_2 x_2 + \cdots$$

If an object is moving, it has momentum. The formal definition of momentum[1] is that it's equal to an object's mass multiplied by that object's velocity. However, a more intuitive way to think about momentum is that it corresponds to the amount of "oomph" an object has in a collision. Regardless of how you think about momentum, the key is this: the momentum of a system upon which no net external force acts is always conserved.

Momentum and Impulse

$$\boxed{\textbf{Momentum: } mv}$$

The units of momentum are kg·m/s, which is the same as N·s. Momentum is a vector quantity, and it is often abbreviated with a p.

$$\boxed{\textbf{Impulse: } \Delta p = F\Delta t}$$

Impulse (designated as I) is an object's change in momentum. It is also equal to the force acting on an object multiplied by the time interval over which that force was applied. The above equation is often referred to as the "impulse–momentum theorem."

The $F\Delta t$ definition of impulse explains why airbags are used in cars and why hitting someone with a pillow is less dangerous than hitting him or her with a cement block. The key is the Δt term. An example will help illustrate this point.

A man jumps off the roof of a building, 3.0 m above the ground. His mass is 70 kg. He estimates (while in free fall) that if he lands stiff-legged, it will take him 3 ms (milliseconds) to come to rest. However, if he bends his knees upon impact, it will take him 100 ms to come to rest. Which way will he choose to land, and why?

This is a multistep problem. We start by calculating the man's velocity the instant before he hits the ground. That's a kinematics problem, so we start by choosing a positive direction—we'll choose "down" to be positive—and by writing out our table of variables.

v_0	0
v_f	?
Δx	3.0 m
a	10 m/s^2
t	?

We have three variables with known values, so we can solve for the other two. We don't care about time, t, so we will just solve for v_f.

$$v_f^2 = v_0^2 + 2a(x - x_0)$$
$$v_f = 7.7 \text{ m/s}$$

Now we can solve for the man's momentum the instant before he hits the ground.

$$p = mv = (70)(7.7) = 540 \text{ kg·m/s}$$

---

[1]This chapter deals only with *linear* momentum. Angular momentum is covered in Chapter 15.

Once he hits the ground, the man quickly comes to rest. That is, his momentum changes from 540 kg·m/s to 0.

$$I = \Delta p = P_f - p_0$$
$$I = -540 \text{ N·s} = F\Delta t$$

If the man does not bend his knees, then

$$-540 = F(0.003 \text{ s})$$
$$F = -180,000 \text{ N}$$

The negative sign in our answer just means that the force exerted on the man is directed in the negative direction: up.

Now, what if he had bent his knees?

$$I = -540 = F\Delta t$$
$$-540 = F(0.10 \text{ seconds})$$
$$F = -5400 \text{ N}$$

If he bends his knees, he allows for his momentum to change more slowly, and as a result, the ground exerts a lot less force on him than had he landed stiff-legged. More to the point, hundreds of thousands of newtons applied to a person's legs will cause major damage—this is the equivalent of almost 20 tons sitting on his legs. So we would assume that the man would bend his knees upon landing, reducing the force on his legs by a factor of 30.

Calculus Version of the Impulse–Momentum Theorem

Conceptually, you should think of impulse as change in momentum, also equal to a force multiplied by the time during which that force acts. This is sufficient when the force in question is constant, or when you can easily define an average force during a time interval.

But what about when a force is changing with time? The relationship between force and momentum in the language of calculus is

$$F = \frac{dp}{dt}, \text{ which then implies that Impulse} = \int F dt$$

A common AP question, then, gives momentum of an object as a function of time, and asks you to take the derivative to find the force on the object.

It's also useful to understand this calculus graphically. Given a graph of momentum vs. time, the slope of the tangent to the graph gives the force at that point in time. Given a graph of force vs. time, the area under that graph is impulse, or change in momentum during that time interval.

Conservation of Momentum

Momentum in an isolated system, where no net external forces act, is always conserved. A rough approximation of a closed system is a billiard table covered with hard tile instead of felt. When the billiard balls collide, they transfer momentum to one another, but the total momentum of all the balls remains constant.

The key to solving conservation of momentum problems is remembering that momentum is a vector.

> A satellite floating through space collides with a small UFO. Before the collision, the satellite was traveling at 10 m/s to the right, and the UFO was traveling at 5 m/s to the left. If the satellite's mass is 70 kg, and the UFO's mass is 50 kg, and assuming that the satellite and the UFO bounce off each other upon impact, what is the satellite's final velocity if the UFO has a final velocity of 3 m/s to the right?

Let's begin by drawing a picture.

10 m/s   5 m/s

Momentum is conserved, so we write

$$p_{satellite} + p_{UFO} = p'_{satellite} + p'_{UFO}$$
$$(m_s)(v_s) + (m_{UFO})(v_{UFO}) = (m_s)(v_s)' + (m_{UFO})(v_{UFO})'$$

The tick marks on the right side of the equation mean "after the collision." We know the momentum of each space traveler before the collision, and we know the UFO's final momentum. So we solve for the satellite's final velocity. (Note that we must define a positive direction; because the UFO is moving to the left, its velocity is plugged in as negative.)

$$(70 \text{ kg})(+10 \text{ m/s}) + (50 \text{ kg})(-5 \text{ m/s}) = (70 \text{ kg})v_s' + (50 \text{ kg})(+3 \text{ m/s})$$
$$v_s' = 4.3 \text{ m/s to the right}$$

Now, what if the satellite and the UFO had stuck together upon colliding? We can solve for their final velocity easily:

$$p_{satellite} + p_{UFO} = p'_{satellite \& UFO}$$
$$(m_s)(v_s) + (m_{UFO})(v_{UFO}) = (m_{s \& UFO})(v_{s \& UFO})'$$
$$(70 \text{ kg})(+10 \text{ m/s}) + (50 \text{ kg})(-5 \text{ m/s}) = (70 \text{ kg} + 50 \text{ kg})(v_{s \& UFO})'$$
$$v'_{s \& UFO} = 3.8 \text{ m/s to the right}$$

Motion of the Center of Mass

The center of mass of a system of objects obeys Newton's second law. Two common examples might illustrate the point:

(1) Imagine that an astronaut on a spacewalk throws a rope around a small asteroid, and then pulls the asteroid toward him. Where will the asteroid and the astronaut collide?

Answer: at the center of mass. Since no forces acted except due to the astronaut and asteroid, the center of mass must have no acceleration. The center of mass started at rest, and stays at rest, all the way until the objects collide.

(2) A toy rocket is in projectile motion, so that it is on track to land 30 m from its launch point. While in the air, the rocket explodes into two identical pieces, one of which lands 35 m from the launch point. Where does the first piece land?

Answer: 25 m from the launch point. Since the only external force acting on the rocket is gravity, the center of mass must stay in projectile motion, and must land 30 m from the launch point. The two pieces are of equal mass, so if one is 5 m beyond the center of mass's landing point, the other piece must be 5 m short of that point.

Finding the Center of Mass

Usually the location of the center of mass (cm) is pretty obvious . . . the formal equation for the cm of several objects is

$$Mx_{cm} = m_1x_1 + m_2x_2 + \cdots$$

Multiply the mass of each object by its position, and divide by the total mass M, and voila, you have the position of the center of mass. What this tells you is that the cm of several equal-mass objects is right in between them; if one mass is heavier than the others, the cm is closer to the heavy mass.

Very rarely, you might have to find the center of mass of a continuous body (like a baseball bat) using calculus. The formula is

$$Mx_{cm} = \int rdm$$

Do not use this equation unless (a) you have plenty of extra time to spend, and (b) you know exactly what you're doing. In the highly unlikely event it's necessary to use this equation to find a center of mass, you will usually be better off just guessing at the answer and moving on to the rest of the problem. (If you want to find out how to do such a problem thoroughly, consult your textbook. This is not something worth reviewing if you don't know how to do it already.)

Elastic and Inelastic Collisions

This brings us to a couple of definitions.

> **Elastic Collision:** A collision in which kinetic energy is conserved

If you're unfamiliar with the concept of kinetic energy (KE), take a few minutes to skim Chapter 13 right now.

When the satellite and the UFO bounced off each other, they experienced a perfectly elastic collision. If kinetic energy is lost to heat or anything else during the collision, it is called an inelastic collision.

> **Inelastic Collision:** A collision in which KE is not conserved

The extreme case of an inelastic collision is called a perfectly inelastic collision.

> **Perfectly Inelastic Collision:** The colliding objects stick together after impact

The second collision between the satellite and the UFO was a perfectly inelastic collision. BUT, MOMENTUM IS STILL CONSERVED, EVEN IN A PERFECTLY INELASTIC COLLISION!

Two-Dimensional Collisions

The key to solving a two-dimensional collision problem is to remember that momentum is a vector, and as a vector it can be broken into x and y components. Momentum in the x-direction is always conserved, and momentum in the y-direction is always conserved.

Maggie has decided to go ice-skating. While cruising along, she trips on a crack in the ice and goes sliding. She slides along the ice at a velocity of 2.5 m/s. In her path is a penguin. Unable to avoid the flightless bird, she collides with it. The penguin is initially at rest and has a mass of 20 kg, and Maggie's mass is 50 kg. Upon hitting the penguin, Maggie is deflected 30° from her initial path, and the penguin is deflected 60° from Maggie's initial path. What is Maggie's velocity, and what is the penguin's velocity, after the collision?

We want to analyze the x-component of momentum and the y-component of momentum separately. Let's begin by defining "right" and "up" to be the positive directions. Now we can look at the x-component.

$$(m_{\text{Maggie}})(v_{\text{Maggie},x}) + (m_{\text{penguin}})(v_{\text{penguin},x}) = (m_M)(v_{M,x})' + (m_p)(v_{p,x})'$$
$$(50 \text{ kg})(+2.5 \text{ m/s}) + (20 \text{ kg})(0) = (50 \text{ kg})(+v'_M \cos 30°) + (20 \text{ kg})(+v'_p \cos 60°)$$
$$125 \text{ kg·m/s} = (50 \text{ kg})(+v'_M)(\cos 30°) + (20 \text{ kg})(+v'_p)(\cos 60°)$$

We can't do much more with the x-component of momentum, so now let's look at the y-component.

$$(m_{\text{Maggie}})(v_{\text{Maggie}, y}) + (m_{\text{penguin}})(v_{\text{penguin}, y}) = (m_M)(v_{M,y})' + (m_p)(v_{p,y})'$$
$$(50 \text{ kg})(0) + (20 \text{ kg})(0) = (50 \text{ kg})(-v'_M \sin 30°) + (20 \text{ kg})(+v'_p \sin 60°)$$

(Note the negative sign on Maggie's y-velocity!)

$$0 = (50 \text{ kg})(-v'_M \sin 30°) + (20 \text{ kg})(+v'_p \sin 60°)$$

Okay. Now we have two equations and two unknowns. It'll take some algebra to solve this one, but none of it is too hard. We will assume that you can do the math on your own, but we will gladly provide you with the answer:

$$v'_M = 2.2 \text{ m/s}$$
$$v'_p = 3.1 \text{ m/s.}$$

The algebra is not particularly important here. Get the conceptual physics down—in a two-dimensional collision, you must treat each direction separately. If you do so, you will receive virtually full credit on an AP problem. If you combine vertical and horizontal momentum into a single conservation equation, you will probably not receive any credit at all.

› Practice Problems

Multiple Choice:

First two questions: A ball of mass M is caught by someone wearing a baseball glove. The ball is in contact with the glove for a time t; the initial velocity of the ball (just before the catcher touches it) is v_0.

1. If the time of the ball's collision with the glove is doubled, what happens to the force necessary to catch the ball?

   (A) It doesn't change.
   (B) It is cut in half.
   (C) It is cut to one-fourth of the original force.
   (D) It quadruples.
   (E) It doubles.

2. If the time of collision remains t, but the initial velocity is doubled, what happens to the force necessary to catch the ball?

   (A) It doesn't change.
   (B) It is cut in half.
   (C) It is cut to one-fourth of the original force.
   (D) It quadruples.
   (E) It doubles.

before collision

3. Two balls, of mass m and $2m$, collide and stick together. The combined balls are at rest after the collision. If the ball of mass m was moving 5 m/s to the right before the collision, what was the velocity of the ball of mass $2m$ before the collision?

   (A) 2.5 m/s to the right
   (B) 2.5 m/s to the left
   (C) 10 m/s to the right
   (D) 10 m/s to the left
   (E) 1.7 m/s to the left

4. Two identical balls have initial velocities $v_1 = 4$ m/s to the right and $v_2 = 3$ m/s to the left, respectively. The balls collide head-on and stick together. What is the velocity of the combined balls after the collision?

   (A) ½ m/s to the right
   (B) ⅔ m/s to the right
   (C) ½ m/s to the right
   (D) ⅔ m/s to the right
   (E) 1 m/s to the right

Free Response:

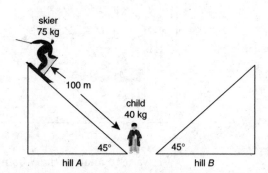

5. A 75-kg skier skis down a hill. The skier collides with a 40-kg child who is at rest on the flat surface near the base of the hill, 100 m from the skier's starting point, as shown above. The skier and the child become entangled. Assume all surfaces are frictionless.

   (a) How fast will the skier be moving when he reaches the bottom of the hill? Assume the skier is at rest when he begins his descent.
   (b) What will be the speed of the skier and child just after they collide?
   (c) If the collision occurs in half a second, how much force will be experienced by each person?

› Solutions to Practice Problems

1. **B**—Impulse is force times the time interval of collision, and is also equal to an object's change in momentum. Solving for force, $F = \Delta p/\Delta t$. Because the ball still has the same mass, and still changes from speed v_0 to speed zero, the ball's momentum change is the same, regardless of the collision time. The collision time, in the denominator, doubled; so the entire expression for force was cut in half.

2. **E**—Still use $F = \Delta p/\Delta t$, but this time it is the numerator that changes. The ball still is brought to rest by the glove, and the mass of the ball is still the same; but the doubled velocity upon reaching the glove doubles the momentum change. Thus, the force doubles.

3. **B**—The total momentum after collision is zero. So the total momentum before collision must be zero as well. The mass m moved 5 m/s to the right, giving it a momentum of $5m$ units; the right-hand mass must have the same momentum to the left. It must be moving half as fast, 2.5 m/s, because its mass it twice as big; then its momentum is $(2m)(2.5) = 5m$ units to the left.

4. **C**—Because the balls are identical, just pretend they each have mass 1 kg. Then the momentum conservation tells us that

$$(1 \text{ kg})(+4 \text{ m/s}) + (1 \text{ kg})(-3 \text{ m/s}) = (2 \text{ kg})(v').$$

The combined mass, on the right of the equation above, is 2 kg; v' represents the speed of the combined mass. Note the negative sign indicating the direction of the second ball's velocity. Solving, $v' = +0.5$ m/s, or 0.5 m/s to the right.

5. (a) This part is not a momentum problem, it's a Newton's second law and kinematics problem. (Or it's an energy problem, if you've studied energy.) Break up forces on the skier into parallel and perpendicular axes—the net force down the plane is $mg(\sin 45°)$. So by Newton's second law, the acceleration down the plane is $g(\sin 45°) = 7.1$ m/s². Using kinematics with intitial velocity zero and distance 100 m, the skier is going 38 m/s(!).

(b) Now use momentum conservation. The total momentum before collision is $(75 \text{ kg})(38 \text{ m/s}) = 2850$ kg·m/s. This must equal the total momentum after collision. The people stick together, with combined mass 115 kg. So after collision, the velocity is 2850 kg·m/s divided by 115 kg, or about 25 m/s.

(c) Change in momentum is force multiplied by time interval . . . the child goes from zero momentum to $(40 \text{ kg})(25 \text{ m/s}) = 1000$ kg·m/s of momentum. Divide this change in momentum by 0.5 seconds, and you get 2000 N, or a bit less than a quarter ton of force. Ouch!

› Rapid Review

- Momentum equals an object's mass multiplied by its velocity. However, you can also think of momentum as the amount of "oomph" a mass has in a collision.

- Impulse equals the change in an object's momentum. It also equals the force exerted on an object multiplied by the time it took to apply that force.

- Momentum is always conserved. When solving conservation of momentum problems, remember that momentum is a vector quantity.

- In an elastic collision, kinetic energy is conserved. When two objects collide and bounce off each other, without losing any energy (to heat, sound, etc.), they have engaged in an elastic collision. In an inelastic collision, kinetic energy is not conserved. The extreme case is a perfectly inelastic collision. When two objects collide and stick together, they have engaged in a perfectly inelastic collision.

Energy Conservation

IN THIS CHAPTER

Summary: While kinematics can be used to predict the speeds of objects with constant acceleration, energy conservation is a more powerful tool that can predict how objects will move even with a changing acceleration.

Key Ideas
- ✪ Work is related to kinetic energy through the work–energy theorem.
- ✪ There are many types of potential energy. Two (due to gravity and due to a spring) are discussed in this chapter.
- ✪ To use conservation of energy, add potential + kinetic energy at two positions in an object's motion. This sum must be the same everywhere.
- ✪ A potential energy function can be derived for any conservative force.

Relevant Equations

The definition of work:

$$W = F \cdot d_{\parallel}$$

The work–energy theorem:

$$W_{\text{net}} = \Delta K$$

The force of a spring:

$$F = -kx$$

Two different types of potential energy:

$$\text{Gravitational PE} = mgh$$
$$\text{Spring PE} = \tfrac{1}{2}kx^2$$

Power:

$$\text{Power} = \frac{\text{work}}{\text{time}} = Fv$$

Relationship between a conservative force F and the potential energy U it creates:

$$F = -\frac{dU}{dx}; \ U = -\int F dx$$

As with momentum, the energy of an isolated system is always conserved. It might change form—potential energy can be converted to kinetic energy, or kinetic energy can be converted to heat—but it'll never simply disappear.

Conservation of energy is one of the most important, fundamental concepts in all of physics . . . translation: it's going to show up all over the AP exam. So read this chapter carefully.

Kinetic Energy and the Work–Energy Theorem

We'll start with some definitions.

> **Energy:** The ability to do work

> **Work:** $F \cdot d_{\parallel}$

What this second definition means is that work equals the product of the distance an object travels and the component of the force acting on that object directed parallel to the object's direction of motion. That sounds more complicated than it really is: an example will help.

A box is pulled along the floor, as shown in Figure 12.1. It is pulled a distance of 10 m, and the force pulling it has a magnitude of 5 N and is directed 30° above the horizontal. So, the force component that is PARALLEL to the 10 m displacement is (5 N)(cos 30°).

$$W = (5 \cos 30° \text{ N})(10 \text{ m})$$
$$W = 43 \text{ N·m}$$

Figure 12.1   Box is pulled along the floor.

One newton · meter is called a joule, abbreviated as 1 J.

- Work is a scalar. So is energy.
- The units of work and of energy are joules.
- Work can be negative . . . this just means that the force is applied in the direction opposite displacement.

> **Kinetic Energy:** Energy of motion, abbreviated K

$$K = \tfrac{1}{2}mv^2$$

This means that the kinetic energy of an object equals one-half the object's mass times its speed squared.

> **Work–Energy Theorem:** $W_{net} = \Delta K$

The net work done on an object is equal to that object's change in kinetic energy. Here's an application:

> A train car with a mass of 200 kg is traveling at 20 m/s. How much force must the brakes exert in order to stop the train car in a distance of 10 m?
>
>

Here, because the only horizontal force is the force of the brakes, the work done by this force is W_{net}.

$$W_{net} = \Delta KE = KE_f - KE_0$$

$$W = \tfrac{1}{2}mv_f^2 - \tfrac{1}{2}mv_0^2$$

$$W = (0) - \tfrac{1}{2}(200 \text{ kg})(20 \text{ m/s})^2$$

$$W = -40{,}000 \text{ J}$$

Let's pause for a minute to think about what this value means. We've just calculated the change in kinetic energy of the train car, which is equal to the net work done on the train car. The negative sign simply means that the net force was opposite the train's displacement. To find the force:

$$-40{,}000 \text{ J} = \text{Force} \cdot \text{distance}$$

$$-40{,}000 \text{ J} = F(10 \text{ m})$$

$$F = -4000 \text{ N, which means 4000 N opposite the}$$
$$\text{direction of displacement}$$

Potential Energy

> **Potential Energy**: Energy of position, abbreviated U

Potential energy comes in many forms: there's gravitational potential energy, spring potential energy, electrical potential energy, and so on. For starters, we'll concern ourselves with gravitational potential energy.

Gravitational PE is described by the following equation:

$$U = mgh$$

In this equation, m is the mass of an object, g is the gravitational field of 10 N/kg on Earth, and h is the height of an object above a certain point (called "the zero of potential").[1] That point can be wherever you want it to be, depending on the problem. For example, let's say a pencil is sitting on a table. If you define the zero of potential to be the table, then the pencil has no gravitational PE. If you define the floor to be the zero of potential, then the pencil has PE equal to mgh, where h is the height of the pencil above the floor. Your choice of the *zero* of potential in a problem should be made by determining how the problem can most easily be solved.

REMINDER: h in the potential energy equation stands for *vertical* height above the zero of potential.

Conservation of Energy: Problem-Solving Approach

Solving energy-conservation problems is relatively simple, as long as you approach them methodically. The general approach is this: write out all the terms for the initial energy of the system, and set the sum of those terms equal to the sum of all the terms for the final energy of the system. Let's practice.

A block of mass m is placed on a frictionless plane inclined at a 30° angle above the horizontal. It is released from rest and allowed to slide 5 m down the plane. What is its final velocity?

If we were to approach this problem using kinematics equations (which we could), it would take about a page of work to solve. Instead, observe how quickly it can be solved using conservation of energy.

---

[1]Note that 10 N/kg is exactly the same as 10 m/s².

$$K_i + U_i = K_f + U_f \begin{pmatrix} i = \text{initial, at the top} \\ f = \text{final, at the bottom} \end{pmatrix}$$

$$\tfrac{1}{2}mv_i^2 + mgh_i = \tfrac{1}{2}mv_f^2 + mgh_f$$

We will define our zero of potential to be the height of the box after it has slid the 5 m down the plane. By defining it this way, the PE term on the right side of the equation will cancel out. Furthermore, because the box starts from rest, its initial KE also equals zero.

$$0 + mgh_i = \tfrac{1}{2}mv_f^2 + 0$$

The initial height can be found using trigonometry: $h_i = (5\text{m})(\sin 30°) = 2.5$ m.

$$mg(2.5\,\text{m}) = \tfrac{1}{2}mv_f^2$$
$$50(\text{m/s})^2 = v_f^2$$
$$v_f = 7\text{m/s}$$

In general, the principle of energy conservation can be stated mathematically like this:

$$\boxed{K_i + U_i + W = K_f + U_f}$$

The term W in this equation stands for work done on an object. For example, if there had been friction between the box and the plane in the previous example, the work done by friction would be the W term. When it comes to the AP exam, *you will include this* W *term only when there is friction (or some other exteral force) involved.* When friction is involved, $W = F_f d$, where F_f is the force of friction on the object, and d is the distance the object travels.

Let's say that there was friction between the box and the inclined plane.

> A box of mass m is placed on a plane inclined at a 30° angle above the horizontal. The coefficient of friction between the box and the plane is 0.20. The box is released from rest and allowed to slide 5.0 m down the plane. What is its final velocity?

We start by writing the general equation for energy conservation:

$$K_i + U_i + W = E_f + U_f$$

W equals $F_f d$, where F_f is the force of friction, and d is 5 m.[2]

$$W = -F_f d = -\mu F_N d$$
$$F_N = (mg\cos\theta), \text{where } \theta = 30°$$

The value for W is negative because friction acts opposite displacement. You may want to draw a free-body diagram to understand how we derived this value for F_N.

Now, plugging in values we have

$$\tfrac{1}{2}mv_i^2 + mgh_i \pm 0.2(mg\cos 30°)(5\,\text{m}) = \tfrac{1}{2}mv_f^2 + mgh_f$$

$$0 + mg(2.5\,\text{m}) - 0.2(mg)(.87)(5\,\text{m}) = \tfrac{1}{2}mv_f^2$$

---

[2]Note this difference carefully. Although potential energy involves only a vertical height, work done by friction includes the *entire* distance the box travels.

We rearrange some terms and cancel out m from each side to get

$$v_f = 5.7 \text{ m/s}$$

This answer makes sense—friction on the plane *reduces* the box's speed at the bottom.

Springs

Gravitational potential energy isn't the only kind of PE around. Another frequently encountered form is spring potential energy.

The force exerted by a spring is directly proportional to the amount that the spring is compressed. That is,

$$\boxed{F_{\text{spring}} = -kx}$$

In this equation, k is a constant (called the spring constant), and x is the distance that the spring has been compressed or extended from its equilibrium state. The negative sign is simply a reminder that the force of a spring always acts opposite to displacement—an extended spring pulls back toward the equilibrium position, while a compressed spring pushes toward the equilibrium position. We call this type of force a restoring force, and we discuss it more in Chapter 15 on simple harmonic motion. However, we can ignore this sign unless we are doing calculus.

When a spring is either compressed or extended, it stores potential energy. The amount of energy stored is given as follows.

$$\boxed{U_{\text{spring}} = \tfrac{1}{2}kx^2}$$

Similarly, the work done by a spring is given by $W_{\text{spring}} = \tfrac{1}{2}kx^2$. Here's an example problem.

A block with a mass of 2 kg is attached to a spring with $k = 1$ N/m. The spring is compressed 10 cm from equilibrium and then released. How fast is the block traveling when it passes through the equilibrium point? Neglect friction.

It's important to recognize that we CANNOT use kinematics to solve this problem! Because the force of a spring changes as it stretches, the block's acceleration is not constant. When acceleration isn't constant, try using energy conservation.

We begin by writing our statement for conservation of energy.

$$K_i + U_i + W = K_f + U_f$$

Now we fill in values for each term. PE here is just in the form of spring potential energy, and there's no friction, so we can ignore the W term. Be sure to plug in all values in meters!

$$0 + \tfrac{1}{2}(k)(0.1\text{m})^2 = \tfrac{1}{2}mv_f^2 + 0$$

$$v_f = \sqrt{\frac{k}{m}(0.1\text{m})^2}$$

Plugging in values for k and m, we have

$$v_f = 0.07 \text{ m/s, that is, 7 cm/s}$$

Power

Whether you walk up a mountain or whether a car drives you up the mountain, the same amount of work has to be done on you. (You weigh a certain number of newtons, and you have to be lifted up the same distance either way!) But clearly there's something different about walking up over the course of several hours and driving up over several minutes. That difference is power.

> **Power:** work/time

Power is, thus, measured in units of joules/second, also known as watts. A car engine puts out hundreds of horsepower, equivalent to maybe 100 kilowatts; whereas, you'd work hard just to put out a power of a few hundred watts.

Potential Energy vs. Displacement Graphs

A different potential energy function can actually be derived for ANY conservative force. (A conservative force means that energy is conserved when this force acts . . . examples are gravity, spring, and electromagnetic forces; friction and air resistance are the most common nonconservative forces.) The potential energy U for a force is given by the following integral:

$$U = -\int F dx$$

Note that this equation works for the gravitational force $F = -mg$ (where $-$ is the down direction) and the spring force $F = -kx$; the potential energy attributable to gravity integrates to mgh, and the spring potential energy becomes $\tfrac{1}{2}kx^2$.

Chris on a Skateboard

Once a potential energy of an object is found as a function of position, making a U vs. x graph tells a lot about the long-term motion of the object. Consider the potential energy of a spring, $\tfrac{1}{2}kx^2$. A graph of this function looks like a parabola, as shown in Figure 12.2.

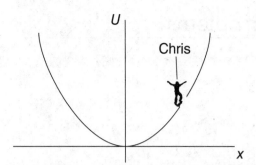

Figure 12.2   Potential energy vs. displacement graph for a spring.

You can get a general feel for how the mass on a spring moves by imagining that Chris is riding a skateboard on a ramp shaped like the graph. A ramp shaped like this looks like a half-pipe. If he starts from some height above the bottom, Chris will oscillate back and forth, going fastest in the middle, and turning around when he runs out of energy at the right or left end. Although this is not precisely how a mass on a spring moves—the mass only moves back and forth, for example—the long-term properties of Chris's motion and the motion of the mass on a spring are the same. The mass oscillates back and forth, with its fastest speed in the middle, just like Chris does.

Thinking about Chris on a skateboard works for all U vs. x graphs. Consider a model of the energy between two atoms that looks like the graph in Figure 12.3.

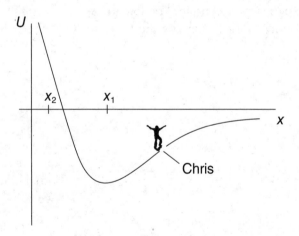

Figure 12.3   Potential energy vs. displacement graph for two atoms.

If Chris on his skateboard released himself from rest near position x_1, he'd just oscillate back and forth, much like in the mass on a spring problem. But if he were to let go near the position labeled x_2, he'd have enough energy to keep going to the right as far as he wants; in fact, he'd make it off the page, never coming back. This is what happens to the atoms in molecules, too. If a second atom is placed pretty close to a distance x_1 from the first atom, it will just oscillate back and forth about that position. However, if the second atom is placed very close to the first atom, it will gain enough energy to escape to a faraway place.

› Practice Problems

Multiple Choice:

Questions 1 and 2:

A block of weight $mg = 100$ N slides a distance of 5.0 m down a 30-degree incline, as shown above.

1. How much work is done on the block by gravity?

(A) 500 J
(B) 430 J
(C) 100 J
(D) 50 J
(E) 250 J

2. If the block experiences a constant friction force of 10 N, how much work is done by the friction force?

(A) −43 J
(B) −25 J
(C) −500 J
(D) −100 J
(E) −50 J

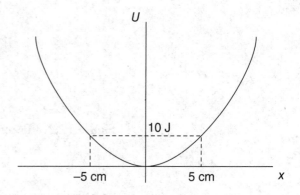

3. A mass experiences a potential energy U that varies with distance x as shown in the graph above. The mass is released from position $x = 0$ with 10 J of kinetic energy. Which of the following describes the long-term motion of the mass?

(A) The mass eventually comes to rest at $x = 0$.
(B) The mass slows down with constant acceleration, stopping at $x = 5$ cm.
(C) The mass speeds up with constant acceleration.
(D) The mass oscillates, never getting farther than 5 cm from $x = 0$.
(E) The mass oscillates, never getting farther than 10 cm from $x = 0$.

4. Two identical balls of mass $m = 1.0$ kg are moving toward each other, as shown above. What is the initial kinetic energy of the system consisting of the two balls?

(A) 0 joules
(B) 1 joules
(C) 12 joules
(D) 18 joules
(E) 36 joules

Free Response:

5. A 1500-kg car moves north according to the velocity–time graph shown.

   (a) Determine the change in the car's kinetic energy during the first 7 s.
   (b) To determine how far the car traveled in these 7 s, the three basic kinematics equations cannot be used. Explain why not.
   (c) Use the velocity–time graph to estimate the distance the car traveled in 7 s.
   (d) What was the net work done on the car in these 7 s?
   (e) Determine the average power necessary for the car to perform this motion.

› Solutions to Practice Problems

1. **E**—The force of gravity is straight down and equal to 100 N. The displacement parallel to this force is the *vertical* displacement, 2.5 m. Work equals force times parallel displacement, 250 J.

2. **E**—The force of friction acts up the plane, and displacement is down the plane, so just multiply force times distance to get 50 J. The negative sign indicates that force is opposite displacement.

3. **D**—Think of Chris on a skateboard—on this graph, he will oscillate back and forth about $x = 0$. Because he starts with a KE of 10 J, he can, at most, have a potential energy of 10 J, which corresponds on the graph to a maximum displacement of 5 cm. (The mass cannot have constant acceleration because constant acceleration only occurs for a constant force; a constant force produces an energy graph that is linear. The mass will not come to rest because we are assuming a conservative force, for which KE can be converted to and from PE freely.)

4. **E**—Kinetic energy is a scalar, so even though the balls move in opposite directions, the KEs cannot cancel. Instead, kinetic energy $\frac{1}{2}(1\text{ kg})(6\text{ m/s})^2$ attributable to different objects adds together algebraically, giving 36 J total.

5. (a) The car started from rest, or zero KE. The car ended up with $\frac{1}{2}(1500\text{ kg})(40\text{ m/s})^2 = 1.2 \times 10^6$ J of kinetic energy. So its change in KE is 1.2×10^6 J.
   (b) The acceleration is not constant. We know that because the velocity–time graph is not linear.
   (c) The distance traveled is found from the area under the graph. It is easiest to approximate by counting boxes, where one of the big boxes is 10 m. There are, give-or-take, 19 boxes underneath the curve, so the car went 190 m.
   (d) We cannot use work = force × distance here, because the net force is continually changing (because acceleration is changing). But $W_{net} = \Delta KE$ is always valid. In part (a) the car's change in KE was found to be 1.2×10^6 J; so the net work done on the car is also 1.2×10^6 J.
   (e) Power is work divided by time, or 1.2×10^6 J/7 s = 170 kW. This can be compared to the power of a car, 220 horsepower.

› Rapid Review

- Energy is the ability to do work. Both energy and work are scalars.

- The work done on an object (or by an object) is equal to that object's change in kinetic energy.

- Potential energy is energy of position, and it comes in a variety of forms; for example, there's gravitational potential energy and spring potential energy.

- The energy of a closed system is conserved. To solve a conservation of energy problem, start by writing $K_i + U_i + W = K_f + U_f$, where "$i$" means "initial," "$f$" means "final," and W is the work done by friction or an externally applied force. Think about what type of U you're dealing with; there might even be more than one form of U in a single problem!

- Power is the rate at which work is done, measured in watts. Power is equal to work/time, which is equivalent to force multiplied by velocity.

- If the functional form of a conservative force is known, then the potential energy attributable to that force is given by

$$U = -\int F dx$$

When this U is graphed against displacement, the motion of an object can be predicted by imagining "Chris on a skateboard" skating on the graph.

CHAPTER 13

Gravitation and Circular Motion

IN THIS CHAPTER

Summary: When an object moves in a circle, it is accelerating toward the center of the circle. Any two massive objects attract each other due to gravity.

Key Ideas
- Centripetal (center-seeking) acceleration is equal to $\dfrac{v^2}{r}$.
- Circular motion (and gravitation) problems still require a free-body diagram and the four-step problem-solving process.
- The gravitational force between two objects is bigger for bigger masses, and smaller for larger separations between the objects.
- Kepler's laws apply to the orbits of planets.

Relevant Equations

Centripetal acceleration:

$$a = \frac{v^2}{r}$$

Gravitational force between any two masses:

$$F = \frac{Gm_1 m_2}{r^2}$$

Gravitational potential energy a long way from a planet:

$$U = -\frac{Gm_1 m_2}{r}$$

It might seem odd that we're covering gravitation and circular motion in the same chapter. After all, one of these topics relates to the attractive force exerted between two massive objects, and the other one relates to, well, swinging a bucket over your head.

However, as you're probably aware, the two topics have plenty to do with each other. Planetary orbits, for instance, can be described only if you understand both gravitation and circular motion. And, sure enough, the AP exam frequently features questions about orbits.

So let's look at these two important topics, starting with circular motion.

Velocity and Acceleration in Circular Motion

Remember how we defined acceleration as an object's change in velocity in a given time? Well, velocity is a vector, and that means that an object's velocity can change either in magnitude or in direction (or both). In the past, we have talked about the magnitude of an object's velocity changing. Now, we discuss what happens when the direction of an object's velocity changes.

When an object maintains the same speed but turns in a circle, the magnitude of its acceleration is constant and directed **toward the center** of the circle. This means that the acceleration vector is perpendicular to the velocity vector at any given moment, as shown in Figure 13.1.

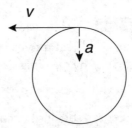

Figure 13.1   Velocity and acceleration of an object traveling in uniform circular motion.

The velocity vector is always directed tangent to the circle, and the acceleration vector is always directed toward the center of the circle. There's a way to prove that statement mathematically, but it's complicated, so you'll just have to trust us. (You can refer to your textbook for the complete derivation.)

Centripetal Acceleration

On to a few definitions.

> **Centripetal acceleration:** The acceleration keeping an object in uniform circular motion, abbreviated a_c

We know that the net force acting on an object is related to the object's acceleration by $F_{net} = ma$. And we know that the acceleration of an object in circular motion points toward the center of the circle. So we can conclude that the centripetal force acting on an object also points toward the center of the circle.

The formula for centripetal acceleration is

$$a_c = \frac{v^2}{r}$$

In this equation, v is the object's velocity, and r is the radius of the circle in which the object is traveling.

> **Centrifugal acceleration:** As far as you're concerned, nonsense. Acceleration in circular motion is always **toward**, not away from, the center.

Centripetal acceleration is real; centrifugal acceleration is nonsense, unless you're willing to read a multipage discussion of "non-inertial reference frames" and "fictitious forces." So for our purposes, there is no such thing as a centrifugal (center-fleeing) acceleration. *When an object moves in a circle, the acceleration (and also the net force) must point to the center of the circle.*

The main thing to remember when tackling circular motion problems is that a *centripetal force is simply whatever force is directed toward the center of the circle in which the object is traveling.* So, first label the forces on your free-body diagram, and then find the net force directed toward the center of the circle. That net force is the centripetal force. But NEVER label a free-body diagram with "F_c."

> **Exam tip from an AP Physics veteran:**
> On a free-response question, do not label a force as "centripetal force," even if that force does act toward the center of a circle; you will not earn credit. Rather, label with the actual source of the force; i.e., tension, friction, weight, electric force, etc.
> —*Mike, high school junior*

Mass on a String

> A block of mass $M = 2$ kg is swung on a rope in a vertical circle of radius r at constant speed v. When the block is at the top of the circle, the tension in the rope is measured to be 10 N. What is the tension in the rope when the block is at the bottom of the circle?
>
>

Let's begin by drawing a free-body diagram of the block at the top of the circle and another of the block at the bottom of the circle.

Next, we write Newton's second law for each diagram. Acceleration is always toward the center of the circle.

$$Mg + T_{top} = Ma \qquad T_{bottom} - Mg = Ma$$

The acceleration is centripetal, so we can plug in v^2/r for both accelerations.

$$Mg + T_{top} = Mv^2/r \qquad T_{bottom} - Mg = Mv^2/r$$

At both top and bottom, the speed v and the radius r are the same. So Mv^2/r has to be the same at both the top and bottom, allowing us to set the left side of each equation equal to one another.

$$Mg + T_{top} = T_{bottom} - Mg$$

With $M = 2$ kg and $T_{top} = 10$ N, we solve to get $T_{bottom} = 50$ N.

Car on a Curve

This next problem is a bit easier than the last one, but it's still good practice.

> A car of mass m travels around a flat curve that has a radius of curvature r. What is the necessary coefficient of friction such that the car can round the curve with a velocity v?

Before we draw our free-body diagram, we should consider how friction is acting in this case. Imagine this: what would it be like to round a corner quickly while driving on ice? You would slide off the road, right? Another way to put that is to say that without friction, you would be unable to make the turn. Friction provides the centripetal force necessary to round the corner. Bingo! The force of friction must point in toward the center of the curve.

We can now write some equations and solve for μ, the coefficient of friction.

The net force in the horizontal direction is F_f, which can be set equal to mass times (centripetal) acceleration.

$$F_f = ma$$
$$F_f = ma = m\left(\frac{v^2}{r}\right)$$

We also know that $F_f = \mu F_N$. So,

$$\mu F_N = \frac{mv^2}{r}$$

Furthermore, we know that the car is in vertical equilibrium—it is neither flying off the road nor being pushed through it—so $F_N = mg$.

$$\mu mg = \frac{mv^2}{r}$$

Solving for μ we have

$$\mu = \frac{v^2}{gr}$$

Note that this coefficient doesn't depend on mass. Good—if it did, we'd need tires made of different materials depending on how heavy the car is.

Newton's Law of Gravitation

We now shift our focus to gravity. Gravity is an amazing concept—you and the Earth attract each other just because you both have mass!—but at the level tested on the AP exam, it's also a pretty easy concept. In fact, there are only a couple equations you need to know. The first is for gravitational force:

$$F_G = \frac{Gm_1 m_2}{r^2}$$

This equation describes the gravitational force that one object exerts on another object. m_1 is the mass of one of the objects, m_2 is the mass of the other object, r is the distance between the center of mass of each object, and G is called the "Universal Gravitational Constant" and is equal to 6.67×10^{-11} (G does have units—they are $\text{N·m}^2/\text{kg}^2$—but most problems won't require your knowing them). The negative sign indicates that the force is attractive. We can leave it off unless we are doing calculus with the equation.

The mass of the Earth, M_E, is 5.97×10^{24} kg. The mass of the sun, M_S, is 1.99×10^{30} kg. The two objects are about 154,000,000 km away from each other. How much gravitational force does Earth exert on the sun?

This is simple plug-and-chug (remember to convert km to m).

$$F_G = \frac{GM_E M_S}{r^2}$$
$$F_G = \frac{6.67 \times 10^{-11}(5.97 \times 10^{24})(1.99 \times 10^{30})}{(1.54 \times 10^{11})^2}$$
$$F_G = 3.3 \times 10^{22}\,\text{N}$$

Notice that the amount of force that the Earth exerts on the sun is exactly the same as the amount of force the sun exerts on the Earth.

We can combine our knowledge of circular motion and of gravity to solve the following type of problem.

> What is the speed of the Earth as it revolves in orbit around the sun?

The force of gravity exerted by the sun on the Earth is what keeps the Earth in motion—it is the centripetal force acting on the Earth.

$$F_G = M_E a = M_E \left(\frac{v^2}{r} \right)$$

$$\frac{GM_E M_S}{r^2} = \frac{M_E v^2}{r}$$

$$\frac{GM_S}{r} = v^2$$

$$v = \sqrt{\frac{GM_S}{r}}$$

$v = 29{,}000$ m/s. (Wow, fast . . . that converts to about 14 miles every second—much faster than, say, a school bus.)

Along with the equation for gravitational force, you need to know the equation for gravitational potential energy.

$$U_G = \frac{-Gm_1 m_2}{r}$$

Why negative? Objects tend get pushed toward the lowest available potential energy. A long way away from the sun, the r term gets big, so the potential energy gets close to zero. But, since a mass is *attracted* to the sun by gravity, the potential energy of the mass must get lower and lower as r gets smaller.

We bet you're thinking something like, "Now hold on a minute! You said a while back that an object's gravitational potential energy equals *mgh*. What's going on?"

Good point. An object's gravitational PE equals *mgh* when that object is near the surface of the Earth. But it equals $\frac{-Gm_1 m_2}{r}$ no matter where that object is.

Similarly, the force of gravity acting on an object equals *mg* (the object's weight) only when that object is near the surface of the Earth.

The force of gravity on an object, however, *always* equals $\frac{Gm_1 m_2}{r^2}$ regardless of location.

Kepler's Laws

Johannes Kepler, the late 1500s theorist, developed three laws of planetary motion based on the detailed observations of Tycho Brahe. You need to understand each law and its consequences.

1. *Planetary orbits are ellipses, with the sun at one focus.* Of course, we can apply this law to a satellite orbiting Earth, in which case the orbit is an ellipse, with Earth at one focus. (We mean the center of the Earth—for the sake of Kepler's laws, we consider the orbiting bodies to be point particles.) In the simple case of a circular orbit, this law still applies because a circle is just an ellipse with both foci at the center.

2. *An orbit sweeps out equal areas in equal times.* If you draw a line from a planet to the sun, this line crosses an equal amount of area every minute (or hour, or month, or whatever)—see Figure 13.2. The consequence here is that when a planet is close to the sun, it must speed up, and when a planet is far from the sun, it must slow down. This applies to the Earth as well. In the Northern Hemisphere winter, when the Earth is slightly closer to the sun,[1] the Earth moves faster in its orbit. (You may have noticed that the earliest sunset in wintertime occurs about two weeks before the solstice—this is a direct consequence of Earth's faster orbit.)

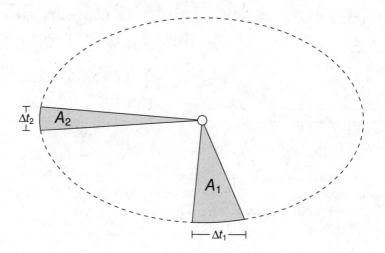

Figure 13.2   Kepler's second law. The area "swept out" by a planet in its orbit is shaded. In equal time intervals $\triangle t_1$ and $\triangle t_2$, these swept areas A_1 and A_2 are the same.

3. *A planet's orbital period squared is proportional to its orbital radius cubed.* In mathematics, we write this as $T^2 = cR^3$. Okay, how do we define the "radius" of a non-circular orbit? Well, that would be average distance from the sun. And what is this constant c? It's a different value for every system of satellites orbiting a single central body. Not worth worrying about, except that you can easily derive it for the solar system by solving the equation above for c and plugging in data from Earth's orbit: $c = 1$ year^2/AU^3, where an "AU" is the distance from Earth to the sun. If you *really* need to, you can convert this into more standard units, but we wouldn't bother with this right now.

Energy of Closed Orbits

When an object of mass m is in orbit around the sun, its potential energy is $U = -\dfrac{GMm}{r}$, where M is the mass of the sun, and r is the distance between the centers of the two masses.

The kinetic energy of the orbiting mass, of course, is $K = \frac{1}{2}mv^2$. The total mechanical energy of the mass in orbit is defined as $U + K$. When the mass is in a stable orbit, the total

---

[1]*Please* don't say you thought the Earth must be farther away from the sun in winter because it's cold. When it's winter in the United States, it's summer in Australia, and we're all the same distance from the sun!

mechanical energy must be less than zero. A mass with positive total mechanical energy can escape the "gravitational well" of the sun; a mass with negative total mechanical energy is "bound" to orbit the sun.[2]

All of the above applies to the planets orbiting in the solar system. It also applies to moons or satellites orbiting planets, when (obviously) we replace the "sun" by the central planet. A useful calculation using the fact that total mechanical energy of an object in orbit is the potential energy plus the kinetic energy is to find the "escape speed" from the surface of a planet . . . at r equal to the radius of the planet, set kinetic plus potential energy equal to zero, and solve for v. This is the speed that, if it is attained at the surface of the planet (neglecting air resistance), will cause an object to attain orbit.

› Practice Problems

Multiple Choice:

Questions 1 and 2:

Two stars, each of mass M, form a binary system. The stars orbit about a point a distance R from the center of each star, as shown in the diagram above. The stars themselves each have radius r.

1. What is the force each star exerts on the other?

(A) $G\dfrac{M^2}{(2r+2R)^2}$

(B) $G\dfrac{M^2}{(R+r)^2}$

(C) $G\dfrac{M^2}{R^2}$

(D) $G\dfrac{M^2}{4R^2}$

(E) $G\dfrac{M^2}{2R^2}$

2. In terms of each star's tangential speed v, what is the centripetal acceleration of each star?

(A) $\dfrac{v^2}{2R}$

(B) $\dfrac{v^2}{(r+R)}$

(C) $\dfrac{v^2}{2(r+R)}$

(D) $\dfrac{v^2}{2r}$

(E) $\dfrac{v^2}{R}$

Questions 3 and 4: In the movie *Return of the Jedi*, the Ewoks throw rocks using a circular-motion device. A rock is attached to a string. An Ewok whirls the rock in a horizontal circle above his head, then lets go, sending the rock careening into the head of an unsuspecting stormtrooper.

3. What force provides the rock's centripetal acceleration?

(A) The vertical component of the string's tension
(B) The horizontal component of the string's tension
(C) The entire tension of the string
(D) The gravitational force on the rock
(E) The horizontal component of the gravitational force on the rock

---

[2]It can be shown that for a planet in a stable, *circular* orbit, the kinetic energy is half the absolute value of the potential energy. This isn't something important enough to memorize, but it might help you out sometime if you happen to remember.

4. The Ewok whirls the rock and releases it from a point above his head and to his right. The rock initially goes straight forward. Which of the following describes the subsequent motion of the rock?

(A) It will continue in a straight line forward, while falling due to gravity.
(B) It will continue forward but curve to the right, while falling due to gravity.
(C) It will continue forward but curve to the left, while falling due to gravity.
(D) It will fall straight down to the ground.
(E) It will curve back toward the Ewok and hit him in the head.

5. A Space Shuttle orbits Earth 300 km above the surface. Why can't the Shuttle orbit 10 km above Earth?

(A) The Space Shuttle cannot go fast enough to maintain such an orbit.
(B) Kepler's laws forbid an orbit so close to the surface of the Earth.
(C) Because r appears in the denominator of Newton's law of gravitation, the force of gravity is much larger closer to the Earth; this force is too strong to allow such an orbit.
(D) The closer orbit would likely crash into a large mountain such as Everest because of its elliptical nature.
(E) Much of the Shuttle's kinetic energy would be dissipated as heat in the atmosphere, degrading the orbit.

Free Response:

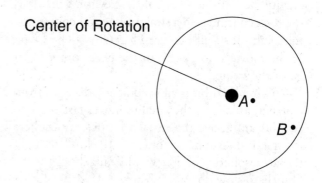

Center of Rotation

6. Consider two points on a rotating turntable: Point A is very close to the center of rotation, while point B is on the outer rim of the turntable. Both points are shown above. A penny could be placed on the turntable at either point A or point B.

(a) In which case would the speed of the penny be greater, if it were placed at point A, or if it were placed at point B? Explain.
(b) At which point would the penny require the larger centripetal force to remain in place? Justify your answer.
(c) Point B is 0.25 m from the center of rotation. If the coefficient of friction between the penny and the turntable is $\mu = 0.30$, calculate the maximum linear speed the penny can have there and still remain in circular motion.

❭ Solutions to Practice Problems

1. D—In Newton's law of gravitation,

$$F = G\frac{m_1 m_2}{r^2},$$

the distance used is the distance between the centers of the planets; here that distance is $2R$. But the denominator is squared, so $(2R)^2 = 4R^2$ in the denominator here.

2. E—In the centripetal acceleration equation

$$a_c = \frac{v^2}{r},$$

the distance used is the radius of the circular motion. Here, because the planets orbit around

a point right in between them, this distance is simply R.

3. B—Consider the vertical forces acting on the rock. The rock has weight, so mg acts down. However, because the rock isn't falling down, something must counteract the weight. That something is the vertical component of the rope's tension. The rope must not be perfectly horizontal, then. Because the circle is horizontal, the centripetal force must be horizontal as well. The only horizontal force here is the horizontal component of the tension. (Gravity acts *down*, last we checked, and so cannot have a horizontal component.)

4. A—Once the Ewok lets go, no forces (other than gravity) act on the rock. So, by Newton's first law, the rock continues in a straight line. Of course, the rock still must fall because of gravity. (The Ewok in the movie who got hit in the head forgot to let go of the string.)

5. E—A circular orbit is allowed at any distance from a planet, as long as the satellite moves fast enough. At 300 km above the surface Earth's atmosphere is practically nonexistent. At 10 km, though, the atmospheric friction would quickly cause the Shuttle to slow down.

6. (a) Both positions take the same time to make a full revolution. But point B must go farther in that same time, so the penny must have bigger speed at point B.

(b) The coin needs more centripetal force at point B. The centripetal force is equal to mv^2/r. However, the speed itself depends on the radius of the motion, as shown in part (a). The speed of a point at radius r is the circumference divided by the time for one rotation T, $v = 2\pi r/T$. So the net force equation becomes, after algebraic simplification, $F_{net} = 4m\pi^2 r/T^2$. Because both positions take equal times to make a rotation, the coin with the larger distance from the center needs more centripetal force.

(c) The force of friction provides the centripetal force here, and is equal to μ times the normal force. Because the only forces acting vertically are F_N and mg, $F_N = mg$. The net force is equal to mv^2/r, and also to the friction force μmg. Setting these equal and solving for v,

$$v = \sqrt{\mu rg}$$

Plug in the values given ($r = 0.25$ m, $\mu = 0.30$) to get $v = 0.87$ m/s. If the speed is faster than this, then the centripetal force necessary to keep the penny rotating increases, and friction can no longer provide that force.

❯ Rapid Review

- When an object travels in a circle, its velocity vector is directed tangent to the circle, and its acceleration vector points toward the center of the circle.

- A centripetal force keeps an object traveling in a circle. The centripetal force is simply whatever net force is directed toward the center of the circle in which the object is traveling.

- Newton's law of gravitation states that the gravitational force between two objects is proportional to the mass of the first object multiplied by the mass of the second divided by the square of the distance between them. This also means that the gravitational force felt by one object is the same as the force felt by the second object.

- Predictions of Kepler's laws: Planets undergo elliptical orbits with the sun at one focus; at points in an orbit closer to the sun, a planet moves faster; the smaller a planet's mean distance from the sun, the shorter its orbital period, by $T^2 \propto R^3$. (The symbol "$\propto$" means "is proportional to.")

CHAPTER 14

Rotational Motion

IN THIS CHAPTER

Summary: The mechanics of rotating objects make up a significant chunk of the AP Physics C exam. But, rotational motion has many direct analogs from linear motion. If you understand the mechanics unit from your first-year physics course, rotational motion can be learned by analogy.

Key Ideas

✪ Rotational kinematics uses essentially the same equations as kinematics, but distances, speeds, and accelerations are rotational quantities expressed with radians instead of with meters.

✪ The rotational inertia defines an object's resistance to rotation. It is the rotational analog of mass.

✪ An object can possess rotational kinetic energy in addition to translational kinetic energy.

✪ Angular momentum is conserved anytime no external torque acts on a system of objects. This includes planets in orbit.

Relevant Equations

Rotational kinematics equations.
First, for constant angular acceleration:

$$\omega_f = \omega_o + \alpha t$$
$$\Delta\theta = \omega_o t + \tfrac{1}{2}\alpha t^2$$
$$\omega_f^2 = \omega_o^2 + 2\alpha\Delta\theta$$

And, in all cases:

$$\theta = \int \omega \, dt$$

$$\omega = \frac{d\theta}{dt} = \int \alpha \, dt$$

$$\alpha = \frac{d\omega}{dt}$$

Conversion between linear and rotational variables:

$$x = r\theta$$
$$v = r\omega$$
$$a = r\alpha$$

Rotational inertia:

$$I = mr^2 \qquad\qquad \text{for a point particle}$$
$$I = \int r^2 \, dm \qquad\qquad \text{for a continuous body}$$

Newton's second law for rotation:

$$\tau_{\text{net}} = I\alpha$$

Rotational kinetic energy:

$$K_{\text{rot}} = \tfrac{1}{2} I\omega^2$$

Angular momentum:

$$L = I\omega = mvr$$

Okay, you now have thoroughly studied how an object moves; that is, if the object can be treated as a point particle. But what happens when an object is spinning? How does that affect motion? Now is the time to learn.

You'll find clear similarities between the material in this chapter and what you already know. In fact, you'll see that every concept, every variable, every equation for rotational motion has an analog in our study of translational motion. The best way to understand rotational motion is simply to apply the concepts of linear motion to the case of a spinning object.

Rotational Kinematics

For an object moving in a straight line, we defined five variables.

v_0	initial velocity
v_f	final velocity
Δx	displacement
a	acceleration
t	time interval

Now consider a fixed object spinning, like a compact disc. The relevant variables become the following:

ω_0 initial *angular* velocity, measured in radians per second
ω_f final *angular* velocity, measured in radians per second
$\Delta\theta$ the total *angle* through which the spinning object rotates, measured in radians
α *angular* acceleration, telling how *angular* velocity changes with time
t time interval

These variables are related via the following three equations. Obviously, these equations differ from the "star equations" used for kinematics . . . but they're nonetheless very similar:

$$\omega_f = \omega_0 + \alpha t$$

$$\Delta\theta = \omega_0 t + \tfrac{1}{2}\alpha t^2$$

$$\omega_f^2 = \omega_0^2 + 2\alpha\Delta\theta$$

So try this example:

A bicycle has wheels with radius 50 cm. The bike starts from rest, and the wheels speed up uniformly to 200 revolutions per minute in 10 seconds. How far does the bike go?

In any linear kinematics problem, the units should be in meters and seconds; in rotational kinematics, the units MUST be in RADIANS and seconds. So convert revolutions per minute to radians per second. To do so, recall that there are 2π radians in every revolution:

$$200 \text{ rev/min} \times 2\pi \text{ rad/rev} \times 1 \text{ min/60 s} = 21 \text{ rad/s}.$$

Now identify variables in a chart:

ω_0	0 rad/s
ω_f	21 rad/s
$\Delta\theta$	?
α	?
t	10 s

We want to solve for $\Delta\theta$ because if we know the angle through which the wheel turns, we can figure out how far the edge of the wheel has gone. We know we can solve for $\Delta\theta$, because we have three of the five variables. Plug and chug into the rotational kinematics equations:

$$\omega_f = \omega_0 + \alpha t$$

$$\alpha = 2.1 \text{ rad/s}^2$$

$$\Delta\theta = \omega_0 t + \tfrac{1}{2}\alpha t^2$$

$$\Delta\theta = 105 \text{ radians}$$

What does this answer mean? Well, if there are 2π (that is, 6.2) radians in one revolution, then 105 radians is about 17 revolutions through which the wheel has turned.

Now, because the wheel has a radius of 0.50 m, the wheel's circumference is $2\pi r = 3.1$ m; every revolution of the wheel moves the bike 3.1 meters forward. And the wheel made 17 revolutions, giving a total distance of about 53 meters.

Is this reasonable? Sure—the biker traveled across about half a football field in 10 seconds.

There are a few other equations you should know. If you want to figure out the linear position, speed, or acceleration of a spot on a spinning object, or an object that's rolling without slipping, use these three equations:

$$x = r\theta$$
$$v = r\omega$$
$$a = r\alpha$$

where r represents the distance from the spot you're interested in to the center of the object.

So in the case of the bike wheel above, the top speed of the bike was $v = (0.5 \text{ m})$ (21 rad/s) = 11 m/s, or about 24 miles per hour—reasonable for an average biker. *Note: To use these equations, angular variable units must involve radians, not degrees or revolutions!!!*

The rotational kinematics equations, just like the linear kinematics equations, are only valid when acceleration is constant. If acceleration is changing, then the same calculus equations that were used for linear kinematics apply here:

$$\theta = \int \omega \, dt$$
$$\omega = \frac{d\theta}{dt} = \int \alpha \, dt$$
$$\alpha = \frac{d\omega}{dt}$$

Rotational Inertia

Newton's second law states that $F_{\text{net}} = ma$; this tells us that the greater the mass of an object, the harder it is to accelerate. This tendency for massive objects to resist changes in their velocity is referred to as inertia.

Well, spinning objects also resist changes in their *angular* velocity. But that resistance, that rotational inertia, depends less on the mass of an object than on how that mass is distributed. For example, a baseball player often warms up by placing a weight on the outer end of the bat—this makes the bat more difficult to swing. But he does not place the weight on the bat handle, because extra weight in the handle hardly affects the swing at all.

The rotational inertia, I, is the rotational equivalent of mass. It tells how difficult it is for an object to speed up or slow its rotation. For a single particle of mass m a distance r from the axis of rotation, the rotational inertia is

$$I = mr^2 \quad I \text{ for a point object.}$$

To find the rotational inertia of several masses—for example, two weights connected by a thin, light rod—just add the I due to each mass.

For a complicated, continuous body, like a sphere or a disk, I can be calculated through integration:

$$I = \int r^2 \, dm \quad I \text{ for a continuous body.}$$

Exam tip from an AP Physics veteran:
On the AP exam, you will only very occasionally have to use calculus to derive a rotational inertia. Usually you will either be able to sum the I due to several masses, or you will be given I for the object in question.

—*Joe, college physics student and Physics C alumnus*

Torque

Torque occurs when a force is applied to an object, and that force can cause the object to rotate.

$$\textbf{Torque} = Fd$$

In other words, the torque exerted on an object equals the force exerted on that object (F) multiplied by the distance between where the force is applied and the fulcrum (d) as long as the force acts perpendicular to the object.

> **Fulcrum:** The point about which an object rotates

Figure 14.1 shows what we mean:

Figure 14.1   The torque applied to this bar equals *Fd*.

The unit of torque is the newton-meter.
Here's an example.

Bob is standing on a bridge. The bridge itself weighs 10,000 N. The span between pillars A and B is 80 m. Bob is 20 m from the center of the bridge. His mass is 100 kg. Assuming that the bridge is in equilibrium, find the force exerted by pillar B on the bridge.

Step 1: Free-body diagram.

We'll use point A as the fulcrum to start with. Why? In a static equilibrium situation, since the bridge isn't *actually* rotating, any point on the bridge could serve as a fulcrum. But we have two unknown forces here, the forces of the supports A and B. We choose the location of one of these supports as the fulcrum, because now that support provides zero torque—the distance from the fulcrum becomes zero! Now all we have to do is solve for the force of support B.

The diagram below isn't a true "free-body diagram," because it includes both distance and forces, but it is useful for a torque problem. Bob's weight acts downward right where he stands.

The bridge's weight is taken into account with a force vector acting at the bridge's center of mass; that is, 40 m to the right of pillar A. This is a generally valid approach—replace the weight of an extended object with a single weight vector acting at the center of mass.

Step 2: Vector components.

We don't have to worry about vector components here. (We would have if the forces had not acted perpendicular to the bridge.)

Step 3: Equations.

$$\text{counterclockwise torque} = \text{clockwise torque}$$
$$F_B(80 \text{ m}) = (1000 \text{ N})(20 \text{ m}) + (10,000 \text{ N})(40 \text{ m})$$

Step 4: Solve. $F_B = 5300 \text{ N}$

This is reasonable because pillar B is supporting *less* than half of the 11,000 N weight of the bridge and Bob. Because Bob is closer to pillar A, and otherwise the bridge is symmetric, A should bear the majority of the weight.

The Physics C exam will often expect you to find the torque provided by a force that acts at an angle. For example, consider a force F acting on a bar at an angle θ, applied a distance x from a pivot. How much torque does this force provide? See Figure 14.2.

Figure 14.2   Force F acting on a bar at an angle θ.

To solve, break the force vector into horizontal and vertical components, as shown in Figure 14.3.

Figure 14.3   Break the force vector into horizontal and vertical components.

The vertical component of F applies a torque of $(F \sin \theta)x$. The horizontal component of F does not apply any torque, because it could not cause the bar to rotate. So, the total torque provided by F is $(F \sin \theta)x$.

Lever Arm

The "lever arm" for a force is the closest distance from the fulcrum to the line of that force. Then, the torque provided by a force is the force times the lever arm.

Consider Figure 14.4, which represents the same situation as Figure 14.2. Instead of breaking F into components, continue the line of the force. The torque is F times the lever arm shown in the diagram. By trigonometry, you can see that the lever arm is equal to $x \sin \theta$. No matter how you look at it, the torque provided by F is still $(F \sin \theta)x$.

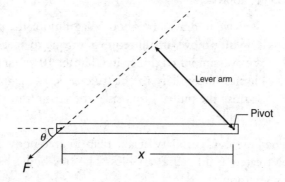

Figure 14.4 Force F acting on a bar at an angle θ.

Newton's Second Law for Rotation

For linear motion, Newton says $F_{net} = ma$; for rotational motion, the analog to Newton's second law is

$$\tau_{net} = I\alpha$$

where τ_{net} is the net torque on an object. Perhaps the most common application of this equation involves pulleys with mass.

A 2.0-kg block on a smooth table is connected to a hanging 3.0-kg block with a light string. This string passes over a pulley of mass 0.50 kg, as shown in the diagram below. Determine the acceleration of the masses. (The rotational inertia for a solid disc of mass m and radius r is $\frac{1}{2}mr^2$.)

We learned how to approach this type of problem in Chapter 10—draw a free-body diagram for each block, and use $F_{net} = ma$. So we start that way.

The twist in this problem is the massive pulley, which causes two changes in the problem-solving approach:

1. We have to draw a free-body diagram for the pulley as well as the blocks. Even though it doesn't move, it still requires torque to accelerate its spinning speed.
2. We oversimplified things in Chapter 10 when we said, "One rope = one tension." The Physics C corollary to this rule says, ". . . unless the rope is interrupted by a mass." Because the pulley is massive, the tension in the rope may be *different* on each side of the pulley.

The Physics C corollary means that the free-body diagrams indicate T_1 and T_2, which must be treated as different variables. The free-body diagram for the pulley includes only these two tensions:

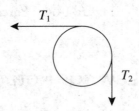

Now, we write Newton's second law for each block:

$$T_1 - 0 = (2 \text{ kg})a$$

$$(3 \text{ kg})g - T_2 = (3 \text{ kg})a.$$

For the pulley, because it is *rotating*, we write Newton's second law for rotation. The torque provided by each rope is equal to the tension in the rope times the distance to the center of rotation; that is, the radius of the pulley. (We're not given this radius, so we'll just call it R for now and hope for the best.)

$$T_2 R - T_1 R = \tfrac{1}{2}(0.5 \text{ kg})R^2 \alpha$$

The acceleration of each block must be the same because they're connected by a rope; the linear acceleration of a point on the edge of the pulley must also be the same as that of the blocks. So, in the pulley equation, replace α by a/R. Check it out, all the R terms cancel! Thank goodness, too, because the radius of the pulley wasn't even given in the problem.

The pulley equation, thus, simplifies to

$$T_2 - T_1 = \tfrac{1}{2}(0.5 \text{ kg})a$$

Now we're left with an algebra problem: three equations and three variables (T_1, T_2, and a). Solve using addition or substitution. Try adding the first two equations together—this gives a $T_1 - T_2$ term that meshes nicely with the third equation.

The acceleration turns out to be 5.6 m/s². If you do the problem neglecting the mass of the pulley (try it!) you get 5.9 m/s². This makes sense—the more massive the pulley, the harder it is for the system of masses to speed up.

Rotational Kinetic Energy

The pulley in the last example problem had kinetic energy—it was moving, after all—but it didn't have *linear* kinetic energy, because the velocity of its center of mass was zero. When an object is rotating, its rotational kinetic energy is found by the following equation:

$$KE_{rotational} = \tfrac{1}{2}I\omega^2$$

Notice that this equation is very similar to the equation for linear kinetic energy. But, because we're dealing with rotation here, we use rotational inertia in place of mass and angular velocity in place of linear velocity.

If an object is moving linearly at the same time that it's rotating, its total kinetic energy equals the sum of the linear KE and the rotational KE.

$$KE_{total} = KE_{linear} + KE_{rotational}$$

Let's put this equation into practice. Try this example problem.

A ball of mass m sits on an inclined plane, with its center of mass at a height h above the ground. It is released from rest and allowed to roll without slipping down the plane. What is its velocity when it reaches the ground? $I_{ball} = (2/5)mr^2$.

This is a situation you've seen before, except there's a twist: this time, when the object moves down the inclined plane, it gains both linear and rotational kinetic energy. However, it's still just a conservation of energy problem at heart. Initially, the ball just has gravitational potential energy, and when it reaches the ground, it has both linear kinetic and rotational kinetic energy.

$$mgh = \tfrac{1}{2}mv^2 + \tfrac{1}{2}I\omega^2$$

$$mgh = \tfrac{1}{2}mv^2 + \tfrac{1}{2}(2/5\ mr^2)(v/r)^2$$

A bit of algebra, and we find that

$$v = \sqrt{\frac{10}{7}gh}$$

If the ball in this problem hadn't rolled down the plane—if it had just slid—its final velocity would have been $\sqrt{2gh}$. (Don't believe us? Try the calculation yourself for practice!) So it makes sense that the final velocity of the ball when it *does* roll down the plane is less than $\sqrt{2gh}$; only a fraction of the initial potential energy is converted to linear kinetic energy.

Angular Momentum and Its Conservation

It probably won't surprise you by this point that momentum, too, has a rotational form. It's called angular momentum (abbreviated, oddly, as L), and it is found by this formula:

$$\boxed{L = I\omega}$$

This formula makes intuitive sense. If you think of angular momentum as, roughly, the amount of effort it would take to make a rotating object stop spinning, then it should seem logical that an object with a large rotational inertia or with a high angular velocity (or both) would be pretty tough to bring to rest.

For a point particle, this formula can be rewritten as

$$\boxed{L = mvr}$$

where v is linear velocity, and r is either (1) the radius of rotation, if the particle is moving in a circle, or (2) distance of closest approach if the particle is moving in a straight line. (See Figure 14.5.)

Figure 14.5   Angular momentum.

Wait a minute! How can an object moving in a straight line have *angular* momentum?!? Well, for the purposes of the AP exam, it suffices just to know that if a particle moves in a straight line, then relative to some point P not on that line, the particle has an angular momentum. But if you want a slightly more satisfying—if less precise—explanation, consider this image. You're standing outside in an open field, and an airplane passes high overhead. You first see it come over the horizon far in front of you, then it flies toward you until it's directly over where you're standing, and then it keeps flying until it finally disappears beneath the opposite horizon. Did the plane fly in an arc over your head or in a straight path? It would be hard for you to tell, right? In other words, when a particle moves in a straight line, an observer who's not on that line would think that the particle sort of looked like it were traveling in a circle.

As with linear momentum, angular momentum is conserved in a closed system; that is, when no external torques act on the objects in the system. Among the most famous examples of conservation of angular momentum is a satellite's orbit around a planet. As shown in Figure 14.6, a satellite will travel in an elliptical orbit around a planet. This means that the satellite is closer to the planet at some times than at others.

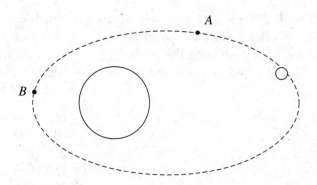

Figure 14.6   Elliptical orbit.

Obviously, at point *A*, the satellite is farther from the center of rotation than at point *B*. Conservation of angular momentum tells us that, correspondingly, the angular speed at point *A* must be less than at point *B*.[1]

The other really famous example of conservation of angular momentum involves a spinning figure skater. When a skater spinning with his or her arms outstretched suddenly brings the arms in close to the body, the speed of rotation dramatically increases. Rotational inertia decreased, so angular speed increased.

You can demonstrate this phenomenon yourself! Sit in a desk chair that spins, and with your legs outstretched, push off forcefully and start spinning. Then tuck in your feet. Dizzying, isn't it?

› Practice Problems

Multiple Choice:

1. All of the objects mentioned in the choices below have the same total mass and length. Which has the greatest rotational inertia about its midpoint?

   (A) a very light rod with heavy balls attached at either end
   (B) a uniform rod
   (C) a nonuniform rod, with the linear density increasing from one end to the other
   (D) a nonuniform rod, with the linear density increasing from the middle to the ends
   (E) a very light rod with heavy balls attached near the midpoint

Camera

2. A pool ball is struck at one end of the table; it moves at constant speed to the far end of the table. A camera is mounted at the side pocket at the table's midpoint, as shown. From the camera's point of view, the pool ball travels from right to left. At which point in its motion does the ball have the greatest angular momentum about the camera's position?

   (A) when the ball was first struck
   (B) at the midpoint of the table
   (C) the angular momentum is the same throughout the motion
   (D) at the far end of the table
   (E) one-quarter of the way across the table, and then again three-quarters of the way across the table

---

[1]Note the consistency with Kepler's law of equal areas in equal times, as discussed in Chapter 13.

3. A ladder of length L leans against a wall at an angle of θ from the horizontal, as shown earlier. The normal force F_N applied from the ground on the ladder applies what torque about the ladder's center of mass?

(A) $F_N \cdot (L/2)$
(B) $F_N \cdot L \cos \theta$
(C) $F_N \cdot L \sin \theta$
(D) $F_N \cdot (L/2) \cos \theta$
(E) $F_N \cdot (L/2) \sin \theta$

4. The front wheel on an ancient bicycle has a radius of 0.5 m. It moves with angular velocity given by the function $\omega(t) = 2 + 4t^2$, where t is in seconds. About how far does the bicycle move between $t = 2$ and $t = 3$ seconds?

(A) 36 m
(B) 27 m
(C) 21 m
(D) 14 m
(E) 7 m

Free Response:

5. A stick of mass M and length L is pivoted at one end. A small mass $m \ll M$ is attached to the right-hand end of the stick. The stick is held horizontally and released from rest.

(a) Given that the rotational inertia of a uniform rod pivoted around one end is $(1/3)ML^2$, determine the rotational inertia of the described contraption.

(b) Calculate the angular velocity of the contraption when it reaches a vertical position.

(c) Calculate the linear velocity of the small mass m when it is at its lowest position.

(d) The figure below represents the stick at its lowest position. On this figure, draw a vector to represent the net force on the rod's center of mass at this point. Justify your answer.

› Solutions to Practice Problems

1. A—The farther the mass from the midpoint, the larger its contribution to the rotational inertia. In choice A the mass is as far as possible from the midpoint; because all items have the same mass, A must have the largest I.

2. C—The angular momentum of a point particle moving in a straight line about a position near the particle is mvr, where r is the distance of closest approach. This value is constant as long as the particle keeps going in a straight line, which our pool ball does.

3. D—Torque is force times the distance to the fulcrum. The force in question is F_N, and acts straight up at the base of the ladder. The distance used is the distance *perpendicular* to the normal force; this must be $(L/2) \cos \theta$, as shown below:

4. D—The angular position function is given by the integral of the angular velocity function with respect to time. The limits on the integral are 2 and 3 seconds:

$$\int_{2}^{3} (2 + 4t^2)dt = 2t + \frac{4t^3}{3}\bigg|_{2}^{3}$$

this evaluates to approximately 27 radians. Using $x = r\theta$, the distance traveled is closest to 14 m.

5. (a) The rotational inertia of the entire contraption is the sum of the moments of inertia for each part. I for the rod is given; I for a point mass a distance L from the pivot is mL^2. So, $I_{total} = (1/3) ML^2 + mL^2$. Be sure to differentiate between M and m.

(b) Rotational kinematics won't work here because angular acceleration isn't constant. We must use energy.

$$U_1 + K_1 = U_2 + K_2$$

Define $U = 0$ at the bottom of the contraption when it hangs vertically. Then, U_2 is only caused by the rod's mass, which is concentrated $L/2$ above the zero point, so $U_2 = MgL/2$. U_1 is due to all of the mass, concentrated L above the zero point: $U_1 = (M + m)gL$. $K_1 = 0$, and K_2 is unknown.

$$(M + m)gL + 0 = MgL/2 + \tfrac{1}{2}I\omega^2$$

Plug in I from part (*a*) and solve for ω to get

$$\omega = \sqrt{\frac{g}{L}\left(\frac{M + 2m}{\frac{1}{3}M + m}\right)}$$

(c) Just use $v = r\omega$. Here, $r = L$ because the center of rotation is L away from the mass.

$$\text{Answer: } v = \sqrt{gL\left(\frac{M + 2m}{\frac{1}{3}M + m}\right)}$$

(d) At this position, the mass is instantaneously in uniform circular motion. So, acceleration (and therefore net force) must be centripetal. Net force is straight up, toward the center of rotation.

› Rapid Review

- Rotational kinematics is very similar to linear kinematics. But instead of linear velocity, you work with angular velocity (in radians/s); instead of linear acceleration, you work with angular acceleration (in radians/s^2); and instead of linear displacement, you work with angular displacement (in radians).

- When doing rotation problems, work in radians, not degrees.

- Rotational inertia is the rotational equivalent of mass—it's a measure of how difficult it is to start or stop an object spinning.

- The rotational equivalent of Newton's second law says that the NET torque on an object equals that object's rotational inertia multiplied by its angular acceleration.

- To solve problems involving a massive pulley, make sure you draw a free-body diagram of the pulley. Also, when a rope passes over a massive pulley, the tension in the rope on one side of the pulley won't be the same as the tension on the other side.

- The total kinetic energy of a rolling object is equal to the sum of its linear kinetic energy and its rotational kinetic energy.

- Angular momentum in a closed system is conserved. An object doesn't necessarily need to travel in a circle to have angular momentum.

CHAPTER 15

Simple Harmonic Motion

IN THIS CHAPTER

Summary: An object whose position–time graph makes a sine or cosine function is in simple harmonic motion. The period of such motion can be calculated.

Key Ideas

✪ There are three conditions for something to be in simple harmonic motion. All are equivalent.

1. The object's position–time graph is a sine or cosine graph.
2. The restoring force on the object is proportional to its displacement from equilibrium.
3. The energy vs. position graph is parabolic, or nearly so.

✪ The mass on a spring is the most common example of simple harmonic motion.

✪ The pendulum is in simple harmonic motion for small amplitudes.

Relevant Equations

Period of a mass on a spring:

$$T = 2\pi \sqrt{\frac{m}{k}}$$

Period of a pendulum:

$$T = 2\pi \sqrt{\frac{L}{g}}$$

Relationship between period and frequency:

$$T = \frac{1}{f}$$

What's so simple about simple harmonic motion (SHM)? Well, the name actually refers to a type of movement—regular, back and forth, and tick-tock tick-tock kind of motion. It's simple compared to, say, a system of 25 springs and masses and pendulums all tied to one another and waggling about chaotically.

The other reason SHM is simple is that, on the AP exam, there are only a limited number of situations in which you'll encounter it. Which means only a few formulas to memorize, and only a few types of problems to really master. We hope you'll agree that most of this material is, relatively, simple.

Amplitude, Period, and Frequency

Simple harmonic motion is the study of oscillations. An **oscillation** is motion of an object that regularly repeats itself over the same path. For example, a pendulum in a grandfather clock undergoes oscillation: it travels back and forth, back and forth, back and forth . . . Another term for oscillation is "periodic motion."

Objects undergo oscillation when they experience a **restoring force**. This is a force that restores an object to the equilibrium position. In the case of a grandfather clock, the pendulum's equilibrium position—the position where it would be if it weren't moving—is when it's hanging straight down. When it's swinging, gravity exerts a restoring force: as the pendulum swings up in its arc, the force of gravity pulls on the pendulum, so that it eventually swings back down and passes through its equilibrium position. Of course, it only remains in its equilibrium position for an instant, and then it swings back up the other way. A restoring force doesn't need to bring an object to rest in its equilibrium position; it just needs to make that object pass through an equilibrium position.

If you look back at the chapter on conservation of energy (Chapter 12), you'll find the equation for the force exerted by a spring, $F = -kx$. The negative sign simply signifies that F is a restoring force: It tries to pull or push whatever is on the end of the spring back to the spring's equilibrium position. So if the spring is stretched out, the restoring force tries to squish it back in, and if the spring is compressed, the restoring force tries to stretch it back out.

One repetition of periodic motion is called a **cycle**. For the pendulum of a grandfather clock, one cycle is equal to one back-and-forth swing.

The maximum displacement from the equilibrium position during a cycle is the **amplitude**. In Figure 15.1, the equilibrium position is denoted by "0," and the maximum displacement of the object on the end of the spring is denoted by "A."

Figure 15.1   Periodic motion of a mass connected to a spring.

The time it takes for an object to pass through one cycle is the period, abbreviated T. Going back to the grandfather clock example, the period of the pendulum is the time it takes to go back and forth once: one second. Period is related to frequency, which is the number of cycles per second. The frequency of the pendulum of the grandfather clock is $f = 1$ cycle/s, where f is the standard abbreviation for frequency; the unit of frequency, the cycle per second, is called a hertz, abbreviated Hz. Period and frequency are related by this equation:

$$T = \frac{1}{f}$$

Vibrating Mass on a Spring

A mass attached to the end of a spring will oscillate in simple harmonic motion. The period of the oscillation is found by this equation:

$$T = 2\pi \sqrt{\frac{m}{k}}$$

In this equation, m is the mass of the object on the spring, and k is the "spring constant." As far as equations go, this is one of the more difficult ones to memorize, but once you have committed it to memory, it becomes very simple to use.

A block with a mass of 10 kg is placed on the end of a spring that is hung from the ceiling. When the block is attached to the spring, the spring is stretched out 20 cm from its rest position. The block is then pulled down an additional 5 cm and released. What is the block's period of oscillation, and what is the speed of the block when it passes through its rest position?

Let's think about how to solve this problem methodically. We need to find two values, a period and a speed. Period should be pretty easy—all we need to know is the mass of the block (which we're given) and the spring constant, and then we can plug into the formula. What about the speed? That's going to be a conservation of energy problem—potential energy in the stretched-out spring gets converted to kinetic energy—and here again, to calculate the potential energy, we need to know the spring constant. So let's start by calculating that.

First, we draw our free-body diagram of the block.

We'll call "up" the positive direction. Before the mass is oscillating, the block is in equilibrium, so we can set F_s equal to mg. (Remember to convert centimeters to meters!)

$$kx = mg$$
$$k \, (0.20 \text{ m}) = (10 \text{ kg})(10 \text{ m/s}^2)$$
$$k = 500 \text{ N/m}$$

Now that we have solved for k, we can go on to the rest of the problem. The period of oscillation can be found by plugging into our formula.

$$T = 2\pi \sqrt{\frac{m}{k}}$$
$$T = 2\pi \sqrt{\frac{10 \text{ kg}}{500 \text{ N/m}}}$$
$$T = 0.89 \text{ s}$$

To compute the velocity at the equilibrium position, we can now use conservation of energy.

$$K_a + U_a = K_b + U_b$$

When dealing with a vertical spring, it is best to define the rest position as $x = 0$ in the equation for potential energy of the spring. If we do this, then gravitational potential energy can be ignored. Yes, gravity still acts on the mass, and the mass changes gravitational potential energy. So what we're really doing is taking gravity into account in the spring potential energy formula by redefining the $x = 0$ position, where the spring is stretched out, as the resting spot rather than where the spring is unstretched.

In the equation above, we have used a subscript "a" to represent values when the spring is stretched out the extra 5 cm, and "b" to represent values at the rest position.

When the spring is stretched out the extra 5 cm, the block has no kinetic energy because it is being held in place. So, the KE term on the left side of the equation will equal 0. At this point, all of the block's energy is entirely in the form of potential energy. (The equation for the PE of a spring is $\frac{1}{2}kx^2$, remember?) And at the equilibrium position, the block's energy will be entirely in the form of kinetic energy. Solving, we have

$$\tfrac{1}{2}mv_a^2 + \tfrac{1}{2}kx_a^2 = \tfrac{1}{2}mv_b^2 + \tfrac{1}{2}kx_b^2$$
$$0 + \tfrac{1}{2} \, (500 \text{ N/m}) \, (0.05 \text{ m})^2 = \tfrac{1}{2} \, (10 \text{ kg})v^2 + 0$$
$$v = 0.35 \text{ m/s}.$$

Pendulums

Simple Pendulums

Problems that involve simple pendulums—in other words, basic, run-of-the-mill, grandfather clock–style pendulums—are actually really similar to problems that involve springs. For example, the formula for the period of a simple pendulum is this:

$$T = 2\pi \sqrt{\frac{L}{g}}$$

Looks kind of like the period of a mass on a spring, right? In this equation, L is the length of the pendulum, and g is the acceleration attributable to gravity (about 10 m/s²). Of course, if your pendulum happens to be swinging on another planet, g will have a different value.[1]

One interesting thing about this equation: the period of a pendulum does not depend on the mass of whatever is hanging on the end of the pendulum. So if you had a pendulum of length L with a peanut attached to the end, and another pendulum of length L with an elephant attached to the end, both pendulums would have the same period in the absence of air resistance.

A string with a bowling ball tied to its end is attached to the ceiling. The string is pulled back such that it makes a 10° angle with the vertical, and it is then released. When the bowling ball reaches its lowest point, it has a speed of 2 m/s. What is the frequency of this bowling ball pendulum?

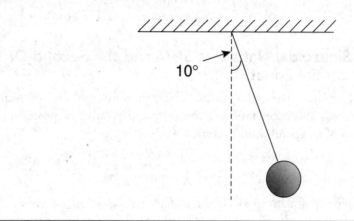

To calculate the period of this pendulum, we must know the length of the string. We can calculate this using conservation of energy. Then, we'll convert the period to a frequency.

Before the string is released, all of the bowling ball's energy is in the form of gravitational PE. If we define the zero of potential to be at the ball's lowest point, then at that point all the bowling ball's energy is in the form of KE. We will use a subscript "a" to represent values before the bowling ball is released and "b" to represent values when the bowling ball is at its lowest point.

$$K_a + U_a = K_b + U_b$$
$$\tfrac{1}{2}mv_a^2 + mgh_a = \tfrac{1}{2}mv_b^2 + mgh_b$$
$$0 + mgh_a = \tfrac{1}{2}mv_b^2 + 0$$

The height of the bowling ball before it is released, h_a, can be calculated using trigonometry.

$$h_a = L - L\cos\theta$$

So, getting back to our previous equation, we have

$$0 + mg(L - L\cos\theta) = \tfrac{1}{2}mv_b^2 + 0$$

---

[1] But even if you did travel to another planet, do you really think you would remember to pack your pendulum?

We know θ and we know v_b, so we can solve for L.

$$L - L \cos\theta = (1/g)\ {}^1\!/_2 v_b^2$$

$$L\,(1 - \cos\theta) = (1/g)\ {}^1\!/_2 v_b^2$$

$$L = 13.2 \text{ m}$$

Now that we know L, we can find the frequency.

$$T = 2\pi\sqrt{\frac{L}{g}}$$

$$T = 2\pi\sqrt{\frac{13.2}{100}}$$

$$T = 7.2 \text{ s; frequency is } 1/T, \text{ or } 0.14 \text{ Hz}$$

The Sinusoidal Nature of SHM and the Second-Order Differential Equation

Consider the force acting on an object in simple harmonic motion: $F_{net} = -kx$. Well, $F_{net} = ma$, and acceleration is the second derivative of position. So the equation for the motion of the pendulum becomes

$$\frac{d^2x}{dt^2} = \frac{-k}{m}x$$

This type of equation is called a differential equation, where a derivative of a function is proportional to the function itself. Specifically, since the **second** derivative is involved, this is called a "second-order" differential equation.

You don't necessarily need to be able to solve this equation from scratch. However, you should be able to verify that the solution $x = A\cos(\omega t)$ satisfies the equation, where

$$\omega = \sqrt{\frac{k}{m}}$$

(How do you verify this? Take the first derivative to get $dx/dt = -A\omega\sin(\omega t)$; then take the second derivative to get $-A\omega^2\cos(\omega t)$. This second derivative is, in fact, equal to the original function multiplied by $-k/m$.)

What does this mean? Well, for one thing, the position–time graph of an object in simple harmonic motion is a cosine graph, as you might have been shown in your physics class. But more interesting is the period of that cosine function. The cosine function repeats every 2π radians. So, at time $t = 0$ and at time $t = 2\pi/\omega$, the position is the same. Therefore, the time $2\pi/\omega$ is the period of the simple harmonic motion. And plugging in the ω value shown above, you see that—*voila!*—

$$T = 2\pi\sqrt{\frac{m}{k}}$$

as listed on the equation sheet!

The Compound Pendulum

The basic approach to pendulums detailed above refers to "simple" pendulums for which the dimensions of the hanging mass are irrelevant. If the hanging mass has a size approaching the length of the string, the period of this "compound" pendulum is

$$2\pi\sqrt{\frac{I}{mgd}}$$

where I is the rotational inertia of the hanging mass, m is the hanging mass, and d is the distance from the center of mass to the top of the string. Only use this equation if you have to. The vast majority of Physics C pendulums involve long strings and masses small enough to make the simple pendulum approximation valid. After all, for a "point" mass on the end of the string, the rotational inertia is $I = mL^2$, meaning that even the compound formula reduces to

$$T = 2\pi\sqrt{\frac{L}{g}}$$

› Practice Problems

1. A basketball player dribbles the ball so that it bounces regularly, twice per second. Is this ball in simple harmonic motion? Explain.

Multiple Choice:

2. A pendulum has a period of 5 seconds on Earth. On Jupiter, where $g \sim 30 \text{ m/s}^2$, the period of this pendulum would be closest to

   (A) 1 s
   (B) 3 s
   (C) 5 s
   (D) 8 s
   (E) 15 s

3. A pendulum and a mass on a spring are designed to vibrate with the same period T. These devices are taken onto the Space Shuttle in orbit. What is the period of each on the Space Shuttle?

pendulum	mass on a spring
(A) will not oscillate	T
(B) T	will not oscillate
(C) will not oscillate	will not oscillate
(D) $\sqrt{2} \cdot T$	T
(E) T	$\dfrac{T}{\sqrt{2}} \cdot T$

4. A mass on a spring has a frequency of 2.5 Hz and an amplitude of 0.05 m. In one complete period, what distance does the mass traverse? (This question asks for the actual distance, not the displacement.)

   (A) 0.05 cm
   (B) 0.01 cm
   (C) 20 cm
   (D) 10 cm
   (E) 5 cm

5. Increasing which of the following will increase the period of a simple pendulum?

   I. the length of the string
   II. the local gravitational field
   III. the mass attached to the string

   (A) I only
   (B) II only
   (C) III only
   (D) I and II only
   (E) I, II, and III

Free Response:

6. A mass m is attached to a horizontal spring of spring constant k. The spring oscillates in simple harmonic motion with amplitude A. Answer the following in terms of A.

   (a) At what displacement from equilibrium is the speed half of the maximum value?
   (b) At what displacement from equilibrium is the potential energy half of the maximum value?
   (c) When is the mass farther from its equilibrium position, when its speed is half maximum, or when its potential energy is half maximum?

❯ Solutions to Practice Problems

1. The ball is *not* in simple harmonic motion. An object in SHM experiences a force that pushes toward the center of the motion, pushing harder the farther the object is from the center; and, an object in SHM oscillates smoothly with a sinusoidal position–time graph. The basketball experiences only the gravitational force, except for the brief time that it's in contact with the ground. Its position–time graph has sharp peaks when it hits the ground.

2. **B**—The period of a pendulum is

$$T = 2\pi\sqrt{\frac{L}{g}}$$

All that is changed by going to Jupiter is *g*, which is multiplied by 3. *g* is in the denominator and under a square root, so the period on Jupiter will be *reduced* by a factor of $\sqrt{3}$. So the original 5-second period is cut by a bit less than half, to about 3 seconds.

3. **A**—The restoring force that causes a pendulum to vibrate is gravity. Because things float in the Space Shuttle rather than fall to the floor, the pendulum will not oscillate at all. However, the restoring force that causes a *spring* to vibrate is the spring force itself, which does not depend on gravity. The period of a mass on a spring also depends on mass, which is unchanged in the Space Shuttle, so the period of vibration is unchanged as well.

4. **C**—The amplitude of an object in SHM is the distance from equilibrium to the maximum displacement. In one full period, the mass traverses this distance four times: starting from max displacement, the mass goes down to the equilibrium position, down again to the max displacement on the opposite side, back to the equilibrium position, and back to where it started from. This is four amplitudes, or 0.20 m, or 20 cm.

5. **A**—The period of a pendulum is

$$T = 2\pi\sqrt{\frac{L}{g}}$$

Because *L*, the length of the string, is in the numerator, increasing *L* increases the period. Increasing *g* will actually *decrease* the period because *g* is in the denominator; increasing the mass on the pendulum

has no effect because mass does not appear in the equation for period.

6. (a) The maximum speed of the mass is at the equilibrium position, where PE = 0, so all energy is kinetic. The maximum potential energy is at the maximum displacement *A*, because there the mass is at rest briefly and so has no KE. At the equilibrium position all of the PE has been converted to KE, so

$$\tfrac{1}{2}kA^2 = \tfrac{1}{2}mv^2_{max}$$

Solving for v_{max}, it is found that

$$v_{max} = A\sqrt{\frac{k}{m}}$$

Now that we have a formula for the maximum speed, we can solve the problem. Call the spot where the speed is half-maximum position 2. Use conservation of energy to equate the energy of the maximum displacement and position 2:

$$\tfrac{1}{2}kA^2 = \tfrac{1}{2}mv_2^2 + \tfrac{1}{2}kx_2^2$$

The speed v_2 is half of the maximum speed we found earlier, or $\tfrac{1}{2}\left(A\sqrt{\dfrac{k}{m}}\right)$. Plug that in and solve for x_2:

$$\tfrac{1}{2}kA^2 = \tfrac{1}{2}m\left(\tfrac{1}{2}A\sqrt{\frac{k}{m}}\right)^2 + \tfrac{1}{2}kx_2^2$$

$$\tfrac{1}{2}kA^2 = \tfrac{1}{4}mA^2\frac{k}{m} + \tfrac{1}{2}kx_2^2$$

The *m*'s and the *k*'s cancel. The result is $x_2 = A\sqrt{\dfrac{3}{4}}$, or about 86% of the amplitude.

(b) The total energy is $\tfrac{1}{2}kA^2$. At some position *x*, the potential energy will be $\tfrac{1}{2}$ of its maximum value. At that point, $\tfrac{1}{2}kx^2 = \tfrac{1}{2}(\tfrac{1}{2}kA^2)$. Canceling and solving for *x*, it is found that

$$x = \frac{1}{\sqrt{2}}A$$

This works out to about 70% of the maximum amplitude.

(c) Since we solved in terms of A, we can just look at our answers to (a) and (b). The velocity is half maximum at $\sqrt{\dfrac{3}{4}}$, or 86%, of A; the potential energy is half maximum at $\dfrac{1}{\sqrt{2}}$ or 71%, of A. Therefore, the mass is farther from equilibrium when velocity is half maximum.

› Rapid Review

- An oscillation is motion that regularly repeats itself over the same path. Oscillating objects are acted on by a restoring force.

- One repetition of periodic motion is called a cycle. The maximum displacement of an oscillating object during a cycle is the object's amplitude. The time it takes for an object to go through a cycle is the period of oscillation.

- Period is related to frequency: $T = 1/f$, and $f = 1/T$.

- When solving problems that involve springs or simple pendulums, be on the lookout for ways to apply conservation of energy. Not every simple harmonic motion problem will require you to use conservation of energy, but many will.

- The position–time graph of an object in simple harmonic motion is a cosine graph. Specifically, the position of the object is found by the equation $x = A \cos(\omega t)$, where

$$\omega = \sqrt{\dfrac{k}{m}}$$

CHAPTER 16

Electrostatics

IN THIS CHAPTER

Summary: An electric field provides a force on a charged particle. Electric potential, also called voltage, provides energy to a charged particle. Once you know the force or energy experienced by a charged particle, Newtonian mechanics (i.e., kinematics, conservation of energy, etc.) can be applied to predict the particle's motion.

Key Ideas

- ✪ The electric force on a charged particle is qE, regardless of what produces the electric field. The electric potential energy of a charged particle is qV.
- ✪ Positive charges are forced in the direction of an electric field; negative charges, opposite the field.
- ✪ Positive charges are forced from high to low potential; negative charges, low to high.
- ✪ Point charges produce non-uniform electric fields. Parallel plates produce a uniform electric field between them.
- ✪ Electric field is a vector, and electric potential is a scalar.

Relevant Equations

Electric force on a charge in an electric field:

$$F = qE$$

Electric field produced by a point charge[1]:

$$E = \frac{\frac{1}{4\pi\varepsilon_0}Q}{r^2}$$

Electric field produced by parallel plates:

$$E = \frac{V}{d}$$

Electric potential energy in terms of voltage:

$$PE = qV$$

Voltage produced by a point charge:

$$V = \frac{\frac{1}{4\pi\varepsilon_0}Q}{r}$$

Charge stored on a capacitor:

$$Q = CV$$

Capacitance of a parallel plate capacitor:

$$C = \frac{\varepsilon_0 A}{d}$$

Electricity literally holds the world together. Sure, gravity is pretty important, too, but the primary reason that the molecules in your body stick together is because of electric forces. A world without electrostatics would be no world at all.

This chapter introduces a lot of the vocabulary needed to discuss electricity, and it focuses on how to deal with electric charges that aren't moving: hence the name, electro*statics*. We'll look at moving charges in the next chapter, when we discuss circuits.

Electric Charge

All matter is made up of three types of particles: protons, neutrons, and electrons. Protons have an intrinsic property called "positive charge." Neutrons don't contain any charge, and electrons have a property called "negative charge."

The unit of charge is the coulomb, abbreviated C. One proton has a charge of 1.6×10^{-19} coulombs.

Most objects that we encounter in our daily lives are electrically neutral—things like couches, for instance, or trees, or bison. These objects contain as many positive charges as negative charges. In other words, they contain as many protons as electrons.

When an object has more protons than electrons, though, it is described as "positively charged"; and when it has more electrons than protons, it is described as "negatively charged." The reason that big objects like couches and trees and bison don't behave like charged particles is because they contain so many bazillions of protons and electrons that an extra few here or there won't really make much of a difference. So even though they might have a slight electric charge, that charge would be much too small, relatively speaking, to detect.

---

[1]The actual equation sheet for the AP exam includes this equation: $F = \frac{1}{4\pi\varepsilon_0}\frac{q_1 q_2}{r^2}$. To interpret this (and other point charge equations), recognize that this equation for the force between two point charges is an amalgamation of the first two equations above: combine $F = qE$ with $E = \frac{\frac{1}{4\pi\varepsilon_0}Q}{r^2}$ and you get $F = \frac{1}{4\pi\varepsilon_0}\frac{q_1 q_2}{r^2}$.

Tiny objects, like atoms, more commonly carry a measurable electric charge, because they have so few protons and electrons that an extra electron, for example, would make a big difference. Of course, you can have very large charged objects. When you walk across a carpeted floor in the winter, you pick up lots of extra charges and become a charged object yourself . . . until you touch a doorknob, at which point all the excess charge in your body travels through your finger and into the doorknob, causing you to feel a mild electric shock.

Electric charges follow a simple rule: *Like charges repel; opposite charges attract.* Two positively charged particles will try to get as far away from each other as possible, while a positively charged particle and a negatively charged particle will try to get as close as possible.

You can also have something called "induced charge." An induced charge occurs when an electrically neutral object becomes polarized—when negative charges pile up in one part of the object and positive charges pile up in another part of the object. The drawing in Figure 16.1 illustrates how you can create an induced charge in an object.

Figure 16.1   Creation of an induced charge.

Electric Fields

Before we talk about electric fields, we'll first define what a field, in general, is.

> **Field:** A property of a region of space that can apply a force to objects found in that region of space

A gravitational field is a property of the space that surrounds any massive object. There is a gravitational field that you are creating and which surrounds you, and this field extends infinitely into space. It is a weak field, though, which means that it doesn't affect other objects very much—you'd be surprised if everyday objects started flying toward each other because of gravitational attraction. The Earth, on the other hand, creates a strong gravitational field. Objects are continually being pulled toward the Earth's surface due to gravitational attraction. However, the farther you get from the center of the Earth, the weaker the gravitational field, and, correspondingly, the weaker the gravitational attraction you would feel.

An **electric field** is a bit more specific than a gravitational field: it only affects charged particles.

> **Electric Field:** A property of a region of space that applies a force to *charged* objects in that region of space. A charged particle in an electric field will experience an electric force.

Unlike a gravitational field, an electric field can either push or pull a charged particle, depending on the charge of the particle. Electric field is a vector; so, electric fields are always drawn as arrows.

Every point in an electric field has a certain value called, surprisingly enough, the "electric field value," or E, and this value tells you how strongly the electric field at that point would affect a charge. The units of E are newtons/coulomb, abbreviated N/C.

Force of an Electric Field

The force felt by a charged particle in an electric field is described by a simple equation:

$$F = qE$$

In other words, the force felt by a charged particle in an electric field is equal to the charge of the particle, q, multiplied by the electric field value, E.

An electron, a proton, and a neutron are each placed in a uniform electric field of magnitude 60 N/C, directed to the right. What is the magnitude and direction of the force exerted on each particle?

The direction of the force on a positive charge is in the same direction as the electric field; the direction of the force on a negative charge is opposite the electric field.

Let's try this equation on for size. Here's a sample problem:

The solution here is nothing more than plug-and-chug into $F = qE$. Notice that we're dealing with a *uniform* electric field—the field lines are evenly spaced throughout the whole region. This means that, no matter where a particle is within the electric field, it always experiences an electric field of exactly 60 N/C.

Also note our problem-solving technique. To find the magnitude of the force, we plug in *just the magnitude* of the charge and the electric field—no negative signs allowed! To find the direction of the force, use the reasoning in the box above (positive charges are forced in the direction of the E field, negative charges opposite the E field).

Let's start with the electron, which has a charge of 1.6×10^{-19} C (no need to memorize, you can look this up on the constant sheet):

$$F = qE$$
$$F = (1.6 \times 10^{-19} \text{ C})(60 \text{ N/C})$$
$$F = 9.6 \times 10^{-18} \text{ N to the LEFT}$$

Now the proton:

$$F = (1.6 \times 10^{-19} \text{ C})(60 \text{ N/C})$$
$$F = 9.6 \times 10^{-18} \text{ N to the RIGHT}$$

And finally the neutron:

$$F = (0 \text{ C})(60 \text{ N/C}) = 0 \text{ N}$$

Notice that the proton feels a force in the direction of the electric field, but the electron feels the same force in the opposite direction.

Don't state a force with a negative sign. Signs just indicate the direction of a force, anyway. So, just plug in the values for q and E, then state the direction of the force in words.

Electric Potential

When you hold an object up over your head, that object has gravitational potential energy. If you were to let it go, it would fall to the ground.

Similarly, a charged particle in an electric field can have electrical potential energy. For example, if you held a proton in your right hand and an electron in your left hand, those two particles would want to get to each other. Keeping them apart is like holding that object over your head; once you let the particles go, they'll travel toward each other just like the object would fall to the ground.

In addition to talking about electrical potential energy, we also talk about a concept called electric potential.

> **Electric Potential:** Potential energy provided by an electric field per unit charge; also called *voltage*

Electric potential is a scalar quantity. The units of electric potential are volts. 1 volt = 1 J/C.

Just as we use the term "zero of potential" in talking about gravitational potential, we can also use that term to talk about voltage. We cannot solve a problem that involves voltage unless we know where the zero of potential is. Often, the zero of electric potential is called "ground."

Unless it is otherwise specified, the zero of electric potential is assumed to be far, far away. This means that if you have two charged particles and you move them farther and farther from each another, ultimately, once they're infinitely far away from each other, they won't be able to feel each other's presence.

The electrical potential energy of a charged particle is given by this equation:

$$\boxed{\text{PE} = qV}$$

Here, q is the charge on the particle, and V is the voltage.

It is extremely important to note that electric potential and electric field are not the same thing. This example should clear things up:

Three points, labeled A, B, and C, are found in a uniform electric field. At which point will a positron (a positively charged version of an electron) have the greatest electrical potential energy?

Electric field lines point in the direction that a positive charge will be forced, which means that our positron, when placed in this field, will be pushed from left to right. So, just as an object in Earth's gravitational field has greater potential energy when it is higher off the ground (think "*mgh*"), our positron will have the greatest electrical potential energy when it is farthest from where it wants to get to. The answer is A.

We hope you noticed that, even though the electric field was the same at all three points, the electric potential was different at each point.

How about another example?

A positron is given an initial velocity of 6×10^6 m/s to the right. It travels into a uniform electric field, directed to the left. As the positron enters the field, its electric potential is zero. What will be the electric potential at the point where the positron has a speed of 1×10^6 m/s?

This is a rather simple conservation of energy problem, but it's dressed up to look like a really complicated electricity problem.

As with all conservation of energy problems, we'll start by writing our statement of conservation of energy.

$$K_i + U_i = K_f + U_f$$

Next, we'll fill in each term with the appropriate equations. Here the potential energy is not due to gravity (*mgh*), nor due to a spring ($1/2\ kx^2$). The potential energy is electric, so it should be written as qV.

$$\tfrac{1}{2}\,mv_i^2 + qV_i = \tfrac{1}{2}\,mv_f^2 + qV_f$$

Finally, we'll plug in the corresponding values. The mass of a positron is exactly the same as the mass of an electron, and the charge of a positron has the same magnitude as the charge of an electron, except a positron's charge is positive. Both the mass and the charge of an electron are given to you on the "constants sheet." Also, the problem told us that the positron's initial potential V_i was zero.

$$\tfrac{1}{2}\,(9.1 \times 10^{-31}\ \text{kg})(6 \times 10^6\ \text{m/s})^2 + (1.6 \times 10^{-19}\ \text{C})(0) =$$
$$\tfrac{1}{2}\,(9.1 \times 10^{-31}\ \text{kg})(1 \times 10^6\ \text{m/s})^2 + (1.6 \times 10^{-19}\ \text{C})(V_f)$$

Solving for V_f, we find that V_f is about 100 V.

For *forces,* a negative sign simply indicates direction. For potentials, though, a negative sign is important. -300 V is less than -200 V, so a proton will seek out a -300 V position in preference to a -200 V position. So, be careful to use proper $+$ and $-$ signs when dealing with potential.

Just as you can draw electric field lines, you can also draw equipotential lines.

> **Equipotential Lines:** Lines that illustrate every point at which a charged particle would experience a given potential

Figure 16.2 shows a few examples of equipotential lines (shown with solid lines) and their relationship to electric field lines (shown with dotted lines):

Figure 16.2   Two examples of equipotential lines (in bold) and electric field lines (dotted).

On the left in Figure 16.2, the electric field points away from the positive charge. At any particular distance away from the positive charge, you would find an equipotential line that circles the charge—we've drawn two, but there are an infinite number of equipotential lines around the charge. If the potential of the outermost equipotential line that we drew was, say, 10 V, then a charged particle placed anywhere on that equipotential line would experience a potential of 10 V.

On the right in Figure 16.2, we have a uniform electric field. Notice how the equipotential lines are drawn perpendicular to the electric field lines. In fact, equipotential lines are always drawn perpendicular to electric field lines, but when the field lines aren't parallel (as in the drawing on the left), this fact is harder to see.

Moving a charge from one equipotential line to another takes energy. Just imagine that you had an electron and you placed it on the innermost equipotential line in the drawing. If you then wanted to move it to the outer equipotential line, you'd have to push pretty hard, because your electron would be trying to move toward, and not away from, the positive charge in the middle.

In the diagram above, point *A* and point *B* are separated by a distance of 30 cm. How much work must be done by an external force to move a proton from point *A* to point *B*?

The potential at point B is higher than at point A; so moving the positively charged proton from A to B requires work to change the proton's potential energy. The question here really is asking how much more potential energy the proton has at point B.

Well, potential energy is equal to qV; here, q is 1.6×10^{-19} C, the charge of a proton. The potential energy at point A is $(1.6 \times 10^{-19}$ C$)(50$ V$) = 8.0 \times 10^{-18}$ J; the potential energy at point B is $(1.6 \times 10^{-19}$ C$)(60$ V$) = 9.6 \times 10^{-18}$ J. Thus, the proton's potential is 1.6×10^{-18} J higher at point B, so it takes 1.6×10^{-18} J of work to move the proton there.

Um, didn't the problem say that points A and B were 30 cm apart? Yes, but that's irrelevant. Since we can see the equipotential lines, we know the potential energy of the proton at each point; the distance separating the lines is irrelevant.

Special Geometries for Electrostatics

There are two situations involving electric fields that are particularly nice because they can be described with some relatively easy formulas. Let's take a look:

Parallel Plates

If you take two metal plates, charge one positive and one negative, and then put them parallel to each other, you create a uniform electric field in the middle, as shown in Figure 16.3:

Figure 16.3   Electric field between charged, parallel plates.

The electric field between the plates has a magnitude of

$$E = \frac{V}{d}$$

V is the voltage difference between the plates, and d is the distance between the plates. Remember, this equation only works for parallel plates.

Charged parallel plates can be used to make a **capacitor**, which is a charge-storage device. When a capacitor is made from charged parallel plates, it is called, logically enough, a "parallel-plate capacitor." A schematic of this type of capacitor is shown in Figure 16.4.

The battery in Figure 16.4 provides a voltage across the plates; once you've charged the capacitor, you disconnect the battery. The space between the plates prevents any charges from jumping from one plate to the other while the capacitor is charged. When you want to discharge the capacitor, you just connect the two plates with a wire.

The amount of charge that each plate can hold is described by the following equation:

$$Q = CV$$

Figure 16.4   Basic parallel-plate capacitor.

Q is the charge on each plate, C is called the "capacitance," and V is the voltage across the plates. The capacitance is a property of the capacitor you are working with, and it is determined primarily by the size of the plates and the distance between the plates, as well as by the material that fills the space between the plates. The units of capacitance are farads, abbreviated F; 1 coulomb/volt = 1 farad.

The only really interesting thing to know about parallel-plate capacitors is that their capacitance can be easily calculated. The equation is:

$$C = \frac{\varepsilon_0 A}{d}$$

In this equation, A is the area of each plate (in m²), and d is the distance between the plates (in m). The term ε_0 (pronounced "epsilon-naught") is called the "permittivity of free space." This term will show up again soon, when we introduce the constant k. The value of ε_0 is 8.84×10^{-12} C/V·m, which is listed on the constants sheet.

Capacitors become important when we work with circuits. So we'll see them again in Chapter 17.

Point Charges

As much as the writers of the AP exam like parallel plates, they *love* point charges. So you'll probably be using these next equations quite a lot on the test.

But, please don't go nuts. . . . The formulas for force on a charge in an electric field ($F = qE$) and a charge's electrical potential energy ($PE = qV$) are your first recourse, your fundamental tools of electrostatics. On the AP exam, most electric fields are NOT produced by point charges! Only use the equations in this section when you have convinced yourself that a point charge is *creating* the electric field or the voltage in question.

First, the value of the electric field at some distance away from a point charge:

$$E = \frac{1}{4\pi\varepsilon_0}\frac{Q}{r^2}$$

Q is the charge of your point charge, ε_0 is the permittivity of free space (on the table of information), and r is the distance away from the point charge.[2] *The field produced by*

---

[2]For calculations, it might be easier to recognize that $\frac{1}{4\pi\varepsilon_0} = 9\times10^9\,N\frac{m^2}{C^2}$. This value, often labeled as k, shows up repeatedly in point-charge problems.

a positive charge points away from the charge; the field produced by a negative charge points toward the charge. When finding an electric field with this equation, do NOT plug in the sign of the charge or use negative signs at all.

Second, the electric potential at some distance away from a point charge:

$$V = \frac{1}{4\pi\varepsilon_0}\frac{Q}{r}$$

When using this equation, you *must* include a + or − sign on the charge creating the potential. (See Figure 16.5.)

Figure 16.5   Electric field produced by point charges.

And third, the force that one point charge exerts on another point charge:

$$F = \frac{1}{4\pi\varepsilon_0}\frac{Q_1 Q_2}{r^2}$$

In this equation, Q_1 is the charge of one of the point charges, and Q_2 is the charge on the other one. This equation is known as Coulomb's Law.

To get comfortable with these three equations, we'll provide you with a rather comprehensive problem.

Two point charges, labeled "A" and "B," are located on the *x*-axis. "A" has a charge of −3 μC, and "B" has a charge of +3 μC. Initially, there is no charge at point *P*, which is located on the *y*-axis as shown in the diagram.

(a)   What is the electric field at point *P* due to charges "A" and "B"?

(b)   If an electron were placed at point *P*, what would be the magnitude and direction of the force exerted on the electron?

(c)   What is the electric potential at point *P* due to charges "A" and "B"?

This is a monster problem. But if we take it one part at a time, you'll see that it's really not too bad.

Part 1—Electric Field

Electric field is a vector quantity. So we'll first find the electric field at point P due to charge "A," then we'll find the electric field due to charge "B," and then we'll add these two vector quantities. One note before we get started: to find r, the distance between points P and "A" or between P and "B," we'll have to use the Pythagorean theorem. We won't show you our work for that calculation, but you should if you were solving this on the AP exam.

$$E_{\text{due to "A"}} = \frac{(9\times10^9)(3\times10^{-6}\text{C})}{(\sqrt{53}\ \text{m})^2} = 510\frac{\text{N}}{\text{C}}, \text{pointing } \textit{toward} \text{ charge A}$$

$$E_{\text{due to "B"}} = \frac{(9\times10^9)(3\times10^{-6}\text{C})}{(\sqrt{53}\ \text{m})^2} = 510\frac{\text{N}}{\text{C}}, \text{pointing } \textit{away from} \text{ charge B}$$

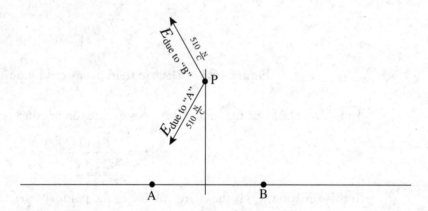

Note that we didn't plug in any negative signs! Rather, we calculated the magnitude of the electric field produced by each charge, and showed the direction on the diagram.

Now, to find the net electric field at point P, we must add the electric field vectors. This is made considerably simpler by the recognition that the y-components of the electric fields cancel . . . both of these vectors are pointed at the same angle, and both have the same magnitude. So, let's find just the x-component of one of the electric field vectors:

$$E_x = E\cos\theta, \text{ where } \theta \text{ is measured from the horizontal.}$$

E = 510 N/C

E$_x$ (= 140 N/C)

θ

Some quick trigonometry will find $\cos\theta$ . . . since $\cos\theta$ is defined as $\dfrac{\text{adjacent}}{\text{hypotenuse}}$, inspection of the diagram shows that $\cos\theta = \dfrac{2}{\sqrt{53}}$. So, the horizontal electric field $E_x = (510\text{ m})$ $\left(\dfrac{2}{\sqrt{53}}\right)$ . . . this gives 140 N/C.

And now finally, there are *TWO* of these horizontal electric fields adding together to the left—one due to charge "A" and one due to charge "B." The total electric field at point P, then, is

$$280 \text{ N/C, to the left.}$$

Part 2—Force

The work that we put into Part 1 makes this part easy. Once we have an electric field, it doesn't matter what caused the E field—just use the basic equation $F = qE$ to solve for the force on the electron, where q is the charge of the electron. So,

$$F = (1.6 \times 10^{-19} \text{ C}) \, 280 \text{ N/C} = 4.5 \times 10^{-17} \text{ N}.$$

The direction of this force must be OPPOSITE the E field because the electron carries a negative charge; so, **to the right**.

Part 3—Potential

The nice thing about electric potential is that it is a scalar quantity, so we don't have to concern ourselves with vector components and other such headaches.

$$V_{\text{due to "A"}} = \frac{(9 \times 10^9)(-3 \times 10^{-6} \text{C})}{\sqrt{53}\text{m}} = -3700 \text{ V}$$

$$V_{\text{due to "B"}} = \frac{(9 \times 10^9)(+3 \times 10^{-6} \text{C})}{\sqrt{53}\text{m}} = +3700 \text{ V}$$

The potential at point P is just the sum of these two quantities. $V = $ zero!

Notice that when finding the electric potential due to point charges, you must include negative signs . . . negative potentials can cancel out positive potentials, as in this example.

Gauss's Law

A more thorough understanding of electric fields comes from Gauss's law. But before looking at Gauss's law itself, it is necessary to understand the concept of electric flux.

> **Electric Flux:** The amount of electric field that penetrates an area
> $$\Phi_E = E \cdot A$$

The electric flux, Φ_E, equals the electric field multiplied by the surface area through which the field penetrates.

Flux only exists if the electric field lines penetrate *straight* through a surface. (Or, if the electric field lines have a component that's perpendicular to a surface.) If an electric field exists parallel to a surface, there is zero flux through that surface. One way to think about this is to imagine that electric field lines are like arrows, and the surface you're considering is like an archer's bull's-eye. There would be flux if the arrows hit the target; but if the archer is standing at a right angle to the target (so that his arrows zoom right on past the target without even nicking it) there's no flux.

In words, Gauss's law states that the net electric flux through a closed surface is equal to the charge enclosed divided by ε_0. This is often written as

$$\int E \cdot dA = \frac{Q_{\text{enclosed}}}{\varepsilon_0}$$

How and When to Use Gauss's Law

Gauss's law is valid the universe over. However, in most cases Gauss's law is not in any way useful—no one expects you to be able to evaluate a three-dimensional integral with a dot product! ONLY use Gauss's law when the problem has spherical, cylindrical, or planar symmetry.

First, identify the symmetry of the problem. Then draw a closed surface, called a "Gaussian surface," that the electric field is everywhere pointing straight through. A Gaussian surface isn't anything real . . . it's just an imaginary closed surface that you'll use to solve the problem. The net electric flux is just E times the area of the Gaussian surface you drew.

> *You should NEVER, ever, try to evaluate the integral* $\int E \cdot dA$ *in using Gauss's law!*

Here is an example problem.

> Consider a metal sphere of radius R that carries a surface charge density σ. What is the magnitude of the electric field as a function of the distance from the center of the sphere?

There are two possibilities here. One possibility is that the function describing the electric field will be a smooth, continuous function. The other possibility is that the function inside the sphere will be different from the function outside the sphere (after all, they're different environments—inside the sphere you're surrounded by charge, and outside the sphere you're not). So we'll assume that the function is different in each environment, and we'll consider the problem in two parts: inside the sphere and outside the sphere. If it turns out that the function is actually smooth and continuous, then we'll have done some extra work, but we'll still get the right answer.

Inside the sphere, draw a Gaussian sphere of any radius. No charge is enclosed, because in a conductor, all the charges repel each other until all charge resides on the outer edge. So, by Gauss's law since the enclosed charge is zero, the term $E \cdot A$ has to be zero as well. A refers to the area of the Gaussian surface you drew, which sure as heck has a surface area.

The electric field inside the conducting sphere must be zero everywhere. This is actually a general result that you should memorize—the electric field inside a conductor is always zero.

Outside the sphere, draw a Gaussian sphere of radius r. This sphere, whatever its radius, always encloses the full charge of the conductor. What is that charge? Well, σ represents the charge per area of the conductor, and the area of the conductor is $4\pi R^2$. So the charge on the conductor is $\sigma 4\pi R^2$. Now, the Gaussian surface of radius r has area $4\pi r^2$. Plug all of this into Gauss's law:

$$E \cdot 4\pi r^2 = \sigma 4\pi R^2 / \varepsilon_0.$$

All the variables are known, so just solve for electric field: $E = \sigma R^2 / \varepsilon_0 r^2$.

Now we can state our answer, where r is the distance from the center of the charged sphere:

$$E = \begin{cases} 0, \text{ when } 0 \leq r < R \\ \dfrac{\sigma R^2}{\varepsilon_0 r^2}, \text{ when } R \leq r \end{cases}$$

What is interesting about this result? We solved in terms of the charge density σ on the conductor. If we solve instead in terms of Q, the total charge on the conductor, we recover the formula for the electric field of a point charge:

$$E = \frac{1}{4\pi\varepsilon_0} \frac{Q}{r^2}!$$

» Practice Problems

Multiple Choice:

Questions 1 and 2:

Two identical positive charges Q are separated by a distance a, as shown above.

1. What is the electric field at a point halfway between the two charges?

    (A) kQ/a^2
    (B) $2kQ/a^2$
    (C) zero
    (D) kQQ/a^2
    (E) $2kQ/a$

2. What is the electric potential at a point halfway between the two charges?

    (A) kQ/a
    (B) $2kQ/a$
    (C) zero
    (D) $4kQ/a$
    (E) $8kQ/a$

Questions 3 and 4:

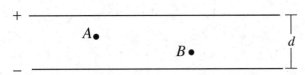

The diagram above shows two parallel metal plates that are separated by distance d. The potential difference between the plates is V. Point A is twice as far from the negative plate as is point B.

3. Which of the following statements about the electric potential between the plates is correct?

    (A) The electric potential is the same at points A and B.
    (B) The electric potential is two times larger at A than at B.
    (C) The electric potential is two times larger at B than at A.
    (D) The electric potential is four times larger at A than at B.
    (E) The electric potential is four times larger at B than at A.

4. Which of the following statements about the electric field between the plates is correct?

    (A) The electric field is the same at points A and B.
    (B) The electric field is two times larger at A than at B.
    (C) The electric field is two times larger at B than at A.
    (D) The electric field is four times larger at A than at B.
    (E) The electric field is four times larger at B than at A.

5. A very long cylindrical conductor is surrounded by a very long cylindrical conducting shell, as shown above. A length L of the inner conductor carries positive charge Q. The same length L of the outer shell carries total charge $-3Q$. How much charge is distributed on a length L of the outside surface of the outer shell?

(A) none
(B) $-Q$
(C) $-2Q$
(D) $-3Q$
(E) $-4Q$

Free Response:

6. Two conducting metal spheres of different radii, as shown below, each have charge $-Q$.

(a) Consider one of the spheres. Is the charge on that sphere likely to clump together or to spread out? Explain briefly.

(b) Is charge more likely to stay inside the metal spheres or on the surface of the metal spheres? Explain briefly.

(c) If the two spheres are connected by a metal wire, will charge flow from the big sphere to the little sphere, or from the little sphere to the big sphere? Explain briefly.

(d) Which of the following two statements is correct? Explain briefly.
   i. If the two spheres are connected by a metal wire, charge will stop flowing when the electric field at the surface of each sphere is the same.
   ii. If the two spheres are connected by a metal wire, charge will stop flowing when the electric potential at the surface of each sphere is the same.

(e) Explain how the correct statement you chose from part (d) is consistent with your answer to (c).

> Solutions to Practice Problems

1. C—Electric field is a *vector*. Look at the field at the center due to each charge. The field due to the left-hand charge points away from the positive charge; i.e., to the right; the field due to the right-hand charge points to the left. Because the charges are equal and are the same distance from the center point, the fields due to each charge have equal magnitudes. So the electric field vectors cancel! $E = 0$.

2. D—Electric potential is a *scalar*. Look at the potential at the center due to each charge: Each charge is distance $a/2$ from the center point, so the potential due to each is $kQ/(a/2)$, which works out to $2kQ/a$. The potentials due to both charges are positive, so add these potentials to get $4kQ/a$.

3. B—If the potential difference between plates is, say, 100 V, then we could say that one plate is at $+100$ V and the other is at 0 V. So, the potential *must* change at points in between the plates. The electric field is uniform and equal to V/d (d is the distance between plates). Thus, the potential increases linearly between the plates, and A must have twice the potential as B.

4. A—The electric field by definition is *uniform* between parallel plates. This means the field must be the same everywhere inside the plates.

5. C—We have cylindrical symmetry, so use Gauss's law. Consider a Gaussian surface drawn within the outer shell. Inside a conducting shell, the electric field must be zero, as discussed in the chapter. By Gauss's law, this means the Gaussian surface we drew must enclose zero net charge. Because the inner cylinder carries charge $+Q$, the inside surface of the shell must carry charge $-Q$ to get zero net charge enclosed by the Gaussian surface. What happens to the $-2Q$ that is left over on the conducting shell? It goes to the outer surface.

6. (a) Like charges repel, so the charges are more likely to spread out from each other as far as possible.

(b) "Conducting spheres" mean that the charges are free to move anywhere within or onto the surface of the spheres. But because the charges try to get as far away from each other as possible, the charge will end up on the surface of the spheres. This is actually a property of conductors—charge will always reside on the surface of the conductor, not inside.

(c) Charge will flow from the smaller sphere to the larger sphere. Following the reasoning from parts (a) and (b), the charges try to get as far away from each other as possible. Because both spheres initially carry the same charge, the charge is more concentrated on the smaller sphere; so the charge will flow to the bigger sphere to spread out. (The explanation that negative charge flows from low to high potential, and that potential is less negative at the surface of the bigger sphere, is also acceptable here.)

(d) The charge will flow until the potential is equal on each sphere. By definition, negative charges flow from low to high potential. So, if the potentials of the spheres are equal, no more charge will flow.

(e) The potential at the surface of each sphere is $-kQ/r$, where r is the radius of the sphere. Thus, the potential at the surface of the smaller sphere is initially more negative, and the charge will initially flow low-to-high potential to the larger sphere.

› Rapid Review

- Matter is made of protons, neutrons, and electrons. Protons are positively charged, neutrons have no charge, and electrons are negatively charged.

- Like charges repel, opposite charges attract.

- An induced charge can be created in an electrically neutral object by placing that object in an electric field.

- Electric field lines are drawn from positive charges toward negative charges. Where an electric field is stronger, the field lines are drawn closer together.

- The electric force on an object depends on both the object's charge and the electric field it is in.

- Unless stated otherwise, the zero of electric potential is at "infinity" which just means a very big distance from whatever else is around.

- Equipotential lines show all the points where a charged object would feel the same electric force. They are always drawn perpendicular to electric field lines.

- The electric field between two charged parallel plates is constant. The electric field around a charged particle depends on the distance from the particle.

- Gauss's law says that the net electric flux through a closed surface is equal to the charge enclosed divided by ε_0. To solve a problem using Gauss's law, look for planar, cylindrical, or spherical symmetry.

CHAPTER 17

Circuits

IN THIS CHAPTER

Summary: Electric charge flowing through a wire is called current. An electrical circuit is built to control current. In this chapter, you will learn how to predict the effects of current flow.

Key Ideas

- ✪ The current in series resistors is the same through each, whereas the voltage across series resistors adds to the total voltage.
- ✪ The voltage across parallel resistors is the same across each, whereas the current through parallel resistors adds to the total current.
- ✪ The brightness of a light bulb depends on the power dissipated by the bulb.
- ✪ A capacitor blocks current once it has been connected for a while.
- ✪ Physics C students need to know that the time constant of an RC circuit is *RC*.

Relevant Equations

Definition of current:

$$I = \frac{dQ}{dt}$$

Resistance of a wire in terms of its properties:

$$R = \rho \frac{L}{A}$$

Ohm's law:

$$V = IR$$

Power in a circuit:

$$P = IV$$

Time constant for an RC circuit:

$$\tau = RC$$

In the last chapter, we talked about situations where electric charges don't move around very much. Isolated point charges, for example, just sit there creating an electric field. But what happens when you get a lot of charges all moving together? That, at its essence, is what goes on in a circuit.

Besides discussing circuits in general, this chapter presents a powerful problem-solving technique: the *V-I-R* chart. As with the chart of variables we used when solving kinematics problems, the *V-I-R* chart is an incredibly effective way to organize a problem that involves circuits. We hope you'll find it helpful.

Current

A circuit is simply any path that will allow charge to flow.

> **Current:** The flow of electric charge. In a circuit, the current is the amount of charge passing a given point per unit time.

Technically, a current is defined as the flow of positive charge. We don't think this makes sense, because electrons—and not protons or positrons—are what flow in a circuit. But physicists have their rationale, and no matter how wacky, we won't argue with it.

In more mathematical terms, current is defined as follows:

$$I = \frac{\Delta Q}{\Delta t}$$

What this means is that the current, *I,* equals the amount of charge flowing past a certain point divided by the time interval during which you're making your measurement. This definition tells us that current is measured in coulombs/second. 1 C/s = 1 ampere, abbreviated as 1 A.

Resistance and Ohm's Law

You've probably noticed that just about every circuit drawn in your physics book contains a battery. The reason most circuits contain a battery is because batteries create a potential difference between one end of the circuit and the other. In other words, if you connect the

Figure 17.1   Flow of charge in a wire connected to a battery.

terminals of a battery with a wire, the part of the wire attached to the "+" terminal will have a higher electric potential than the part of the wire attached to the "−" terminal. And positive charge flows from high potential to low potential. So, in order to create a current, you need a battery. (See Figure 17.1.)

In general, the greater the potential difference between the terminals of the battery, the more current flows.

The amount of current that flows in a circuit is also determined by the resistance of the circuit.

Resistance: A property of a circuit that resists the flow of current

---

Resistance is measured in ohms. One ohm is abbreviated as 1 Ω.

If we have some length of wire, then the resistance of that wire can be calculated. Three physical properties of the wire affect its resistance:

- The material the wire is made out of: the **resistivity**, ρ, of a material is an intrinsic property of that material. Good conducting materials, like gold, have low resistivities.[1]
- The length of the wire, L: the longer the wire, the more resistance it has.
- The cross-sectional area A of the wire: the wider the wire, the less resistance it has.

We put all of these properties together in the equation for resistance of a wire:

$$R = \rho \frac{L}{A}$$

Now, this equation is useful only when you need to calculate the resistance of a wire from scratch. Usually, on the AP exam or in the laboratory, you will be using resistors that have a pre-measured resistance.

Resistor: Something you put in a circuit to change the circuit's resistance

---

[1]Resistivity would be given on the AP exam if you need a value. Nothing here to memorize.

Resistors are typically ceramic, a material that doesn't allow current to flow through it very easily. Another common type of resistor is the filament in a light bulb. When current flows into a light bulb, it gets held up in the filament. While it's hanging out in the filament, it makes the filament extremely hot, and the filament gives off light.

The way that a resistor (or a bunch of resistors) affects the current in a circuit is described by Ohm's law.

$$\textbf{Ohm's law: } V = IR$$

V is the voltage across the part of the circuit you're looking at, I is the current flowing through that part of the circuit, and R is the resistance in that part of the circuit. Ohm's law is the most important equation when it comes to circuits, so make sure you know it well.

When current flows through a resistor, electrical energy is being converted into heat energy. The rate at which this conversion occurs is called the power dissipated by a resistor. This power can be found with the equation

$$P = IV$$

This equation says that the power, P, dissipated in part of a circuit equals the current flowing through that part of the circuit multiplied by the voltage across that part of the circuit.

Using Ohm's law, it can be easily shown that $IV = I^2R = V^2/R$. It's only worth memorizing the first form of the equation, but any one of these could be useful.

Resistors in Series and in Parallel

In a circuit, resistors can either be arranged in series with one another or parallel to one another. Before we take a look at each type of arrangement, though, we need first to familiarize ourselves with circuit symbols, shown in Figure 17.2.

Figure 17.2   Common circuit symbols.

First, let's examine resistors in series. In this case, all the resistors are connected in a line, one after the other after the other:

Figure 17.3   Example of series resistors.

To find the equivalent resistance of series resistors, we just add up all the individual resistors.

$$R_{eq} = R_1 + R_2 + R_{3...}$$

For the circuit in Figure 17.3, $R_{eq} = 3000\ \Omega$. In other words, using three 1000 Ω resistors in series produces the same total resistance as using one 3000 Ω resistor.

Parallel resistors are connected in such a way that you create several paths through which current can flow. For the resistors to be truly in parallel, the current must split, then immediately come back together.

Figure 17.4   Example of parallel resistors.

The equivalent resistance of parallel resistors is found by this formula:

$$\frac{1}{R_{eq}} = \frac{1}{R_1} + \frac{1}{R_2} + \frac{1}{R_3} \cdots$$

For the circuit in Figure 17.4, the equivalent resistance is 333 Ω. So hooking up three 1000 Ω resistors in parallel produces the same total resistance as using one 333 Ω resistor. (Note that the equivalent resistance of parallel resistors is *less than* any individual resistor in the parallel combination.)

A Couple of Important Rules

Rule #1—When two resistors are connected in SERIES, the amount of current that flows through one resistor equals the amount of current that flows through the other resistor.

Rule #2—When two resistors are connected in PARALLEL, the voltage across one resistor is the same as the voltage across the other resistor, and is equal to the total voltage across the parallel combination.

The *V-I-R* Chart

Here it is—the trick that will make solving circuits a breeze. Use this method on your homework. Use this method on your quizzes and tests. But most of all, use this method on the AP exam. It works.

The easiest way to understand the *V-I-R* chart is to see it in action, so we'll go through a problem together, filling in the chart at each step along the way.

Find the voltage across each resistor in the circuit shown below.

We start by drawing our *V-I-R* chart, and we fill in the known values. Right now, we know the resistance of each resistor, and we know the total voltage (it's written next to the battery).

	V	*I*	*R*
R_1			5 Ω
R_2			7 Ω
R_3			10 Ω
Total	12 V		

Next, we simplify the circuit. This means that we calculate the equivalent resistance and redraw the circuit accordingly. We'll first find the equivalent resistance of the parallel part of the circuit:

$$\frac{1}{R_{eq}} = \frac{1}{7\,\Omega} + \frac{1}{10\,\Omega}.$$

Use your calculator to get $1/R_{eq} = (0.24)$.

Taking the reciprocal and rounding to one significant figure, we get

$$R_{eq} = 4 \, \Omega.$$

So we can redraw our circuit like this:

Next, we calculate the equivalent resistance of the entire circuit. Following our rule for resistors in series, we have

$$R_{eq} = 4 \, \Omega + 5 \, \Omega = 9 \, \Omega.$$

We can now fill this value into the *V-I-R* chart.

	V	I	R
R_1			5Ω
R_2			7Ω
R_3			10Ω
Total	12 V		9Ω

Notice that we now have two of the three values in the "Total" row. Using Ohm's law, we can calculate the third. That's the beauty of the *V-I-R* chart: *Ohm's law is valid whenever two of the three entries in a row are known.*

Then we need to put on our thinking caps. We know that all the current that flows through our circuit will also flow through R_1. (You may want to take a look back at the original drawing of our circuit to make sure you understand why this is so.) Therefore, the *I* value in the "R_1" row will be the same as the *I* in the "Total" row. We now have two of the three values in the "R_1" row, so we can solve for the third using Ohm's law.

	V	I	R
R_1	6.5 V	1.3 A	5Ω
R_2			7Ω
R_3			10Ω
Total	12 V	1.3 A	9Ω

Finally, we know that the voltage across R_2 equals the voltage across R_3, because these resistors are connected in parallel. The total voltage across the circuit is 12 V, and the voltage across R_1 is 6.5 V. So the voltage that occurs between R_1 and the end of the circuit is

$$12 \, V - 6.5 \, V = 5.5 \, V.$$

Therefore, the voltage across R_2, which is the same as the voltage across R_3, is 5.5 V. We can fill this value into our table. Finally, we can use Ohm's law to calculate I for both R_2 and R_3. The finished V-I-R chart looks like this:

	V	I	R
R_1	6.5 V	1.3 A	5 Ω
R_2	5.5 V	0.8 A	7 Ω
R_3	5.5 V	0.6 A	10 Ω
Total	12 V	1.3 A	9 Ω

To answer the original question, which asked for the voltage across each resistor, we just read the values straight from the chart.

Now, you might be saying to yourself, "This seems like an awful lot of work to solve a relatively simple problem." You're right—it is.

However, there are several advantages to the V-I-R chart. The major advantage is that, by using it, you force yourself to approach every circuit problem exactly the same way. So when you're under pressure—as you will be during the AP exam—you'll have a tried-and-true method to turn to.

Also, if there are a whole bunch of resistors, you'll find that the V-I-R chart is a great way to organize all your calculations. That way, if you want to check your work, it'll be very easy to do.

Finally, free-response problems that involve circuits generally ask you questions like these.

(a) What is the voltage across each resistor?
(b) What is the current flowing through resistor #4?
(c) What is the power dissipated by resistor #2?

By using the V-I-R chart, you do all your calculations once, and then you have all the values you need to solve any question that the AP writers could possibly throw at you.

Tips for Solving Circuit Problems Using the *V-I-R* Chart

- First, enter all the given information into your chart. If resistors haven't already been given names (like "R_1"), you should name them for easy reference.
- Next simplify the circuit to calculate R_{eq}, if possible.
- Once you have two values in a row, you can calculate the third using Ohm's law. *You CANNOT use Ohm's law unless you have two of the three values in a row.*
- Remember that if two resistors are in series, the current through one of them equals the current through the other. And if two resistors are in parallel, the voltage across one equals the voltage across the other.

Kirchoff's Laws

Kirchoff's laws help you solve complicated circuits. They are especially useful if your circuit contains two batteries.

Kirchoff's laws say:

1. At any junction, the current entering equals the current leaving.
2. The sum of voltages around a closed loop is 0.

The first law is called the "junction rule," and the second is called the "loop rule." To illustrate the junction rule, we'll revisit the circuit from our first problem. (See Figure 17.5.)

Figure 17.5   Circuit illustrating Kirchoff's junction rule.

According to the junction rule, whatever current enters Junction "A" must also leave Junction "A." So let's say that 1.25 A enters Junction "A," and then that current gets split between the two branches. If we measured the current in the top branch and the current in the bottom branch, we would find that the total current equals 1.25 A. And, in fact, when the two branches came back together at Junction "B," we would find that exactly 1.25 A was flowing out through Junction "B" and through the rest of the circuit.

Kirchoff's junction rule says that charge is conserved: you don't lose any current when the wire bends or branches. This seems remarkably obvious, but it's also remarkably essential to solving circuit problems.

Kirchoff's loop rule is a bit less self-evident, but it's quite useful in sorting out difficult circuits.

As an example, we'll show you how to use Kirchoff's loop rule to find the current through all the resistors in the circuit.

We will follow the steps for using Kirchoff's loop rule:

- Arbitrarily choose a direction of current. Draw arrows on your circuit to indicate this direction.

- Follow the loop in the direction you chose. When you cross a resistor, the voltage is $-IR$, where R is the resistance, and I is the current flowing through the resistor. This is just an application of Ohm's law. (If you have to follow a loop *against* the current, though, the voltage across a resistor is written $+IR$.)

- When you cross a battery, if you trace from the $-$ to the $+$ add the voltage of the battery, subtract the battery's voltage if you trace from $+$ to $-$.

- Set the sum of your voltages equal to 0. Solve. If the current you calculate is negative, then the direction you chose was wrong—the current actually flows in the direction opposite to your arrows.

In the case of Figures 17.6a and 17.6b, we'll start by collapsing the two parallel resistors into a single equivalent resistor of 170 Ω. You don't *have* to do this, but it makes the mathematics much simpler.

Next, we'll choose a direction of current flow. But which way? In this particular case, you can probably guess that the 9-V battery will dominate the 1.5-V battery, and thus the current will be clockwise. But even if you aren't sure, just choose a direction and stick with it—if you get a negative current, you chose the wrong direction.

Figure 17.6a Example circuit for using Kirchoff's loop rule.

Figure 17.6b Circuit ready for analysis via Kirchoff's loop rule.

Here is the circuit redrawn with the parallel resistors collapsed and the assumed direction of current shown. Because there's now only one path for current to flow through, we have labeled that current I.

Now let's trace the circuit, starting at the top left corner and working clockwise:

- The 170 Ω resistor contributes a term of $-(170\ \Omega)\ I$.
- The 1.5-V battery contributes the term of -1.5 volts.
- The 100 Ω resistor contributes a term of $-(100\ \Omega)\ I$.
- The 200 Ω resistor contributes a term of $-(200\ \Omega)\ I$.
- The 9-V battery contributes the term of $+9$ volts.

Combine all the individual terms, and set the result equal to zero. The units of each term are volts, but units are left off below for algebraic clarity:

$$0 = (-170)I + (-1.5) + (-100)I + (-200)I + (+9).$$

By solving for I, the current in the circuit is found to be 0.016 A; that is, 16 milliamps, a typical laboratory current.

The problem is not yet completely solved, though—16 milliamps go through the 100 Ω and 200 Ω resistors, but what about the 300 Ω and 400 Ω resistors? We can find that the voltage across the 170 Ω equivalent resistance is $(0.016\ \text{A})(170\ \Omega) = 2.7$ V. Because the voltage across parallel resistors is the same for each, the current through each is just 2.7 V divided by the resistance of the actual resistor: 2.7 V/300 Ω = 9 mA, and 2.7 V/400 Ω = 7 mA. Problem solved!

Oh, and you might notice that the 9 mA and 7 mA through each of the parallel branches adds to the total of 16 mA—as required by Kirchoff's junction rule.

Circuits from an Experimental Point of View

When a real circuit is set up in the laboratory, it usually consists of more than just resistors—light bulbs and motors are common devices to hook to a battery, for example. For the purposes of computation, though, we can consider pretty much any electronic device to act like a resistor.

But what if your purpose is *not* computation? Often on the AP exam, as in the laboratory, you are asked about observational and measurable effects. The most common questions involve the brightness of light bulbs and the measurement (not just computation) of current and voltage.

Brightness of a Bulb

The brightness of a bulb depends solely on the power dissipated by the bulb. (Remember, power is given by any of the equations I^2R, IV, or V^2/R.) You can remember that from your own experience—when you go to the store to buy a lightbulb, you don't ask for a "400-ohm" bulb, but for a "100-watt" bulb. And a 100-watt bulb is brighter than a 25-watt bulb. But be careful—a bulb's power can change depending on the current and voltage it's hooked up to. Consider this problem.

A lightbulb is rated at 100 W in the United States, where the standard wall outlet voltage is 120 V. If this bulb were plugged in in Europe, where the standard wall outlet voltage is 240 V, which of the following would be true?

(A) The bulb would be one-quarter as bright.
(B) The bulb would be one-half as bright.
(C) The bulb's brightness would be the same.
(D) The bulb would be twice as bright.
(E) The bulb would be four times as bright.

Your first instinct might be to say that because brightness depends on power, the bulb is exactly as bright. But that's not right! The power of a bulb can change.

The resistance of a lightbulb is a property of the bulb itself, and so will not change no matter what the bulb is hooked to.

Since the resistance of the bulb stays the same while the voltage changes, by V^2/R, the power goes up, and the bulb will be brighter. How much brighter? Since the voltage in Europe is doubled, and because voltage is squared in the equation, the power is multiplied by 4—choice E.

Ammeters and Voltmeters

Ammeters measure current, and voltmeters measure voltage. This is pretty obvious, because current is measured in amps, voltage in volts. It is *not* necessarily obvious, though, how to connect these meters into a circuit.

Remind yourself of the properties of series and parallel resistors—voltage is the same for any resistors in parallel with each other. So if you're going to measure the voltage across a resistor, you must put the voltmeter in *parallel* with the resistor. In Figure 17.7, the meter labeled V_2 measures the voltage across the 100 Ω resistor, while the meter labeled V_1 measures the potential difference between points A and B (which is also the voltage across R_1).

Figure 17.7 Measuring voltage with a voltmeter.

Current is the same for any resistors in *series* with one another. So, if you're going to measure the current through a resistor, the ammeter must be in series with that resistor. In Figure 17.8, ammeter A_1 measures the current through resistor R_1, while ammeter A_2 measures the current through resistor R_2.

Figure 17.8 Measuring current with an ammeter.

As an exercise, ask yourself, is there a way to figure out the current in the other three resistors based only on the readings in these two ammeters? The answer is in the footnote.[2]

---

[2] The current through R_5 must be the same as through R_1, because both resistors carry whatever current came directly from the battery. The current through R_3 and R_4 can be determined from Kirchoff's junction rule: subtract the current in R_2 from the current in R_1, and that's what's left over for the right-hand branch of the circuit.

RC Circuits: Steady-State Behavior

When you have both resistors and capacitors in a circuit, the circuit is called an "RC circuit." If you remember, we introduced capacitors in Chapter 17, when we talked about charged, parallel plates.

The simplest problems with capacitors in circuits involve "steady-state behavior." This just means that the circuit has been connected for a while. In these cases, the only thing you'll generally need to worry about is how to deal with capacitors in series and in parallel.

When capacitors occur in series, you add them inversely. The charge stored on each capacitor in series must be the same.

$$\frac{1}{C_{eq}} = \frac{1}{C_1} + \frac{1}{C_2} + \frac{1}{C_3} + \cdots$$

Figure 17.9 Example of capacitors in series.

For the circuit in Figure 17.9, the equivalent capacitance is $C_{eq} = 1.5\ \mu F$.

When capacitors occur in parallel, you add them algebraically. The voltage across each capacitor in parallel must be the same.

$$C_{eq} = C_1 + C_2 + C_3 + \cdots$$

Figure 17.10 Example of capacitors in parallel.

The equivalent capacitance for the circuit in Figure 17.10 is $18\ \mu F$.

You should also know that the energy stored by a capacitor is

$$E = \frac{1}{2}\,CV^2$$

Once the circuit has been connected for a long time, capacitors stop current from flowing. To find the charge stored on or the voltage across a capacitor, just use the equation for capacitors, $Q = CV$.

For example, imagine that you hook up a 10-V battery to a 5 Ω resistor in series with an uncharged 1 F capacitor. (1 F capacitors are rarely used in actual electronics application—most capacitances are micro- or nanofarads—but they are commonly used for physics class demonstrations!) When the circuit is first hooked up, the capacitor is empty—it is ready and waiting for as much charge as can flow to it. Thus, initially, the circuit behaves as if the capacitor weren't there. In this case, then, the current through the resistor starts out at 10 V/5 Ω = 2 A.

But, after a long time, the capacitor blocks current. The resistor might as well not be there; we might as well just have a capacitor right across the battery. After a long time, the capacitor takes on the voltage of the battery, 10 V. (So the charge stored on the capacitor is $Q = CV = 10$ C.)

RC Circuits: Transitional Behavior

Okay, the obvious question here is, "What happens during the in-between times, while the capacitor is charging?" That's a more complicated question, one that is approached in Physics C. It's easiest if we start with a discussion of a capacitor *discharging*. (See Figure 17.11.)

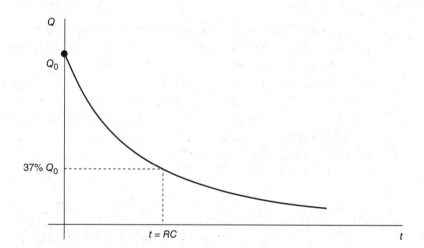

Figure 17.11   Graph of a capacitor discharging.

Consider a circuit with just a resistor R and a capacitor C. (That's what we mean by an RC circuit.) The capacitor is initially charged with charge Q_0. Apply Kirchoff's voltage rule:

$$-IR + V_c = 0$$

where V_c is the voltage across the capacitor, equal to Q/C by the equation for capacitors.

By definition, current is the time derivative of charge,

$$I = \frac{dQ}{dt}$$

So substituting this value for I into the Kirchoff equation we wrote above, and rearranging a bit, we get

$$\frac{dQ}{dt} = \frac{Q}{RC}$$

This is a differential equation. On the AP exam you will only rarely have to carry out the algorithmic solution to such an equation; however, you must recognize that the solution will have an exponential term, and you should be able to use limiting case reasoning to guess at the precise form of the solution. See the section on air resistance in Chapter 10 for details.

Here, the charge on the capacitor as a function of time is $Q = Q_0 e^{-t/RC}$. What does this mean?

Well, look at the limiting cases. At the beginning of the discharge, when $t = 0$, the exponential term becomes $e^0 = 1$; so $Q = Q_0$, as expected. After a long time, the exponential term becomes very small (e gets raised to a large negative power), and the charge goes to zero on the capacitor. Of course—that's what is meant by discharging.

And in between times? Try graphing this on your calculator. You get a function that looks like exponential decay.

What's cool here is that the product RC has special meaning. The units of RC are seconds: this is a time. RC is called the time constant of the RC circuit. The time constant gives us an idea of how long it will take to charge or discharge a capacitor. (Specifically, after one time constant the capacitor will have $1/e = 37\%$ of its original charge remaining; if the capacitor is charging rather than discharging, it will have charged to 63% of its full capacity.)

So there's no need to memorize the numerous complicated exponential expressions for charge, voltage, and current in an RC circuit. Just remember that all these quantities vary exponentially, and approach the "after a long time" values asymptotically.

What does the graph of charge vs. time for a *charging* capacitor look like? (See Figure 17.12.) Think about it a moment. At $t = 0$, there won't be any charge on the capacitor, because you haven't started charging it yet. And after a long time, the capacitor will be fully charged, and you won't be able to get more charge onto it. So the graph must start at zero and increase asymptotically.

Figure 17.12   Graph of a capacitor charging.

The charge asymptotically approaches the maximum value, which is equal to CV (V is the final voltage across the capacitor). After one time constant, the charge is $1/e = 37\%$ away from its maximum value.

Inductors in Circuits

An inductor makes use of induced EMF (see Chapter 19) to resist changes in current in a circuit. If part of a circuit is coiled, then the magnetic field produced by the coils induces a "back EMF" in the rest of the circuit . . . that EMF depends on how fast the current is changing, by Faraday's law. An inductor in a circuit is drawn as a little coil, as shown in Figure 17.13.

$$L$$

Figure 17.13 Symbol for an inductor in a circuit.

The voltage drop across an inductor is

$$V = L\frac{dI}{dt}$$

where L is called the inductance of the inductor. Inductance is measured in units of henrys.

What does this equation mean? If the current is changing rapidly, as when a circuit is first turned on or off, the voltage drop across the inductor is large; if the current is barely changing, as when a circuit has been on for a long time, the inductor's voltage drop is small.

We can think of an inductor as storing energy in the magnetic field it creates. When current begins to flow through the inductor, it stores up as much energy as it can. After a while, it has stored all the energy it can, so the current just goes through the inductor without trouble. The energy stored in an inductor is found by this equation.

$$E = \frac{1}{2}LI^2$$

For the AP Physics C exam, you need to understand circuits with inductors and resistors, as well as circuits with inductors and capacitors.

Other Circuits

RL Circuits

RL circuits contain just an inductor and a resistor, and perhaps a battery, as shown in Figure 17.14.

Figure 17.14 An RL circuit.

Imagine that we connect the switch in the circuit in Figure 17.15 at time $t = 0$. At that point, the current will change rapidly from zero to some nonzero value. So, because $\frac{dI}{dt}$

is large, the inductor has a large voltage drop, the resistor has very little voltage drop, and the current cannot immediately reach its maximum value. After a while, though, the current changes less rapidly, the voltage drop across the inductor becomes small, the voltage drop across the resistor gets bigger, and the current in the circuit becomes large.

A graph of current vs. time for this circuit is shown in Figure 17.15.

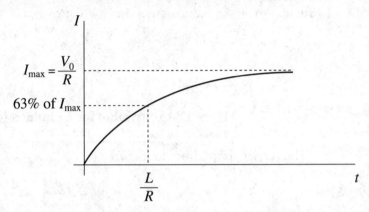

Figure 17.15   Graph of current vs. time for a simple RL circuit.

What would happen if we disconnected the battery? Well, the inductor would discharge its energy through the resistor. At first, the inductor would resist the decrease in current; but after a long time, the current would reach zero, as shown in Figure 17.16.

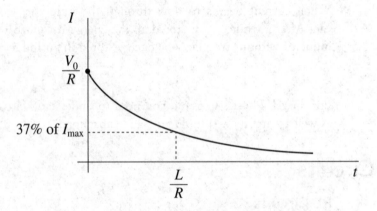

**Figure 17.16   Graph of current vs. time for a simple
RL circuit once the battery is disconnected.**

Note that the current in an RL circuit looks much like that in an RC circuit. In fact, we can define a time constant for an RL circuit, just as we did for the RC circuit, as the time for the current to lose 63% of its value (or to reach 37% of its maximum value when increasing). The time constant for an RL circuit is L/R.

LC Circuits

In a circuit consisting of just a capacitor and an inductor, both the capacitor and inductor try to store energy. They take turns storing the energy in the circuit—the capacitor charges, then discharges, then charges again . . .

In fact, the charge on the capacitor oscillates from maximum to minimum sinusoidally with period $2\pi\sqrt{LC}$. You may have to write the solution to a second-order differential equation, just like you did for the mass on a spring in Chapter 16.

› Practice Problems

Multiple Choice:

1. A 100 Ω, 120 Ω, and 150 Ω resistor are connected to a 9-V battery in the circuit shown above. Which of the three resistors dissipates the most power?

   (A) the 100 Ω resistor
   (B) the 120 Ω resistor
   (C) the 150 Ω resistor
   (D) both the 120 Ω and 150 Ω
   (E) all dissipate the same power

2. A 1.0-F capacitor is connected to a 12-V power supply until it is fully charged. The capacitor is then disconnected from the power supply, and used to power a toy car. The average drag force on this car is 2 N. About how far will the car go?

   (A) 36 m
   (B) 72 m
   (C) 144 m
   (D) 24 m
   (E) 12 m

3. Three resistors are connected to a 10-V battery as shown in the diagram above. What is the current through the 2.0 Ω resistor?

   (A) 0.25 A
   (B) 0.50 A
   (C) 1.0 A
   (D) 2.0 A
   (E) 4.0 A

4. Three capacitors are connected as shown in the diagram above. $C_1 = 2\,\mu F$; $C_2 = 4\,\mu F$; $C_3 = 6\,\mu F$. If the battery provides a potential of 9 V, how much charge is stored by this system of capacitors?

   (A) 3.0 μC
   (B) 30 μC
   (C) 2.7 μC
   (D) 27 μC
   (E) 10 μC

5. What is the resistance of an ideal ammeter and an ideal voltmeter?

	Ideal Ammeter	Ideal Voltmeter
(A)	zero	infinite
(B)	infinite	zero
(C)	zero	zero
(D)	infinite	infinite
(E)	1 Ω	1 Ω

Free Response:

6.

(a) Simplify the above circuit so that it consists of one equivalent resistor and the battery.

(b) What is the total current through this circuit?

(c) Find the voltage across each resistor. Record your answers in the spaces below.
   Voltage across 200 Ω resistor: _____
   Voltage across 300 Ω resistor: _____
   Voltage across 400 Ω resistor: _____
   Voltage across 500 Ω resistor: _____

(d) Find the current through each resistor. Record your answers in the spaces below.
   Current through 200 Ω resistor: _____
   Current through 300 Ω resistor: _____
   Current through 400 Ω resistor: _____
   Current through 500 Ω resistor: _____

(e) The 500 Ω resistor is now removed from the circuit. State whether the current through the 200 Ω resistor would increase, decrease, or remain the same. Justify your answer.

› Solutions to Practice Problems

1. **A**—On one hand, you could use a *V-I-R* chart to calculate the voltage or current for each resistor, then use $P = IV$, I^2R, or V^2/R to find power. On the other hand, there's a quick way to reason through this one. Voltage changes across the 100 Ω resistor, then again across the parallel combination. Because the 100 Ω resistor has a bigger resistance than the parallel combination, the voltage across it is larger as well. Now consider each resistor individually. By power $= V^2/R$, the 100 Ω resistor has both the biggest voltage and the smallest resistance, giving it the most power.

2. **A**—The energy stored by a capacitor is $\frac{1}{2}CV^2$. By powering a car, this electrical energy is converted into mechanical work, equal to force times parallel displacement. Solve for displacement, you get 36 m.

3. **C**—To use Ohm's law here, simplify the circuit to a 10-V battery with the 10 Ω equivalent resistance. We can use Ohm's law for the entire circuit to find that 1.0 A is the total current. Because all the resistors are in series, this 1.0 A flows through each resistor, including the 2 Ω resistor.

4. **D**—First, simplify the circuit to find the equivalent capacitance. The parallel capacitors add to 6 μF. Then the two series capacitors combine to 3 μF. So we end up with 9 V across a 3 μF equivalent capacitance. By the basic equation for capacitors, $Q = CV$, the charge stored on these capacitors is 27 μC.

5. **A**—An ammeter is placed in series with other circuit components. In order for the ammeter not to itself resist current and change the total current in the circuit, you want the ammeter to have as little resistance as possible—in the ideal case, zero resistance. But a voltmeter is placed in parallel with other circuit components. If the voltmeter has a low resistance, then current will flow through the voltmeter instead of through the rest of the circuit. Therefore, you want it to have as high a resistance as possible, so the voltmeter won't affect the circuit being measured.

6. (a) Combine each of the sets of parallel resistors first. You get 120 Ω for the first set, 222 Ω for the second set, as shown in the diagram below. These two equivalent resistances add as series resistors to get a total resistance of 342 Ω.

(b) Now that we've found the total resistance and we were given the total voltage, just use Ohm's law to find the total current to be 0.026 A (also known as 26 mA).

(c) and (d) should be solved together using a V-I-R chart. Start by going back one step to when we began to simplify the circuit: a 9-V battery, a 120 Ω combination, and a 222 Ω combination, shown above. The 26-mA current flows through each of these . . . so use V = IR to get the voltage of each: 3.1 V and 5.8 V, respectively.

Now go back to the original circuit. We know that voltage is the same across parallel resistors. So both the 200 Ω and 300 Ω resistors have a 3.1-V voltage across them. Use Ohm's law to find that 16 mA goes through the 200 Ω resistor, and 10 mA through the 300 Ω. Similarly, both the 400 Ω and 500 Ω resistors must have 5.8 V across them. We get 15 mA and 12 mA, respectively.

Checking these answers for reasonability: the total voltage adds to 8.9 V, or close enough to 9.0 V with rounding. The current through each set of parallel resistors adds to just about 26 mA, as we expect.

(e) Start by looking at the circuit as a whole. When we remove the 500 Ω resistor, we actually *increase* the overall resistance of the circuit because we have made it more difficult for current to flow by removing a parallel path. The total voltage of the circuit is provided by the battery, which provides 9.0 V no matter what it's hooked up to. So by Ohm's law, if total voltage stays the same while total resistance increases, total current must *decrease* from 26 mA.

Okay, now look at the first set of parallel resistors. Their equivalent resistance doesn't change, yet the total current running through them decreases, as discussed above. Therefore, the voltage across each resistor decreases, and the current through each decreases as well.

› Rapid Review

- Current is the flow of positive charge. It is measured in amperes.

- Resistance is a property that impedes the flow of charge. Resistance in a circuit comes from the internal resistance of the wires and from special elements inserted into circuits known as "resistors."

- Resistance is related to current and voltage by Ohm's law: $V = IR$.

- When resistors are connected in series, the total resistance equals the sum of the individual resistances. And the current through one resistor equals the current through any other resistor in series with it.

- When resistors are connected in parallel, the inverse of the total resistance equals the sum of the inverses of the individual resistances. The voltage across one resistor equals the voltage across any other resistor connected parallel to it.

Exam tip from an AP Physics veteran:

Many AP problems test your ability to use Ohm's law correctly. Ohm's law cannot be used unless the voltage, current, and resistance all refer to the same circuit element; on a *V-I-R* chart, this means that Ohm's law can only be used across a single row of the chart.

— *Chat, college junior and physics major*

- The *V-I-R* chart is a convenient way to organize any circuit problem.

- Kirchoff's junction rule says that any current coming into a junction will leave the junction. This is a statement of conservation of charge. Kirchoff's loop rule says that the sum of the voltages across a closed loop equals zero. This rule is helpful especially when solving problems with circuits that contain more than one battery.

- Ammeters measure current, and are connected in series; voltmeters measure voltage, and are connected in parallel.

- When capacitors are connected in series, the inverse of the total capacitance equals the sum of the inverses of the individual capacitances. When they are connected in parallel, the total capacitance just equals the sum of the individual capacitances.

- A capacitor's purpose in a circuit is to store charge. After it has been connected to a circuit for a long time, the capacitor becomes fully charged and prevents the flow of current.

- A capacitor gains or loses charge exponentially. The "time constant" of an RC circuit is equal to the resistance times the capacitance, and gives a characteristic time for the charging or discharging to occur.

- An inductor resists the change of current in a circuit. In an RL circuit, when the battery is first connected, the current increases asymptotically from zero up to a final value of *V/R*. When the battery is disconnected, the current decreases asymptotically to zero with a time constant of $\frac{L}{R}$. In an LC circuit, the charge on the capacitor oscillates from maximum to minimum sinusoidally with period $2\pi\sqrt{LC}$.

CHAPTER 18

Magnetism

IN THIS CHAPTER

Summary: Magnetic fields produce forces on moving charges; moving charges, such as current-carrying wires, can create magnetic fields. This chapter discusses the production and the effects of magnetic fields.

KEY IDEA

Key Ideas

✪ The force on a moving charge due to a magnetic field is qvB.
✪ The direction of the magnetic force on a moving charge is given by a right-hand rule, and is NOT in the direction of the magnetic field.
✪ Current-carrying wires produce magnetic fields.
✪ When the magnetic flux through a wire changes, a voltage is induced.
✪ An inductor inhibits the change in the current running through it. After a long time, the inductor acts as a bare wire.

Relevant Equations

Force on a charged particle in a magnetic field:

$$F = qvB$$

Force on a current-carrying wire:

$$F = ILB$$

Magnetic field due to a long, straight, current-carrying wire:

$$B = \frac{\mu_0 I}{2\pi r}$$

Magnetic flux:

$$\Phi_B = BA$$

Induced EMF:

$$\varepsilon = N\frac{\Delta\Phi}{\Delta t}$$

Induced EMF for a rectangular wire moving into or out of a magnetic field:

$$\varepsilon = BLv$$

Time constant for an LR circuit:

$$\tau = \frac{L}{R}$$

When most people think of magnets, they imagine horseshoe-shaped objects that can pick up bits of metal. Or maybe they visualize a refrigerator door. But not a physics ace like you! You know that magnetism is a wildly diverse topic, involving everything from bar magnets to metal coils to mass spectrometers. Perhaps you also know that magnetism is a subject filled with countless "right-hand rules," many of which can seem difficult to use or just downright confusing. So our goal in this chapter—besides reviewing all of the essential concepts and formulas that pertain to magnetism—is to give you a set of easy-to-understand, easy-to-use right-hand rules that are guaranteed to earn you points on the AP exam.

Magnetic Fields

All magnets are dipoles, which means that they have two "poles," or ends. One is called the north pole, and the other is the south pole. Opposite poles attract, and like poles repel.

You can never create a magnet with just a north pole or just a south pole. If you took the magnet in Figure 18.1

Figure 18.1   Bar magnet.

and cut it down the middle, you would not separate the poles. Instead, you would create two magnets like those shown in Figure 18.2.

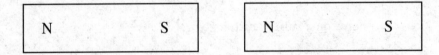

Figure 18.2   Cutting the bar magnet in Figure 18.1 in half just gives you two smaller bar magnets. You can never get an isolated north or south pole.

A magnet creates a magnetic field. (See Figure 18.3.) Unlike electric field lines, which either go from a positive charge to a negative charge or extend infinitely into space, magnetic field lines form loops. These loops point away from the north end of a magnet, and toward the south end. Near the magnet the lines point nearly straight into or out of the pole.

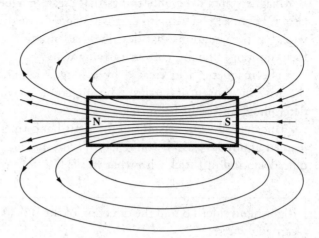

Figure 18.3   Magnetic field lines created by a bar magnet.

Just as we talk about the value of an electric field at a certain point, we can also talk about the value of a magnetic field at a certain point. The value of a magnetic field is a vector quantity, and it is abbreviated with the letter B. The value of a magnetic field is measured in teslas.

Often, the writers of the AP exam like to get funky about how they draw magnetic field lines. Rather than putting a magnetic field in the plane of the page, so that the field would point up or down or left or right, the AP writers will put magnetic fields perpendicular to the page. This means that the magnetic field either shoots out toward you or shoots down into the page.

When a magnetic field line is directed out of the page, it is drawn as shown in Figure 18.4a,

Figure 18.4a   Symbol for a magnetic field line directed out of the page.

and when a magnetic field line is directed into the page, it is drawn as shown in Figure 18.4b.

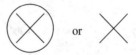

Figure 18.4b   Symbol for a magnetic field line directed into the page.

Supposedly, the drawing in Figure 18.4a is intended to look like the tip of an arrow coming out of a page, and the drawing in Figure 18.4b is intended to look like the tail of an arrow going into a page.[1] These symbols can be used to describe other ideas, such as electric fields going into or out of the page, or currents flowing into or out of the page, but they are most often used to describe magnetic fields.

---

[1]If you're not too impressed by these representations, just remember how physicists like to draw hippopotomuses. There's a reason why these science folks weren't accepted into art school.

Long, Straight, Current-Carrying Wires

Bar magnets aren't the only things that create magnetic fields—current-carrying wires do also. Of course, you can also create a magnetic field using a short, curvy, current-carrying wire, but the equations that describe that situation are a little more complicated, so we'll focus on long, straight, current-carrying wires.

The magnetic field created by a long, straight, current-carrying wire loops around the wire in concentric circles. The direction in which the magnetic field lines loop is determined by a right-hand rule.

(Incidentally, our versions of the right-hand rules may not be the same as what you've learned in physics class. If you're happy with the ones you already know, you should ignore our advice and just stick with what works best for you.)

> Right-hand rule: To find the direction of the B field produced by long, straight, current-carrying wires.
>
> Pretend you are holding the wire with your right hand. Point your thumb in the direction of the current. Your fingers wrap around your thumb the same way that the magnetic field wraps around the wire.

Here's an example. A wire is directed perpendicular to the plane of this page (that is, it's coming out straight toward you). The current in this wire is flowing out of the page. What does the magnetic field look like?

To solve this, we first pretend that we are grabbing the wire. If it helps, take your pencil and place it on this page, with the eraser touching the page and the point of the pencil coming out toward you. This pencil is like the wire. Now grab the pencil with your right hand. The current is coming out of the page, so make sure that you have grabbed the pencil in such a way that your thumb is pointing away from the page. If it looks like you're giving someone a "thumbs-up sign," then you're doing this correctly. Finally, look at how your fingers are wrapped around the pencil. From a bird's-eye view, it should look like your fingers are wrapping counterclockwise. So this tells us the answer to the problem, as shown in Figure 18.5.

Figure 18.5   Magnetic field (dotted lines) generated by a long, straight, current-carrying wire oriented perpendicular to the plane of the page.

Here's another example. What does the magnetic field look like around a wire in the plane of the page with current directed upward?

We won't walk you through this one; just use the right-hand rule, and you'll be fine. The answer is shown in Figure 18.6.

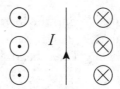

Figure 18.6   Magnetic field around a wire in the plane of the page with current directed upward.

The formula that describes the magnitude of the magnetic field created by a long, straight, current-carrying wire is the following:

$$B = \frac{\mu_0 I}{2\pi r}$$

In this formula, B is the magnitude of the magnetic field, μ_0 is a constant called the "permeability of free space" ($\mu_0 = 4\pi \times 10^{-7}$ T·m/A), I is the current flowing in the wire, and r is the distance from the wire.

Moving Charged Particles

The whole point of defining a magnetic field is to determine the forces produced on an object by the field. You are familiar with the forces produced by bar magnets—like poles repel, opposite poles attract. We don't have any formulas for the amount of force produced in this case, but that's okay, because this kind of force is irrelevant to the AP exam.

Instead, we must focus on the forces produced by magnetic fields on charged particles, including both isolated charges and current-carrying wires. (After all, current is just the movement of positive charges.)

A magnetic field exerts a force on a charged particle if that particle is moving perpendicular to the magnetic field. A magnetic field does not exert a force on a stationary charged particle, nor on a particle that is moving parallel to the magnetic field.

$$F = qvB$$

The magnitude of the force exerted on the particle equals the charge on the particle, q, multiplied by the velocity of the particle, v, multiplied by the magnitude of the magnetic field.

This equation is sometimes written as $F = qvB(\sin \theta)$. The θ refers to the angle formed between the velocity vector of your particle and the direction of the magnetic field. So, if a particle moves in the same direction as the magnetic field lines, $\theta = 0°$, $\sin 0° = 0$, and *that particle experiences no magnetic force!*

Nine times out of ten, you will not need to worry about this "sin θ" term, because the angle will either be zero or 90°. However, if a problem explicitly tells you that your particle is *not* traveling perpendicular to the magnetic field, then you will need to throw in this extra "sin θ" term.

> Right-hand rule: To find the force on a charged particle.
>   Point your right hand, with fingers extended, in the direction that the charged particle is traveling. Then, bend your fingers so that they point in the direction of the magnetic field.
>
> - If the particle has a POSITIVE charge, your thumb points in the direction of the force exerted on it.
> - If the particle has a NEGATIVE charge, your thumb points opposite the direction of the force exerted on it.

The key to this right-hand rule is to remember the sign of your particle. This next problem illustrates how important sign can be.

> An electron travels through a magnetic field, as shown below. The particle's initial velocity is 5×10^6 m/s, and the magnitude of the magnetic field is 0.4 T. What are the magnitude and direction of the particle's acceleration?

This is one of those problems where you're told that the particle is *not* moving perpendicular to the magnetic field. So the formula we use to find the magnitude of the force acting on the particle is

$$F = qvB(\sin \theta)$$
$$F = (1.6 \times 10^{-19} \text{ C})(5 \times 10^6 \text{ m/s})(0.4 \text{ T})(\sin 30°)$$
$$F = 1.6 \times 10^{-13} \text{ N}.$$

Note that we never plug in the negative signs when calculating force. The negative charge on an electron will influence the direction of the force, which we will determine in a moment. Now we solve for acceleration:

$$F_{net} = ma$$
$$a = 1.8 \times 10^{17} \text{ m/s}^2.$$

Wow, you say . . . a bigger acceleration than anything we've ever dealt with. Is this unreasonable? After all, in less than a second the particle would be moving faster than the speed of light, right? The answer is still reasonable. In this case, the acceleration is perpendicular to the velocity. This means the acceleration is *centripetal*, and the particle must move in a circle at constant speed. But even if the particle were speeding up at this rate, either the acceleration wouldn't act for very long, or relativistic effects would prevent the particle from traveling faster than light.

Finally, we solve for direction using the right-hand rule. We point our hand in the direction that the particle is traveling—to the right. Next, we curl our fingers upward, so that they point in the same direction as the magnetic field. Our thumb points out of the page. BUT WAIT!!! We're dealing with an electron, which has a negative charge. So the force acting on our particle, and therefore the particle's acceleration, points in the opposite direction. The particle is accelerating into the page.

Magnetic Force on a Wire

A current is simply the flow of positive charges. So, if we put a current-carrying wire perpendicular to a magnetic field, we have placed moving charges perpendicular to the field, and these charges experience a force. The wire can be pulled by the magnetic field!

The formula for the force on a long, straight, current-carrying wire in the presence of a magnetic field is

$$F = ILB$$

This equation says that the force on a wire equals the current in the wire, I, multiplied by the length of the wire, L, multiplied by the magnitude of the magnetic field, B, in which the wire is located.

Sometimes you'll see this equation written as $F = ILB(\sin \theta)$. Just like the equation for the force on a charge, the θ refers to the angle between the wire and the magnetic field. You normally don't have to worry about this θ because, in most problems, the wire is perpendicular to the magnetic field, and $\sin 90° = 1$, so the term cancels out.

The direction of the force on a current-carrying wire is given by the same right-hand rule as for the force on a charged particle because current is simply the flow of positive charge.

What would happen if you had two long, straight, current-carrying wires side by side? This is a question that the writers of the AP exam love to ask, so it is a great idea to learn how to answer it.

The trick that makes answering this question very easy is that you have to draw the direction of the magnetic field that one of the wires creates; then consider the force on the other wire. So, for example . . .

Two wires are placed parallel to each other. The direction of current in each wire is indicated above. How will these wires interact?

(A) They will attract each other.
(B) They will repel each other.
(C) They will not affect each other.
(D) This question cannot be answered without knowing the length of each wire.
(E) This question cannot be answered without knowing the current in each wire.

Let's follow our advice and draw the magnetic field created by the left-hand wire.

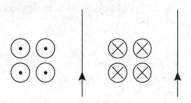

Now, a wire's field cannot produce a force on itself. The field that we drew is *caused by* the left wire, but produces a force on the right-hand wire. Which direction is that force? Use the right-hand rule for the force on a charged particle. The charges are moving up, in the direction of the current. So point up the page, and curl your fingers toward the magnetic field, into the page. The right wire is forced to the LEFT. Newton's third law says that the force on the left wire by the right wire will be equal and opposite.[2] So, the wires attract, answer A.

Often, textbooks give you advice such as, "Whenever the current in two parallel wires is traveling in the same direction, the wires will attract each other, and vice versa." Use it if you like, but this advice can easily be confused.

Mass Spectrometry: More Charges Moving Through Magnetic Fields

A magnetic field can make a charged particle travel in a circle. Here's how it performs this trick.

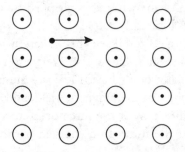

Figure 18.7a   Positively charged particle moving in a magnetic field directed out of the page.

Let's say you have a proton traveling through a uniform magnetic field coming out of the page, and the proton is moving to the right, like the one we drew in Figure 18.7a. The magnetic field exerts a downward force on the particle (use the right-hand rule). So the path of the particle begins to bend downward, as shown in Figure 18.7b.

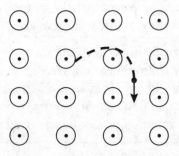

Figure 18.7b   Curving path of a positively charged particle moving in a magnetic field directed out of the page.

---

[2]You could also figure out the force on the left wire by using the same method we just used for the force on the right wire: draw the magnetic field produced by the right wire, and use the right-hand rule to find the direction of the magnetic force acting on the left wire.

Now our proton is moving straight down. The force exerted on it by the magnetic field, using the right-hand rule, is now directed to the left. So the proton will begin to bend leftward. You probably see where this is going—a charged particle, traveling perpendicular to a uniform magnetic field, will follow a circular path.

We can figure out the radius of this path with some basic math. The force of the magnetic field is causing the particle to go in a circle, so this force must cause centripetal acceleration. That is, $qvB = mv^2/r$.

We didn't include the "$\sin \theta$" term because the particle is always traveling perpendicular to the magnetic field. We can now solve for the radius of the particle's path:

$$r = \frac{mv}{qB}$$

The real-world application of this particle-in-a-circle trick is called a mass spectrometer. A mass spectrometer is a device used to determine the mass of a particle.

A mass spectrometer, in simplified form, is drawn in Figure 18.8.

Figure 18.8   Basic mass spectrometer.

A charged particle enters a uniform electric field (shown at the left in Figure 18.8). It is accelerated by the electric field. By the time it gets to the end of the electric field, it has acquired a high velocity, which can be calculated using conservation of energy. Then the particle travels through a tiny opening and enters a uniform magnetic field. This magnetic field exerts a force on the particle, and the particle begins to travel in a circle. It eventually hits the wall that divides the electric-field region from the magnetic-field region. By measuring where on the wall it hits, you can determine the radius of the particle's path. Plugging this value into the equation we derived for the radius of the path, you can calculate the particle's mass, $r = mv/qB$.

You may see a problem on the free-response section that involves a mass spectrometer. These problems may seem intimidating, but, when you take them one step at a time, they're not very difficult.

Induced EMF

A changing magnetic field produces a current. We call this occurrence **electromagnetic induction**.

So let's say that you have a loop of wire in a magnetic field. Under normal conditions, no current flows in your wire loop. However, if you change the magnitude of the magnetic field, a current will begin to flow.

We've said in the past that current flows in a circuit (and a wire loop qualifies as a circuit, albeit a simple one) when there is a potential difference between the two ends of the circuit. Usually, we need a battery to create this potential difference. But we don't have a battery hooked up to our loop of wire. Instead, the changing magnetic field is doing the same thing as a battery would. So rather than talking about the voltage of the battery in this circuit, we talk about the "voltage" created by the changing magnetic field. The technical term for this "voltage" is **induced EMF**.

> **Induced EMF:** The potential difference created by a changing magnetic field that causes a current to flow in a wire. EMF stands for Electro-Motive Force, but is *NOT* a force.

For a loop of wire to "feel" the changing magnetic field, some of the field lines need to pass through it. The amount of magnetic field that passes through the loop is called the **magnetic flux**. This concept is pretty similar to electric flux.

> **Magnetic Flux:** The number of magnetic field lines that pass through an area

The units of flux are called webers; 1 weber = 1 T·m². The equation for magnetic flux is

$$\Phi_B = BA$$

In this equation, Φ_B is the magnetic flux, B is the magnitude of the magnetic field, and A is the area of the region that is penetrated by the magnetic field.

Let's take a circular loop of wire, lay it down on the page, and create a magnetic field that points to the right, as shown in Figure 18.9.

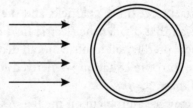

Figure 18.9   Loop of wire in the plane of a magnetic field.

No field lines go through the loop. Rather, they all hit the edge of the loop, but none of them actually passes through the center of the loop. So we know that our flux should equal zero.

Okay, this time we will orient the field lines so that they pass through the middle of the loop. We'll also specify the loop's radius = 0.2 m, and that the magnetic field is that of the Earth, $B = 5 \times 10^{-5}$ T. This situation is shown in Figure 18.10.

Figure 18.10   Loop of wire with magnetic field lines going through it.

Now all of the area of the loop is penetrated by the magnetic field, so A in the flux formula is just the area of the circle, πr^2.

The flux here is

$$\Phi_B = (5 \times 10^{-5})(\pi)\,(0.2^2) = 6.2 \times 10^{-6} \text{ T·m}^2.$$

Sometimes you'll see the flux equation written as $BA\cos\theta$. The additional cosine term is only relevant when a magnetic field penetrates a wire loop at some angle that's not 90°. The angle θ is measured between the magnetic field and the "normal" to the loop of wire . . . if you didn't get that last statement, don't worry about it. Rather, know that the cosine term goes to 1 when the magnetic field penetrates directly into the loop, and the cosine term goes to zero when the magnetic field can't penetrate the loop at all.

Because a loop will only "feel" a changing magnetic field if some of the field lines pass through the loop, we can more accurately say the following: *A changing magnetic **flux** creates an induced EMF.*

Faraday's Law tells us exactly how much EMF is induced by a changing magnetic flux.

$$\varepsilon = \frac{N \cdot \Delta\Phi_B}{\Delta t} \text{[3]}$$

ε is the induced EMF, N is the number of loops you have (in all of our examples, we've only had one loop), and Δt is the time during which your magnetic flux, Φ_B, is changing.

Up until now, we've just said that a changing magnetic flux creates a current. We haven't yet told you, though, in which direction that current flows. To do this, we'll turn to **Lenz's Law**.

Lenz's Law: States that the direction of the induced current opposes the increase in flux

When a current flows through a loop, that current creates a magnetic field. So what Lenz said is that the current that is induced will flow in such a way that the magnetic field it creates points opposite to the direction in which the already existing magnetic flux is changing.

---

[3]But the calculus version of the induced EMF formula states: $\varepsilon = -N\dfrac{d\Phi}{dt}$. If you're given magnetic flux as a function of time, then take the *negative* time derivative to find the induced EMF.

Sound confusing?[4] It'll help if we draw some good illustrations. So here is Lenz's Law in pictures.

We'll start with a loop of wire that is next to a region containing a magnetic field (Figure 18.11a). Initially, the magnetic flux through the loop is zero.

Figure 18.11a Loop of wire next to a region containing a magnetic field pointing out of the page.

Now, we will move the wire into the magnetic field. When we move the loop toward the right, the magnetic flux will increase as more and more field lines begin to pass through the loop. The magnetic flux is increasing out of the page—at first, there was no flux out of the page, but now there is some flux out of the page. Lenz's Law says that the induced current will create a magnetic field that opposes this increase in flux. So the induced current will create a magnetic field into the page. By the right-hand rule, the current will flow clockwise. This situation is shown in Figure 18.11b.

Figure 18.11b Current induced in loop of wire as it moves into a magnetic field directed out of the page.

After a while, the loop will be entirely in the region containing the magnetic field. Once it enters this region, there will no longer be a changing flux, because no matter where it is within the region, the same number of field lines will always be passing through the loop. Without a changing flux, there will be no induced EMF, so the current will stop. This is shown in Figure 18.11c.

Figure 18.11c Loop of wire with no current flowing, because it is not experiencing a changing magnetic flux.

---

[4]"Yes."

To solve a problem that involves Lenz's Law, use this method:

- Point your right thumb in the initial direction of the magnetic field.
- Ask yourself, "Is the flux increasing or decreasing?"
- If the flux is decreasing, then just curl your fingers (with your thumb still pointed in the direction of the magnetic field). Your fingers show the direction of the induced current.
- If flux is increasing in the direction you're pointing, then flux is decreasing in the other direction. So, point your thumb in the opposite direction of the magnetic field, and curl your fingers. Your fingers show the direction of the induced current.

Induced EMF in a Rectangular Wire

Consider the example in Figures 18.11a–c with the circular wire being pulled through the uniform magnetic field. It can be shown that if instead we pull a *rectangular* wire into or out of a uniform field B at constant speed v, then the induced EMF in the wire is found by

$$\varepsilon = BLv$$

Here, L represents the length of the side of the rectangle that is NOT entering or exiting the field, as shown below in Figure 18.12.

Figure 18.12   Rectangular wire moving through a uniform magnetic field.

Some Words of Caution

We say this from personal experience. First, when using a right-hand rule, use big, easy-to-see gestures. A right-hand rule is like a form of advertisement: it is a way that your hand tells your brain what the answer to a problem is. You want that advertisement to be like a billboard—big, legible, and impossible to misread. Tiny gestures will only lead to mistakes. Second, when using a right-hand rule, *always* use your right hand. *Never use your left hand!* This will cost you points!

Exam tip from an AP Physics veteran:
Especially if you hold your pencil in your right hand, it's easy accidentally to use your left hand. Be careful!

—*Jessica, college sophomore*

The Biot-Savart Law and Ampere's Law

So far we've only discussed two possible ways to create a magnetic field—use a bar magnet, or a long, straight, current-carrying wire. And of these, we only have an equation to find the magnitude of the field produced by the wire.

Biot-Savart Law

The Biot-Savart Law provides a way, albeit a complicated way, to find the magnetic field produced by pretty much any type of current. It's not worth worrying about using the law because it's got a horrendously complicated integral with a cross product included. Just know the conceptual consequence: a little element of wire carrying a current produces a magnetic field that (a) wraps around the current element via the right-hand rule, and (b) decreases in magnitude as $1/r^2$, r being the distance from the current element.

So why does the magnetic field caused by a long, straight, current-carrying wire drop off as $1/r$ rather than $1/r^2$? Because the $1/r^2$ drop-off is for the magnetic field produced just by a teeny little bit of current-carrying wire (in calculus terminology, by a differential element of current). When we include the contributions of every teeny bit of a very long wire, the net field drops off as $1/r$.

Ampere's Law

Ampere's Law gives an alternative method for finding the magnetic field caused by a current. Although Ampere's Law is valid everywhere that current is continuous, it is only *useful* in a few specialized situations where symmetry is high. There are three important results of Ampere's Law:

1. The magnetic field produced by a very long, straight current is

$$B = \frac{\mu_0 I}{2\pi r}$$

outside the wire; inside the wire, the field increases linearly from zero at the wire's center.

2. A solenoid is set of wound wire loops. A current-carrying solenoid produces a magnetic field. Ampere's Law can show that the magnetic field due to a solenoid is shaped like that of a bar magnet; and the magnitude of the magnetic field inside the solenoid is approximately uniform, $B_{solenoid} = \mu_0\, nI$. (Here I is the current in the solenoid, and n is the number of coils per meter in the solenoid.)

3. The magnetic field produced by a wire-wrapped torus (a "donut" with wire wrapped around it [see Figure 18.13]) is zero everywhere outside the torus, but nonzero within the torus. The direction of the field inside the torus is around the donut.

Figure 18.13   A wire-wrapped torus.

Maxwell's Equations

Okay, we'll get this out of the way right now: *You will not have to solve Maxwell's equations on the AP Physics exam.* These four equations include integrals the likes of which you will not be able to solve until well into college physics, if then. However, you *can* understand the basic point of each equation, and, most importantly, understand the equations' greatest consequence.

Accelerating charges produce oscillations of electric and magnetic fields. These oscillations propagate as waves, with speed

$$c = \frac{1}{\sqrt{\mu_0 \varepsilon_0}}$$

Maxwell obtained this wave speed as a mathematical result from the equations. He noticed that, when the experimentally determined constants were plugged in, the speed of his "electromagnetic waves" was identical to the speed of light.[5] Maxwell's conclusion was that light must be an electromagnetic wave.

What are Maxwell's equations? We're not even going to write them out, for fear that you might throw down your book in trepidation. If you're really interested in the integral or differential form of the equations, you will find them in your physics book (or on a rather popular T-shirt). While we won't write the equations, we'll gladly summarize what they are and what they mean.

- *Maxwell equation 1* is simply Gauss's Law: the net electric flux through a closed surface is proportional to the charge enclosed by that surface.
- *Maxwell equation 2* is sometimes called Gauss's Law for magnetism: the net magnetic flux through a closed surface must always be zero. The consequence of this equation is that magnetic poles come in north/south pairs—you cannot have an isolated north magnetic pole.
- *Maxwell equation 3* is simply Faraday's Law: a changing magnetic flux through a loop of wire induces an EMF.
- *Maxwell equation 4* is partly Ampere's Law, but with an addition called "displacement current" that allows the equation to be valid in all situations. The principal consequence is that just as a changing magnetic field can produce an electric field, a changing electric field can likewise produce a magnetic field.

---

[5]Which had first been accurately measured in the late 1600s using observations of the moons of Jupiter.

› Practice Problems

Multiple Choice:

1. A point charge of $+1\ \mu C$ moves with velocity v into a uniform magnetic field B directed to the right, as shown above. What is the direction of the magnetic force on the charge?

   (A) to the right and up the page
   (B) directly out of the page
   (C) directly into the page
   (D) to the right and into the page
   (E) to the right and out of the page

2. A uniform magnetic field B points up the page, as shown above. A loop of wire carrying a clockwise current is placed at rest in this field as shown above, and then let go. Which of the following describes the motion of the wire immediately after it is let go?

   (A) The wire will expand slightly in all directions.
   (B) The wire will contract slightly in all directions.
   (C) The wire will rotate, with the top part coming out of the page.
   (D) The wire will rotate, with the left part coming out of the page.
   (E) The wire will rotate clockwise, remaining in the plane of the page.

3. An electron moves to the right in a uniform magnetic field that points into the page. What is the direction of the electric field that could be used to cause the electron to travel in a straight line?

   (A) down toward the bottom of the page
   (B) up toward the top of the page
   (C) into the page
   (D) out of the page
   (E) to the left

Free Response:

4. A circular loop of wire of negligible resistance and radius $R = 20$ cm is attached to the circuit shown above. Each resistor has resistance 10 Ω. The magnetic field of the Earth points up along the plane of the page in the direction shown, and has magnitude $B = 5.0 \times 10^{-5}$ T.

   The wire loop rotates about a horizontal diameter, such that after a quarter rotation the loop is no longer in the page, but perpendicular to it. The loop makes 500 revolutions per second, and remains connected to the circuit the entire time.

   (a) Determine the magnetic flux through the loop when the loop is in the orientation shown.
   (b) Determine the maximum magnetic flux through the loop.
   (c) Estimate the average value of the induced EMF in the loop.
   (d) Estimate the average current through resistor C.

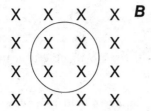

5. A loop of wire is located inside a uniform magnetic field, as shown above. Name at least four things you could do to induce a current in the loop.

› Solutions to Practice Problems

1. **C**—Use the right-hand rule for the force on charged particles. You point in the direction of the velocity, and curl your fingers in the direction of the magnetic field. This should get your thumb pointing into the page. Because this is a positive charge, no need to switch the direction of the force.

2. **C**—Use the right-hand rule for the force on a wire. Look at each part of this wire. At the leftmost and rightmost points, the current is along the magnetic field lines. Thus, these parts of the wire experience no force. The topmost part of the wire experiences a force out of the page (point to the right, fingers curl up the page, the thumb points out of the page). The bottommost part of the wire experiences a force *into* the page. So, the wire will rotate.

3. **A**—Use the right-hand rule for the force on a charge. Point in the direction of velocity, curl the fingers into the page, the thumb points up the page . . . but this is a *negative* charge, so the force on the charge is down the page. Now, the electric force must cancel the magnetic force for the charge to move in a straight line, so the electric force should be up the page. (E and B *fields* cannot cancel, but forces sure can.) The direction of an *electric* force on a negative charge is opposite the field; so the field should point down, toward the bottom of the page.

4. (a) Flux equals zero because the field points along the loop, not ever going straight through the loop.
   (b) Flux is maximum when the field *is* pointing straight through the loop; that is, when the loop is perpendicular to the page. Then flux will be just $BA = 5.0 \times 10^{-5}$

   $T \cdot \pi (0.20 \text{ m})^2 = 6.3 \times 10^{-6}$ T·m². (Be sure your units are right!)
   (c) Induced EMF for this one loop is change in flux over time interval. It takes 1/500 of a second for the loop to make one complete rotation; so it takes $1/4$ of that, or 1/2000 of a second, for the loop to go from zero to maximum flux. Divide this change in flux by 1/2000 of a second . . . this is 6.3×10^{-6} T·m²/0.0005 s = 0.013 V. (That's 13 mV.)
   (d) Now we can treat the circuit as if it were attached to a battery of voltage 13 mV. The equivalent resistance of the parallel combination of resistors B and C is 5 Ω; the total resistance of the circuit is 15 Ω. So the current in the whole circuit is 0.013 V/15 W = 8.4×10^{-4} A. (This can also be stated as 840 μA.) The current splits evenly between resistors B and C since they're equal resistances, so we get 420 μA for resistor C.

5. The question might as well be restated, "Name four things you could do to change the flux through the loop," because only a changing magnetic flux induces an EMF.

   (a) Rotate the wire about an axis in the plane of the page. This will change the θ term in the expression for magnetic flux, $BA \cos \theta$.
   (b) Pull the wire out of the field. This will change the area term, because the magnetic field lines will intersect a smaller area of the loop.
   (c) Shrink or expand the loop. This also changes the area term in the equation for magnetic flux.
   (d) Increase or decrease the strength of the magnetic field. This changes the B term in the flux equation.

› Rapid Review

- Magnetic fields can be drawn as loops going from the north pole of a magnet to the south pole.

- A long, straight, current-carrying wire creates a magnetic field that wraps around the wire in concentric circles. The direction of the magnetic field is found by a right-hand rule.

- Similarly, loops of wire that carry current create magnetic fields. The direction of the magnetic field is, again, found by a right-hand rule.

- A magnetic field exerts a force on a charged particle if that particle is moving perpendicular to the magnetic field.

- When a charged particle moves perpendicular to a magnetic field, it ends up going in circles. This phenomenon is the basis behind mass spectrometry.

- A changing magnetic flux creates an induced EMF, which causes current to flow in a wire.

- Lenz's Law says that when a changing magnetic flux induces a current, the direction of that current will be such that the magnetic field it induces is pointed in the opposite direction of the original change in magnetic flux.

- The Biot–Savart Law has as its consequence that a little element of wire carrying a current produces a magnetic field that (1) wraps around the current element via the right-hand rule, and (2) decreases in magnitude as $1/r^2$, r being the distance from the current element. This is applicable to Physics C only.

- Ampere's Law has as its consequence that (1) the magnetic field produced by a very long, straight current is

$$B_{\text{wire}} = \frac{\mu_0 I}{2\pi r}$$

outside the wire; inside the wire, the field increases linearly from zero at the wire's center, and (2) the magnetic field produced by a wire-wrapped torus is zero everywhere outside the torus, but nonzero within the torus. The direction of the field inside the torus is around the donut.

Build Your Test-Taking Confidence

PHYSICS **C**—Mechanics Practice Exam 1—Multiple-Choice Questions

PHYSICS **C**—Mechanics Practice Exam 1—Free-Response Questions

PHYSICS **C**—Electricity and Magnetism Practice Exam 1—Multiple-Choice Questions

PHYSICS **C**—Electricity and Magnetism Practice Exam 1—Free-Response Questions

PHYSICS **C**—Mechanics Practice Exam 1—Multiple-Choice Solutions

PHYSICS **C**—Mechanics Practice Exam 1—Free-Response Solutions

PHYSICS **C**—Electricity and Magnetism Practice Exam 1—Multiple-Choice Solutions

PHYSICS **C**—Electricity and Magnetism Practice Exam 1—Free-Response Solutions

Physics C—Mechanics Practice Exam 1—Multiple-Choice Questions

ANSWER SHEET

1 (A) (B) (C) (D) (E)
2 (A) (B) (C) (D) (E)
3 (A) (B) (C) (D) (E)
4 (A) (B) (C) (D) (E)
5 (A) (B) (C) (D) (E)
6 (A) (B) (C) (D) (E)
7 (A) (B) (C) (D) (E)
8 (A) (B) (C) (D) (E)
9 (A) (B) (C) (D) (E)
10 (A) (B) (C) (D) (E)
11 (A) (B) (C) (D) (E)
12 (A) (B) (C) (D) (E)

13 (A) (B) (C) (D) (E)
14 (A) (B) (C) (D) (E)
15 (A) (B) (C) (D) (E)
16 (A) (B) (C) (D) (E)
17 (A) (B) (C) (D) (E)
18 (A) (B) (C) (D) (E)
19 (A) (B) (C) (D) (E)
20 (A) (B) (C) (D) (E)
21 (A) (B) (C) (D) (E)
22 (A) (B) (C) (D) (E)
23 (A) (B) (C) (D) (E)
24 (A) (B) (C) (D) (E)

25 (A) (B) (C) (D) (E)
26 (A) (B) (C) (D) (E)
27 (A) (B) (C) (D) (E)
28 (A) (B) (C) (D) (E)
29 (A) (B) (C) (D) (E)
30 (A) (B) (C) (D) (E)
31 (A) (B) (C) (D) (E)
32 (A) (B) (C) (D) (E)
33 (A) (B) (C) (D) (E)
34 (A) (B) (C) (D) (E)
35 (A) (B) (C) (D) (E)

Physics C—Mechanics Practice Exam 1—Multiple-Choice Questions

Time: 45 minutes. You may refer to the constants sheet and the equation sheet, both of which are found in the appendix. You may use a calculator.

1. A cannon is mounted on a truck that moves forward at a speed of 5 m/s. The operator wants to launch a ball from a cannon so the ball goes as far as possible before hitting the level surface. The muzzle velocity of the cannon is 50 m/s. At what angle from the horizontal should the operator point the cannon?

   (A) 5°
   (B) 41°
   (C) 45°
   (D) 49°
   (E) 85°

2. A car moving with speed v reaches the foot of an incline of angle θ. The car coasts up the incline without using the engine. Neglecting friction and air resistance, which of the following is correct about the magnitude of the car's horizontal acceleration a_x and vertical acceleration a_y?

   (A) $a_x = 0$; $a_y < g$
   (B) $a_x = 0$; $a_y = g$
   (C) $a_x < g$; $a_y < g$
   (D) $a_x < g$; $a_y = g$
   (E) $a_x < g$; $a_y > g$

3. A bicycle slows down with an acceleration whose magnitude increases linearly with time. Which of the following velocity–time graphs could represent the motion of the bicycle?

4. A cart is sliding down a low friction incline. A device on the cart launches a ball, forcing the ball perpendicular to the incline, as shown above. Air resistance is negligible. Where will the ball land relative to the cart, and why?

   (A) The ball will land in front of the cart, because the ball's acceleration component parallel to the plane is greater than the cart's acceleration component parallel to the plane.
   (B) The ball will land in front of the cart, because the ball has a greater magnitude of acceleration than the cart.
   (C) The ball will land in the cart, because both the ball and the cart have the same component of acceleration parallel to the plane.
   (D) The ball will land in the cart, because both the ball and the cart have the same magnitude of acceleration.
   (E) The ball will land behind the cart, because the ball slows down in the horizontal direction after it leaves the cart.

GO ON TO THE NEXT PAGE

5. The quantity "jerk," j, is defined as the time derivative of an object's acceleration,

$$j = \frac{da}{dt} = \frac{d^3x}{dt^3}.$$

What is the physical meaning of the area under a graph of jerk vs. time?

(A) The area represents the object's acceleration.
(B) The area represents the object's change in acceleration.
(C) The area represents the object's change in velocity.
(D) The area represents the object's velocity.
(E) The area represents the object's change in position.

6. A particle moves along the x-axis with a position given by the equation $x(t) = 5 + 3t$, where x is in meters, and t is in seconds. The positive direction is east. Which of the following statements about the particle is FALSE?

(A) The particle is east of the origin at $t = 0$.
(B) The particle is at rest at $t = 0$.
(C) The particle's velocity is constant.
(D) The particle's acceleration is constant.
(E) The particle will never be west of position $x = 0$.

7. A mass hangs from two ropes at unequal angles, as shown above. Which of the following makes correct comparisons of the horizontal and vertical components of the tension in each rope?

	Horizontal Tension	Vertical Tension
(A)	greater in rope B	greater in rope B
(B)	equal in both ropes	greater in rope A
(C)	greater in rope A	greater in rope A
(D)	equal in both ropes	equal in both ropes
(E)	greater in rope B	equal in both ropes

8. The force of air resistance F on a mass is found to obey the equation $F = bv^2$, where v is the speed of the mass, for the range of speeds investigated in an experiment. A graph of F vs. v^2 is shown above. What is the value of b?

(A) 0.83 kg/m
(B) 1.7 kg/m
(C) 3.0 kg/m
(D) 5.0 kg/m
(E) 1.0 kg/m

9. A box sits on an inclined plane without sliding. As the angle of the plane (measured from the horizontal) increases, the normal force

(A) increases linearly
(B) decreases linearly
(C) does not change
(D) decreases nonlinearly
(E) increases nonlinearly

10. Which of the following conditions are necessary for an object to be in static equilibrium?

I. The vector sum of all torques on the object must equal zero.
II. The vector sum of all forces on the object must equal zero.
III. The sum of the object's potential and kinetic energies must be zero.

(A) I only
(B) II only
(C) III only
(D) I and II only
(E) I, II, and III

GO ON TO THE NEXT PAGE

Push = 50 N

35

11. A student pushes a big 16-kg box across the floor at constant speed. He pushes with a force of 50 N angled 35° from the horizontal, as shown in the diagram above. If the student pulls rather than pushes the box at the same angle, while maintaining a constant speed, what will happen to the force of friction?

(A) It must increase.
(B) It must decrease.
(C) It must remain the same.
(D) It will increase only if the speed is greater than 3.1 m/s.
(E) It will increase only if the speed is less than 3.1 m/s.

12. Consider a system consisting only of the Earth and a bowling ball, which moves upward in a parabola above Earth's surface. The downward force of Earth's gravity on the ball, and the upward force of the ball's gravity on the Earth, form a Newton's third law force pair. Which of the following statements about the ball is correct?

(A) The ball must be in equilibrium since the upward forces must cancel downward forces.
(B) The ball accelerates toward the Earth because the force of gravity on the ball is greater than the force of the ball on the Earth.
(C) The ball accelerates toward the Earth because the force of gravity on the ball is the only force acting on the ball.
(D) The ball accelerates away from Earth because the force causing the ball to move upward is greater than the force of gravity on the ball.
(E) The ball accelerates away from Earth because the force causing the ball to move upward plus the force of the ball on the Earth are together greater than the force of gravity on the ball.

13. A mass m is attached to a mass $3m$ by a rigid bar of negligible mass and length L. Initially, the smaller mass is located directly above the larger mass, as shown above. How much work is necessary to flip the rod 180° so that the larger mass is directly above the smaller mass?

(A) $4mgL$
(B) $2mgL$
(C) mgL
(D) $4\pi mgL$
(E) $2\pi mgL$

14. A ball rolls horizontally with speed v off of a table a height h above the ground. Just before the ball hits the ground, what is its speed?

(A) $\sqrt{2gh}$

(B) $v\sqrt{2gh}$

(C) $\sqrt{v^2 + 2gh}$

(D) v

(E) $v + \sqrt{2gh}$

GO ON TO THE NEXT PAGE

15. A pendulum is launched into simple harmonic motion in two different ways, as shown above, from a point that is a height h above its lowest point. During both launches, the bob is given an initial speed of 3.0 m/s. On the first launch, the initial velocity of the bob is directed upward along the pendulum's path, and on the second launch it is directed downward along the pendulum's path. Which launch will cause the pendulum to swing with the larger amplitude?

(A) the first launch
(B) the second launch
(C) Both launches produce the same amplitude.
(D) The answer depends on the initial height h.
(E) The answer depends on the length of the supporting rope.

16. The mass M is moving to the right with velocity v_0 at position $x = x_0$. Neglect friction. The spring has force constant k. What is the total mechanical energy of the block at this position?

(A) $\frac{1}{2}mv_0^2$
(B) $\frac{1}{2}mv_0^2 + \frac{1}{2}kx_0^2$
(C) $\frac{1}{2}mv_0^2 + \frac{1}{2}kx_0^2 + mgx_0$
(D) $mgx_0 + \frac{1}{2}mv_0^2$
(E) $mgx_0 + \frac{1}{2}kx_0^2$

17. A sphere, a cube, and a cylinder, all of equal mass, are released from rest from the top of a short incline. The surface of the incline is extremely slick, so much so that the objects do not rotate when released, but rather slide with negligible friction. Which reaches the base of the incline first?

(A) the sphere
(B) the cube
(C) the cylinder
(D) All reach the base at the same time.
(E) The answer depends on the relative sizes of the objects.

18. Block B is at rest on a smooth tabletop. It is attached to a long spring, which is in turn anchored to the wall. Block A slides toward and collides with block B. Consider two possible collisions:

Collision I: Block A bounces back off of block B.
Collision II: Block A sticks to block B.

Which of the following is correct about the speed of block B immediately after the collision?

(A) It is faster in case II than in case I ONLY if block B is heavier.
(B) It is faster in case I than in case II ONLY if block B is heavier.
(C) It is faster in case II than in case I regardless of the mass of each block.
(D) It is faster in case I than in case II regardless of the mass of each block.
(E) It is the same in either case regardless of the mass of each block.

GO ON TO THE NEXT PAGE

6.0 m/s

bird

ball .50 kg

30 m/s

19. A 0.30-kg bird is flying from right to left at 30 m/s. The bird collides with and sticks to a 0.50-kg ball that is moving straight up with speed 6.0 m/s. What is the magnitude of the momentum of the ball/bird combination immediately after collision?

(A) 12.0 N·s
(B) 9.5 N·s
(C) 9.0 N·s
(D) 6.0 N·s
(E) 3.0 N·s

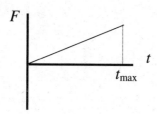

F

t

t_{max}

20. The force F on a mass is shown above as a function of time t. Which of the following methods can be used to determine the impulse experienced by the mass?

  I. multiplying the average force by t_{max}
  II. calculating the area under the line on the graph

  III. taking the integral $\int_{0}^{t_{max}} F \cdot dt$

    (A) II only
    (B) III only
    (C) II and III only
    (D) I and II only
    (E) I, II, and III

21. A projectile is launched on level ground in a parabolic path so that its range would normally be 500 m. When the projectile is at the peak of its flight, the projectile breaks into two pieces of equal mass. One of these pieces falls straight down, with no further horizontal motion. How far away from the launch point does the other piece land?

(A) 250 m
(B) 375 m
(C) 500 m
(D) 750 m
(E) 1000 m

Questions 22 and 23:

$\dfrac{2L}{3}$

m

L

A rigid rod of length L and mass M is floating at rest in space far from a gravitational field. A small blob of putty of mass $m < M$ is moving to the right, as shown above. The putty hits and sticks to the rod a distance $2L/3$ from the top end.

22. How will the rod/putty contraption move after the collision?

(A) The contraption will have no translational motion, but will rotate about the rod's center of mass.
(B) The contraption will have no translational motion, but will rotate about the center of mass of the rod and putty combined.
(C) The contraption will move to the right and rotate about the position of the putty.
(D) The contraption will move to the right and rotate about the center of mass of the rod and putty combined.
(E) The contraption will move to the right and rotate about the rod's center of mass.

GO ON TO THE NEXT PAGE

23. What quantities are conserved in this collision?

    (A) linear and angular momentum, but not kinetic energy
    (B) linear momentum only
    (C) angular momentum only
    (D) linear and angular momentum, and linear but not rotational kinetic energy
    (E) linear and angular momentum, and linear and rotational kinetic energy

24. A car rounds a banked curve of uniform radius. Three forces act on the car: a friction force between the tires and the road, the normal force from the road, and the weight of the car. Which provides the centripetal force which keeps the car in circular motion?

    (A) the friction force alone
    (B) the normal force alone
    (C) the weight alone
    (D) a combination of the normal force and the friction force
    (E) a combination of the friction force and the weight

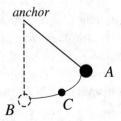

25. A ball of mass m anchored to a string swings back and forth to a maximum position A, as shown above. Point C is partway back to the vertical position. What is the direction of the mass's acceleration at point C?

    (A) along the mass's path toward point B
    (B) toward the anchor
    (C) away from the anchor
    (D) between a line toward the anchor and a line along the mass's path
    (E) along the mass's path toward point A

26. In a carnival ride, people of mass m are whirled in a horizontal circle by a floorless cylindrical room of radius r, as shown in the diagram above. If the coefficient of friction between the people and the tube surface is μ, what minimum speed is necessary to keep the people from sliding down the walls?

    (A) $\sqrt{\mu r g}$

    (B) $\sqrt{\dfrac{rg}{\mu}}$

    (C) $\sqrt{\dfrac{\mu}{rg}}$

    (D) $\sqrt{\dfrac{1}{\mu rg}}$

    (E) $\sqrt{\mu mg}$

GO ON TO THE NEXT PAGE

Questions 27 and 28:

The uniform, rigid rod of mass *m*, length *L*, and rotational inertia *I* shown above is pivoted at its left-hand end. The rod is released from rest from a horizontal position.

27. What is the linear acceleration of the rod's center of mass the moment after the rod is released?

(A) $\dfrac{mgL^2}{2I}$

(B) $\dfrac{mgL^2}{4I}$

(C) $\dfrac{mgL^2}{I}$

(D) $\dfrac{mgL}{2I}$

(E) $\dfrac{2mgL^2}{I}$

28. What is the linear speed of the rod's center of mass when the mass passes through a vertical position?

(A) $\sqrt{\dfrac{mgL^3}{8I}}$

(B) $\sqrt{\dfrac{mg\pi L^3}{4I}}$

(C) $\sqrt{\dfrac{mg\pi L^3}{8I}}$

(D) $\sqrt{\dfrac{mgL^3}{4I}}$

(E) $\sqrt{\dfrac{mgL^3}{2I}}$

29. The 1.0-m-long nonuniform plank, shown above, has weight 1000 N. It is to be supported by two rods, *A* and *B*, as shown above. The center of mass of the plank is 30 cm from the right edge. Each support bears half the weight of the plank. If support *B* is 10 cm from the right-hand edge, how far from the left-hand edge should support *A* be?

(A) 0 cm
(B) 10 cm
(C) 30 cm
(D) 50 cm
(E) 70 cm

30. A mass *m* on a spring oscillates on a horizontal surface with period *T*. The total mechanical energy contained in this oscillation is *E*. Imagine that instead a new mass *4m* oscillates on the same spring with the same amplitude. What is the new period and total mechanical energy?

	Period	Total Mechanical Energy
(A)	*T*	*E*
(B)	2*T*	*E*
(C)	2*T*	2*E*
(D)	*T*	4*E*
(E)	2*T*	16*E*

GO ON TO THE NEXT PAGE

31. A mass m is attached to a horizontal spring of spring constant k. The spring oscillates in simple harmonic motion with amplitude A. What is the maximum speed of this simple harmonic oscillator?

    (A) $2\pi\sqrt{\dfrac{m}{k}}$

    (B) $2\pi A\sqrt{\dfrac{m}{k}}$

    (C) $2\pi A\sqrt{\dfrac{k}{m}}$

    (D) $A\sqrt{\dfrac{k}{m}}$

    (E) $A\sqrt{\dfrac{m}{k}}$

32. An empty bottle goes up and down on the surface of the ocean, obeying the position function $x = A\cos(\omega t)$. How much time does this bottle take to travel once from its lowest position to its highest position?

    (A) $\dfrac{2\pi}{\omega}$

    (B) $\dfrac{\pi}{\omega}$

    (C) $\dfrac{4\pi}{\omega}$

    (D) $\dfrac{\pi}{2\omega}$

    (E) $\dfrac{\pi}{4\omega}$

33. The Space Shuttle orbits 300 km above the Earth's surface; the Earth's radius is 6400 km. What is the acceleration due to Earth's gravity experienced by the Space Shuttle?

    (A) 4.9 m/s^2
    (B) 8.9 m/s^2
    (C) 9.8 m/s^2
    (D) 10.8 m/s^2
    (E) zero

34. An artificial satellite orbits Earth just above the atmosphere in a circle with constant speed. A small meteor collides with the satellite at point P in its orbit, increasing its speed by 1%, but not changing the instantaneous direction of the satellite's velocity. Which of the following describes the satellite's new orbit?

    (A) The satellite now orbits in an ellipse, with P as the farthest approach to Earth.
    (B) The satellite now orbits in an ellipse, with P as the closest approach to Earth.
    (C) The satellite now orbits in a circle of larger radius.
    (D) The satellite now orbits in a circle of smaller radius.
    (E) The satellite cannot maintain an orbit, so it flies off into space.

35. Mercury orbits the sun in about one-fifth of an Earth year. If 1 AU is defined as the distance from the Earth to the sun, what is the approximate distance between Mercury and the sun?

    (A) (1/25) AU
    (B) (1/9) AU
    (C) (1/5) AU
    (D) (1/3) AU
    (E) (1/2) AU

STOP. End of Physics C—Mechanics Practice Exam 1—Multiple-Choice Questions

Physics C—Mechanics Practice Exam 1—Free-Response Questions

Time: 45 minutes. You may refer to the constants sheet and the equation, both of which are found in the appendix. You may use a calculator.

CM 1

Two 5-kg masses are connected by a light string over two massless, frictionless pulleys. Each block sits on a frictionless inclined plane, as shown above. The blocks are released from rest.

(a) Determine the magnitude of the acceleration of the blocks.

Now assume that the 30° incline provides a resistive force which depends on speed v. This resistive force causes the entire system's acceleration to be given by the expression

$$a = 1.8 - 0.03v$$

where a speed v in m/s gives an acceleration in m/s^2. The blocks are again released from rest.

(b) i. On the axes below, sketch a graph of the speed of the 5-kg block as a function of time. Label important values, including any asymptotes and intercepts.

   ii. Explain how the expression for acceleration leads to the graph you drew.

(c) Explain how to figure out the terminal speed of the 5-kg block.

(d) The terminal speed is 60 m/s—that's a typical speed in automobile racing. Explain briefly why this result is physically reasonable, even though the blocks are on a track in a physics laboratory.

GO ON TO THE NEXT PAGE

CM 2

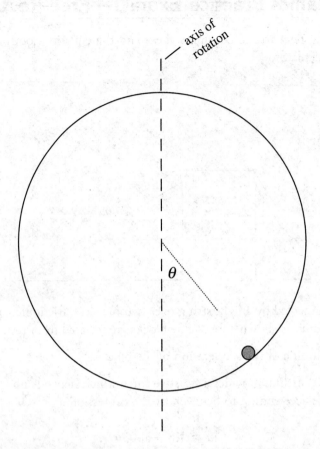

A hollow glass sphere of radius 8.0 cm rotates about a vertical diameter with frequency 5 revolutions per second. A small wooden ball of mass 2.0 g rotates inside the sphere, as shown in the diagram above.

(a) Draw a free-body diagram indicating the forces acting on the wooden ball when it is at the position shown in the picture above.
(b) Calculate the angle θ, shown in the diagram above, to which the ball rises.
(c) Calculate the linear speed of the wooden ball as it rotates.
(d) The wooden ball is replaced with a steel ball of mass 20 g. Describe how the angle θ to which the ball rises will be affected. Justify your answer.

GO ON TO THE NEXT PAGE

CM 3

A heavy ball of mass m is attached to a light but rigid rod of length L. The rod is pivoted at the top and is free to rotate in a circle in the plane of the page, as shown above.

(a) The mass oscillates to a maximum angle θ. On the picture of the mass m below, draw a vector representing the direction of the NET force on the mass while it is at angle θ. Justify your choice of direction.

●

(b) Is the magnitude of the net force at the maximum displacement equal to $mg \sin\theta$ or $mg \cos\theta$? Choose one and justify your choice.

(c) Derive an expression for the ball's potential energy U as a function of the angle θ. Assume that a negative angle represents displacement from the vertical in the clockwise direction.

(d) On the axes below, sketch a graph of the mass's potential energy U as a function of the angle θ for angles between $-90°$ and $+360°$. Label maximum and minimum values on the vertical axis.

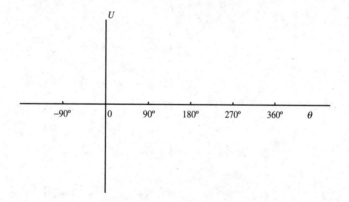

(e) The pendulum is considered a classic example of simple harmonic motion when it undergoes small-amplitude oscillation. With specific reference to the graph you made in part (d), explain why the assumption of simple harmonic motion is valid.

STOP. End of Physics C—Mechanics Practice Exam 1—Free-Response Questions

Physics C—Electricity and Magnetism Practice Exam 1—Multiple-Choice Questions

ANSWER SHEET

1 (A) (B) (C) (D) (E)   13 (A) (B) (C) (D) (E)   25 (A) (B) (C) (D) (E)
2 (A) (B) (C) (D) (E)   14 (A) (B) (C) (D) (E)   26 (A) (B) (C) (D) (E)
3 (A) (B) (C) (D) (E)   15 (A) (B) (C) (D) (E)   27 (A) (B) (C) (D) (E)
4 (A) (B) (C) (D) (E)   16 (A) (B) (C) (D) (E)   28 (A) (B) (C) (D) (E)
5 (A) (B) (C) (D) (E)   17 (A) (B) (C) (D) (E)   29 (A) (B) (C) (D) (E)
6 (A) (B) (C) (D) (E)   18 (A) (B) (C) (D) (E)   30 (A) (B) (C) (D) (E)
7 (A) (B) (C) (D) (E)   19 (A) (B) (C) (D) (E)   31 (A) (B) (C) (D) (E)
8 (A) (B) (C) (D) (E)   20 (A) (B) (C) (D) (E)   32 (A) (B) (C) (D) (E)
9 (A) (B) (C) (D) (E)   21 (A) (B) (C) (D) (E)   33 (A) (B) (C) (D) (E)
10 (A) (B) (C) (D) (E)   22 (A) (B) (C) (D) (E)   34 (A) (B) (C) (D) (E)
11 (A) (B) (C) (D) (E)   23 (A) (B) (C) (D) (E)   35 (A) (B) (C) (D) (E)
12 (A) (B) (C) (D) (E)   24 (A) (B) (C) (D) (E)

Physics C—Electricity and Magnetism Practice Exam 1— Multiple-Choice Questions

Time: 45 minutes. You may refer to the constants sheet and the equation sheet, both of which are found in the appendix. You may use a calculator.

1. Experimenter A uses a very small test charge q_o, and experimenter B uses a test charge $2q_o$ to measure an electric field produced by two parallel plates. A finds a field that is

    (A) greater than the field found by B
    (B) the same as the field found by B
    (C) less than the field found by B
    (D) either greater or less than the field found by B, depending on the accelerations of the test charges
    (E) either greater or less than the field found by B, depending on the masses of the test charges

2. A solid conducting sphere has radius R and carries positive charge Q. Which of the following graphs represents the electric field E as a function of the distance r from the center of the sphere?

    (A)

    (B)

    (C)

    (D)

    (E)

3. An electron moving at constant velocity enters the region between two charged plates, as shown above. Which of the paths above correctly shows the electron's trajectory after leaving the region between the charged plates?

    (A) A
    (B) B
    (C) C
    (D) D
    (E) E

4. Two isolated particles, A and B, are 4 m apart. Particle A has a net charge of $2Q$, and B has a net charge of Q. The ratio of the magnitude of the electric force on A to that on B is

    (A) 4:1
    (B) 2:1
    (C) 1:1
    (D) 1:2
    (E) 1:4

GO ON TO THE NEXT PAGE

5. A uniform electric field points to the left. A small metal ball charged to -2 mC hangs at a $30°$ angle from a string of negligible mass, as shown above. The tension in the string is measured to be 0.1 N. What is the magnitude of the electric field? (sin $30° = 0.50$; cos $30° = 0.87$; tan $30° = 0.58$.)

(A) 25 N/C
(B) 50 N/C
(C) 2500 N/C
(D) 5000 N/C
(E) 10,000 N/C

6. A thin semicircular conductor of radius R holds charge $+Q$. What is the magnitude and direction of the electric field at the center of the circle?

(A) $\dfrac{kQ}{R^2}$ ↑

(B) $\dfrac{kQ}{R^2}$ ↓

(C) $\dfrac{kQ}{\pi R^2}$ ↑

(D) $\dfrac{kQ}{\pi R^2}$ ↓

(E) The electric field is zero at the center.

7. Above an infinitely large plane carrying charge density σ, the electric field points up and is equal to $\sigma/2\varepsilon_o$. What is the magnitude and direction of the electric field below the plane?

(A) $\sigma/2\varepsilon_o$, down
(B) $\sigma/2\varepsilon_o$, up
(C) σ/ε_o, down
(D) σ/ε_o, up
(E) zero

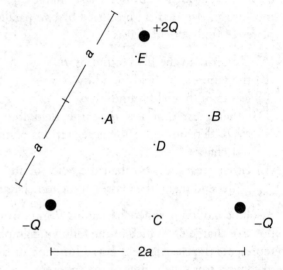

8. Three charges are arranged in an equilateral triangle, as shown above. At which of these points is the electric potential smallest?

(A) A
(B) B
(C) C
(D) D
(E) E

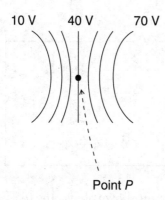

Point *P*

9. The diagram shows a set of equipotential surfaces. At point *P*, what is the direction of the electric field?

(A) left
(B) right
(C) up the page
(D) down the page
(E) either left or right, which one cannot be determined

10. A metal sphere carries charge *Q*; a nonconducting sphere of equal size carries the same charge *Q*, uniformly distributed throughout the sphere. These spheres are isolated from each other. Consider the electric field at the center of the spheres, within the spheres, and outside the spheres. Which of these electric fields will be the same for both spheres, and which will be different?

	At the Center	Elsewhere Within the Sphere	Outside the Sphere
(A)	Same	Same	Same
(B)	Same	Same	Different
(C)	Same	Different	Same
(D)	Different	Different	Same
(E)	Different	Different	Different

11. Under what conditions is the net electric flux through a closed surface proportional to the enclosed charge?

(A) under any conditions
(B) only when the enclosed charge is symmetrically distributed
(C) only when all nearby charges are symmetrically distributed
(D) only when there are no charges outside the surface
(E) only when enclosed charges can be considered to be point charges

radius *r*

axis

12. A hollow metal ring of radius *r* carries charge *q*. Consider an axis straight through the center of the ring. At what point(s) along this axis is/are the electric field equal to zero?

(A) only at the center of the ring
(B) only at the center of the ring, and a very long distance away
(C) only a very long distance away
(D) only at the center of the ring, a distance *r* away from the center, and a very long distance away
(E) everywhere along this axis

13. A parallel plate capacitor consists of identical rectangular plates of dimensions *a* × *b*, separated by a distance *c*. To cut the capacitance of this capacitor in half, which of these quantities should be doubled?

(A) *a*
(B) *b*
(C) *c*
(D) *ab*
(E) *abc*

14. Two identical capacitors are hooked in parallel to an external circuit. Which of the following quantities must be the same for both capacitors?

I. the charge stored on the capacitor
II. the voltage across the capacitor
III. the capacitance of the capacitor
    (A) I only
    (B) II only
    (C) II and III only
    (D) I and III only
    (E) I, II, and III

GO ON TO THE NEXT PAGE

15. A 2-µF capacitor is connected directly to a battery. When the capacitor is fully charged, it stores 600 µC of charge. An experimenter replaces the 2-µF capacitor with three 18-µF capacitors in series connected to the same battery. Once the capacitors are fully charged, what charge is stored on each capacitor?

(A) 100 µC
(B) 200 µC
(C) 600 µC
(D) 1200 µC
(E) 1800 µC

16. A spherical conductor carries a net charge. How is this charge distributed on the sphere?

(A) The charge is evenly distributed on the surface.
(B) The charge resides on the surface only; the distribution of charge on the surface depends on what other charged objects are near the sphere.
(C) The charge moves continually within the sphere.
(D) The charge is distributed uniformly throughout the sphere.
(E) The charge resides within the sphere; the distribution of charge within the sphere depends on what other charged objects are near the sphere.

17. Three resistors are connected to a battery as shown in the diagram above. The switch is initially open. When the switch is closed, what happens to the total voltage, current, and resistance in the circuit?

	Voltage	Current	Resistance
(A)	increases	increases	increases
(B)	does not change	does not change	does not change
(C)	does not change	decreases	increases
(D)	does not change	increases	decreases
(E)	decreases	decreases	decreases

18. In the circuit shown above, the 0.5-F capacitor is initially uncharged. The switch is closed at time $t = 0$. What is the time constant (the time for the capacitor to charge to 63% of its maximum charge) for the charging of this capacitor?

(A) 5 s
(B) 10 s
(C) 20 s
(D) 30 s
(E) 40 s

19. In the circuit shown above, what is the current through the 3 Ω resistor?

(A) 0 A
(B) 0.5 A
(C) 1.0 A
(D) 1.5 A
(E) 2.0 A

20. A lightbulb rated at 100 W is twice as bright as a bulb rated at 50 W when both are connected in parallel directly to a 100-V source. Now imagine that these bulbs are instead connected in series with each other. Which is brighter, and by how much?

(A) The bulbs have the same brightness.
(B) The 100-W bulb is twice as bright.
(C) The 50-W bulb is twice as bright.
(D) The 100-W bulb is four times as bright.
(E) The 50-W bulb is four times as bright.

GO ON TO THE NEXT PAGE

21. A uniform magnetic field *B* is directed into the page. An electron enters this field with initial velocity *v* to the right. Which of the following best describes the path of the electron while it is still within the magnetic field?

(A) It moves in a straight line.
(B) It bends upward in a parabolic path.
(C) It bends downward in a parabolic path.
(D) It bends upward in a circular path.
(E) It bends downward in a circular path.

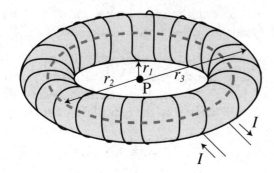

22. Wire is wound around an insulated circular donut, as shown above. A current *I* flows in the wire in the direction indicated by the arrows. The inner, average, and outer radii of the donut are indicated by r_1, r_2, and r_3, respectively. What is the magnitude and direction of the magnetic field at point *P*, the center of the donut?

(A) zero

(B) $\frac{\mu_o I}{2r_1}$

(C) $\frac{\mu_o I}{2r_2}$

(D) $\frac{\mu_o I}{2r_3}$

(E) $\frac{\mu_o I}{2\pi r_2}$

23. A wire carries a current toward the top of the page. An electron is located to the right of the wire, as shown above. In which direction should the electron be moving if it is to experience a magnetic force toward the wire?

(A) into the page
(B) out of the page
(C) toward the bottom of the page
(D) toward the top of the page
(E) to the right

24. Which of the following statements about electric and magnetic fields is FALSE?

(A) A charge moving along the direction of an electric field will experience a force, but a charge moving along the direction of a magnetic field will not experience a force.
(B) All charges experience a force in an electric field, but only moving charges can experience a force in a magnetic field.
(C) A positive charge moves in the direction of an electric field; a positive charge moves perpendicular to a magnetic field.
(D) All moving charges experience a force parallel to an electric field and perpendicular to a magnetic field.
(E) A negative charge experiences a force opposite the direction of an electric field; a negative charge experiences a force perpendicular to a magnetic field.

25. Which of these quantities decreases as the inverse square of distance for distances far from the objects producing the fields?

(A) the electric field produced by a finite-length charged rod
(B) the electric field produced by an infinitely long charged cylinder
(C) the electric field produced by an infinite plane of charge
(D) the magnetic field produced by an infinitely long, straight current-carrying wire
(E) the magnetic field produced by a wire curled around a torus

GO ON TO THE NEXT PAGE

26. A proton enters a solenoid. Upon entry, the proton is moving in a straight line along the axis of the solenoid. Which of the following is a correct description of the proton's motion within the solenoid?

    (A) The proton will be bent in a parabolic path.
    (B) The proton will be bent in a circular path.
    (C) The proton will continue in its straight path at constant velocity.
    (D) The proton will continue in its straight path and slow down.
    (E) The proton will continue in its straight path and speed up.

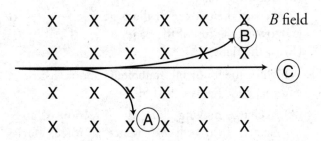

27. A uniform magnetic field points into the page. Three subatomic particles are shot into the field from the left-hand side of the page. All have the same initial speed and direction. These particles take paths A, B, and C, as labeled in the diagram above. Which of the following is a possible identity for each particle?

	$\underline{A}$	$\underline{B}$	$\underline{C}$
(A)	antiproton	proton	electron
(B)	antiproton	positron	neutron
(C)	proton	electron	neutron
(D)	positron	antiproton	neutron
(E)	electron	proton	neutron

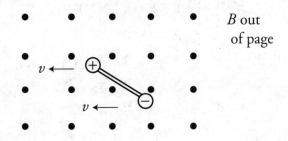

28. The electric dipole shown above consists of equal-magnitude charges and has an initial leftward velocity v in a uniform magnetic field pointing out of the page, as shown above. The dipole experiences

    (A) a clockwise net torque, and a net force to the left
    (B) a counterclockwise net torque, and a net force to the left
    (C) no net torque, and a net force to the left
    (D) a counterclockwise net torque, and no net force
    (E) a clockwise net torque, and no net force

29. A beam of electrons has speed 10^7 m/s. It is desired to use the magnetic field of the Earth, 5×10^{-5} T, to bend the electron beam into a circle. What will be the radius of this circle?

    (A) 1 nm
    (B) 1 μm
    (C) 1 mm
    (D) 1 m
    (E) 1 km

30. A very small element of wire of length dL carries a current I. What is the direction of the magnetic field produced by this current element at point P, shown above?

    (A) to the right
    (B) toward the top of the page
    (C) into the page
    (D) out of the page
    (E) There is no magnetic field produced at point P by this element.

GO ON TO THE NEXT PAGE

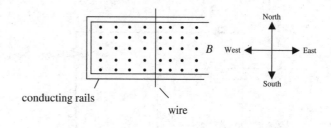

31. A loop of wire surrounds a hole in a table, as shown above. A bar magnet is dropped, north end down, from far above the table through the hole. Let the positive direction of current be defined as counterclockwise as viewed from above. Which of the following graphs best represents the induced current I in the loop?

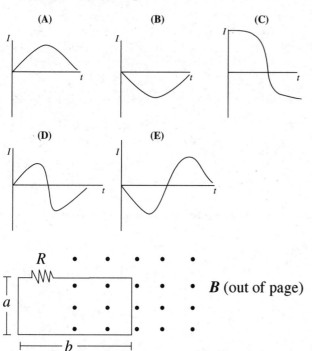

33. A conducting wire sits on smooth metal rails, as shown above. A variable magnetic field points out of the page. The strength of this magnetic field is increased linearly from zero. Immediately after the field starts to increase, what will be the direction of the current in the wire and the direction of the wire's motion?

	Current in the Wire	Motion of the Wire
(A)	north	no motion
(B)	north	east
(C)	north	west
(D)	south	west
(E)	south	east

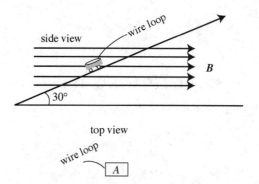

side view

top view

34. A uniform magnetic field B points parallel to the ground. A toy car is sliding down a frictionless plane inclined at 30°. A loop of wire of resistance R and cross-sectional area A lies in the flat plane of the car's body, as shown above. What is the magnetic flux through the wire loop?

(A) zero
(B) $BA \cos 30°$
(C) $BA \cos 60°$
(D) BA
(E) $(BA \cos 60°)/R$

32. A rectangular loop of wire has dimensions $a \times b$ and includes a resistor R. This loop is pulled with speed v from a region of no magnetic field into a uniform magnetic field B pointing through the loop, as shown above. What is the magnitude and direction of the current through the resistor?

(A) Bav/R, left-to-right
(B) Bbv/R, left-to-right
(C) Bav/R, right-to-left
(D) Bbv/R, right-to-left
(E) Bba/R, right-to-left

GO ON TO THE NEXT PAGE

35. If the two equal resistors R_1 and R_2 are connected in parallel to a 10-V battery with no other circuit components, the current provided by the battery is I. In the circuit shown above, an inductor of inductance L is included in series with R_2. What is the current through R_2 after the circuit has been connected for a long time?

(A) zero

(B) $(1/4)\, I$

(C) $(1/2)\, I$

(D) I

(E) $I\dfrac{R_1 + R_2}{LR_2}$

STOP. End of Physics C—Electricity and Magnetism Practice Exam 1—Multiple-Choice Questions

Physics C—Electricity and Magnetism Practice Exam 1—Free-Response Questions

Time: 45 minutes. You may refer to the constants sheet and the equation sheet, both of which are found in the appendix. You may use a calculator.

E&M 1

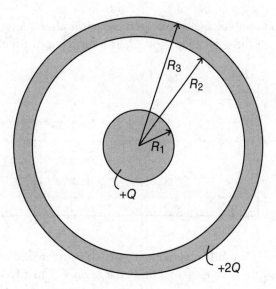

A metal sphere of radius R_1 carries charge $+Q$. A concentric spherical metal shell, of inner radius R_2 and outer radius R_3, carries charge $+2Q$.

(a) Let r represent the distance from the center of the spheres. Calculate the electric field as a function of r in each of the following four regions:

1. between $r = 0$ and $r = R_1$
2. between $r = R_1$ and $r = R_2$
3. between $r = R_2$ and $r = R_3$
4. between $r = R_3$ and $r = 0$

(b) How much charge is on each surface of the outer spherical shell? Justify your answer.
(c) Determine the electric potential of the outer spherical shell.
(d) Determine the electric potential of the inner metal sphere.

GO ON TO THE NEXT PAGE

E&M 2

A 1-MΩ resistor is connected to the network of capacitors shown above. The circuit is hooked to a 10-V battery. The capacitors are initially uncharged. The battery is connected, and the switch is closed at time $t = 0$.

(a) Determine the equivalent capacitance of C_1, C_2, and C_3.

(b) Determine the charge on and voltage across each capacitor after a long time has elapsed.

(c) On the axes below, sketch the total charge on C_3 as a function of time.

(d) After the capacitors have been fully charged, the switch is opened, disconnecting C_1 and C_2 from the circuit. What happens to the voltage across and charge on C_3? Justify your answer.

GO ON TO THE NEXT PAGE

E&M 3

In the laboratory, far from the influence of other magnetic fields, the Earth's magnetic field has a value of 5.00×10^{-5} T. A compass in this lab reads due north when pointing along the direction of Earth's magnetic field.

A long, straight current-carrying wire is brought close to the compass, deflecting the compass to the position shown above, 48° west of north.

(a) Describe one possible orientation of the wire and the current it carries that would produce the deflection shown.

(b) Calculate the magnitude B_{wire} of the magnetic field produced by the wire that would cause the deflection shown.

(c) The distance d from the wire to the compass is varied, while the current in the wire is kept constant; a graph of B_{wire} vs. d is produced. On the axes below, sketch the shape of this graph.

(d) It is desired to adjust this plot so that the graph becomes a straight line. The vertical axis is to remain B_{wire}, the magnetic field produced by the wire. How could the quantity graphed on the horizontal axis be adjusted to produce a straight-line graph? Justify your answer.

(e) The current carried by the wire is 500 mA. Determine the slope of the line on the graph suggested in part (d).

STOP. End of Physics C—Electricity and Magnetism Practice Exam 1—Free-Response Questions

Physics C—Mechanics Practice Exam 1—Multiple-Choice Solutions

1. **D**—A projectile has its maximum range when it is shot at an angle of 45° relative to the ground. The cannon's initial velocity relative to the ground in this problem is given by the vector sum of the man's 5 m/s forward motion and the cannon's 50 m/s muzzle velocity. To get a resultant velocity of 45°, the man must shoot the cannon at only a slightly higher angle, as shown in the diagram below.

2. **C**—The car stays on the plane, and slows down as it goes up the plane. Thus, the net acceleration is in the direction down the plane, which has both a nonzero horizontal and vertical component. The car is not in free fall, so its vertical acceleration is less than g.

3. **E**—Acceleration is the slope of the v–t graph. Because acceleration increases, the slope of the v–t graph must get steeper, eliminating choices A and B. The bike slows down, so the speed must get closer to zero as time goes on, eliminating choices C and D.

4. **C**—The cart's acceleration is $g\sin\theta$, down the plane, the ball's acceleration is g, straight down. (So the magnitudes of acceleration are different and choice D is wrong.) The component of the ball's acceleration along an axis parallel to the plane is also $g\sin\theta$, equal to the ball's acceleration component.

5. **B**—The area under a jerk–time graph is the quantity jdt. The derivative

$$j = \frac{da}{dt}$$

can be interpreted as a change in acceleration over a time interval,

$$j = \frac{\Delta a}{\Delta t}.$$

Solving algebraically, $j\Delta t$ is Δa, meaning the change in acceleration.

6. **B**—At $t = 0$, $x = +5$ m, so the particle is east of the origin to start with. The velocity is given by the derivative of the position function, $v(t) = 3$ m/s. This is a constant velocity; the acceleration is thus zero (and constant), but at $t = 0$ the velocity is also 3 m/s, so choice B is false.

7. **B**—Consider the horizontal and vertical forces separately. The only horizontal forces are the horizontal components of the tensions. Because the block is in equilibrium, these horizontal tensions must be *equal*, meaning only choices B and D can be right. But the ropes can't have equal horizontal AND vertical tensions, otherwise they'd hang at equal angles. So D can't be the right choice, and B must be right.

8. **B**—The equation $F = bv^2$ is of the form $y = mx$, the equation of a line. Here F is the vertical axis, v^2 is the horizontal axis, so b is the slope of the line. Looking at the graph, the slope is 5.0 N/3.0 m²/s² = 1.7 kg/m.

9. **D**—Because no forces act perpendicular to the incline except for the normal force and the perpendicular component of weight, and there is no acceleration perpendicular to the incline, the normal force is equal to the perpendicular component of weight, which is $mg\cos\theta$. As the angle increases, the cosine of the angle decreases. This decrease is nonlinear because a graph of F_N vs. θ would show a curve, not a line.

10. **D**—In equilibrium, the net force and the net torque must both be zero. *Static* equilibrium means the object is stationary, so kinetic energy must be zero. However, potential energy can take on any value—a sign suspended above a roadway is in static equilibrium, yet has potential energy relative to Earth's surface.

11. **B**—The friction force is equal to the coefficient of friction times the normal force. The coefficient of friction is a property of the surfaces in contact, and thus will not change here. However, the normal force decreases when the cart is pulled rather than pushed—the surface must apply more force to the box when there is a downward component to the applied force than when there is an upward component. Speed is irrelevant because equilibrium in the vertical direction is maintained regardless.

12. **C**—The ball accelerates *toward* the Earth because, although it is moving upward, it must be slowing down. The only force acting on the ball is Earth's gravity. Yes, the ball exerts a force on the Earth, but that force acts on the Earth, not the ball. According to Newton's third law, force pairs always act on different objects, and thus can never cancel.

13. **B**—The work done on an object by gravity is independent of the path taken by the object and is equal to the object's weight times its vertical displacement. Gravity must do $3mgL$ of work to raise the large mass, but must do $mg(-L)$ of work to lower the small mass. The net work done is thus $2mgL$.

14. **C**—Use conservation of energy. Position 1 will be the top of the table; position 2 will be the ground. $PE_1 + KE_1 = PE_2 + KE_2$. Take the PE at the ground to be zero. Then $\frac{1}{2}mv_2^2 = \frac{1}{2}mv_1^2 + mgh$. The ms cancel. Solving for v_2, you get choice C. (Choice E is wrong because it's illegal algebra to take a squared term out of a square root when it is added to another term.)

15. **C**—Consider the conservation of energy. At the launch point, the potential energy is the same regardless of launch direction. The kinetic energy is also the same because KE depends on speed alone and not direction. So, both balls have the same amount of kinetic energy to convert to potential energy, bringing the ball to the same height in every cycle.

16. **B**—Total mechanical energy is defined as kinetic energy plus potential energy. The KE here is $\frac{1}{2}mv_0^2$. The potential energy is provided entirely by the spring—gravitational potential energy requires a *vertical* displacement, which doesn't occur here. The PE of the spring is $\frac{1}{2}kx_0^2$.

17. **D**—When an object rotates, some of its potential energy is converted to rotational rather than linear kinetic energy, and thus it moves more slowly than a non-rotating object when it reaches the bottom of the plane. However, here none of the objects rotate! The acceleration does not depend on mass or size.

18. **D**—Momentum must be conserved in the collision. If block *A* bounces, it changes its momentum by a larger amount than if it sticks. This means that block *B* picks up more momentum (and thus more speed) when block *A* bounces. The mass of the blocks is irrelevant because the comparison here is just between bouncing and not bouncing. So *B* goes faster in collision I regardless of mass.

19. **B**—The momentum of the bird before collision is 9 N·s to the left; the momentum of the ball is initially 3 N·s up. The momentum after collision is the *vector* sum of these two initial momentums. With a calculator you would use the Pythagorean theorem to get 9.5 N·s; without a calculator you should just notice that the resultant vector must have magnitude less than 12 N·s (the algebraic sum) and more than 9 N·s.

20. **E**—Impulse is defined on the equation sheet as the integral of force with respect to time, so III is right. The meaning of this integral is to take the area under a *F* vs. *t* graph, so II is right. Because the force is increasing linearly, the average force will be halfway between zero and the maximum force, and the rectangle formed by this average force will have the same area as the triangle on the graph as shown, so I is right.

21. **D**—The center of mass of the projectile must maintain the projectile path and land 500 m from the launch point. The first half of the projectile fell straight down from the peak of its flight, which is halfway to the maximum range, or 250 m from the launch point. So the second half of equal mass must be 250 m beyond the center of mass upon hitting the ground, or 750 m from the launch point.

22. **D**—By conservation of linear momentum, there is momentum to the right before collision, so there must be momentum to the right after collision as well. A free-floating object rotates about its center of mass; because the putty is attached to the rod, the combination will rotate about its combined center of mass.

23. **A**—Linear and angular momentum are conserved in *all* collisions (though often angular momentum conservation is irrelevant). Kinetic energy, though, is only conserved in an elastic collision. Because the putty sticks to the rod, this collision cannot be elastic. Some of the kinetic energy must be dissipated as heat.

24. **D.**

plane of circular motion

The centripetal force must act toward the center of the car's circular path. This direction is NOT down the plane, but rather is purely horizontal. The friction force acts down the plane and thus has a horizontal component; the normal force acts perpendicular to the plane and has a horizontal component. So BOTH F_N and F_f contribute to the centripetal force.

25. **D**—The mass's acceleration has two components here. Some acceleration must be centripetal (i.e., toward the anchor) because the mass's path is circular. But the mass is also speeding up, so it must have a tangential component of acceleration toward point *B*. The vector sum of these two components must be in between the anchor and point *B*.

26. **B**—The free-body diagram for a person includes F_N toward the center of the circle, mg down, and the force of friction up:

Because the person is not sliding down, $mg = F_f$. And because the motion of the person is circular, the normal force is a centripetal force, so $F_N = mv^2/r$. The force of friction by definition is μF_N. Combining these equations, we have $mg = \mu mv^2/r$; solve for v to get answer choice B. Note: Without any calculation, you could recognize that only choices A and B have units of speed, so you would have had a good chance at getting the answer right just by guessing one of these two!

27. **B**—Use Newton's second law for rotation, $\tau_{net} = I\alpha$. The only torque about the pivot is the rod's weight, acting at the rod's center; this torque is thus $mgL/2$. So the angular acceleration, α, of the rod is $mgL/2I$. But the question asks for a linear acceleration, $a = r\alpha$, where r is the distance to the center of rotation. That distance here is $L/2$. So combining, you get $a = (L/2)(mgL/2I) = mgL^2/4I$.

28. **D**—We cannot use rotational kinematics here because the net torque, and thus the angular acceleration, is not constant. Use conservation of energy instead. The potential energy at the release point is $mg(L/2)$ ($L/2$ because the rod's center of mass is that far vertically above its lowest point). This potential energy is converted entirely into rotational kinetic energy $\frac{1}{2}I\omega^2$. The rod's angular velocity ω is equal to $v/(L/2)$, where v is the linear speed of the center of mass that we're solving for. Plugging in, you get $mgL/2 = \frac{1}{2}I(v^2/[L/2]^2)$. Solving for v, choice D emerges from the mathematics.

29. **D**—Choose any point at all as the fulcrum; say, the center of mass. Rod B supports 500 N, and is located 20 cm from the fulcrum, producing a total counterclockwise torque of 10,000 N·cm. Rod A also supports 500 N; call its distance from the fulcrum "x". So $10,000 = 500x$, and $x = 20$ cm. This means Rod A is located 20 cm left of the center of mass, or 50 cm from the left edge.

30. **B**—The period of a mass on a spring is

$$2\pi\sqrt{\frac{m}{k}}$$

with the mass under the square root. So when the mass is quadrupled, the period is only multiplied by two. The total mechanical energy is the sum of potential plus kinetic energy. At the greatest displacement from equilibrium (i.e., at the amplitude), the mass's speed is zero and all energy is potential; potential energy of a spring is $\frac{1}{2}kx^2$ and does not depend on mass. So, because the amplitude of oscillation remains the same, the total mechanical energy does not change.

31. **D**—The maximum potential energy of the mass is at the amplitude, and equal to $\frac{1}{2}kA^2$. This is entirely converted to kinetic energy at the equilibrium position, where the speed is maximum. So set $\frac{1}{2}kA^2 = \frac{1}{2}mv^2_{max}$. Solving for v_{max}, you get choice D. (Note: Only choices C and D have units of velocity! So guess between these if you have to!)

32. **B**—The bottle's lowest position is $x = -A$, and its highest position is $x = +A$. When $t = 0$, $\cos(0) = 1$ and the bottle is at $x = +A$. So, find the time when the cosine function goes to -1. This is when $\omega t = \pi$, so $t = \pi/\omega$.

33. **B**—Don't try to calculate the answer by saying $mg = GMm/r^2$! Not only would you have had to memorize the mass of the Earth, but you have no calculator and you only have a minute or so, anyway. So think: the acceleration must be less than 9.8 m/s², because that value is calculated at the surface of the Earth, and the Shuttle is farther from Earth's center than that. But the added height of 300 km is a small fraction (~5%) of the Earth's radius. So the gravitational acceleration will not be THAT much less. The best choice is thus 8.9 m/s². (By the way, acceleration is not zero—if it were, the Shuttle would be moving in a straight line, and not orbiting.)

34. **B**—The orbit can no longer be circular—circular orbits demand a specific velocity. Because the satellite gains speed while at its original distance from the planet, the orbit is now elliptical. Because the direction of the satellite's motion is still tangent to the former circular path, in the next instant the satellite will be farther from Earth than at point P, eliminating answer choice A. The satellite will not "fly off into space" unless it reaches escape velocity, which cannot be 1% greater than the speed necessary for a low circular orbit.

35. **D**—Kepler's third law states that for all planets in the same system, their period of orbit squared is proportional to the average distance from the sun cubed. Using units of years and AU, for Earth, $(1 \text{ year})^2 = (1 \text{ AU})^3$. For Mercury, we have $(\frac{1}{5} \text{ year})^2 = (? \text{ AU})^3$. Solving for the question mark, you find that the distance from Mercury to the sun is the cube root of $\frac{1}{25}$ AU, which is closest to $\frac{1}{3}$ AU.

Physics C—Mechanics Practice Exam 1—Free-Response Solutions

Notes on grading your free-response section

For answers that are numerical, or in equation form:

*For each part of the problem, look to see if you got the right answer. If you did, and you showed any reasonable (and correct) work, give yourself full credit for that part. It's okay if you didn't explicitly show EVERY step, as long as some steps are indicated and you got the right answer. However:

*If you got the WRONG answer, then look to see if you earned partial credit. Give yourself points for each step toward the answer as indicated in the rubrics below. Without the correct answer, you must show each intermediate step explicitly in order to earn the point for that step. (See why it's so important to show your work?)

*If you're off by a decimal place or two, not to worry—you get credit anyway, as long as your approach to the problem was legitimate. This isn't a math test. You're not being evaluated on your rounding and calculator-use skills.

*You do not have to simplify expressions in variables all the way. Square roots in the denominator are fine; fractions in nonsimplified form are fine. As long as you've solved properly for the requested variable, and as long as your answer is algebraically equivalent to the rubric's, you earn credit.

*Wrong, but consistent: Often you need to use the answer to part (a) in order to solve part (b). But you might have the answer to part (a) wrong. If you follow the correct procedure for part (b), plugging in your incorrect answer, then you will usually receive *full credit* for part (b). The major exceptions are when your answer to part (a) is unreasonable (say, a car moving at 10^5 m/s, or a distance between two cars equal to 10^{-100} meters), or when your answer to part (a) makes the rest of the problem trivial or irrelevant.

For answers that require justification:

*Obviously your answer will not match the rubric word-for-word. If the general gist is there, you get credit.

*But the reader is not allowed to interpret for the student. If your response is vague or ambiguous, you will NOT get credit.

*If your response consists of both correct and incorrect parts, you will usually not receive credit. It is not possible to try two answers, hoping that one of them is right. ☺ (See why it's so important to be concise?)

CM 1

(a)

1 pt: Write Newton's second law for the direction along the plane for each block.
For the right block, $T - mg\sin 30° = ma$
For the left block $mg\sin 60° - T = ma$

1 pt: for including consistent directions for both equations

1 pt: for including a trig function in both equations, even if it's the wrong function

1 pt: solve these equations simultaneously to get the acceleration

1 pt: answer is $a = 1.8$ m/s². (An answer of $a = -1.8$ m/s² is incorrect because the magnitude of a vector cannot be negative.)
(Alternatively you can just recognize that $mg\sin 60°$ pulls left, while $mg\sin 30°$ pulls right, and use Newton's second law directly on the combined system. Be careful, though, because the mass of the ENTIRE system is 10 kg, not 5 kg!)

(b)
i.

1 pt: for a graph that starts at $v = 0$, has exponential form, and sort of levels off to a maximum speed.

1 pt: for indicating that the asymptote represents the terminal speed, or 60 m/s.

ii.

1 pt: since acceleration is dv/dt, we have a differential equation: $dv/dt = 1.8 - 0.03v$. We need to find the expression for v.

1 pt: In a differential equation where the derivative is proportional to the function itself, the solution has an exponential term.

1 pt: In the solution e is raised to the $-0.03t$ power because 0.03 is what multiplies the v.

1 pt: Since the blocks start at rest and speed up, the solution includes $(1-e^{-0.03t})$ not just $e^{-0.03t}$.

[Those previous three points could be earned for a direct algorithmic solution for v, using separation of variables and integration.]

1 pt: For large t, the exponential term goes to zero, and so $(1-e^{-0.03t})$ should be multiplied by the terminal velocity. That's why there's an asymptote.

(c)

1 pt: The terminal velocity is when acceleration equals zero.

1 pt: solve the equation $0 = 1.8 - 0.03v$. (You get 60 m/s.)

(d)

1 pt: The blocks only reach this terminal speed after a long time. An incline in a physics lab can't be more than a couple of meters long, meaning the blocks don't have the time and space to reach 60 m/s.

CM 2

(a)

1 pt: The weight of the ball acts down.

1 pt: The normal force acts up and left, perpendicular to the surface of the glass.

1 pt: No other forces act.

(b)

1 pt: The normal force can be broken into vertical and horizontal components, where the vertical is $F_N \cos \theta$ and the horizontal is $F_N \sin \theta$. (The vertical direction goes with cosine here because θ is measured from the vertical.)

1 pt: The net vertical force is zero because the ball doesn't rise or fall on the glass. Setting up forces equal to down, $F_N \cos \theta = mg$.

1 pt: The horizontal force is a centripetal force, so $F_N \sin \theta = mv^2/r \sin \theta$.

1 pt: For using $r \sin \theta$ and not just r. (Why? Because you need to use the radius of the actual circular motion, which is not the same as the radius of the sphere.)

1 pt: The tangential speed "v" is the circumference of the circular motion divided by the period. Since period is $1/f$, and because the radius of the circular motion is $r \sin \theta$, this speed $v = 2\pi r \sin \theta f$.

1 pt: Now divide the vertical and horizontal force equations to get rid of the F_N term:

$$\sin \theta / \cos \theta = v^2 / r \sin \theta g.$$

1 pt: Plug in the speed and the $\sin \theta$ terms cancel, leaving $\cos \theta = g/4\pi^2 r f^2$.

1 pt: Plugging in the given values (including $r = 0.08$ m), $\theta = 83°$.

(c)

1 pt: From part (a), the linear speed is $2\pi r \sin \theta f$.

1 pt: Plugging in values, the speed is 2.5 m/s. (If you didn't get the point in part (a) for figuring out how to calculate linear speed, but you do it right here, then you can earn the point here.)

(d)

1 pt: The angle will not be affected.

1 pt: Since the mass of the ball does not appear in the equation to calculate the angle in part (b), the mass does not affect the angle.

CM 3

(a)

1 pt: The net force is at an angle down and to the left, perpendicular to the rod.

1 pt: Because the ball is instantaneously at rest, the direction of the velocity in the next instant must also be the direction of the acceleration; this direction is along the arc of the ball's motion.

(b)

1 pt: The magnitude of the net force is $mg \sin \theta$.

1 pt: It's easiest to use a limiting argument: When $\theta = 90°$, then the net force would be simply the weight of the ball, mg. $mg \sin 90° = mg$, while $mg \cos 90° = $ zero; hence the correct answer.

(c)

1 pt: The force on the mass is $-mg \sin \theta$, the negative arising because the force is always opposite the displacement.

1 pt: Potential energy is derived from force by
$$U = -\int F dx.$$

1 pt: The distance displaced $x = L\theta$.

1 pt: The differential dx becomes $L \, d\theta$.

1 pt: The integral becomes $\int mgL \sin \theta \, d\theta$, which evaluates to $-mgL \cos \theta$. (Here the constant of integration can be taken to be any value at all because the zero of potential energy can be chosen arbitrarily.)
[Alternate solution: Using geometry, it can be found that the height of the bob above the lowest point is $L - L \cos \theta$. Thus, the potential energy is $mgh = mg(L - L \cos \theta)$. This gives the same answer, but has defined the arbitrary constant of integration as mgL.]

(d)

1 pt: The graph should look like some sort of sine or cosine function, oscillating smoothly. The graph may be shifted up or down and still receive full credit.

1 pt: The graph should have an amplitude of mgL, though the graph can be shifted arbitrarily up or down on the vertical axis.

1 pt: The graph should have a minimum at $\theta = 0$.

1 pt: The graph should have a maximum at $\theta = 180°$.

(e)

1 pt: For simple harmonic motion, the restoring force must be linearly proportional to the displacement, like $F = -kx$. This yields an energy function that is quadratic: $-(-kx) \cdot dx$ integrates to give $U = \frac{1}{2}kx^2$. The graph of the energy of a simple harmonic oscillator is, thus, parabolic.

1 pt: Near the $\theta = 0$ position, the graph in part (e) is shaped much like a parabola, only deviating from a parabolic shape at large angles; so the pendulum is a simple harmonic oscillator as long as the energy graph approximates a parabola.

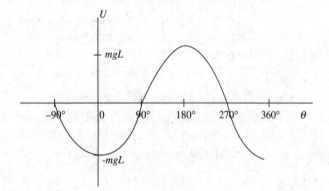

AP Physics C—Mechanics
Full Exam Scoring

Multiple-Choice: Number Correct_____(35 max)

Free-Response: Question 1_____(15 max)
Question 2_____(15 max)
Question 3_____(15 max)

Total Free-Response_____(45 max)

$1.286 \times$ Multiple-Choice + Free-Response = Raw Score_____(90 max)

59–90	5
45–58	4
35–44	3
23–34	2
0–22	1

Physics C—Electricity and Magnetism Practice Exam 1—Multiple-Choice Solutions

1. **B**—An electric field exists regardless of the amount of charge placed in it, and regardless of whether any charge at all is placed in it. So both experimenters must measure the same field (though they will measure different forces on their test charges).

2. **D**—You could use Gauss's law to show that the field outside the sphere has to decrease as $1/r^2$, eliminating choices B and E. But it's easier just to remember that an important result of Gauss's law is that the *electric field inside a conductor is always zero everywhere*, so D is the only possibility.

3. **B**—While in the region between the plates, the negatively charged electron is attracted to the positive plate, so bends upward. But after leaving the plates, there is no more force acting on the electron. Thus, the electron continues in motion in a straight line by Newton's first law.

4. **C**—This is a Newton's third law problem! The force of A on B is equal (and opposite) to the force of B on A. Or, we can use Coulomb's law: The field due to A is $k(2Q)/(4\text{ m})^2$. The force on B is $QE = k2QQ/(4\text{ m})^2$. We can do the same analysis finding the field due to B and the force on A to get the same result.

5. **A**—The charge is in equilibrium, so the horizontal component of the tension must equal the electric force. This horizontal tension is 0.1 N times sin 30° (not cosine because 30° was measured from the *vertical*), or 0.05 N. The electric force is qE, where q is 0.002 C. So the electric field is 0.050 N/0.002 C. Reduce the expression by moving the decimal to get 50/2, or 25 N/C.

6. **D**—The answer could, in principle, be found using the integral form of Coulomb's law. But you can't do that on a one-minute multiple-choice problem. The electric field will point down the page—the field due to a positive charge points away from the charge, and there's an equal amount of charge producing a rightward field as a leftward field, so horizontal fields cancel. So, is the answer B or D? Choice B is not correct because electric fields add as vectors. Only the vertical component of the field due to each little charge element contributes to the net electric field, so the net field must be *less than* kQ/R^2.

7. **A**—Use the symmetry of the situation to see the answer. Because the infinitely large plane looks the same on the up side as the down side, its electric field must look the same, too—the field must point away from the plane and have the same value.

8. **C**—Another way to look at this question is, "Where would a small positive charge end up if released near these charges?" because positive charges seek the smallest potential. The positive charge would be repelled by the $+2Q$ charge and attracted to the $-Q$ charges, so would end up at point C. Or, know that potential due to a point charge is kq/r. Point C is closest to both $-Q$ charges, so the r terms will be smallest, and the negative contribution to the potential will be largest; point C is farthest from the $+2Q$ charge, so the r term will be large, and the positive contribution to the potential will be smallest.

9. **A**—A positive charge is forced from high to low potential, which is generally to the left; and the force on a positive charge is in the direction of the electric field. At point P itself the electric field is directly to the left because an electric field is always perpendicular to equipotential surfaces.

10. **C**—The charge on the metal sphere distributes uniformly on its surface. Because the nonconducting sphere also has a uniform charge distribution, by symmetry the electric fields will cancel to zero at the center. Outside the spheres we can use Gauss's law: $E \cdot A = Q_{enclosed}/\varepsilon_o$. Because the charge enclosed by a Gaussian surface outside either sphere will be the same, and the spheres are the same size, the electric field will be the same everywhere outside either sphere. But within the sphere? A Gaussian surface drawn inside the conducting sphere encloses no charge, while a Gaussian surface inside the nonconducting sphere does enclose some charge. The fields inside must *not* be equal.

11. **A**—That's what Gauss's law says: net flux through a closed surface is equal to the charge enclosed divided by ε_o. Though Gauss's law is only *useful* when all charge within or without a Gaussian surface is symmetrically distributed, Gauss's law is *valid* always.

12. **B**—The electric field at the center of the ring is zero because the field caused by any charge element is canceled by the field due to the charge on the other side of the ring. The electric field decreases as $1/r^2$ by Coulomb's law, so a long distance away from the ring the field goes to zero. The field is nonzero near the ring, though, because each charge element creates a field pointing away from the ring, resulting in a field always along the axis.

13. **C**—Capacitance of a parallel-plate capacitor is $\varepsilon_o A/d$, where A is the area of the plates, and d is the separation between plates. To halve the capacitance, we must halve the area or double the plate separation. The plate separation in the diagram is labeled c, so double distance c.

14. **E**—We are told that the capacitors are identical, so their capacitances must be equal. They are hooked in parallel, meaning the voltages across them must be equal as well. By $Q = CV$, the charge stored by each must also be equal.

15. **E**—First determine the voltage of the battery by $Q = CV$. This gives $V = 600 \ \mu C/2 \ \mu F = 300$ V. This voltage is hooked to the three series capacitors, whose equivalent capacitance is 6 μF (series capacitors add inversely, like parallel resistors). So the total charge stored now is $(6 \ \mu F)(300 \ V) = 1800 \ \mu C$. This charge is *not* split evenly among the capacitors, though! Just as the current through series resistors is the same through each and equal to the total current through the circuit, the charge on series capacitors is the same and equal to the total.

16. **B**—The charge does reside on the surface, and, if the conductor is alone, will distribute evenly. But, if there's another nearby charge, then this charge can repel or attract the charge on the sphere, causing a redistribution.

17. **D**—The voltage must stay the same because the battery by definition provides a constant voltage. Closing the switch adds a parallel branch to the network of resistors. Adding a parallel resistor *reduces* the total resistance. By Ohm's law, if voltage stays the same and resistance decreases, total current must increase.

18. **C**—The time constant for an RC circuit is equal to RC. The resistance used is the resistance encountered by charge that's flowing to the capacitor; in this case, 40 Ω. So $RC = 20$ s.

19. **E**—Assume that the current runs clockwise in the circuit, and use Kirchoff's loop rule. Start with the 7-V battery and trace the circuit with the current: $+7V - I(3 \ \Omega) + 3V - I(2 \ \Omega) = 0$. Solve for I to get 2.0 A.

20. **C**—The intrinsic property of the light bulb is *resistance*; the power dissipated by a bulb depends on its voltage and current. When the bulbs are connected to the 100-V source, we can use the expression for power $P = V^2/R$ to see that the bulb rated at 50 watts has twice the resistance of the other bulb. Now in series, the bulbs carry the same current. Power is also I^2R; thus the 50-watt bulb with twice the resistance dissipates twice the power, and is twice as bright.

21. **E**—The electron bends downward by the right-hand rule for a charge in a B field—point to the right, curl fingers into the page, and the thumb points up the page. But the electron's negative charge changes the force to down the page. The path is a circle because the direction of the force continually changes, always pointing perpendicular to the electron's velocity. Thus, the force on the electron is a centripetal force.

22. **A**—This is one of the important consequences of Ampere's law. The magnetic field inside the donut is always along the axis of the donut, so the symmetry demands of Ampere's law are met. If we draw an "Amperian Loop" around point P but inside r_1, this loop encloses no current; thus the magnetic field must be zero.

23. **C**—The magnetic field due to the wire at the position of the electron is into the page. Now use the other right-hand rule, the one for the force on a charged particle in a magnetic field. If the charge moves down the page, then the force on a positive charge would be to the right, but the force on a (negative) electron would be left, toward the wire.

24. **C**—A positive charge experiences a force in the direction of an electric field, and perpendicular to a magnetic field; but the direction of a force is not necessarily the direction of motion.

25. **A**—The electric field due to *any* finite-sized charge distribution drops off as $1/r^2$ a long distance away because if you go far enough away, the charge looks like a point charge. This is not true for infinite charge distributions, though. The magnetic field due to an infinitely long wire is given by

$$\frac{\mu_\circ I}{2\pi r}$$

not proportional to $1/r^2$; the magnetic field produced by a wire around a torus is zero outside the torus by Ampere's law.

26. **C**—The magnetic field produced by a single loop of wire at the center of the loop is directly out of the loop. A solenoid is a conglomeration of many loops in a row, producing a magnetic field that is uniform and along the axis of the solenoid. So, the proton will be traveling parallel to the magnetic field. By $F = qvB \sin\theta$, the angle between the field and the velocity is zero, producing no force on the proton. The proton continues its straight-line motion by Newton's first law.

27. **E**—By the right-hand rule for the force on a charged particle in a magnetic field, particle C must be neutral, particle B must be positively charged, and particle A must be negatively charged. Charge B must be more massive than charge A because it resists the change in its motion more than A. A proton is positively charged and more massive than the electron; the neutron is not charged.

28. **E**—The force on the positive charge is upward; the force on the negative charge is downward. These forces will tend to rotate the dipole clockwise, so only A or E could be right. Because the charges and velocities are equal, the magnetic force on each $= qvB$ and is the same. So, there is no net force on the dipole. (Yes, no net force, even though it continues to move to the left.)

29. **D**—The centripetal force keeping the electrons in a circle is provided by the magnetic force. So set $qvB = mv^2/r$. Solve to get $r = (mv)/(qB)$. Just look at orders of magnitude now: $r = (10^{-31}$ kg) $(10^7 \text{m/s})/(10^{-19}\text{C})(10^{-5}\text{ T})$. This gives $r = 10^{24}/10^{24} = 10^0$ m ~ 1 m.

30. **E**—An element of current produces a magnetic field that wraps around the current element, pointing out of the page above the current and into the page below. But right in front (or anywhere along the axis of the current), the current element produces no magnetic field at all.

31. D—A long way from the hole, the magnet produces very little flux, and that flux doesn't change much, so very little current is induced. As the north end approaches the hole, the magnetic field points down. The flux is *increasing* because the field through the wire gets stronger with the approach of the magnet; so, point your right thumb upward (in the direction of *decreasing* flux) and curl your fingers. You find the current flows counterclockwise, defined as positive. Only A or D could be correct. Now consider what happens when the magnet leaves the loop. The south end descends away from the loop. The magnetic field still points down, into the south end of the magnet, but now the flux is *decreasing*. So point your right thumb down (in the direction of decreasing flux) and curl your fingers. Current now flows clockwise, as indicated in choice D. (While the magnet is going through the loop, current goes to zero because the magnetic field of the bar magnet is reasonably constant near the center of the magnet.)

32. A—You remember the equation for the induced EMF in a moving rectangular loop, $\varepsilon = Blv$. Here *l* represents the length of the wire that doesn't change within the field; dimension *a* in the diagram. So the answer is either A or C. To find the direction of induced current, use Lenz's law: The field points out of the page, but the flux through the loop is *increasing* as more of the loop enters the field. So, point your right thumb into the page (in the direction of decreasing flux) and curl your fingers; you find the current is clockwise, or left to right across the resistor.

33. D—Start by finding the direction of the induced current in the wire using Lenz's law: the magnetic field is out of the page. The flux *increases* because the field strength increases. So point your right thumb into the page, and curl your fingers to find the current flowing clockwise, or south in the wire. Now use the right-hand rule for the force on moving charges in a magnetic field (remembering that a current is the flow of positive charge). Point down the page, curl your fingers out of the page, and the force must be to the west.

34. C—There is clearly nonzero flux because the field does pass through the wire loop. The flux is not *BA*, though, because the field does not go *straight* through the loop—the field hits the loop at an angle. So is the answer *BA* cos 30°, using the angle of the plane; or *BA* cos 60°, using the angle from the vertical? To figure it out, consider the extreme case. If the incline were at zero degrees, there would be zero flux through the loop. Then the flux would be *BA* cos 90°, because cos 90° is zero, and cos 0° is one. So don't use the angle of the plane, use the angle from the vertical, *BA* cos 60°.

35. C—The inductor resists changes in current. But after a long time, the current reaches steady state, meaning the current does not change; thus the inductor, after a long time, might as well be just a straight wire. The battery will still provide current *I*, of which half goes through each equal resistor.

Physics C—Electricity and Magnetism Practice
Exam 1—Free-Response Solutions

E&M 1

(a)

1 pt: Inside a conductor, the electric field must always be zero. $E = 0$.

1 pt: Because we have spherical symmetry, use Gauss's law.

1 pt: The area of a Gaussian surface in this region is $4\pi r^2$. The charge enclosed by this surface is Q.

1 pt: So, $E = Q_{enclosed}/\varepsilon_o A = Q/4\pi \varepsilon_o r^2$.

1 pt: Inside a conductor, the electric field must always be zero. $E = 0$.

2 pts: Just as in part 2, use Gauss's law, but now the charge enclosed is $3Q$. $E = 3Q/4\pi \varepsilon_o r^2$.

(b)

1 pt: $-Q$ is on the inner surface.

1 pt: $+3Q$ is on the outer surface.

1 pt: Because $E = 0$ inside the outer shell, a Gaussian surface inside this shell must enclose zero charge, so $-Q$ must be on the inside surface to cancel the $+Q$ on the small sphere. Then to keep the total charge of the shell equal to $+2Q$, $+3Q$ must go to the outer surface.

(c)

1 pt: Because we have spherical symmetry, the potential due to both spheres is $3Q/4\pi \varepsilon_o r$, with potential equal to zero an infinite distance away.

1 pt: So at position R_3, the potential is $3Q/4\pi \varepsilon_o R_3$. (Since $E = 0$ inside the shell, V is the same value everywhere in the shell.)

(d)

1 pt: Integrate the electric field between R_1 and R_2 to get $V = Q/4\pi \varepsilon_o r + a$ constant of integration.

1 pt: To find that constant, we know that $V(R_2)$ was found in part (c), and is $3Q/4\pi \varepsilon_o R_3$. Thus, the constant is

$$\frac{3Q}{4\pi\varepsilon_o R_3} - \frac{Q}{4\pi\varepsilon_o R_2}.$$

1 pt: Then, potential at $R_1 = Q/4\pi \varepsilon_o R_1 +$ the constant of integration.

E&M 2

(a)

1 pt: The series capacitors add inversely,

$$\frac{1}{4 \ \mu F} + \frac{1}{12 \ \mu F} = \frac{1}{C_{eq}},$$

so C_{eq} for the series capacitors is 3 μF.

1 pt: The parallel capacitor just adds in algebraically, so the equivalent capacitance for the whole system is 5 μF.

(b)

1 pt: After a long time, the resistor is irrelevant; no current flows because the fully charged capacitors block direct current.

1 pt: The voltage across C_3 is 10 V (because there's no voltage drop across the resistor without any current).

1 pt: By $Q = CV$ the charge on C_3 is 20 μC.

1 pt: Treating C_1 and C_2 in series; the equivalent capacitance is 3 μF, the voltage is 10 V (in parallel with C_3).

1 pt: The charge on the equivalent capacitance of C_1 and C_2 is 30 μC; thus the charge on $C_1 = 30$ μC, and the charge on C_2 is also 30 μC (charge on series capacitors is the same).

1 pt: Using $Q = CV$, the voltage across C_1 is 7.5 V.

1 pt: Using $Q = CV$, the voltage across C_2 is 2.5 V.

(c)

1 pt: For a graph that starts at $Q = 0$.

1 pt: For a graph that asymptotically approaches 20 μC (or whatever charge was calculated for C_3 in part b).

1 pt: For calculating the time constant of the circuit, RC = 5 s.

1 pt: For the graph reaching about 63% of its maximum charge after one time constant.

(d)

1 pt: For recognizing that the voltage does not change.

1 pt: For explaining that if voltage changed, then Kirchoff's voltage rule would not be valid around a loop including C_3 and the battery (or explaining that voltage is the same across parallel components, so if one is disconnected the other's voltage is unaffected).

E&M 3

(a)

1 pt: For placing the wire along a north–south line.

1 pt: The wire could be placed above the compass, with the current traveling due north. (The wire also could be placed underneath the compass, with current traveling due south.) (Points can also be earned for an alternative correct solution: for example, the wire could be placed perpendicular to the face of the compass (just south of it), with the current running up.)

(b)

1 pt: The B field due to Earth plus the B field caused by the wire, when added together as vectors, must give a resultant direction of 48° west of north.

1 pt: Placing these vectors tail-to-tip, as shown below, $\tan 48° = B_{\text{wire}}/B_{\text{Earth}}$.

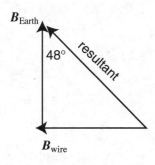

1 pt: So $B_{\text{wire}} = B_{\text{Earth}}\tan 48° = 5.6 \times 10^{-5}$ T.

(c)

1 pt: The magnetic field due to a long, straight, current-carrying wire is given by

$$B = \frac{\mu_o I}{2\pi r},$$

where r is the distance from the wire to the field point, represented in this problem by d.

1 pt: So B is proportional to $1/d$; this results in a hyperbolic graph.

1 pt: This graph should be asymptotic to both the vertical and horizontal axes.

(d)

1 pt: Place $1/d$ on the horizontal axis.

2 pts: The equation for the field due the wire can be written

$$B = \left(\frac{\mu_o I}{2\pi}\right)\left(\frac{1}{d}\right).$$

Everything in the first set of parentheses is constant. So, this equation is of the form $y = mx$, which is the equation of a line, if $1/d$ is put on the x-axis of the graph. (1 point can be earned for a partially complete explanation. On this problem, no points can be earned for justification if the answer is incorrect.)

(e)

1 pt: The slope of the graph, from the equation above, is

$$\frac{\mu_o I}{2\pi}.$$

1 pt: For plugging in values correctly, including 0.5 A or 500 mA.

1 pt: For units on the slope equivalent to magnetic field times distance (i.e., T·m, T·cm, mT·m, etc.).

1 pt: For a correct answer, complete with correct units: 1.0×10^{-7} Tm, or 1.0×10^{-4} mT·m.

AP Physics C—Electricity and Magnetism
Full Exam Scoring

Multiple-Choice: Number Correct_____(35 max)

Free-Response: Question 1_____(15 max)
                 Question 2_____(15 max)
                 Question 3_____(15 max)

Total Free-Response_____(45 max)

$1.286 \times$ Multiple-Choice + Free-Response = Raw Score_____(90 max)

56–90	5
44–55	4
32–43	3
23–34	2
0–22	1

Physics C—Mechanics Practice Exam 2—Multiple-Choice Questions

ANSWER SHEET

1 (A) (B) (C) (D) (E)	13 (A) (B) (C) (D) (E)	25 (A) (B) (C) (D) (E)
2 (A) (B) (C) (D) (E)	14 (A) (B) (C) (D) (E)	26 (A) (B) (C) (D) (E)
3 (A) (B) (C) (D) (E)	15 (A) (B) (C) (D) (E)	27 (A) (B) (C) (D) (E)
4 (A) (B) (C) (D) (E)	16 (A) (B) (C) (D) (E)	28 (A) (B) (C) (D) (E)
5 (A) (B) (C) (D) (E)	17 (A) (B) (C) (D) (E)	29 (A) (B) (C) (D) (E)
6 (A) (B) (C) (D) (E)	18 (A) (B) (C) (D) (E)	30 (A) (B) (C) (D) (E)
7 (A) (B) (C) (D) (E)	19 (A) (B) (C) (D) (E)	31 (A) (B) (C) (D) (E)
8 (A) (B) (C) (D) (E)	20 (A) (B) (C) (D) (E)	32 (A) (B) (C) (D) (E)
9 (A) (B) (C) (D) (E)	21 (A) (B) (C) (D) (E)	33 (A) (B) (C) (D) (E)
10 (A) (B) (C) (D) (E)	22 (A) (B) (C) (D) (E)	34 (A) (B) (C) (D) (E)
11 (A) (B) (C) (D) (E)	23 (A) (B) (C) (D) (E)	35 (A) (B) (C) (D) (E)
12 (A) (B) (C) (D) (E)	24 (A) (B) (C) (D) (E)	

Physics C—Mechanics Practice Exam 2—Multiple-Choice Questions

Time: 45 minutes. You may refer to the constants sheet and the equation sheet, both of which are found in the appendix. You may use a calculator.

1. A jet airplane has mass 300,000 kg. In order to take off, it accelerates uniformly over a horizontal distance of 3000 m, reaching a top speed of 80 m/s. Neglecting drag forces, which of the following is closest to the average horizontal force provided by the airplane's engines?

   (A) 10^6 N
   (B) 10^4 N
   (C) 10^3 N
   (D) 10^5 N
   (E) 10^0 N

2. On a one-dimensional track, a large cart in motion collides with a small cart at rest. The carts bounce off each other. Which of the following is true about linear momentum and kinetic energy?

   (A) Momentum may or may not be conserved; kinetic energy may or may not be conserved.
   (B) Momentum must be conserved; kinetic energy must be conserved.
   (C) Momentum may or may not be conserved; kinetic energy must be conserved.
   (D) Momentum must be conserved; kinetic energy may or may not be conserved.
   (E) Momentum must be conserved; kinetic energy must not be conserved.

3. The escape velocity for a rocket from Earth's surface is 11 km/s. What is the escape velocity for a rocket on the surface of a planet whose mass is the same as Earth's but whose radius is half that of Earth?

   (A) 2.8 km/s
   (B) 6.5 km/s
   (C) 7.8 km/s
   (D) 11 km/s
   (E) 15.4 km/s

Hand pulls up so scale reads 10 N

1 kg

4. A 1-kg block hangs from a string at rest. A person holds a spring scale attached vertically to the string, pulling upward so that the scale reads 10 N. What is the tension in the string?

   (A) 19 N
   (B) 9 N
   (C) 0 N
   (D) 10 N
   (E) 20 N

2 kg   4 kg   6 kg → F = 24 N

5. Three blocks *A*, *B*, and *C* are connected by taut light strings on a frictionless surface, as shown above. A rightward force *F* = 24 N is applied to block *C*. Which of the following correctly ranks the accelerations a_A, a_B, and a_C of each block?

   (A) $a_A > a_B > a_C$
   (B) $a_C > a_B > a_A$
   (C) $a_A = a_B > a_C$
   (D) $a_A = a_B = a_C$
   (E) $a_C > a_B = a_A$

6. A 250-g cart rolls to the right at 100 cm/s and collides with a 500-g cart, which is initially rolling left at 75 cm/s. The carts stick together. What is the speed of the carts right after they collide?

   (A) 75 cm/s
   (B) 83 cm/s
   (C) 25 cm/s
   (D) 17 cm/s
   (E) 50 cm/s

GO ON TO THE NEXT PAGE

7. An object of mass m is constrained to move along the x-axis only. It experiences a potential energy function $U = \frac{1}{2}kx^2 - bx$, where U is in joules and x is in meters. Which of the following represents the net force F on the object?

   (A) $b - kx$

   (B) $kx - b$

   (C) $\frac{kx^3}{6} - bx^2$

   (D) $bx^2 - \frac{kx^3}{6}$

   (E) $kx + b$

8. Three objects, of mass 2 kg, 2 kg, and 4 kg, are arranged as shown in the diagram. Which of the following is closest to the y-coordinate of the three objects' center of mass?

   (A) 2.0 cm
   (B) 3.5 cm
   (C) 1.5 cm
   (D) 0.5 cm
   (E) 1.0 cm

9. A block is released from rest at the top of a ramp on which friction is negligible. At the bottom of the ramp, the block encounters a rough, level surface on which the coefficient of kinetic friction with the block is 0.20. The block slides to rest after traveling 45 cm on the rough surface, as shown in the diagram. From what height vertically above the rough surface was the block released?

   (A) 9 cm
   (B) 22.5 cm
   (C) The answer cannot be determined without knowing the mass of the block.
   (D) 225 cm
   (E) 90 cm

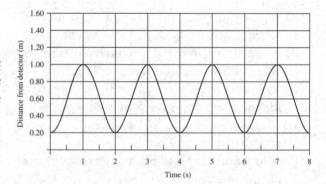

Questions 10 and 11: A 0.20-kg object is attached to a spring, which hangs vertically. A motion detector placed underneath the object records the position-time data shown above.

10. At which of the following times is the object's acceleration downward and at its maximum magnitude?

    (A) 1.5 s
    (B) 2.0 s
    (C) 0.0 s
    (D) 1.0 s
    (E) 0.5 s

11. What is the spring constant of the spring?

(A) 0.9 N/m
(B) 5.0 N/m
(C) 2.5 N/m
(D) 2.0 N/m
(E) 3.9 N/m

12. Which of the following quantities, if any, is a scalar quantity?

(A) A velocity of −2.0 m/s
(B) A potential energy of −2.0 J
(C) A momentum of −2.0 N·s
(D) A displacement of −2.0 m
(E) None of the above is a scalar quantity.

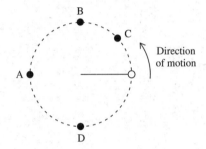

13. A ball of mass m is attached to a light string, as shown above. The ball is whirled counterclockwise in a vertical circle at constant speed. At which labeled position is the tension in the string largest?

(A) A
(B) B
(C) C
(D) D
(E) None of the above; the tension is constant throughout.

14. An object moves along the x-axis according to the potential energy function $U(x) = ax^2 - b$, where a and b are positive constants. Which of the following lists all of the positions in which the particle is in stable equilibrium?

(A) $x = 0$ only
(B) $x = 0$, $x = b$, and $x = -b$
(C) $x = b$ and $x = -b$
(D) $x = 0$, $x = a/b$, and $x = -a/b$
(E) $x = a/b$ and $x = -a/b$

15. A 200-W motor lifts an object at a constant speed of 0.5 m/s. The object ends up 100 m east of where it started and elevated 100 m vertically from its starting point after 20 seconds of elapsed time. What is the mass of the object?

(A) $2\sqrt{2}$ kg
(B) $4\sqrt{2}$ kg
(C) 0.2 kg
(D) 4 kg
(E) 8 kg

16. The velocity of a particle moving along the x-axis is given as a function of time by the expression $v(t) = 4t^2 - 3t + 2$, where v is in units of m/s and t in s. About how far did the particle move between $t = 0$ and $t = 2$ s?

(A) 9 m
(B) 12 m
(C) 24 m
(D) 19 m
(E) 13 m

Questions 17–19: A moon executes an elliptical orbit about its planet. Point P is where the moon is closest to the planet; point A is where the moon is farthest from the planet.

17. As the moon moves from point P to point A and then back to its original position, what happens to its angular momentum about the central planet?

(A) It increases, then decreases.
(B) It decreases, then increases.
(C) It decreases the entire way.
(D) It remains constant.
(E) It increases the entire way.

18. As the moon moves from point P to point A and then back to its original position, what happens to the potential energy of the moon-planet system?

(A) It increases, then decreases
(B) It decreases, then increases
(C) It decreases the entire way.
(D) It remains constant.
(E) It increases the entire way.

GO ON TO THE NEXT PAGE

19. As the planet moves from point P to point A and then back to its original position, what happens to the magnitude of the force of the moon on the planet?

(A) It increases, then decreases
(B) It decreases, then increases
(C) It decreases the entire way.
(D) It remains constant.
(E) It increases the entire way.

20. Block A has mass 4 kg; block B has mass 2 kg. Each block experiences an identical but unknown net force for a time of 3 s. Which of the following correctly compares block A's change in linear momentum Δp_A to block B's change in linear momentum Δp_B?

(A) $\Delta p_A = \Delta p_B \neq 0$
(B) $\Delta p_A = (1/12)\Delta p_B$
(C) $\Delta p_A = \Delta p_B = 0$
(D) $\Delta p_A = (1/2)\Delta p_B$
(E) $\Delta p_A = (1/6)\Delta p_B$

21. A meterstick of nonnegligible mass m is pivoted at its center, as shown. Two blocks, block 1 and block 2, are placed on top of the meterstick. When the meterstick is released from the rest at the position shown, it begins to rotate clockwise. Which of the following statements about the masses of the two blocks is correct?

(A) It cannot be determined which block has greater mass, because the lever arms associated with the torques provided by each block are different.
(B) The blocks are of equal mass, because the magnitude of the angular acceleration of each block is the same.
(C) Block 1 has greater mass, because the lever arm associated with the torque it provides is larger than that of block 2.
(D) Block 2 has greater mass, because more torque is provided by block 2 with a smaller lever arm.
(E) The blocks are of equal mass, because the meterstick's mass is not negligible.

22. In an amusement park ride, people of mass m stand with their backs to the inside of a large cylinder of radius R. The maximum coefficient of static friction between a person's clothes and the cylinder wall is μ. The cylinder rotates fast enough that the floor can drop away and the riders remain "stuck" to the wall without falling. What is the minimum period of rotation for which the riders will "stick" to the wall?

(A) $\dfrac{\mu}{Rg}$

(B) μmg

(C) $\sqrt{\dfrac{\mu}{Rg}}$

(D) $2\pi\sqrt{\dfrac{R\mu}{g}}$

(E) $2\pi\mu\, mg$

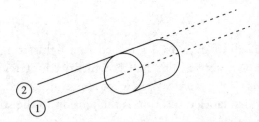

23. The solid disk shown has mass M and radius R. The rotational inertia of the disk about axis 1, which passes through the disk's center, is $(1/2)MR^2$. What is the rotational inertia of the disk about axis 2, which is tangential to the disk's edge?

(A) $(3/2)MR^2$
(B) $(2/5)MR^2$
(C) MR^2
(D) $(1/3)MR^2$
(E) $(2/3)MR^2$

GO ON TO THE NEXT PAGE

24. A 0.50-kg lab cart on a frictionless surface is attached to a spring, as shown in the figure. The rightward direction is considered positive. The spring is neither compressed nor stretched at position $x = 0$. The cart is released from rest at position $x = +0.25$ m at time $t = 0$. Which of the following graphs represents the force applied by the spring as a function of x?

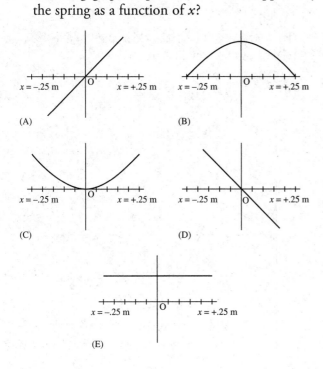

Questions 25 and 26: A ball is thrown off a cliff, with an initial velocity directed at an angle θ downward and to the right.

25. Which of the following is correct about the ball's acceleration from when the ball is released until it hits the ground?

(A) It remains constant and is directed at the angle θ.
(B) It remains constant and is directed downward.
(C) It increases and its direction changes.
(D) It increases and is directed downward.
(E) It increases and is directed at the angle θ.

26. Which of the following graphs represents the vertical position y of the ball as a function of time, where upward is the positive direction?

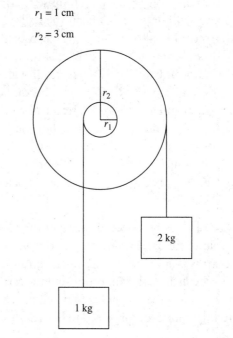

27. A double-pulley consists of pulleys of two different radii attached together such that they rotate together. The radius r_1 of the inner pulley is 1 cm, and the radius r_2 of the outer pulley is 3 cm. A 1-kg object and a 2-kg object are hung from the pulley as shown in the diagram. How much torque must be applied in order to hold the pulley at rest?

(A) 50 N·cm
(B) 7 N·cm
(C) 70 N·cm
(D) 5 N·cm
(E) 30 N·cm

GO ON TO THE NEXT PAGE

28. Identical balls A and B are thrown straight upward with initial speeds v_A and v_B, respectively. Ball A goes three times higher than ball B. What is the relationship between v_A and v_B?

(A) $v_A = 6v_B$
(B) $v_A = 9v_B$
(C) $v_A = 1.7v_B$
(D) $v_A = 2.4v_B$
(E) $v_A = 3v_B$

29. Two identical balls, A and B, fall vertically and hit the floor with speed v_1. Ball A rebounds with speed v_2; ball B does not rebound. Consider the impulse exerted on the floor and the impulse exerted on the ball during these collisions. Which case(s) cause greater magnitude of impulse?

Impulse exerted on the floor	Impulse exerted on the ball
(A) greater in ball B's collision	greater in ball B's collision
(B) greater in ball A's collision	greater in ball A's collision
(C) greater in ball A's collision	greater in ball B's collision
(D) equal in both collisions	equal in both collisions
(E) greater in ball B's collision	greater in ball A's collision

30. A cart of mass m moves to the right on a level surface along the x-axis. The only horizontal force on the cart is that of air resistance, which can be modeled as being linearly proportional to the cart's speed v. Which of the following differential equations could describe Newton's second law for this cart?

(A) $\dfrac{dv}{dt} = -\dfrac{b}{m}v$

(B) $\dfrac{dv}{dt} = \dfrac{b}{m}v$

(C) $\dfrac{dv}{dt} = g - \dfrac{b}{m}v$

(D) $\dfrac{d^2x}{dt^2} = -\dfrac{b}{m}x$

(E) $\dfrac{d^2x}{dt^2} = \dfrac{b}{m}x$

31. Train A is initially traveling east with speed 10 m/s, slowing down with acceleration 5 m/s². Train B is initially at rest a distance of 200 m from train A's starting location. Train B speeds up to the west with identical acceleration 5 m/s². How long does it take for the trains to pass each other?

(A) 80 s
(B) 5 s
(C) 40 s
(D) 10 s
(E) 20 s

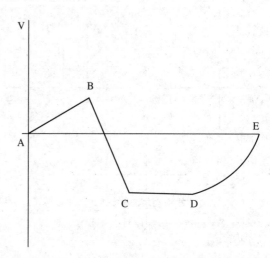

32. An object moves along the x-axis with a velocity v given as a function of time t as shown in the graph. During which section(s) of the graph is the object's acceleration constant, but not zero?

(A) AB and BC only
(B) AB, BC, and DE only
(C) CD only
(D) DE only
(E) AB only

33. A particle of mass m is released from rest at position $x = 0$ at time $t = 0$. The velocity v of the particle is given by the equation $v = \dfrac{3t^2}{m}$. Which of the following functions could represent the net force on the particle?

(A) $6t^3$
(B) t^3
(C) $3t$
(D) $6t$
(E) $(3/2)t$

GO ON TO THE NEXT PAGE

34. A ball can move to the left or right along a track, where right is considered positive. A graph of the ball's velocity as a function of time is shown. Which of the following describes the ball's motion?

(A) The ball slows down to the right, then speeds up to the right.
(B) The ball slows down to the right, then speeds up to the left.
(C) The ball speeds up and then slows down.
(D) The ball slows down to the left, then speeds up to the left.
(E) The ball slows down to the left, then speeds up to the right.

35. A block of mass m experiences a force F, which pushes down and to the right at an angle θ, as shown. The block encounters a rough surface of coefficient of kinetic friction μ. As the block moves a distance d, how much work is done by the net force on the block?

(A) $(F \cos\theta - \mu mg)d$
(B) $(F - \mu mg)d$
(C) Fd
(D) $Fd \cos\theta$
(E) $(F \cos\theta - \mu[mg + F \sin\theta])d$

STOP. End of Physics C—Mechanics Practice Exam 2—Multiple-Choice Questions

Physics C—Mechanics Practice Exam 2—Free-Response Questions

Time: 45 minutes. You may refer to the constants sheet and the equation sheet, both of which are found in the appendix. You may use a calculator.

Top View

1. An end of a uniform rod of length d and mass M is attached to a frictionless horizontal surface by a frictionless pivot, as shown. Point C marks the midpoint of the rod. The rod is initially motionless, but is free to rotate about the pivot.

   (a) Derive an expression for the rotational inertia of the rod about the pivot in terms of given variables and fundamental constants.

   (b) Student 1 slides a clay disk of mass m_1 perpendicular to the rod with speed v_1, as shown. The disk sticks to the rod a distance x from the pivot. Derive an expression for the angular speed ω of the rod-disk system immediately after the collision.

   (c) Student 2 slides a rubber disk of mass m_1 perpendicular to the rod, also with speed v_1. However, this rubber disk bounces off the rod. After which collision, if either, does the rod rotate with greater angular speed?

   _____ after colliding with the clay disk
   _____ after colliding with the rubber disk
   _____ both collisions result in the same angular speed for the rod
   _____ which collision produces greater angular speed for the rod cannot be determined

   Justify your answer.

   For the following two questions, consider collisions involving the clay disk and assume $M \gg m_1$.

   (d) In order to maximize the angular speed of the rod-disk system after collision, should the disk hit the rod left of, right of, or at point C? Briefly justify your answer.

   (e) How, if at all, would your answer to (d) change if the rod's mass distribution were nonuniform, with linear mass density getting larger farther from the pivot? Justify your answer.

GO ON TO THE NEXT PAGE

2. An object of mass m is attached to a spring of spring constant k, as shown in the diagram. The object rests on a horizontal frictionless surface. The spring is compressed a distance d from the equilibrium position, where $x = 0$. The object is then released from rest to oscillate in simple harmonic motion.

(a) Derive a differential equation that can be used to solve for the block's position x as a function of time t.

(b) Write an expression for the block's position x as a function of time that satisfies the differential equation in (a) and the conditions in the problem statement.

(c) The block loses its attachment to the spring when it is at the equilibrium position while moving to the right in its oscillation. The block falls off the table a height y above the ground. Derive an expression for the horizontal distance R that the block lands from the table.

(d) Instead consider that the block lost its attachment to the spring when it was moving to the right in its oscillation, but a distance ½d to the right of the equilibrium position. How, if at all, does the distance R change?

_____ R becomes larger   _____ R becomes smaller   _____ R remains the same

Justify your answer.

(e) On the axes provided, sketch a graph of horizontal position x versus time t for the block that loses attachment a distance ½d to the right of the equilibrium position. Let $t = 0$ be the moment when the spring is fully compressed; continue the graph until the block hits the floor.

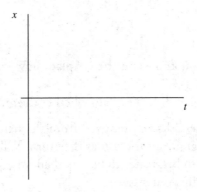

(f) On the axes provided, sketch a graph of speed v versus time t for the block that loses attachment a distance $\frac{1}{2}d$ to the right of the equilibrium position. Let $t = 0$ be the moment when the spring is fully compressed; continue the graph until the block hits the floor.

3. In the laboratory, a block of unknown mass m_1 is attached via a light rope and pulleys to a hanger of known mass m_2. The pulleys are of negligible mass and turn with negligible friction. The block and hanger are released from rest in the configuration shown.

   (a) Describe a procedure for measuring the acceleration of the hanger. You should use equipment usually found in a high school laboratory.

   (b) Is the magnitude of the acceleration of the block greater than, less than, or equal to the magnitude of the acceleration of the hanger? Justify your answer.

   Now m_2 is varied by placing disks of different masses on the hanger. For each value of m_2, the acceleration a of the hanger is measured. A graph is produced with $m_2 g$ on the vertical axis and a on the horizontal axis.

   (c) Is this graph linear?

   ____ yes   ____ no

   - If yes, explain how you know and then explain how you would use a line of best fit to determine the mass m_1.
   - If no, explain why not and then explain whether the graph would be concave-up or concave-down.

   (d) In a final experiment, the disks are removed from the hanger, and the pulleys are replaced with pulleys that do experience significant friction as they turn. Will the acceleration of the hanger in this final experiment be measured to be greater than, less than, or equal to the acceleration of the hanger in the original experiment? Justify your answer.

STOP. End of Physics C—Mechanics Practice Exam 2—Free-Response Questions

Physics C—Electricity and Magnetism Practice Exam 2—Multiple-Choice Questions

ANSWER SHEET

1 Ⓐ Ⓑ Ⓒ Ⓓ Ⓔ	13 Ⓐ Ⓑ Ⓒ Ⓓ Ⓔ	25 Ⓐ Ⓑ Ⓒ Ⓓ Ⓔ
2 Ⓐ Ⓑ Ⓒ Ⓓ Ⓔ	14 Ⓐ Ⓑ Ⓒ Ⓓ Ⓔ	26 Ⓐ Ⓑ Ⓒ Ⓓ Ⓔ
3 Ⓐ Ⓑ Ⓒ Ⓓ Ⓔ	15 Ⓐ Ⓑ Ⓒ Ⓓ Ⓔ	27 Ⓐ Ⓑ Ⓒ Ⓓ Ⓔ
4 Ⓐ Ⓑ Ⓒ Ⓓ Ⓔ	16 Ⓐ Ⓑ Ⓒ Ⓓ Ⓔ	28 Ⓐ Ⓑ Ⓒ Ⓓ Ⓔ
5 Ⓐ Ⓑ Ⓒ Ⓓ Ⓔ	17 Ⓐ Ⓑ Ⓒ Ⓓ Ⓔ	29 Ⓐ Ⓑ Ⓒ Ⓓ Ⓔ
6 Ⓐ Ⓑ Ⓒ Ⓓ Ⓔ	18 Ⓐ Ⓑ Ⓒ Ⓓ Ⓔ	30 Ⓐ Ⓑ Ⓒ Ⓓ Ⓔ
7 Ⓐ Ⓑ Ⓒ Ⓓ Ⓔ	19 Ⓐ Ⓑ Ⓒ Ⓓ Ⓔ	31 Ⓐ Ⓑ Ⓒ Ⓓ Ⓔ
8 Ⓐ Ⓑ Ⓒ Ⓓ Ⓔ	20 Ⓐ Ⓑ Ⓒ Ⓓ Ⓔ	32 Ⓐ Ⓑ Ⓒ Ⓓ Ⓔ
9 Ⓐ Ⓑ Ⓒ Ⓓ Ⓔ	21 Ⓐ Ⓑ Ⓒ Ⓓ Ⓔ	33 Ⓐ Ⓑ Ⓒ Ⓓ Ⓔ
10 Ⓐ Ⓑ Ⓒ Ⓓ Ⓔ	22 Ⓐ Ⓑ Ⓒ Ⓓ Ⓔ	34 Ⓐ Ⓑ Ⓒ Ⓓ Ⓔ
11 Ⓐ Ⓑ Ⓒ Ⓓ Ⓔ	23 Ⓐ Ⓑ Ⓒ Ⓓ Ⓔ	35 Ⓐ Ⓑ Ⓒ Ⓓ Ⓔ
12 Ⓐ Ⓑ Ⓒ Ⓓ Ⓔ	24 Ⓐ Ⓑ Ⓒ Ⓓ Ⓔ	

Physics C—Electricity and Magnetism Practice Exam 2— Multiple-Choice Questions

Time: 45 minutes. You may refer to the constants sheet and the equation sheet, both of which are found in the appendix. You may use a calculator.

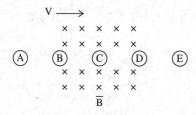

1. A object of charge q moves at constant speed v in a uniform magnetic field B in a circular path of radius R. How much work is done by the field on the object in each revolution?

   (A) $qvBR$
   (B) $\pi R^2 qvB$
   (C) $2\pi R^2 qvB$
   (D) zero
   (E) $2\pi qvBR$

2. A uniform magnetic field B points into the page and is limited to the region shown. A circular loop of wire is pulled to the right such that it maintains a steady speed. At which labeled position is the current in the wire at its largest counterclockwise value?

   (A) A
   (B) B
   (C) C
   (D) D
   (E) E

Questions 3 and 4: Two point objects produce electric potentials at the origin. Object 1, located along the positive x-axis, produces an electric potential of +100 V at the origin; Object 2, located along the negative y-axis, produces an electric potential of +100 V at the origin.

3. What is the net electric potential at the origin?

   (A) +200 V
   (B) 0 V
   (C) $+100\sqrt{2}$ V
   (D) The answer cannot be determined without knowing the relative distances of the charges from the origin.
   (E) $(+200 \text{ V}) (\cos 45°)$

4. The magnitude of the charge on object 1 is twice the magnitude of the charge on object 2. What is the ratio of object 1's distance from the origin to object 2's distance from the origin?

   (A) 2:1
   (B) 1:1
   (C) 1:4
   (D) 4:1
   (E) 1:2

GO ON TO THE NEXT PAGE

Questions 5–7:

Two isolated and identical long, straight, parallel wires carry currents I_1 and I_2 in the directions shown in the top view. The wires are separated by a distance d. The magnitude of current in wire 2 initially is twice the magnitude of current in wire 1. The top wire experiences a force F_1 due to the bottom wire.

5. In the laboratory, I_2 is held constant while I_1 is changed to different values both greater and less than I_2. A force probe measures the force F_1 on the top wire for each different I_1. Which of the following graphs represents F_1 as a function of I_1?

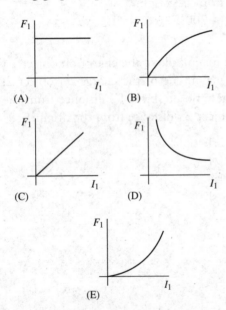

6. Which of the following indicates the magnitude and direction of the force F_2 on wire 2 due to wire 1?

(A) Half F_1 and downward
(B) Twice F_1 and downward
(C) Equal to F_1 and upward
(D) Equal to F_1 and downward
(E) Half F_1 and upward

7. Now the distance d is doubled while the currents I_1 and I_2 remain the same. In terms of F_1, what is the new force of wire 2 on wire 1?

(A) $2F_1$
(B) $(1/8)\,F_1$
(C) $(1/4)\,F_1$
(D) $(1/2)\,F_1$
(E) F_1

8. A very long, straight wire carries a current of I_1 in a direction toward the top of the page, as shown in the diagram. A rectangular coil with two sides parallel to the straight wire carries a current I_2. The near side of the rectangular coil is 2 cm away from the straight wire; the far side is 7 cm from the straight wire. Which of the following correctly sketches the magnetic field magnitude B as a function of the distance x along the *top* segment of the rectangular wire loop?

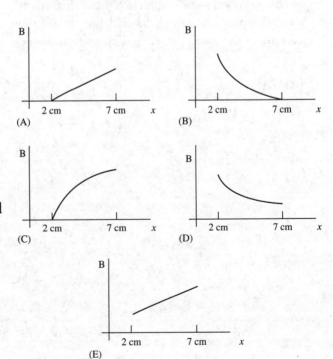

GO ON TO THE NEXT PAGE

9. A magnetic field that is aimed perpendicular to the plane of a wire loop varies as a function of time given by the equation $B(t) = 4t$. Which of the following sketches the emf produced in the loop as a function of time?

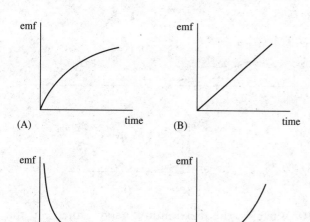

(A)

(B)

(C)

(D)

(E)

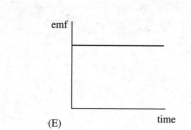

10. A positively charged object moves to the left at constant speed v. The object enters a region containing uniform magnetic and electric fields and continues to move in a straight line at constant speed. The electric field E is directed down toward the bottom of the page, as shown. What is the direction of the magnetic field?

(A) Into the page
(B) Down toward the bottom of the page
(C) Up toward the top of the page
(D) To the right
(E) Out of the page

Questions 11–13: Four objects with charge $+Q$, $-Q$, and $-q$ are placed at the corners of a square of side x, as shown in the diagram.

11. What is the direction of the net electric force on the object of charge $-q$?

(A)   (B)   (C)   (D)   (E)

12. Which of the following represents the magnitude of the electric field due to the other three charges at the location of the $-q$ charge?

(A) $\dfrac{\sqrt{2}kQ}{x^2}$

(B) $\dfrac{5kQ}{x^2}$

(C) $\dfrac{\left(2\sqrt{2}-1\right)kQ}{x^2}$

(D) $\dfrac{kQ}{x^2}$

(E) $\dfrac{3kQ}{2x^2}$

13. Which of the following expressions gives the electric potential at the position of the $-q$ charge due to the other two charges?

(A) $\dfrac{-kQ}{\sqrt{2}x}$

(B) $\dfrac{-kQ}{x}$

(C) $\dfrac{3kQ}{x}$

(D) $\dfrac{\left(1-2\sqrt{2}\right)kQ}{x}$

(E) $\dfrac{\left(2\sqrt{2}-1\right)kQ}{x}$

Questions 14–16: A battery with voltage V, two resistors R_1 and R_2, two switches S_1 and S_2, and an inductor L are connected in a circuit as shown. The resistance of R_2 is twice that of R_1. At time $t = 0$, the switches have been open for a long time and the inductor stores no energy. At time $t = 0$, switch S_1 is closed. At time $t = t_1$ switch S_1 is opened and, simultaneously, switch S_2 is closed.

14. Which of the following expressions represents the voltage across the resistor R_1 as a function of time before t_1?

(A) $Ve^{-\frac{t}{RL}}$

(B) $V(1-e^{-\frac{tR}{L}})$

(C) V

(D) $V(1-e^{-\frac{t}{RL}})$

(E) $Ve^{-\frac{tR}{L}}$

15. Which of the following graphs represents the current I through the inductor as a function of time?

16. What is the maximum energy stored in the inductor?

(A) $\dfrac{LV^2}{2R_1^2}$

(B) zero

(C) $\dfrac{LV^2}{2R_2^2}$

(D) $\dfrac{LV^2}{2\left(\dfrac{R_1R_2}{R_1+R_2}\right)^2}$

(E) $\dfrac{LV^2}{2(R_1+R_2)^2}$

17. Two identical resistors are connected in parallel to a battery of voltage V, dissipating power P. Next, the same resistors are instead connected in series to the same battery. What is the new total voltage and total power in the new circuit?

(A) $4V$, $P/4$
(B) V, P
(C) $4V$, $4P$
(D) V, $4P$
(E) V, $P/4$

GO ON TO THE NEXT PAGE

18. In a region of space, the electric field is zero everywhere. Which of the following MUST be true about the electric potential in this region?

   (A) It must be the same value, either positive or negative, everywhere.
   (B) It must be zero everywhere.
   (C) It must be the same positive value everywhere.
   (D) It must be zero at at least one point in the region.
   (E) It must be the same negative value everywhere.

Questions 19 and 20: Two parallel plate capacitors, each with capacitance C, are connected in series with one another as part of a larger circuit. Each stores charge Q and has voltage difference V between its plates. These two capacitors are then replaced by a single equivalent capacitor and reconnected to the same larger circuit.

19. What is the capacitance of the replacement capacitor?

   (A) C
   (B) $C/2$
   (C) $2C$
   (D) $3C/2$
   (E) $C/\sqrt{2}$

20. What is the charge on and voltage across the replacement capacitor?

	charge	voltage
(A)	$2Q$	$V/2$
(B)	$2Q$	$2V$
(C)	Q	$2V$
(D)	Q	V
(E)	Q	$V/2$

21. Two large oppositely charged parallel plates are initially separated by a distance d. The uniform electric field between the plates has magnitude E. Next, the magnitude of the charge on each plate is doubled, while the separation distance d is doubled. What is the new electric field magnitude?

   (A) E
   (B) $E/4$
   (C) $E/2$
   (D) $4E$
   (E) $2E$

22. Four objects with charge $+Q$ are arranged on the corners of a square, as shown. Three of the objects are fixed in place; the one at the top right of the square is free to move and is released from rest. No external forces act on the four-object system. Which of the following correctly describes the motion of the free object?

   (A) It moves up and to the right with increasing acceleration, always speeding up.
   (B) It moves down and left until it hits the bottom-right object.
   (C) It moves up and to the right with decreasing acceleration until it eventually comes to rest.
   (D) It oscillates about its original position.
   (E) It moves up and to the right with decreasing acceleration, always speeding up.

23. Two hollow metal spheres of different radii initially carry different charges: the larger sphere 1 carries charge $+q_1$, and the smaller sphere 2 carries charge $-q_2$. When the spheres are connected by a long conducting wire, charge will flow until:

   (A) the electric field at each sphere's surface is the same.
   (B) the charge residing on the surface of each sphere is equal.
   (C) the electric field at each sphere's center is the same.
   (D) the charge residing on the surface of each sphere is zero.
   (E) the electric potential at each sphere's surface is the same.

Questions 24 and 25: A parallel-plate capacitor is filled with air. Each plate has area 10 cm². The separation between plates is 2.0 cm. The top plate stores +200 nC of charge, and the bottom plate stores –200 nC of charge.

24. An insulating material of dielectric constant κ is inserted between the plates. What happens to the capacitance of the capacitor?

   (A) $(0.44 \text{ pF})/\kappa$
   (B) $(0.44 \text{ pF}) \cdot \kappa$
   (C) (0.44 pF)
   (D) $(0.44 \text{ pF}) \cdot \kappa^2$
   (E) $(0.44 \text{ pF})/\kappa^2$

GO ON TO THE NEXT PAGE

25. The original capacitor is again filled with air. Now the plates are replaced with new plates of area 20 cm^2 but the same charge and separation. How is the potential difference across the plates affected?

    (A) The potential difference is quadrupled.
    (B) The potential difference is cut in half.
    (C) The potential difference is doubled.
    (D) The potential difference is unchanged.
    (E) The potential difference is reduced to ¼ of its previous value.

26. A square loop of wire with side length 0.10 m is situated in the plane of the page. A uniform magnetic field **B** points into the page, along the z-axis, as shown in the diagram. Which of the following manipulations would increase the magnetic flux through the wire loop?

    (A) Increase the side length of the square loop
    (B) Rotate the loop about the z-axis
    (C) Decrease the magnetic field strength
    (D) Rotate the loop about the x-axis
    (E) Rotate the loop about the y-axis

27. A solid, nonconducting sphere carries a uniform volume charge distribution r. Which of the following is a correct statement?

    (A) All positions in the sphere are at the same electric potential.
    (B) All charge that is not bound to an atom resides on the surface of the sphere.
    (C) The net charge enclosed by any Gaussian surface entirely within the conductor must be zero.
    (D) The electric field just outside the sphere is directed perpendicular to the sphere's surface.
    (E) The electric field magnitude inside the sphere is zero.

28. A proton moving to the right encounters an electric field that points up. What is the direction of the electric force on the proton once the proton enters the electric field?

    (A) At an angle down and to the right
    (B) Down
    (C) At an angle up and to the right
    (D) Right
    (E) Up

29. A solid conducting sphere of radius R contains a distribution of charge $-Q$ along its surface. Although the electric field at the sphere's center is zero, the electric potential is not. Why not?

    (A) Because the electric potential is defined as equal to zero only at a position very far away from the sphere, the potential cannot be zero anywhere else.
    (B) Because the electric field is only zero right at the sphere's center, a changing electric field nearby must create a changing electric potential nearby, too.
    (C) Because in the formula for electric potential R is in the denominator; when $R = 0$ the potential is not zero, it is undefined.
    (D) Because a negative charge would be forced away from the sphere toward $V = 0$ far away, the potential at the sphere's surface is nonzero; and in a conductor, the potential is uniform throughout.
    (E) Because a positive test charge placed at the sphere's center would be attracted to the surface, and positive charges are forced high-to-low potential.

GO ON TO THE NEXT PAGE

30. Can a negatively charged conductor apply an attractive force on an uncharged insulator?

(A) YES – If the uncharged insulator is small enough, the r term in the denominator of Coulomb's law would become small, making the whole expression large and creating a measurable force.

(B) NO – Because charge can't move freely along the insulator's surface, charge separation by induction cannot occur.

(C) NO – Because one of the q terms in Coulomb's law would be zero, it's impossible for a negatively charged object to apply an electric force on an uncharged object.

(D) YES – The positive charges can induce a local negative charge on the near surface of the insulator.

(E) YES – The electrons in the negatively charged conductor can attract the protons in the insulator.

31. Two objects, each with charge $+Q$, are a fixed distance d apart. Each applies an electric force F to the other. Next, an object with charge $-(1/8)Q$ is placed on the midpoint between the first two objects. The new electric force experienced by each of the positively charged objects is:

(A) $(3/4)F$
(B) $3F$
(C) $(1/2)F$
(D) F
(E) zero

32. The electric potential along the y-axis is given by $V = -3y^2 - 2y - 3$, where y is in meters and V is in volts. At what position on the y-axis is the electric field equal to zero?

(A) $+0.33$ m
(B) -3 m
(C) 0 m
(D) -0.33 m
(E) $+3$ m

33. A long, straight wire of circular cross-section with radius α carries a uniform areal current density j. What is the value of the line integral of the magnetic field around the circumference of the wire?

(A) $\mu_0 j \pi \alpha$

(B) $2\mu_0 j \pi \alpha$

(C) $2\mu_0 j \pi \alpha^2$

(D) $\mu_0 j$

(E) $\mu_0 j \pi \alpha^2$

Questions 34 and 35: A 120-V source is connected to three resistors, as shown in the diagram. The resistance of R_3 is twice the resistance of R_2, which is twice the resistance of R_1.

34. Which of the following ranks the power P_1, P_2, and P_3 dissipated by each resistor?

(A) $P_1 > P_3 > P_2$
(B) $P_2 > P_3 > P_1$
(C) $P_1 = P_2 = P_3$
(D) $P_3 > P_2 > P_1$
(E) $P_1 > P_2 > P_3$

35. Which of the following is correct about the equivalent resistance of this circuit?

(A) It is between the resistances of R_2 and R_3.
(B) It is greater than the resistance of R_3.
(C) It is between the resistances of R_1 and R_2.
(D) It is less than the resistance of R_1.
(E) It is equal to the resistance of R_2.

STOP. End of Physics C—Electricity and Magnetism Practice Exam 2—Multiple-Choice Questions

Physics C—Electricity and Magnetism Practice Exam 2—
Free-Response Questions

Time: 45 minutes. You may refer to the constants sheet and the equation sheet, both of which are found in the appendix. You may use a calculator.

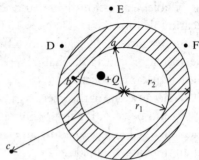

1. A point object carrying positive charge $+Q$ sits in the hollow center of a spherical conducting shell, as shown in the diagram. The inner radius of the shell is r_1, and the outer radius is r_2. Positions A, B, and C are located distances a, b, and c from the shell's center, respectively.

   (a) Determine the magnitude of the electric field at each of the following positions:
       i. Position C
       ii. Position B
       iii. Position A
   (b) Draw a vector indicating the direction and relative magnitude of the electric field at positions D, E, and F. If the electric field is zero, indicate so explicitly.
   (c) Determine the electric potential at each of the following positions:
       i. Position C
       ii. Position B
       iii. Position A
   (d) i. What charge resides on the inner surface of the shell? Justify your answer.
       ii. What charge resides on the outer surface of the shell? Justify your answer.

   (e) Now the charged point object is relocated such that it is off-center, as shown in the diagram.
       i. Describe any changes to the magnitude or direction of the electric fields at positions B and C with the relocated central object. Justify your answer.
       ii. Describe any changes to the amount, sign, or distribution of charge residing on the inner and outer surface of the conducting shell. Justify your answer.

2. An uncharged capacitor is connected to the circuit shown, where $R_A > R_B$. Initially the switch is open, connected neither to position 1 nor to position 2. At time $t = 0$, the switch is thrown to position 1.

   (a) i. What is the current through resistor R_1 immediately after $t = 0$?
       ii. What is the voltage across the capacitor a long time after $t = 0$?
       Now, at time t_2, which is a long time after $t = 0$, the switch is thrown to position 2.

GO ON TO THE NEXT PAGE

(b) i. Which resistor, if either, takes a larger current immediately after time t_2? Justify your answer briefly.

ii. Which resistor, if either, takes a larger voltage immediately after time t_2? Justify your answer briefly.

iii. What is the voltage across the capacitor a long time after time t_2?

(c) i. Show how to use Kirchhoff's rules to write (but do NOT solve) a differential equation for the charge Q on the capacitor as a function of time for all times after t_2.

ii. On the axes provided, sketch a graph of the charge on the capacitor Q as a function of time, beginning at t_2 and ending a long time afterward.

iii. On the axes provided, sketch the magnitude of current through R_A as a function of time, beginning at t_2 and ending a long time afterward.

(d) A student in the laboratory is assigned to verify the current graph in (c) iii. experimentally. The student proposes the following procedure:

I'll hook a digital multimeter set to measure current in series with R_A. I'll start a stopwatch simultaneously with throwing the switch to position 2. I'll call out every 10 s, when my partner will record the ammeter reading.

Explain under what conditions, if any, this procedure will effectively provide evidence for the time-dependent current of the circuit as predicted in (c) iii.

3. (15 points)

A very long wire carries current I_1. Nearby, a square wire loop of side x carries a current I_2, which is produced by a very small battery within the loop as shown. The top side of the square loop is located a distance a from the long wire.

(a) i. In terms of given variables and fundamental constants, calculate the magnitude of the total force applied by the long wire on the wire loop.

ii. Draw a vector indicating the direction of the magnetic force calculated in (a) i.

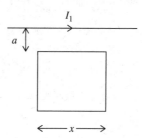

Now the battery in the square loop is removed, and the loop is placed at the same location. For the following, use values $a = 0.02$ m, $x = 0.05$ m, and $I_1 = 0.50$ A.

(b) Calculate the magnetic flux through the square loop.

(c) Calculate the induced current in the square loop.

GO ON TO THE NEXT PAGE

(d) Finally, the square loop is moved from its initial position to a new position, a distance $a + x$ from the long wire. It takes 2 s for the wire to change locations. Using the values $I_1 = 0.50$ A, $a = 0.020$ m, and $x = 0.050$ m, calculate the average EMF induced in the square loop while it changes positions.

STOP. End of Physics C—Electricity and Magnetism Practice Exam 2—Free-Response Questions

Physics C—Mechanics Practice Exam 2—Multiple-Choice Solutions

1. **D**—The airplane's acceleration can be found from kinematics, using $v^2 = v_0^2 + 2a\Delta x$ with $v_0 = 0$. This gives $a = (80$ m/s$)^2/2(3000$ m$) = 1.1$ m/s/s. The net force is ma, so multiply by the 300,000-kg mass to get about 310,000 N. That's 3×10^5 N.

2. **D**—In collisions, momentum generally must be conserved because no net external force acts. But kinetic energy could be converted into internal energy in the collision. Without data to check or an explicit statement of an elastic collision, kinetic energy may or may not be conserved.

3. **E**—For an object of mass m launched with escape velocity, its total mechanical energy at the surface of the planet is kinetic plus potential, or

$$\frac{1}{2}mv^2 + \left(-G\frac{Mm}{r}\right).$$ When the object gets very far

from the planet, its kinetic energy is zero (because escape velocity is the *minimum* speed necessary to leave the planet) and its potential energy is also zero (by definition, any position a long way from the planet has zero potential energy). So set the previous expression equal to zero and solve for v

to get $v = \sqrt{\dfrac{2GM}{r}}$. Now apply semi-quantitative

reasoning—the numerator does not change, but the planet's radius gets cut in half. The radius is in the denominator and under the square root,

meaning the speed is multiplied by $\dfrac{1}{\sqrt{\frac{1}{2}}} = \sqrt{2} = 1.4$.

Or, you can intuit that the gravitational field at the surface of the planet will be stronger because the planet's radius is smaller. That would increase, not decrease, the escape velocity. Probably it's easier the conceptual way.

4. **D**—The block is in equilibrium, at rest. Thus the weight equals the tension, which is 10 N. The scale simply reads this tension. (If you wanted to do a free body diagram of the scale, it would include a 10-N tension pulling down, and the 10-N force of the hand pulling up.)

5. **D**—The blocks are attached together. Acceleration is the change in speed every second. In 1 second, all the blocks must change speed by the same amount; if they didn't, one of the blocks would become unattached. The objects experience different net forces because they are of different mass, but the accelerations must be the same.

6. **D**—The total momentum before collision is (250 g)(100 m/s) = 25,000 g·cm/s to the right and (500 g)(75 cm) = 37,500 g·cm/s to the left. Subtracting, this gives 12,500 g·cm/s total momentum to the left. That's the same momentum as after collision, by conservation. After collision, because the carts stick, the total momentum of 12,500 g·cm/s is the total mass of 750 g times the speed. Dividing, the speed is 17 cm/s.

7. **A**—Take the negative derivative of a potential energy function to get force. Here, the force is $-kx + b$.

8. **E**—Ignore the x direction entirely. In the y direction, there's 4 kg at $y = 0$ and 4 kg at $y = 2$ cm. These equal masses have a center of mass directly in between, at $y = 1$ cm.

9. **A**—The energy conversion here is gravitational potential energy (mgh) to work done by friction (equal to friction force times distance, where friction force is mu times the normal force): $mgh = \mu mgd$. Solving, $h = \mu d$. Here μ is 0.20 and $d = 0.45$ m. That's 0.09 m, or 9 cm.

10. **D**—The vertical axis of the graph indicates that up is the positive direction. The slope of this graph is velocity. When an object slows down, its acceleration is in the opposite direction of its motion; when an object speeds up, its acceleration is in the same direction as its motion. So we want a negative slope that gets steeper (meaning downward, increasing velocity) or a positive slope that gets shallower (meaning upward, decreasing velocity). That's near the top of the peaks of the graph, like at $t = 1.0$ s.

11. D—The period of an object oscillating on a spring is $2\pi\dfrac{\sqrt{m}}{\sqrt{k}}$. The graph shows the period of oscillation—the time for one complete cycle—to be 2.0 s. The mass is given as 0.20 kg. Plug into the equation earlier to get $k = 2.0$ N/m.

12. C—Displacement, velocity, and momentum are vector quantities because their direction matters. When using a negative sign with these, the negative indicates a direction. However, all forms of energy are scalar quantities, just amounts with no direction. The negative sign on potential energy simply means an amount of potential energy less than zero.

13. D—The net force is ma, which in circular motion is mv^2/r. Because speed, radius, and mass don't change throughout the motion, the net force is constant. To find the net force, add or subtract the individual forces on the ball. At the peak, both the tension in the string and the weight pull down: $F_{net} = T + mg$. At the bottom, though, the tension pulls up while the weight pulls down: $F_{net} = T - mg$. With F_{net} and mg constants, the tension at the bottom must be greater—at the bottom, tension is $F_{net} + mg$, whereas at the top, tension is $F_{net} - mg$.

14. A—Stable equilibrium is where the U vs. x graph has a local minimum. This function is an upward-opening parabola, so anywhere where the derivative is zero is a local minimum. Set the derivative $2ax = 0$; solving, $x = 0$.

15. D—Power P is work done per time. The motor must do work to change the object's potential energy by mgh, where h is 100 m. (Not $100\sqrt{2}$ m, because the h in this formula represents vertical height only. No work is done to carry the object horizontally.) The relevant equation becomes $P = \dfrac{mgh}{t}$, where t is the 20-s time interval. Solving, $m = \dfrac{Pt}{gh}$. That's (200 W)(20 s) / (10 m/s/s) (100 m) = 4 kg.

16. A—To get displacement, integrate the velocity function. The limits of the definite integral should be 0 to 2 s. The integral gives $\dfrac{4t^3}{3} - \dfrac{3t^2}{2} + 2t_0^2$. This evaluates to 8.7 m, closest to A.

17. D—The only force on the moon is the force of the planet. This force acts on a line directly through the planet's center; thus, this force provides no torque about the planet. Because no torque acts on the moon, the moon's angular momentum is conserved.

18. A—The formula for the moon-planet potential energy is $-G\dfrac{Mm}{d}$, where M is the planet's mass, m is the moon's mass, and d is the distance between them. The zero of potential energy is taken by convention to be when the moon is a very long way from the planet. As the moon gets closer to the planet, the d term in the denominator decreases. This increases the absolute value of the $G\dfrac{Mm}{d}$ term. But that term is negative, that is, below zero; a smaller d means a smaller potential energy.

19. B—The magnitude of the force of the planet on the moon is $G\dfrac{Mm}{d^2}$. As the moon gets closer to the planet, the d term in the denominator decreases, increasing the amount of the force.

20. A—Force times time is impulse. Both objects experienced the same nonzero force for the same time, so experience the same impulse. Impulse is change in momentum.

21. **D**—Because the pivot is at the meterstick's center of mass, the meterstick's weight provides no torque. The angular acceleration is clockwise; thus, clockwise torques are greater than counterclockwise torques. These torques are equal to the weight of each object times the object's distance from the pivot. Object 2 provides a greater torque, yet its lever arm (the distance from the pivot) is smaller. Thus, object 2 must be more massive.

22. **D**—The centripetal force mv^2/r is the normal force F_n. The friction force, also equal to μF_n, balances the weight. The leads to the equation $\mu \dfrac{mv^2}{r} = mg$. The speed of an object in circular motion is the circumference over the period T, so replace v with $\dfrac{2\pi r}{T}$. Now manipulate algebraically to solve for T.

23. **A**—Use the parallel axis theorem: $I = I_{cm} + Mh^2$, where h is the distance between parallel axes. The rotational inertia through the object's center of mass is $(1/2)MR^2$. The distance between the two axes is R. So $I = (1/2)MR^2 + MR^2 = (3/2)MR^2$.

24. **D**—When the displacement is positive—that is, to the right—the force of the spring is negative, that is, to the left. The magnitude of the force of a spring is kx and so is linear in x. Only choice **D** is linear, with negative force for positive displacement.

25. **B**—Regardless of how it's thrown, once released, the ball is in free-fall: no forces except gravity act on the ball. All objects in free-fall experience a constant acceleration of 10 m/s/s downward.

26. **B**—The slope of the position-time graph is the velocity. Initially, the slope must be nonzero and negative because the ball moves down. And then the graph curves; the slope gets steeper because the ball's speed increases.

27. **A**—The torque provided by each string is force times lever arm. The lever arm in this case is the radius of the pulley. So clockwise torque is (20 N)(3 cm) = 60 N·cm. The counterclockwise torque is (10 N)(1 cm) = 10 N·cm. The net torque is thus (60 − 10) = 50 N·cm.

28. **C**—Use kinematics equation $v_f^2 = v_o^2 + 2a\Delta x$. The ball comes to rest at its peak, $v_f = 0$. So $v_0 = \sqrt{2a\Delta x}$. Here the maximum height Δx is under a square root. So three times higher means $\sqrt{3}$ times bigger speed, and the square root of 3 is 1.7.

29. **B**—Impulse is change in momentum. Both balls lose the same amount of momentum in hitting the floor and coming to rest; however, ball A changes its momentum even more in order to rebound. So ball A changes its momentum by a larger amount, therefore experiencing the greater impulse. Impulse is also force times time of collision. By Newton's third law, the force of the ball on the floor is equal to the force of the floor on the ball, and the same collision takes the same amount of time. So if ball A experiences more impulse in its collision, so does the floor.

30. **A**—Translated to equations, the problem says $F = -bv$, where b is some positive constant. (The term bv is negative, because the force of air resistance must act opposite the direction of velocity.) We know net force $F = ma$, and a is the time derivative of velocity. So rewrite: $m\dfrac{dv}{dt} = -bt$. Rearrange algebraically to get.

31. **E**—The equation for train A's position is derived from $\Delta x = v_0 t + \frac{1}{2}at^2$: $x = 10t - 2.5t^2$, with $x = 0$ at its original location and calling positive x to the east. That makes train A's initial velocity positive and its acceleration negative. Train B's position is given by $x = 200 - 2.5t^2$. This works because at time $t = 0$ $x = 200$; then after 1 s, $x = 197.5$ m, so is moving west as expected. Now set both expressions for x equal to each other: $10t - 2.5t^2 = 200 - 2.5t^2$. This solves to give $t = 20$ s.

32. **A**—Acceleration is the slope of a velocity-time graph. The acceleration is constant when the graph is a line: AB, BC, and CD. But CD's section is horizontal, indicating zero acceleration.

33. **D**—Net force is ma, where a is the time derivative of the velocity function. This derivative gives $v = \dfrac{6t}{m}$. So ma is $6t$.

34. **A**—Here the graph is always above the horizontal axis; this means the motion is always in the positive direction (i.e., right). The vertical axis values get closer to zero, reach zero, and then get farther from zero. Thus, the speed gets closer then farther from zero: the car slows down and speeds up.

35. **E**—The net force on the block includes the horizontal component of F to the right and the friction force to the left. That's $F\cos\theta$ to the right. To the left, the force of friction is μF_n, where the normal force F_n in this case is the weight mg plus the vertical component of F in order to maintain vertical equilibrium. So the friction force to the left is $\mu(mg + F\sin\theta)$. The net force is now $F\cos\theta - \mu(mg + F\sin\theta)$. And this net force is parallel to the displacement d, so multiply these to get the net work: $[F\cos\theta - \mu(mg + F\sin\theta)]d$.

Physics C—Mechanics Practice Exam 2—Free-Response Solutions

Notes on grading your free-response section

For answers that are numerical, or in equation form:

*For each part of the problem, look to see if you got the right answer. If you did, and you showed any reasonable (and correct) work, give yourself full credit for that part. It's okay if you didn't explicitly show EVERY step, as long as some steps are indicated and you got the right answer. However:

*If you got the WRONG answer, then look to see if you earned partial credit. Give yourself points for each step toward the answer as indicated in the rubrics below. Without the correct answer, you must show each intermediate step explicitly in order to earn the point for that step. (See why it's so important to show your work?)

*If you're off by a decimal place or two, not to worry—you get credit anyway, as long as your approach to the problem was legitimate. This isn't a math test. You're not being evaluated on your rounding and calculator-use skills.

*You do not have to simplify expressions in variables all the way. Square roots in the denominator are fine; fractions in nonsimplified form are fine. As long as you've solved properly for the requested variable, and as long as your answer is algebraically equivalent to the rubric's, you earn credit.

*Wrong, but consistent: Often you need to use the answer to part (a) in order to solve part (b). But you might have the answer to part (a) wrong. If you follow the correct procedure for part (b), plugging in your incorrect answer, then you will usually receive *full credit* for part (b). The major exceptions are when your answer to part (a) is unreasonable (say, a car moving at 10^5 m/s, or a distance between two cars equal to 10^{-100} meters), or when your answer to part (a) makes the rest of the problem trivial or irrelevant.

For answers that require justification:

*Obviously your answer will not match the rubric word-for-word. If the general gist is there, you get credit.

*But the reader is not allowed to interpret for the student. If your response is vague or ambiguous, you will NOT get credit.

*If your response consists of both correct and incorrect parts, you will usually not receive credit. It is not possible to try two answers, hoping that one of them is right. ☺ (See why it's so important to be concise?)

1.

(a)

The rotational inertia is given by $I = \int x^2 dm$.

To evaluate the integral, set λ as the constant mass per unit length. Replace dm with λdx, giving $\lambda \int_0^d x^2 dx$. This evaluates to $\dfrac{\lambda d^3}{3}$. Here, λ is m/d, making the final result $I = (1/3)md^2$.

1 pt   for using the correct general calculus expression for I

1 pt   for replacing dm with λdx

1 pt   for setting up an integral with an $x^2 dx$ term and limits from 0 to d

1 pt   for correctly evaluating a correct integral

1 pt   for recognizing that λ is m/d

1 pt   for the correct answer

(b)

Angular momentum is conserved. Before, the total angular momentum is just that of the disk, $m_1 v_1 x$. Afterward, the total angular momentum is the sum of the disk and rod's $I\omega$, which is $\left(\frac{1}{3}Md^2 + m_1 x^2\right)\omega$. Set the expressions equal and solve to get $\omega = \dfrac{m_1 v_1 x}{\left(\frac{1}{3}Md^2 + m_1 x^2\right)\omega}$.

1 pt   for a correct expression for total momentum before collision

1 pt   for a correct expression for I of the rod-disk system

1 pt for setting expressions for total momentum before collision equal to total momentum after.

1 pt for the correct expression for ω

(c)

The rubber disk provides greater angular speed after collision. In both cases the angular momentum before the collision is the same. However, the rubber disk rebounds, which means it has negative momentum after the collision. That means that the rod must have even more positive momentum after the collision in order to subtract the rubber disk's momentum and still get the same total momentum.

1 pt for correct answer
1 pt for correct justification

(d)

To the left of point C. Angular momentum for the disk is $m_1 v_1 x$, and the bigger x, the bigger the total angular momentum that can be transferred into the rod-disk after the collision.

1 pt for correct answer and justification

(e)

The answer wouldn't change. The total angular momentum of the system before collision is still $m_1 v_1 x$. That angular momentum is still transferred to the system after the collision. Because this angular momentum depends on x but not on properties of the rod, the rod's linear density is irrelevant.

1 pt for correct answer
1 pt for correct justification

2.

(a)

The net force is ma, and also is equal to $-kx$ because it's provided by a spring. Acceleration is $\frac{d^2 x}{dt^2}$. Combine to get $\frac{d^2 x}{dt^2} = -\frac{k}{m} x$.

1 pt for setting ma equal to the force of the spring
1 pt for substituting $\frac{d^2 x}{dt^2}$ for a

(b)

The solution to a second-order differential equation is a cosine function. Initially, the compression is maximum and equal to d. So write $x = d \cos(\omega t)$. But ω isn't given in the problem statement. Take two derivatives to get $\frac{d^2 x}{dt^2} = -d \omega^2 \cos(\omega t)$. In order for this expression to match the one in (a), ω must be equal to $\sqrt{\frac{k}{m}}$. The final answer is thus $x = d \cos(\sqrt{\frac{k}{m}} t)$.

1 pt for writing an expression with a cosine or sine term
1 pt for a correct answer

(c)

First, find the speed of the block when it loses contact with the spring. This requires energy conservation, because the block's acceleration while attached to the spring is not constant. Spring potential energy is converted to kinetic energy: $\frac{1}{2} k d^2 = \frac{1}{2} m v^2$. The speed of the block is $d \sqrt{\frac{k}{m}}$. Then when the block leaves the table, it falls for a time given by vertical kinematics with $v_0 = 0$: $y = \frac{1}{2} g t^2$. Solve to get the time $t = \sqrt{\frac{2y}{g}}$.

Horizontally, the block's speed doesn't change; so multiply speed by time to get distance traveled in the air, $R = d \sqrt{\frac{2ky}{mg}}$.

1 pt for using energy to get the block's speed
1 pt for using vertical kinematics to get time
1 pt for the correct expression in terms of given variables

(d)

R becomes smaller. In the first case, all of the spring energy was transferred to the block's kinetic energy. In the new case, the spring stores some energy at release. So the block has less kinetic energy, moves at a slower speed, and covers less horizontal distance in the same time of flight.

1 pt for the correct answer
1 pt for a correct justification

(e)

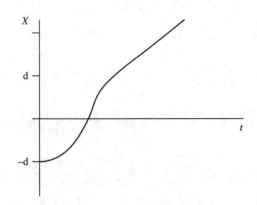

Initially the positon-time graph is sinusoidal, because the block was in simple harmonic motion. When the block is released, it moves at constant speed, represented by an unchanging slope (i.e., a straight line). That slope doesn't change, even after the block leaves the table, because no further horizontal forces act on the block.

1 pt   for the correct sinusoidal shape before release from the spring

1 pt   for a straight line, tangent to the sinusoid, immediately after release

1 pt   for continuing the straight line until the end

(f)

Initially the speed is zero; the velocity-time graph is sinusoidal, because the block was in simple harmonic motion. When the block is released, its speed doesn't change until the block leaves the table. Then, the block gains speed—the vertical velocity increases, so the Pythagorean sum of vertical and horizontal velocities must also increase even though horizontal velocity doesn't change.

1 pt   for the correct sinusoidal shape before release from the spring

1 pt   for a horizontal line continuous with the sinusoid after release

1 pt   for increasing speed when the block leaves the table

3.

(a)
Many approaches. My favorite: Place a sonic motion detector beneath the hanger. Use the detector to make a velocity-time graph while the hanger is in motion. The slope of that graph is the hanger's acceleration.

1 pt   for measuring quantities that could lead to a determination of acceleration

1 pt   for a plausible procedure

1 pt   for a detailed procedure

1 pt   for explaining how to get acceleration from measured quantities

1 pt   for multiple data points (note that any use of a graph satisfies this requirement)

(b)
Equal. Acceleration is the change in an object's speed in some about of time. The objects are connected; if one speeds up, so does the other by the same amount. (Otherwise, they would become disconnected or the rope would go slack.)

1 pt   for the correct answer

1 pt   for a correct justification

(c)
The relevant equation here comes from applying Newton's second law to the two-object system. The net force is $m_2g - m_1g$; the system mass is $m_1 + m_2$. Because the graph has m_2g on the vertical axis, solve for m_2g: $m_2g = (m_1 + m_2)a + m_1g$. Because a appears linearly (i.e., not squared or square rooted) in the numerator, the graph is linear: **yes**. Identify each term with a term in the equation for a line, $y = mx + b$. The y variable is m_2g. The x variable is a. This leaves the slope of the graph as $(m_1 + m_2)$. The b term is the y-intercept and is m_1g. To get m_1, find the vertical intercept of the best-fit line and divide by g.

1 pt   for recognizing that the graph is linear

1 pt   for explaining why the graph is linear

1 pt   for using Newton's second law correctly to get an expression relating m_2g and a

1 pt   for using the vertical intercept to get m_1

1 pt   for explaining in words or mathematics why the vertical intercept is used to get m_1

(d)

The newly measured acceleration would be **less**. Now the net force on the system isn't just $m_2 g - m_1 g$; there's another force, the friction force, that acts opposite the direction of motion. Because the objects are released from rest, that's also opposite the direction of acceleration. So the net force would be smaller than before. Because $a = F_{net} / m$ and the system mass hasn't changed, the acceleration would be smaller.

1 pt   for choosing "less"

1 pt   for explicitly explaining why the net force would be less

1 pt   for relating less net force to less acceleration using Newton's second law

AP Physics C—Mechanics

Full Exam Scoring

Multiple-Choice: Number Correct_____(35 max)

Free-Response: Question 1_____(15 max)
                Question 2_____(15 max)
                Question 3_____(15 max)

Total Free-Response_____(45 max)

$1.286 \times$ Multiple-Choice $+$ Free-Response $=$ Raw Score_____(90 max)

59–90	5
45–58	4
35–44	3
23–34	2
0–22	1

Physics C—Electricity and Magnetism Practice Exam 2— Multiple-Choice Solutions

1. **D**—The magnetic force on the object is indeed qvB. However, that force is always perpendicular to the direction of motion. (This is true for all magnetic forces on moving charged objects.) Work is equal to force times the distance traveled parallel to that force—because the force and motion are never parallel to one another, no work is done.

2. **B**—An emf is only induced in a wire when the flux through the wire is changing; thus the answer must be B or D, where the wire is entering or leaving the magnetic field. To find the direction of the induced current, use Lenz's law—point the right thumb in the direction of the magnetic field, and ask if the flux is decreasing. At position D the flux is decreasing; so curl the fingers to find that at D the current is clockwise. At position B the flux is not decreasing; so flip the direction of the thumb and curl the fingers. That gives a counterclockwise current.

3. **A**—Electric potential is a scalar; thus, electric potentials at a point due to multiple objects are added together.

4. **A**—The potential due to a point charge is $\frac{kQ}{d}$,

    where d is the distance from the charge. Both objects produce the same potential. So the equation with the bigger charge in the numerator must also have a bigger distance in the denominator and by the same factor because the equation has no squares or square roots.

5. **C**—The force of a magnetic field on a current carrying wire is $F = ILB$. Here the I is I_1 because wire 1 is experiencing the force; B is the magnetic field produced by wire 2 at the location of wire 1. That magnetic field is

    $B = \frac{\mu_0 I_2}{2\pi d}$. Combining the equations, we find that

    $F_1 = \frac{I_1 L \mu_0 I_2}{2\pi d}$. All values here are constant except I_1, which is in the numerator and to the first power; the graph is therefore linear.

6. **C**—Newton's third law demands that the force of wire 1 on wire 2 be equal to the force of wire 2 on wire 1; so the magnitude of F_2 is equal to F_1. Wire 1 produces a magnetic field into the page at the location of wire 2 (by the second right-hand rule: point the thumb along I_1 and curl the fingers—the fingers point into the page at the location of wire 2). Then by the first right-hand rule (point in the direction of current, curl the fingers toward the magnetic field, the thumb gives the direction of force), the force on wire 2 is upward, toward wire 1.

7. **D**—Combining the equations for the magnetic field produced by wire 2 at the location of wire 1, and for the force exerted by that magnetic field on

    wire 1, we get $F_1 = \frac{I_1 L \mu_0 I_2}{2\pi d}$. Here, d is in the

    denominator and to the first power, so doubling d simply halves F_1.

8. **D**—The magnetic field produced by a current-

    carrying wire is given by $\frac{\mu_0 I}{2\pi r}$, where r is the

    distance from the wire. So B goes inversely with x here, meaning only B or D could be right. The magnetic field does not go to zero just because a wire ends 7 cm away from another wire.

9. **E**—Emf is the time derivative of magnetic flux. Here, because the area of the loop and the angle of the magnetic field relative to the loop don't change, the time derivative of the magnetic field determines the flux. The time derivative of $4t$ is simply a constant 4—the emf doesn't vary in time.

10. **E**—The electric force on a positive charge is in the direction of the electric field, so downward. To create equilibrium allowing for constant speed, the magnetic force must be upward. Using the first right-hand rule, the fingers point left for the velocity and the thumb points up for the force, so the fingers indicating the magnetic field direction curl out of the page.

11. **D**—The force components are away from the negative charges and toward the positive charge. The negative charges produce equal components right and up, with a resultant 45 degrees up and right. The positive charge produces a force 45 degrees down and left. Because the positive charge is farther from $-q$ than the other charges, the force it produces is smaller, and thus the net force is up and right.

12. **C**—The top-left and bottom-right charges each produce an electric field component of magnitude $\frac{kQ}{x^2}$ directed toward those charges. These perpendicular components add pythagoreanly to $\frac{\sqrt{2}kQ}{x^2}$ down and left, toward the $+Q$ charge. That $+Q$ charge produces an electric field pointing up and right of magnitude $\frac{kQ}{(\sqrt{2}x)^2}$. Because this field is in the opposite direction of the field due to the other two charges, the two fields subtract. Finding a common denominator and subtracting yields choice.

13. **D**—Each of the $-Q$ charges produces a potential of $\frac{-kQ}{x}$ at the position in question. (Potentials add or subtract algebraically; negative charges produce negative potentials.) The $+Q$ charge is $\sqrt{2}x$ away and so produces a potential of $\frac{+kQ}{\sqrt{2}x}$. Get a common denominator and add together $\frac{+kQ}{\sqrt{2}x}$ $\frac{-kQ}{x}$ $\frac{-kQ}{x}$ to get choice.

14. **B**—An inductor resists change in current. Initially, when we close S_1, the current needs to change rapidly from zero to something; so the inductor stores energy initially, leaving zero voltage for the resistor. After a long time, though, when the current reaches a steady state, the circuit behaves as if the inductor weren't there, meaning the voltage across R_1 is just V. Both choices B and D meet these limiting conditions—plug in $t = 0$ and you get a voltage of zero. But the time constant for an RL circuit is L/R, not RL. Thus, the correct choice is not D, but B.

15. **D**—Without the inductor, the current would go from zero to a maximum value instantaneously when S_1 was closed. With the inductor, the current increases to a maximum gradually with an exponential relationship. So only C and D get the first part of the current right. Then the current decreases back to zero exponentially—both C and D show that. What's the difference? The time constant for changes in the current is given by L/R. The bigger the resistance, the shorter the time it takes to reach the steady-state current. Because R_2 is bigger than R_1, the drop in current after the second switch is closed is faster than the rise in current initially.

16. **A**—The energy stored by an inductor is $\frac{LI^2}{2}$. What current I is used? We need the maximum current. That's V/R_1, when S_1 has been closed for a long time but before S_2 is closed. When S_2 is open, the resistor R_2 has no effect on the circuit. After S_2 is closed, the current in the inductor drops, so it cannot be the maximum.

17. **E**—Voltage is provided by a battery; with rare exceptions, this voltage does not depend on what the battery is attached to. Power is V^2/R. The equivalent resistance of the circuit quadruples with the new arrangement. (Originally identical resistors R in parallel give equivalent resistance $R/2$; in series, the equivalent resistance is $2R$.) So the numerator of the power equation doesn't change while the denominator quadruples, causing power to be cut by ¼.

18. **A**—Pretend a positive charge is in fact located in this region. No electric field means no electric force on this charge. Because positive charges are forced high-to-low potential and there's no force on this charge, there can't be "high" and "low" potentials—the potential must be uniform. Uniform potential has the same effect whether it's a uniform potential of zero, +5 V, –10 V, or whatever—only the difference in potential from one position to another is relevant here.

19. **B**—The equivalent resistance of series capacitors is given by $\dfrac{1}{C_{eq}} = \dfrac{1}{C_1} + \dfrac{1}{C_2}$. The shortcut is that the equivalent capacitance of two equal capacitors in series is half of each individual capacitance.

20. **C**—Even though each of the original capacitors stored charge Q, the equivalent capacitor also stores charge Q: capacitors in series each carry the same charge, which is equal to the total charge stored. In the initial situation, each capacitor took voltage $V = Q/C$. Now the equivalent capacitor takes voltage $(Q)/(C/2) = 2Q/C$ = twice the voltage across each individual capacitor.

21. **E**—Start with the equation for capacitance of a parallel plate capacitor, $C = \dfrac{\varepsilon_0 A}{d}$. Doubling d causes the capacitance C to be cut in half. Next, look at the relationship between charge and voltage for a capacitor: $Q = CV$. Here, Q is doubled and C is halved, meaning that V must be increased by a factor of 4. Finally, the electric field between the plates is given by $E = V/d$. The numerator increases by a factor of 4, while the denominator only increases by a factor of 2. So E is doubled.

22. **E**—The acceleration depends on the net force. The net force on the free object decreases as it gets farther from the other objects, because the distance term in the denominator of Coulomb's law gets larger. But the free object will always experience a force up and to the right. A net force in the direction of motion always causes an object to speed up, not to slow down.

23. **E**—Positive charge is forced high-to-low potential; negative charge is forced low-to-high potential. When there's no difference in electric potential, then charge is not forced to flow.

24. **B**—The capacitance of a parallel plate capacitor filled with a vacuum (or air, which is close enough) is $C = \varepsilon_0 \dfrac{A}{d}$, which works out to 0.44 pF – 0.44 × 10^{-12} F in this case. The capacitance is multiplied by the dielectric constant of the material filling the capacitor. Note that there's no need to plug in values into the capacitance equation.

25. **B**—The potential difference (i.e., the voltage) across a capacitor is given by $Q = CV$. In this case, the charge across the plates is unaffected. The capacitance is given by $C = \varepsilon_0 \dfrac{A}{d}$; because A is in the numerator and to the first power, the capacitance doubles when the area of the plates doubles. Back to $Q = CV$, the same Q with doubled C gives half the previous V.

26. **A**—Magnetic flux is BA, where B is the magnetic field strength and A is the area of the loop that is directly penetrated by the magnetic field. So we need to either increase the magnetic field strength or increase the area of the loop directly penetrated by the field. The rotations do not increase that area: rotating about the x- or y-axis would reduce the area of the loop available to the magnetic field penetration. Rotation about the z-axis wouldn't change that area. But increasing the actual physical area of the loop would increase the A term.

27. **D**—Choices (A), (B), (C), and (E) are valid only for a conducting sphere. However, (D) is correct in this case, too, because the charge distribution is uniform; the symmetry of the charge distribution means that at any position on the surface, the charges in the sphere produce horizontal electric field components that cancel. Only the vertical (i.e., perpendicular to the surface) component remains.

28. **E**—A positively charged object is forced in the same direction as the electric field. The direction of motion has nothing to do with the direction of force.

29. **D**—It is correct that electric potential is zero a very long distance away from the sphere, but so what. The electric potential at the surface is given by $V = -kQ/R$; it is negative because it is produced by a negative charge. A negative charge near the surface of the sphere would be forced low-to-high potential, which would be from the negative-potential surface toward zero potential far away. But within the conducting sphere, the electric field is zero, meaning the potential cannot change. The potential at the sphere's center is ALSO $V = -kQ/R$.

30. **B**—Charge separation by induction happens in conductors, in which charge can flow freely along the conductor's surface. This phenomenon allows an uncharged *conductor* to experience attraction to another charged object. However, in an insulator, charges cannot flow freely, so there can't even be a local area in which negative charges attract positive charges.

31. **C**—Consider the leftmost object. It experiences two electric forces, one from the $+Q$ charge and one from the $-(1/8)Q$ charge. Write Coulomb's law for each of these forces, and subtract because the forces act in opposite directions: $\frac{kQQ}{d^2} - \frac{k\frac{1}{8}QQ}{\left(\frac{1}{2}d\right)^2}$.

Simplify the expression to get $\frac{1}{2}\frac{kQQ}{d^2}$, which is half of the force of the two $+Q$ charges on each other.

32. **D**—The electric field is related to the electric potential by $E = -\frac{dV}{dy}$. The negative derivative of the V function is $6y + 2$; set that equal to zero to get $y = -(1/3)$.

33. **E**—Ampere's law says that the line integral of the magnetic field around a closed line is $\mu_0 I_{enclosed}$. How much current is enclosed by the circumference of the wire? The areal current density j times the area enclosed. The cross-sectional area enclosed here is just the area of the circular wire, πa^2.

34. **E**—The power dissipated by a resistor is given by V^2/R. Here the voltage across each resistor is the same, because all are in parallel with each other. Mathematically, then, the smallest resistance will take the largest power. Distance from the battery is irrelevant.

35. **D**—You don't need the equation for equivalent resistance of parallel resistors. No matter the values, the equivalent resistance of parallel resistors is always less than the smallest resistor.

Physics C—Electricity and Magnetism Practice Exam 2— Free-Response Solutions

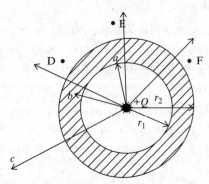

(b) Draw a vector indicating the direction and relative magnitude of the electric field at positions *D, E,* and *F*. If the electric field is zero, indicate so explicitly.

1. (15 points)

A point object carrying positive charge $+Q$ sits in the hollow center of an uncharged spherical conducting shell, as shown in the diagram. The inner radius of the shell is r_1, and the outer radius is r_2. Positions *A, B,* and *C* are located distances *a, b,* and *c* from the shell's center, respectively.

(a) Determine the magnitude of the electric field at each of the following positions:

    i. Position *C*

    Because the conductor itself has no charge, the charge enclosed by a Gaussian surface of radius *c* is just *Q*. Then the reasoning in part i gives $Q/4\pi\varepsilon_0 c^2$ or kQ/c^2.

1 pt for correct answer

    ii. Position *B*

    Fact: The electric field inside a conductor is zero.

1 pt for correct answer

    iii. Position *A*

    Draw a spherical Gaussian surface with radius *a*. It encloses charge *Q* and has surface area $4\pi a2$. By the symmetry of the problem, the integral in Gauss's law becomes multiplication: $EA = Q_{enclosed}/\varepsilon_0$. The electric field is then $Q/4\pi\varepsilon_0 a2$; this is equivalent to $kQ/a2$ using *k* as the Coulomb's law constant.

1 pt for correct answer

1 pt for each vector pointing away from the center of the sphere

1 pt for vectors at D and F being longer than the vector at E

(c) Determine the electric potential at each of the following positions:

    i. Position *C*

    The electric potential a long distance away is zero. Because the electric field outside the shell has the same form as that due to a point charge, so does the electric potential: $+kQ/c$.

1 pt for the correct answer

    ii. Position *B*

    The electric potential at the outer surface of the shell is $+kQ/r_2$. Because the electric field is zero within the shell, the potential cannot change within the shell—it's still the same potential as at either surface. So $+kQ/r_2$.

1 pt for correct answer

    iii. Position *A*

    The electric potential inside a spherical shell of charge is equal to kq/r, where *r* is the radius of the shell. The electric potential due to a point charge is also kq/r, where this *r* represents the distance from the charge. At position *A*, we have three things contributing to the potential: the point charge $+Q$ at the center, the ring of charge $-Q$ on the inside surface, and the ring $+Q$ on the outside surface. Superimpose these three to get a total potential of $+kQ/a - kQ/r_1 + kQ/r_2$.

Note that this works out to give the same potential at the inside surface ($+kQ/r_2$) as at the outer surface.

1 pt for correct answer

(d)

i. A spherical Gaussian surface drawn inside the shell must enclose zero charge, because the electric field inside the shell is zero. We know such a shell encloses $+Q$ from the point object, so the inner surface must carry charge $-Q$ to make the total charge inside that Gaussian surface zero.

1 pt for correct answer
1 pt for a correct justification

ii. What charge resides on the outer surface of the shell? Justify your answer.

We know the shell is uncharged. With $-Q$ on the inner surface, $+Q$ must be on the outer surface to give a net charge of zero on the shell.

1 pt for an answer consistent with i and correct justification

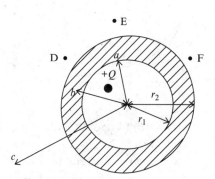

(e) Now the charged point object is relocated such that it is off-center, as shown in the diagram.

i. Describe any changes to the magnitude or direction of the electric fields at positions B and C with the relocated central object. Justify your answer.

The electric field at B is still zero, because B is still inside a conductor. No change.

The electric field at C is unchanged, because the electric field outside a

conductor is perpendicular to the conductor's surface; the symmetry of the problem *outside* the shell is unchanged. A Gaussian sphere drawn through C still encloses the same charge, so no change.

1 pt for correct justification for no change in electric field at B
1 pt for correct justification that there is no change in the electric field at C

ii. Describe any changes to the amount, sign, or distribution of charge residing on the inner and outer surface of the conducting shell. Justify your answer.

The same amount and sign of charge must reside on each surface, according to Gauss's law, in order to get an electric field of zero inside the conductor. However, whereas the outer surface's charge will still be uniformly distributed, the charge on the inner surface will be differently distributed—the point object will induce a denser negative charge on the part of the surface closest to the object.

1 pt justifying the same amount and sign of charge on each surface with Gauss's law
1 pt justifying the different distribution on the inner surface

2. An uncharged capacitor of capacitance C is connected to the circuit shown, where $R_A > R_B$. Initially the switch is open, connected neither to position 1 nor to position 2. At time $t = 0$, the switch is thrown to position 1.

(a)

i. What is the current through resistor R_1 immediately after $t = 0$?

The uncharged capacitor will initially allow current to flow as if the circuit consisted of just the battery and resistor. So by Ohm's law the current is V/R_A.

1 pt for correct answer

ii. What is the voltage across the capacitor a long time after $t = 0$?

After a long time the capacitor will be charged, and thus will block current. Zero.

1 pt for correct answer

Now, at time t_2, which is a long time after $t = 0$, the switch is thrown to position 2.

(b)

i. Which resistor, if either, takes a larger current immediately after time t_2? Justify your answer briefly.

The resistors are in series—they take the same current by definition (or by Kirchhoff's junction rule).

1 pt for answer and brief justification

ii. Which resistor, if either, takes a larger voltage immediately after time t_2? Justify your answer briefly.

In the instant after closing the switch, the capacitor is charged, meaning it has a voltage across it and will act briefly as a battery. Both resistors take the same current as each other. By Ohm's law, then, the bigger resistor takes the bigger voltage. So R_A.

1 pt for correct answer

1 pt for justification

iii. What is the voltage across the capacitor a long time after time t_2?

The voltage is given by Q/C, where Q is the charge on the capacitor. This charge drains over time, so the voltage will also drop, reducing to zero after a long time.

1 pt for correct answer

(c)

i. Show how to use Kirchhoff's rules to write (but do NOT solve) a differential equation for the charge Q on the capacitor as a function of time for all times after t_2.

The sum of the voltage changes will equal zero. Trace the circuit starting with the capacitor, which raises the voltage by Q/C. Each resistor drops the voltage by IR: $Q/C - IR_1 - IR_2 = 0$.

Current is dQ/dt; replace I to get $Q/C - (R_1 + R_2) \, dQ/dt = 0$.

And that is a differential equation for Q. All the variables except for Q and t are constants.

1 pt for writing any equation that tries to sum voltage changes to zero

1 pt for the correct Kirchhoff's equation: $Q/C - IR_1 - IR_2 = 0$

1 pt replacing I with dQ/dt

ii. On the axes provided, sketch a graph of the charge on the capacitor Q as a function of time, beginning at t_2 and ending a long time afterward.

1 pt starting with nonzero Q and ending close to zero Q

1 pt showing something like exponential decay

iii. On the axes provided, sketch the magnitude of current through R_A as a function of time, beginning at t_2 and ending a long time afterward.

The current is initially large—see (d). The current drops to zero—see (e). In between, the current in any RC circuit changes by an exponential function.

1 pt starting with nonzero I and ending close to zero I

1 pt showing something like exponential decay

(d) A student in the laboratory is assigned to verify the current graph in (c) iii. experimentally. The student proposes the following procedure:
The time constant $(R_1 + R_2)C$ for the capacitor's discharge has to be comparable with the 10-s stopwatch call-out time.

1 pt for referencing the time constant of the circuit

1 pt for correctly relating the time constant to the 10-s stopwatch time, that is, they should be somewhat similar

3. (15 points)

A very long wire carries current I_1. Nearby, a square wire loop of side x carries a current I_2, which is produced by a very small battery within the loop as shown. The top side of the square loop is located a distance a from the long wire.

(a)

i. In terms of given variables and fundamental constants, calculate magnitude of the total force applied by the long wire on the wire loop.

The magnetic field produced by I_1 at the location of the wire loop is always into the page, by the right-hand rule associated with $B = \dfrac{\mu_0 I}{2\pi d}$. Thus, by the right-hand rule associated with $F = ILB$, the force on the left-hand side of the loop is to the left; the force on the right-hand side of the loop is to the right. These forces are equal in magnitude, because each element of the loop is the same distance from the long wire. So the side forces cancel.

The force on the top wire is upward and equal to $I_2 xB$, where $B = \dfrac{\mu_0 I_1}{2\pi a}$. The force on the bottom wire is downward and equal to $I_2 xB$, where $B = \dfrac{\mu_0 I_1}{2\pi(a+x)}$.

Subtract the two forces to get $F = I_2 x \dfrac{\mu_0 I_1}{2\pi a} - I_2 x \dfrac{\mu_0 I_1}{2\pi(x+a)}$. No need to simplify—any equivalent form is acceptable.

1 pt for subtracting just force on top and bottom wire portions

1 pt for correct use of $B = \dfrac{\mu_0 I}{2\pi d}$

1 pt for correct use of $F = ILB$

1 pt for combining equations and substituting a and $x + a$ for d, and x for L

ii. Draw a vector indicating the direction of the magnetic force calculated in (a) i.

1 pt for the correct answer

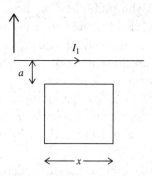

Now the battery in the square loop is removed, and the loop is placed at the same location.

(b) Calculate the magnetic flux through the square loop.

Magnetic flux is $\int B \cdot dA$. Here replace B with $B = \dfrac{\mu_0 I_1}{2\pi r}$ and dA with $x \cdot dr$, where r is a variable representing distance from the long wire: $x \int_{a}^{x+a} \dfrac{\mu_0 I_1}{2\pi r} dr$. Take the integral to get

$\dfrac{x\mu_0 I_1}{2\pi} \ln r$, evaluated from a to $x + a$. That's $\dfrac{x\mu_0 I_1}{2\pi} \ln\left(\dfrac{x+a}{a}\right)$. Any form of answer is acceptable, as long as the integral is actually evaluated—no integral notation on the final answer.

1 pt for substituting $B = \dfrac{\mu_0 I_1}{2\pi r}$ into any form of the magnetic flux equation

1 pt for attempting to use calculus rather than straight multiplication because the magnetic field term is not constant

1 pt for evaluating the integral to some sort of logarithmic function, even if not entirely correct

1 pt for entirely correct solution, including correct substitution of integral limits

(c) Calculate the induced emf in the square loop.

Induced emf is the time derivative of the magnetic flux. This flux does not change in time, because the field and the area of the loop that the field penetrates don't change in time. So zero induced current.

1 pt for using any form of the emf equation, either in words or variables (not just writing it, using it)

1 pt for explaining or showing that the ΔBA term is zero (i.e., the magnetic flux doesn't change in time)

(d) Finally, the square loop is moved from its initial position to a new position, a distance $a + x$ from the long wire. It takes 2 s for the wire to change locations. Using the values I_1 = 0.50 A, a = 0.020 m, and x = 0.050 m, calculate the average EMF induced in the square loop while it changes positions.

Using the solution in (c), we know the initial magnetic flux. Plugging into the result, the $\dfrac{x\mu_0 I_1}{2\pi}$ term gives 5.0×10^{-9} in standard units. The natural log term becomes ln (7/2) = 1.3. So the initial flux is 6.3×10^{-9} Tm^2.

The final flux is calculated using the same formula, just plugging in the different locations of the loop: $x + x + a$ and $x + a$. That's 0.12 m and 0.07 m. The natural log term this time becomes ln (12/7) = 0.53. So the final flux is 2.7×10^{-9} Tm^2.

Subtract final minus initial flux to get the change in flux of 3.6×10^{-9} Tm^2.

But induced emf is change in flux divided by the time interval over which the flux changed—divide by 2 s to get the final answer: the induced emf is 1.8×10^{-9} V (i.e., 1.8 nV).

1 pt for plugging the correct values into whatever equation they came up with in (c) for the initial flux.

1 pt for plugging the correct values into whatever equation they came up with in (c) for the final flux

1 pt for dividing any defined change in flux by 2 s

1 pt for the correct numerical answer (i.e., somewhere between 1.5 and 2.0 nV); the answer must have correct units, but may be in any form

AP Physics C—Electricity and Magnetism
Full Exam Scoring

Multiple-Choice: Number Correct_____(35 max)

Free-Response: Question 1_____(15 max)
Question 2_____(15 max)
Question 3_____(15 max)

Total Free-Response_____(45 max)

1.286 × Multiple-Choice + Free-Response = Raw Score_____(90 max)

56–90	5
44–55	4
32–43	3
23–34	2
0–22	1

Physics C—Mechanics Practice Exam 3—Multiple-Choice Questions

ANSWER SHEET

1 (A) (B) (C) (D) (E)
2 (A) (B) (C) (D) (E)
3 (A) (B) (C) (D) (E)
4 (A) (B) (C) (D) (E)
5 (A) (B) (C) (D) (E)
6 (A) (B) (C) (D) (E)
7 (A) (B) (C) (D) (E)
8 (A) (B) (C) (D) (E)
9 (A) (B) (C) (D) (E)
10 (A) (B) (C) (D) (E)
11 (A) (B) (C) (D) (E)
12 (A) (B) (C) (D) (E)

13 (A) (B) (C) (D) (E)
14 (A) (B) (C) (D) (E)
15 (A) (B) (C) (D) (E)
16 (A) (B) (C) (D) (E)
17 (A) (B) (C) (D) (E)
18 (A) (B) (C) (D) (E)
19 (A) (B) (C) (D) (E)
20 (A) (B) (C) (D) (E)
21 (A) (B) (C) (D) (E)
22 (A) (B) (C) (D) (E)
23 (A) (B) (C) (D) (E)
24 (A) (B) (C) (D) (E)

25 (A) (B) (C) (D) (E)
26 (A) (B) (C) (D) (E)
27 (A) (B) (C) (D) (E)
28 (A) (B) (C) (D) (E)
29 (A) (B) (C) (D) (E)
30 (A) (B) (C) (D) (E)
31 (A) (B) (C) (D) (E)
32 (A) (B) (C) (D) (E)
33 (A) (B) (C) (D) (E)
34 (A) (B) (C) (D) (E)
35 (A) (B) (C) (D) (E)

Physics C—Mechanics Practice Exam 3—Multiple-Choice Questions

Time: 45 minutes. You may refer to the constants sheet and the equation sheet, both of which are found in the appendix. You may use a calculator.

1. An object moves along the positive x-axis. The net force on the object as a function of time t measured in seconds is given in newtons by the function $F(t) = 3t^2 + t + 2$. What is the impulse delivered to the object during the first second of motion?

   (A) 4.0 N·s
   (B) 3.5 N·s
   (C) 0 N·s
   (D) 7.0 N·s
   (E) 6.0 N·s

2. A cart moves along a straight track. Its position x as a function of time is given in meters by the equation $x = 2t^3 + t^2 - 2t$. What is the cart's acceleration at time $t = 4$ s?

   (A) 102 m/s²
   (B) 10 m/s²
   (C) 133 m/s²
   (D) 12 m/s²
   (E) 50 m/s²

3. An object of mass m is attached to a vertical spring, as shown above. When the string is unstretched, it is of length L. When the object is gently attached and allowed to hang from rest, the string is of length $L + x$. Now the object is attached, released from rest while the spring is at its unstretched length L, and allowed to oscillate. What is the maximum length of the spring during the oscillations?

   (A) $L + \sqrt{2}x$
   (B) $2L + 2x$
   (C) $2L + \sqrt{2}x$
   (D) $L + 2x$
   (E) $L + 4x$

Overhead view

Questions 4 and 5: Two carts move along a smooth surface as shown above. Cart A of mass 3.1 kg moves west with speed 1.2 m/s. Cart B of mass 1.3 kg moves north with speed 2.2 m/s. The carts collide and stick together, moving at angle θ above west.

4. What is the speed of the center of mass of the two-cart system before collision?

   (A) 2.5 m/s
   (B) 3.4 m/s
   (C) 1.1 m/s
   (D) 1.6 m/s
   (E) 2.3 m/s

5. Which of the following methods will calculate the angle θ?

   (A) Divide cart B's speed by cart A's speed, and take the inverse tangent of the result.
   (B) Calculate the momentum of each cart by multiplying mass times speed. Then divide cart B's momentum by cart A's momentum, and take the inverse tangent of the result.
   (C) Calculate the kinetic energy of each cart by multiplying ½ by its mass times its speed squared. Then divide the cart B's kinetic energy by cart A's kinetic energy, and take the inverse tangent of the result.
   (D) Divide the square of cart B's speed by the square of cart A's speed, and take the inverse tangent of the result.
   (E) Divide cart B's mass by cart A's mass, and take the inverse tangent of the result.

GO ON TO THE NEXT PAGE

6. A pendulum and a spring both oscillate in harmonic motion with small amplitude. Which of the following shows correct graphs of how the period T of the harmonic motion depends on the mass m of the object in oscillation for the pendulum and the spring?

Pendulum   Spring

(A)

(B)

(C)

(D)

(E)

7. Cart A is initially moving to the right toward stationary cart B. The carts collide and bounce off one another. Which of the following is correct about whether the horizontal linear momentum and the kinetic energy of the two-cart system are conserved in the collision?

(A) Linear momentum must be conserved. Kinetic energy may possibly be conserved.
(B) Linear momentum may possibly be conserved. Kinetic energy must be conserved.
(C) Linear momentum may possibly be conserved. Kinetic energy may possibly be conserved.
(D) Linear momentum must be conserved. Kinetic energy must be conserved.
(E) Linear momentum must be conserved. Kinetic energy must not be conserved.

8. A block slides down a frictionless ramp on Earth's surface. The ramp makes an angle θ above the horizontal, and the block's acceleration down the incline is a. Now, the block slides down the same ramp near a different planet's surface. The ramp still makes an angle θ above the horizontal. This different planet has twice the density of Earth but the same radius. What is the acceleration of the block sliding down the ramp on the different planet?

(A) $(1/2)a$
(B) $2a$
(C) a
(D) $(1/4)a$
(E) $4a$

GO ON TO THE NEXT PAGE

Questions 9–11: A particle moves clockwise in a horizontal circle of radius 2.0 m, as shown above. At the moment in which the particle is at the position shown, its speed is 3.0 m/s, and its speed is increasing by 2.5 m/s per second.

9. Which of the following vectors could represent the direction of the particle's instantaneous velocity at the position shown?

(A)

(B)

(C)

(D)

(E)

10. Which of the following vectors could represent the direction of the net force on the particle at the position shown?

(A)

(B)

(C)

(D)

(E)

11. What is the magnitude of the particle's instantaneous acceleration at the position shown?

(A) 3.6 m/s^2
(B) 1.5 m/s^2
(C) 4.5 m/s^2
(D) 5.1 m/s^2
(E) 2.5 m/s^2

12. Two blocks move across a rough table at constant speed. Friction is NOT negligible on any surface. The bottom block is pulled to the right with force F. Which of the following could indicate the direction of the total force of the bottom block on the top block?

(A)

(B)

(C)

(D)

(E)

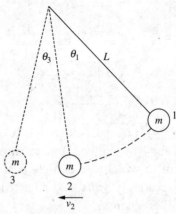

13. Three stones are thrown from a cliff with velocity vectors v_A, v_B, and v_C. The magnitude of the initial velocity for each stone is the same, but the directions of initial velocity are shown in the diagram. Which of the following correctly ranks the stones according to their speed upon hitting the level ground below the cliff, and by the magnitude of their vertical components of velocity upon hitting the ground?

	Speed at ground	Magnitude of vertical velocity at ground
(A)	B > C = A	A > B > C
(B)	A = B = C	A = B = C
(C)	C > B > A	A = B = C
(D)	C > B > A	A > B > C
(E)	A = B = C	A > B > C

Questions 14–16: An object of mass m is connected to a string of length L. The string is pulled back to an angle θ_1 and released from rest at position 1. Air resistance is NOT negligible. When the string is vertical, the object moves left. The object comes to rest again at position 3 when the string is at angle θ_3.

14. Which of the following is a correct expression for the work done by the air on the object between positions 1 and 2?

(A) $\frac{1}{2}mv_2^2$
(B) $mgL\theta_3$
(C) $\frac{1}{2}mv_2^2 - mgL\theta_3$
(D) $\frac{1}{2}mv_2^2 - mgL\theta_1$
(E) $mgL\theta_3 - mgL\theta_1$

15. Is the angle θ_3 greater than, less than, or equal to θ_1?

(A) θ_3 is greater than $\frac{1}{2}\theta_1$.
(B) θ_3 is equal to half of θ_1.
(C) θ_3 is less than $\frac{1}{2}\theta_1$.
(D) The answer cannot be determined, but could be determined if we knew whether the force of air resistance were proportional to v or v^2.
(E) The answer cannot be determined, even if we knew whether the force of air resistance were proportional to v or v^2.

GO ON TO THE NEXT PAGE

16. Now consider that the force of air resistance is equal to cv. Which of the following is a differential equation that could be used to solve for the angle θ as a function of time while the string is between angles θ_1 and θ_2?

(A) $mg\theta - cv = m\dfrac{d^2\theta}{dt^2}$

(B) $mg\sin\theta - cv = m\dfrac{d^2}{dt^2}(L\theta)$

(C) $mg\sin\theta + cv = m\dfrac{d^2}{dt^2}(L\theta)$

(D) $mg\sin\theta - cv = m\dfrac{d^2\theta}{dt^2}$

(E) $mg\sin\theta + cv = m\dfrac{d^2\theta}{dt^2}$

Questions 17–18: A cart moves along a straight road according to the velocity-time graph shown above.

17. What is the average acceleration of this car between time 0 and time 10 s?

(A) $+0.3$ m/s^2
(B) 0.0 m/s^2
(C) $+0.6$ m/s^2
(D) $+1.0$ m/s^2
(E) $+3.0$ m/s^2

18. What is the average velocity of this car between time 0 and time 10 s?

(A) 1.2 m/s
(B) 24 m/s
(C) 12 m/s
(D) 2.4 m/s
(E) 1.0 m/s

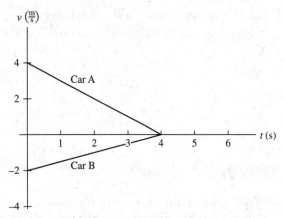

19. Car A and Car B start at the same position as each other at time $t = 0$, then move according to the velocity v vs. time graphs above. How far apart are the cars at time $t = 4$ s?

(A) 10 m
(B) 24 m
(C) 8 m
(D) 12 m
(E) 4 m

Questions 20–22: A string of length L is attached to an object of unknown mass. The string is pulled back to a small unknown angle and released from rest. An astronaut takes this apparatus to the surface of Planet X, where the gravitational field is 4.9 N/kg.

20. The time for the object to first reach the vertical position on Earth is t_e. On the surface of Planet X, what is the time for the object to first reach the vertical position?

(A) t_e
(B) $2t_e$
(C) $\dfrac{t_e}{\sqrt{2}}$
(D) $4t_e$
(E) $\sqrt{2}\,t_e$

GO ON TO THE NEXT PAGE

21. Let the maximum speed of the object on Earth be v_e. What is the maximum speed of the object on Planet X?

    (A) v_e

    (B) $2v_e$

    (C) $\dfrac{v_e}{\sqrt{2}}$

    (D) $4v_e$

    (E) $\sqrt{2}v_e$

22. What measurements in addition to the string length L must be measured to determine an experimental value for g on this planet?

    I. The time for the object to pass through the vertical position two consecutive times
    II. The speed of the object as it passes the vertical position
    III. The mass of the object

    (A) II only
    (B) II and III
    (C) III only
    (D) I only
    (E) I and III

23. A ball is dropped from a skyscraper. Between the time of the drop and the time at which the ball reaches terminal velocity, which of the following is true about the magnitudes of the ball's velocity and acceleration vectors?

    (A) velocity remains constant while acceleration remains constant
    (B) velocity increases while acceleration decreases
    (C) velocity decreases while acceleration decreases
    (D) velocity increases while acceleration remains constant
    (E) velocity remains constant while acceleration decreases

GO ON TO THE NEXT PAGE

Questions 24 and 25: A small dart of mass M_2 is fired into a hanging object of mass M_1, which is initially at rest. The dart sticks, and the combined dart-object system moves to a maximum vertical height h above their initial position.

24. Which of the following is a correct expression for the speed of the combined dart-object system immediately after collision?

(A) $\sqrt{\dfrac{M_2}{(M_1+M_2)}gh}$

(B) $\sqrt{\dfrac{2M_1}{M_1+M_2}gh}$

(C) $\sqrt{2gh}$

(D) $\sqrt{\dfrac{M_1}{M_1+M_2}gh}$

(E) $\sqrt{\dfrac{2M_2}{M_1+M_2}gh}$

25. Which of the following is a correct expression for the speed of the dart before the collision?

(A) $\sqrt{\dfrac{2(M_1+M_2)}{M_1}gh}$

(B) $\sqrt{\dfrac{2(M_1+M_2)}{M_2}gh}$

(C) $\dfrac{M_1+M_2}{M_2}\sqrt{2gh}$

(D) $\sqrt{2gh}$

(E) $\dfrac{M_1+M_2}{M_1}\sqrt{2gh}$

26. A hoop of mass m is released from rest at the top of a ramp, a vertical distance h above the bottom of the ramp. The hoop rolls without slipping to the bottom of the ramp, where it has speed v and total mechanical energy E. Next, a solid disk, also of mass m, is released from the same position, and likewise rolls without slipping. Which of the following is correct about the speed and mechanical energy of the disk compared to the hoop?

	Speed of the disk	Mechanical energy of the disk
(A)	greater than v	equal to E
(B)	less than v	less than E
(D)	less than v	equal to E
(C)	equal to v	equal to E
(E)	equal to v	less than E

27. In the laboratory, disk 1 spins on a vertical axle with minimal friction. Disk 2 is initially not spinning and drops from above onto disk 1. The disks collide and rotate together after collision. How does the angular momentum and the rotational kinetic energy of the two-disk system compare before and after collision?

	System angular momentum	System rotational kinetic energy
(A)	same before and after collision	same before and after collision
(B)	smaller after collision	smaller after collision
(C)	greater after collision	greater after collision
(D)	same before and after collision	smaller after collision
(E)	smaller after collision	same before and after collision

GO ON TO THE NEXT PAGE

Questions 28 and 29: Three spheres are arranged in deep space as shown above, far away from any planet or star.

28. Which of the following diagrams shows the correct relative magnitudes and directions of the forces F_C (the gravitational force of sphere C on sphere A) and F_B (the gravitational force of sphere B on sphere A)?

29. In units of Gm^2/x^2, which of the following represents the net gravitational force of spheres B and C on sphere A?

(A) 7/18
(B) 7/3
(C) 1/6
(D) 4/3
(E) 11/18

Questions 30 and 31: An object of mass 2 kg moves in one dimension according to the velocity v vs. time t function $v(t) = c - bt^2$, where $c = +2$ m/s, and $b = +3$ m/s^3. The positive direction is to the right.

30. Which of the following is an expression for the net force (in SI units) acting on the object as a function of time?

(A) $-6t$
(B) $4 - 6t^2$
(C) $-12t$
(D) $2t - t^3$
(E) $4t - 2t^2$

31. Which of the following descriptions of the object's motion starting at time $t = 0$ and immediately thereafter is correct?

(A) The object initially is moving to the left at 2 m/s and is speeding up.
(B) The object initially is moving to the right at 2 m/s and is speeding up.
(C) The object initially is at rest, then speeds up.
(D) The object initially is moving to the left at 2 m/s and is slowing down.
(E) The object initially is moving to the right at 2 m/s and is slowing down.

32. A 5000 kg satellite changes its orbital speed by firing a thruster for one minute. In that time, the satellite's speed changes from 7600 m/s to 7500 m/s. What is the force provided by the thruster?

(A) 8300 N
(B) 500,000 N
(C) 50,000 N
(D) 30,000 N
(E) 83 N

33. A satellite of mass m_s is placed in geosynchronous orbit, meaning it remains over the same position on Earth's surface at all times. The mass of Earth is m_e, and the period of Earth's orbit is T. Which of the following is a correct expression for the radius of the satellite's orbit?

(A) $\sqrt{\dfrac{Gm_sT^2}{4\pi^2}}$

(B) $\dfrac{Gm_eT}{2\pi}$

(C) $\sqrt[3]{\dfrac{Gm_sT^2}{4\pi^2}}$

(D) $\sqrt{\dfrac{Gm_eT^2}{4\pi^2}}$

(E) $\sqrt[3]{\dfrac{Gm_eT^2}{4\pi^2}}$

GO ON TO THE NEXT PAGE

34. A student reports the results of an experiment:

A ball of mass 1.0 kg initially moves horizontally at a speed of 2.0 m/s. The ball bounces off the stationary wall of a building, rebounding horizontally with speed 2.0 m/s.

Which of the following is a correct statement about horizontal linear momentum conservation in this collision?

(A) The momentum of the ball was not conserved, but the momentum of the ball-Earth system was conserved.

(B) The momentum of the ball was not conserved, and neither was the momentum of the ball-Earth system.

(C) The momentum of the ball was conserved, and the momentum of the ball-Earth system was also conserved.

(D) The momentum of the ball was conserved, but the momentum of the ball-Earth system was not conserved.

(E) The momentum of the ball was conserved, but the data provided don't provide enough evidence to draw a conclusion about whether momentum of the ball-Earth system was conserved.

35. Satellite A undergoes circular orbit around Earth. The satellite maintains a distance above Earth's surface equal to one Earth radius. Satellite B undergoes circular orbit a distance above Earth's surface equal to two Earth radii. What is the ratio of the orbital speed of satellite A to the orbital speed of satellite B?

(A) 1:1
(B) 3:2
(C) $\sqrt{2}$:1
(D) 2:1
(E) $\sqrt{3}$:$\sqrt{2}$

STOP. End of Physics C—Mechanics Practice Exam 3—Multiple-Choice Questions

Physics C—Mechanics Practice Exam 3—Free-Response Questions

Time: 45 minutes. You may refer to the constants sheet and the equation sheet, both of which are found in the appendix. You may use a calculator.

1. An object of mass 2 kg moves in one dimension along the x-axis, experiencing a resistive force. Its velocity v in meters per second as a function of time t in seconds is given by the expression $v(t) = +1.4e^{-bt}$.

   (a) What are the units of the constant b?
   (b) Determine the magnitude of the object's initial velocity.
   (c) Is the object moving in the positive or negative direction initially? Briefly justify your answer.
   (d) Immediately after time $t = 0$, is the object speeding up, slowing down, or moving with steady speed? Briefly justify your answer.
   (e) Immediately after time $t = 0$, is the magnitude of the object's acceleration increasing, decreasing, or remaining constant? Briefly justify your answer.
   (f) On the axes below, sketch the shape of a graph of the net force on this object as a function of time for the first 4 seconds of motion. Label the graph with expressions for any vertical or horizontal intercepts.

   (g) In terms of b, derive an expression for the total distance traveled by the object after a very long time.
   (h) Calculate the total energy dissipated by the resistive force after a very long time.

GO ON TO THE NEXT PAGE

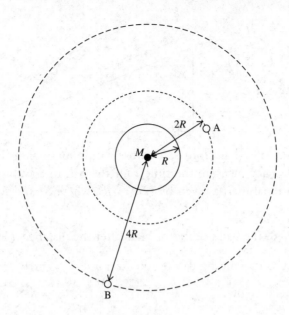

2. Satellites A and B are in circular orbit around a planet of mass M and radius R. Satellite A has mass m_A and orbital radius $2R$. Satellite B has mass m_B and orbital radius $4R$.

(a) Derive an expression for the orbital speed v_A of satellite A in terms of given variables and fundamental constants.

(b) The orbital speed of satellite B is v_B. Can the ratio $v_B:v_A$ be calculated? If so, calculate this ratio. If not, explain what additional information would be needed and why.

(c) Derive an expression for the work necessary to move satellite A into satellite B's orbit.

(d) Let the period of satellite A's orbit be T_A and the period of satellite B's orbit be T_B. Calculate the ratio T_B/T_A.

(e) Now assume each satellite has the same mass m_A. In that case, which satellite has a larger total mechanical energy in its orbit? Justify your answer.

(f) Derive an expression for the minimum speed that satellite A must have at the location shown in order to end up a very long way away from the planet.

GO ON TO THE NEXT PAGE

3. In the laboratory, students roll a ball from rest without slipping down a surface inclined at an unknown angle θ to the horizontal. They measure the time t for the ball to travel a distance d measured along the incline. The ball has rotational inertia given by $(2/3)MR^2$, where M and R are the mass and radius of the ball, respectively.

(a) Show that the speed v of the ball's center of mass after the distance d is given by $v = \sqrt{\frac{6}{5} gd \sin\theta}$.

(b) Show that d is related to t according to the equation $d = \frac{3}{10} g \sin\theta t^2$.

The students collect the data below.

d (m)	t (s)		
0.10	0.52		
0.20	0.75		
0.30	0.97		
0.40	1.10		
0.50	1.25		
0.60	1.36		

(c) Indicate below which quantities could be graphed to yield a straight line whose slope could be used to calculate the angle θ.

Vertical axis: _____
Horizontal axis: _____

Use the remaining rows in the table provided, as needed, to record any quantities you indicated that are not given in the table. Label each row you use and include units.

GO ON TO THE NEXT PAGE

(d) Plot the data points for the quantities indicated in part (c) on the graph below. Clearly scale and label all axes, including units if appropriate. Draw a straight line that best represents the data.

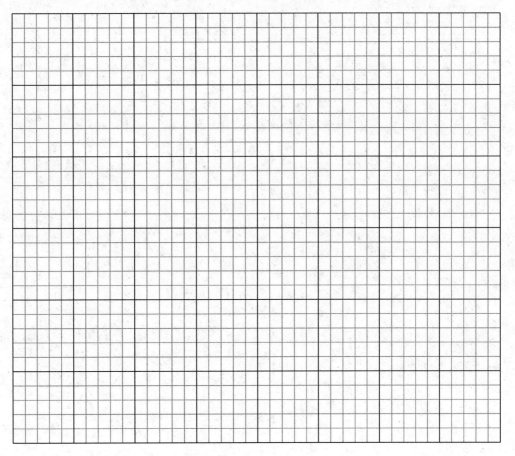

(e) Using the straight line, calculate an experimental value for θ.

STOP. End of Physics C—Mechanics Practice Exam 3—Free-Response Questions

Physics C—Electricity and Magnetism Practice Exam 3—Multiple-Choice Questions

ANSWER SHEET

1 (A) (B) (C) (D) (E)
2 (A) (B) (C) (D) (E)
3 (A) (B) (C) (D) (E)
4 (A) (B) (C) (D) (E)
5 (A) (B) (C) (D) (E)
6 (A) (B) (C) (D) (E)
7 (A) (B) (C) (D) (E)
8 (A) (B) (C) (D) (E)
9 (A) (B) (C) (D) (E)
10 (A) (B) (C) (D) (E)
11 (A) (B) (C) (D) (E)
12 (A) (B) (C) (D) (E)

13 (A) (B) (C) (D) (E)
14 (A) (B) (C) (D) (E)
15 (A) (B) (C) (D) (E)
16 (A) (B) (C) (D) (E)
17 (A) (B) (C) (D) (E)
18 (A) (B) (C) (D) (E)
19 (A) (B) (C) (D) (E)
20 (A) (B) (C) (D) (E)
21 (A) (B) (C) (D) (E)
22 (A) (B) (C) (D) (E)
23 (A) (B) (C) (D) (E)
24 (A) (B) (C) (D) (E)

25 (A) (B) (C) (D) (E)
26 (A) (B) (C) (D) (E)
27 (A) (B) (C) (D) (E)
28 (A) (B) (C) (D) (E)
29 (A) (B) (C) (D) (E)
30 (A) (B) (C) (D) (E)
31 (A) (B) (C) (D) (E)
32 (A) (B) (C) (D) (E)
33 (A) (B) (C) (D) (E)
34 (A) (B) (C) (D) (E)
35 (A) (B) (C) (D) (E)

Physics C—Electricity and Magnetism Practice Exam 3— Multiple-Choice Questions

Time: 45 minutes. You may refer to the constants sheet and the equation sheet, both of which are found in the appendix. You may use a calculator.

<u>Questions 1 and 2:</u> The circuit above consists of three capacitors and a battery, which has been connected for a long time.

1. What is the charge stored on the 6 nF capacitor?

   (A) 96 nC
   (B) 48 nC
   (C) 432 nC
   (D) 4 nC
   (E) 144 nC

2. What is the voltage across the 8 nF capacitor?

   (A) 2 V
   (B) 12 V
   (C) 16 V
   (D) 8 V
   (E) 3 V

<u>Questions 3 and 4:</u> Two long, straight wires are separated by a distance d. The left-hand wire carries a current I directed into the page; the right-hand wire carries a current I directed out of the page. Points R and P are positions in space, located as shown in the diagram.

3. What is the magnitude of the net magnetic field produced at point P?

   (A) $\dfrac{3\mu_0 I}{2\pi d}$

   (B) $\dfrac{\mu_0 I}{2\pi d}$

   (C) $\dfrac{\mu_0 I}{4\pi d}$

   (D) $\dfrac{\mu_0 I}{\pi d}$

   (E) $\dfrac{3\mu_0 I}{4\pi d}$

GO ON TO THE NEXT PAGE

4. What is the direction of the net magnetic field produced at point R?

   (A) ⟵
   (B) Zero
   (C) ↙
   (D) ⟶
   (E) ↘

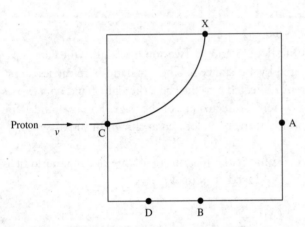

Questions 5 and 6: A proton initially moving right with speed v enters a region in which the magnetic field is uniform. The proton is deflected along the path shown, exiting the magnetic field at position X. Next, an electron initially moving right with identical speed v enters the magnetic field from the same position.

5. Which of the labeled positions is closest to where the electron will exit the magnetic field?

   (A) A
   (B) B
   (C) C
   (D) D
   (E) X

6. The speed of the proton a very short time t after entering the magnetic field is v_p; the speed of the electron the same time t after entering the magnetic field is v_e. Which of the following correctly compares v_p and v_e?

   (A) v_p is smaller than v_e by more than a factor of 10
   (B) v_p is equal to v_e
   (C) v_p is larger than v_e by less than a factor of 10
   (D) v_p is larger than v_e by more than a factor of 10
   (E) v_p is smaller than v_e by less than a factor of 10

Questions 7 and 8: A capacitor C_1 is initially connected to a 12 V battery for a long time, as in diagram 1. Next, in diagram 2 the battery is disconnected, and in diagram 3 C_1 is connected instead to capacitor C_2, which has an initial charge.

7. Which of the following must be identical quantities in diagram 3?

   I. The charge on each capacitor
   II. The voltage across each capacitor
   III. The capacitance of each capacitor

   (A) I only
   (B) II only
   (C) III only
   (D) I and II only
   (E) I, II, and III

GO ON TO THE NEXT PAGE

8. Which of the following must be identical quantities for capacitor C_1 in circuits 1 and 3?

I. The voltage across C_1
II. The charge on C_1
III. The capacitance of C_1

(A) I only
(B) II only
(C) III only
(D) I and II only
(E) I, II, and III

Questions 9 and 10 refer to the circuit above.

9. What is the resistance of R_2?

(A) 33 Ω
(B) 3 Ω
(C) 150 Ω
(D) 100 Ω
(E) 20 Ω

10. What is the voltage measured by the voltmeter?

(A) 200 V
(B) 20 V
(C) 60 V
(D) 100 V
(E) 250 V

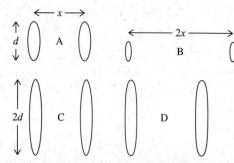

11. Four parallel-plate capacitors had different plate diameters d and distances x between the plates, as shown above. Which of the following ranks the capacitors according to their capacitance?

(A) C = B > A > D
(B) C > A > D > B
(C) C > D > A > B
(D) D > C = B > A
(E) D > C > B > A

12. A parallel plate capacitor has capacitance C. Each plate of the capacitor holds a charge of magnitude Q. Which of the following expressions gives the energy stored in this capacitor?

(A) $\frac{1}{2}Q^2/C$
(B) Q^2/C
(C) QC
(D) $\frac{1}{2}QC^2$
(E) $\frac{1}{2}Q/C$

GO ON TO THE NEXT PAGE

Region 1   Region 2

13. In region 1, a uniform electric field of magnitude E_1 points right. In region 2, another uniform electric field of smaller magnitude E_2 points to the left, as shown above. A positive charge $+q$ is released from rest at the position indicated, at the far left of region 1. Which of the following graphs shows the speed v of the charge as a function of time?

(A)

(B)

(C)

(D)

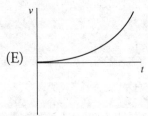

(E)

14. Consider a long, straight wire of circular cross section. The current through the wire has uniform current density across its cross-sectional area. Let the distance from the center of the wire along a cross-sectional slice be r. The magnetic field inside the wire is proportional to which of the following?

(A) r^2
(B) $r^{1/2}$
(C) r
(D) r^{-2}
(E) r^{-1}

15. The diagram above shows a cross section of a three-dimensional closed surface. While no electric charges are inside the surface, several point charges outside the surface produce the nonuniform electric field E shown above. Consider the vector dA to have a magnitude equal to a small element of surface area, and direction pointed normal to the surface as shown. Which of the following is true about $\int E \cdot dA$ evaluated for the entire surface?

(A) It is positive, because the net charge of the objects producing this electric field must have been positive.
(B) It is zero, because no charge is enclosed within the surface
(C) It is negative, because the smaller electric field intersects more surface area than the larger electric field.
(D) It is undefined, because the E is not always parallel to dA.
(E) It is positive, because the larger electric field intersects more surface area than the smaller electric field.

GO ON TO THE NEXT PAGE

16. A uniform electric field of magnitude 400 N/C points to the right. Positions 1 and 2 are located in the electric field as shown. An object of charge +1.0 mC moves from position 1 to position 2. How much work is done on the object by the field?

(A) –0.84 J
(B) +0.84 J
(C) +1.2 J
(D) –1.2 J
(E) 0 J

17. Two objects carry opposite charges of the same magnitude. Both objects move up the page with speed v, as shown above. Which of the following indicates the direction of the instantaneous electric and magnetic fields, if any, at point P directly between the objects?

Magnetic field	Electric field
(A) out of the page	zero
(B) into the page	zero
(C) zero	zero
(D) zero	to the right
(E) into the page	to the right

18. Four isolated charge arrangements are shown above. Which of the following correctly ranks the magnitude of the electric force F exerted by each charge on the other in its arrangement?

(A) $F_1 > F_3 > F_2 > F_4$
(B) $F_1 > F_2 > F_3 > F_4$
(C) $F_1 = F_3 > F_2 = F_4$
(D) $F_3 > F_4 > F_1 = F_2$
(E) $F_1 = F_2 > F_3 = F_4$

19. A parallel plate capacitor is connected to a battery and charged fully. While still connected to the battery, a dielectric slab is inserted between the plates of the capacitor. Which of the following quantities will change when the slab is inserted?

 I. The magnitude of the electric field between the plates
 II. The charge stored on the capacitor
 III. The potential difference between the plates

(A) I only
(B) II only
(C) III only
(D) I and III only
(E) I, II, and III

Negatively charged glass rod
Wire 1
Metal sphere
Insulating stand
Metal desk

20. A metal sphere is attached to an insulating stand. Conducting wire 1 is connected between the sphere and a very large metal desk in electrical contact with the ground. A negatively charged glass rod is brought very close to the sphere without touching it, as shown. Next, wire 1 is cut. Finally, the glass rod is moved far away from the sphere. Which of the pictures of the sphere models the sign and distribution of charge on the surface of the sphere at the end of this process?

(A)

(B)

(C)

(D)

(E)

21. A circular wire of radius r is completely inside a magnetic field B, which increases with time t according to the function $B = 3t^2$. Which of the following is a correct expression for the EMF induced in the wire?

(A) $12\pi r^2 t$
(B) $6\pi r^2 t$
(C) $6\pi r t^2$
(D) $12\pi r t$
(E) $3\pi r^2 t^2$

$E = 80\ \dfrac{N}{C}$

A   P

←————— 16 cm —————→

22. Two parallel plates—the positive plate on the right—produce a uniform electric field of 80 N/C. The plates are separated by 16 cm. Point A is next to the positive plate, while point P is directly between the plates. How much kinetic energy is gained by a proton that is released from rest at point A when it reaches point P?

(A) 1.0×10^{-18} J
(B) 1.4×10^{-6} J
(C) 2.1×10^{-6} J
(D) 0 J
(E) 2.0×10^{-18} J

1   2

Questions 23 and 24: Two metal spheres, labeled 1 and 2, have different radii, as shown above. The spheres initially each carried positive charge $+Q$, but have been in electrical contact by means of a long metal wire for a long time.

I

23. A rectangular wire loop is located above a wire carrying a current I, which increases with time t according to the equation $I = 3t$. Which of the following is correct about the current induced in the wire loop?

(A) It is counterclockwise and increasing.
(B) It is clockwise and increasing.
(C) It remains zero.
(D) It is counterclockwise and constant.
(E) It is clockwise and constant.

GO ON TO THE NEXT PAGE

24. Which of the following statements is true about the electric potential at the center of each sphere?

    (A) It is greater for sphere 1.
    (B) It is zero for both spheres.
    (C) It is the same positive value for both spheres.
    (D) It is the same negative value for both spheres.
    (E) It is greater for sphere 2.

25. Which of the following is true about the charge on each sphere after a long time?
    (A) Both spheres are positively charged, but sphere 1 holds a greater magnitude of charge.
    (B) Both spheres hold zero charge.
    (C) Sphere 2 holds positive charge, while sphere 1 holds negative charge.
    (D) Both spheres are positively charged, but sphere 2 holds a greater magnitude of charge.
    (E) Both spheres hold equal positive charge.

26. Circuit 1 above shows three identical resistors labeled X, Y, and Z. In circuit 2, resistor Z is removed. Which of the following correctly compares the current through and voltage across resistor Y in circuit 2 compared to circuit 1?

Current through resistor Y	Voltage across resistor Y
(A) Greater in circuit 2	Greater in circuit 2
(B) Equal in both circuits	Equal in both circuits
(C) Greater in circuit 2	Smaller in circuit 2
(D) Smaller in circuit 2	Smaller in circuit 2
(E) Greater in circuit 2	Equal in both circuits

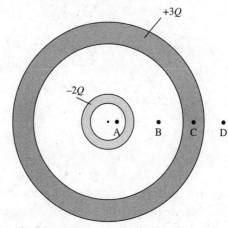

Questions 27 and 28: The diagram above shows two concentric spherical conducting shells. The net charge on the inner sphere is $-2Q$. The net charge on the outer sphere is $+3Q$.

27. What is the charge that resides on the outer surface of the outer shell?

    (A) $+2Q$
    (B) zero
    (C) $+Q$
    (D) $+3Q$
    (E) $+5Q$

28. Four positions are labeled in the diagram. Which of the following correctly ranks those positions by the magnitude of the electric field at each position?

    (A) A > B > D > C
    (B) D > C > B > A
    (C) A > B > C > D
    (D) D = B > A = C
    (E) B > D > A = C

GO ON TO THE NEXT PAGE

29. A uniform magnetic field of magnitude B points at a 60° angle above the plane of a rectangular wire loop of dimensions x by y as shown above. What is the magnetic flux through the loop?

(A) Bxy

(B) Bx

(C) $\frac{1}{2}Bxy$

(D) $\frac{\sqrt{3}}{2}Bxy$

(E) By

30. A 50 V battery is connected to a 70 Ω resistor and a 0.50 μF capacitor in the circuit shown above. The capacitor is uncharged when the switch is closed. Sometime later when the current through the resistor is 0.43 A, how much charge is stored on the capacitor?

(A) 0 μC

(B) 35 μC

(C) 25 μC

(D) 15 μC

(E) 10 μC

Questions 31 and 32: In the circuit above, the switch S has initially been closed for a very long time. Then the switch is opened.

31. Immediately before the switch is opened, what is the current through R_1?

(A) 1.5 A

(B) 0.33 A

(C) 1.0 A

(D) 0.5 A

(E) 0 A

32. Immediately after the switch is opened, what is the current through R_1?

(A) 1.5 A

(B) 0.33 A

(C) 1.0 A

(D) 0.5 A

(E) 0 A

33. An electron is initially moving to the left with speed v parallel to a wire carrying a constant rightward current I as shown above. Which of the following indicates the direction of the magnetic force on the electron at the instant shown, and whether the long-term path of the electron is circular or not circular?

Direction of force	Electron's long-term path
(A) rightward	circular
(B) downward	circular
(C) upward	not circular
(D) upward	circular
(E) downward	not circular

Questions 34 and 35: Two small objects, each carrying negative electric charge of magnitude 2.0 μC, are placed on the x-axis at positions $x_a = +4.0$ cm and $x_b = -4.0$ cm.

34. What is the electric potential at position $x = 0$?

(A) +900,000 V
(B) +450,000 V
(C) 0 V
(D) −450,000 V
(E) −900,000 V

35. What is the magnitude of the electric field at position $x = 0$?

(A) 44 N/C
(B) 2.2 million N/C
(C) 1.1 million N/C
(D) 0 N/C
(E) 22 N/C

STOP. End of Physics C—Electricity and Magnetism Practice Exam 3—Multiple-Choice Questions

Physics C—Electricity and Magnetism Practice Exam 3—Free-Response Questions

Time: 45 minutes. You may refer to the constants sheet and the equation sheet, both of which are found in the appendix. You may use a calculator.

1. A rod of length L carrying positive charge has uniform linear charge density ℓ. Points A and B are located distances d and $2d$, respectively, from the center of the line.

   (a) Consider the situation when L is much, much greater than d.
      i. Derive an expression for the magnitude of the electric field at point A. Express your answer in terms of given variables and fundamental constants.
      ii. On the dot below, draw the direction of the electric field at point A.

   iii. Let the magnitude of the electric field at point A be E_{A1}. Is the magnitude of the electric field at point B greater than, less than, or equal to $\frac{1}{2}E_{A1}$? Justify your answer.
      iv. Derive an expression for the electric potential difference between points A and B. Express your answer in terms of given variables and fundamental constants.

   (b) Now consider the situation when L is NOT much greater than d.
      i. In terms of given variables and fundamental constants, derive an integral with limits that could be evaluated to determine the magnitude of the electric field at point A.
      ii. On the dot below, draw the direction of the electric field at point A.

   iii. Let the magnitude of the electric field in this case at point A be E_{A2}. Is E_{A2} greater than, less than, or equal to E_{A1}? Justify your answer.

2. A single rectangular copper coil of dimensions s by ℓ is moving to the right with speed v. Let position $x = 0$ be where the right-hand edge of the coil enters a uniform magnetic field of magnitude B pointing into the page. Let position $x = D$ be where the left-hand edge of the coil exits the field.

   (a) i. On the axes below, sketch the shape of a graph of the current induced in the coil as a function of position, from $x = 0$ to $x = D + \ell$. Represent clockwise current as positive.

GO ON TO THE NEXT PAGE

ii. Justify the shape of your graph for the region $x = 0$ to $x = \ell$.

iii. In terms of given variables and fundamental constants, write an expression for the maximum induced EMF in the coil.

(b) Describe any changes to your graph if instead a copper coil of the same rectangular dimensions but consisting of two loops of wire moved with speed v through the magnetic field. Justify your response.

(c) Now the original single coil enters the field as before, but the coil speeds up with acceleration a starting from rest at position $x = 0$.

i. Consider only the time during which the coil is entering the magnetic field. Derive an expression for the induced EMF in the coil as a function of position x. Express your answer in terms of given variables and fundamental constants.

ii. Sketch the shape of a graph of the current induced in this coil as a function of position, from $x = 0$ to $x = D + \ell$.

3. In the laboratory, you are given a wire coil of unknown inductance. You have available digital ammeters, digital voltmeters, and a variety of known resistors and capacitors.

(a) Using the available equipment, describe an experimental procedure that could determine the inductance of the wire coil. Give enough detail that another student could reproduce your method.

(b) Draw a labeled diagram showing how the inductor is connected to the other equipment in your procedure.

(c) Explain how the inductance of the coil will be determined from the measurements made.

(d) The coil is determined to have an inductance of 25 mH. It is connected to a 15 V battery, a 100 Ω resistor, and a 50 Ω resistor in the circuit shown. The circuit has been connected for a long time with the switch in position A. Next, the switch is thrown to position B.

i. Determine the current through the inductor immediately before the switch is thrown. Briefly justify your answer.

ii. Determine the current through the inductor immediately after the switch is thrown. Briefly justify your answer.

iii. Determine the current through the inductor after the switch has been in position B for a long time. Briefly justify your answer.

STOP. End of Physics C—Electricity and Magnetism Practice Exam 3—Free-Response Questions

Physics C—Mechanics Practice Exam 3—Multiple-Choice Solutions

1. **B**—Impulse is the integral of force with respect to time. That's $t^3 + t^2/2 + 2t$, evaluated from 0 to 1 second: $1 + ½ + 2 = 3.5$ N·s.

2. **E**—Acceleration is the second time derivative of position. The second derivative of the given function is $a = 12t + 2$. Plug in $t = 4$ s to get an acceleration of 50 m/s².

3. **D**—The equilibrium position is the midpoint of any oscillations. So $L + x$ is the equilibrium position. The object was released a distance x above the equilibrium position, meaning x is the amplitude of the oscillations. The spring will reach a distance x both above and below the equilibrium, meaning the spring will oscillate between a length L and $(L + x) + x$. That's $L + 2x$ as the maximum length.

4. **C**—Use conservation of momentum to find the total momentum before collision. Momentum is mass times velocity. For cart A before collision that's 3.72 N·s west; for cart B before collision that's 2.86 N·s north. The total momentum before collision is the Pythagorean sum of these—because momentum is a vector, direction matters. So total momentum before collision is 4.69 N·s at the angle θ. Conservation of momentum means that this is also the total momentum after collision. Since the carts stick together, just divide this by the 4.4 kg mass to get the speed after collision of 1.07 m/s. And since no external forces act on the two-cart system, its center of mass always moves at this speed. So answer is closest to C.

5. **B**—Momentum is a vector and is conserved separately in each direction in a collision. The total momentum on the vertical axis is just cart B's momentum, and on the horizontal axis, just cart A's momentum. The inverse tangent of these momentum components gives the direction of the total momentum vector. And the direction of a velocity—of movement—is always the same as the direction of momentum. (You can't just use the inverse tangent on the velocity components, because velocity isn't conserved in a collision!)

6. **C**—The period of a pendulum is $2\pi\sqrt{\dfrac{L}{g}}$; mass is irrelevant, so the graph of period vs. mass is a horizontal line. The period of an object on a spring is $2\pi\sqrt{\dfrac{m}{k}}$, which depends on the square root of m, as in **C**.

7. **A**—Linear momentum is conserved in any collision because there are no external forces acting on the two-cart system. By definition, elastic collisions conserve kinetic energy. It's true that for a collision to be elastic, the carts must bounce, but just because carts bounce doesn't mean the collision *must* be elastic.

8. **B**—The unbalanced force down the incline is $mg\sin\theta$. Newton's second law shows that the acceleration is then $g\sin\theta$. So however g changes, that's how the acceleration changes. The formula for the gravitational field near a planet is $g = GM/r^2$. But we're given density, not mass! Density is mass per volume. So multiply numerator and denominator by r to get $g = GMr/r^3$. Now M/r^3 is density . . . so $g = G(density)r$. The universal gravitation constant G can't change, the problem says the radius r doesn't change, but the density doubles—so the whole term for g doubles. And so does the acceleration.

9. **B**—The instantaneous velocity is in the direction the object is moving at this instant. That's straight down the page.

10. **E**—The net force is in the direction of acceleration. The acceleration has two components here: one toward the center (the "centripetal" acceleration) and another in the direction of motion because the particle is speeding up (the "tangential" acceleration). So the acceleration, and the net force, points somewhat left toward the center and somewhat down.

11. **D**—The acceleration has two components, which must be added using the Pythagorean theorem. The centripetal component is v^2/r, which is $(3 \text{ m/s})^2/(2 \text{ m}) = 4.5$ m/s². The tangential component is given as 2.5 m/s². So add $4.5^2 + 2.5^2$ and take the square root to get 5.1 m/s².

12. **D**—The blocks move at constant speed and so experience balanced forces both vertically and horizontally. Vertically, the force of the bottom block on the top block has to balance the top block's weight—and so has an upward component. Horizontally, the bottom block can't exert a force on the top block, because there's no other object to exert a balancing force. Thus no horizontal forces can act on the top block at all.

13. **E**—For the magnitude of vertical velocity, start with the vertical component of initial velocity—A's is largest, B's is next largest, C's is zero. Look at which goes highest: Kinematics equations simplify to $x = v^2/2a$ for final speed of zero, so the stone with the greatest initial vertical speed goes highest. Similarly, the one that goes highest hits the ground with greatest vertical speed. So the *vertical* velocity at ground is ranked A > B > C. As for speed at ground, it's easiest to see this through energy conservation. All three rocks gain the same potential energy because they're at the same vertical height from the ground. All three rocks start with the same initial kinetic energy because their speeds are the same. So the blocks must end up with the same kinetic energy as each other at the bottom, meaning also the same speed.

14. **E**—From position 1 to 2, the mechanical energy goes from all potential to all kinetic. Work is done by the air to reduce this mechanical energy. The reduction in mechanical energy is the difference between the kinetic energy at the bottom $(\frac{1}{2}mv_2^2)$ and the potential energy at the top $(mgL\theta_1)$.

15. **E**—If there's a teeny bit of air resistance, then mechanical energy is almost conserved, and θ_3 is almost equal to θ_1. If there's a lot of air resistance, then mechanical energy is barely conserved at all, and θ_3 is nearly zero. The form of the air resistance function doesn't matter; the pure amount of work done by air resistance matters. We don't know anything about that.

16. **B**—The forces in the direction of the object's motion at any position have components $mg \sin\theta$ along the object's path and cv against the object's path. So the net force is $mg \sin\theta - cv$. Set this equal to mass times acceleration, where acceleration is the second derivative of position. But we don't want the derivative of the angle θ, we want the derivative of the distance along the arc. That's $L\theta$.

17. **C**—Acceleration is the slope of the velocity-time graph. "Average" acceleration would be the slope from the beginning to the end of the graph, disregarding what's in between. That's the slope from (0, –3) to (10, 3) which is 6/10 = 0.6 m/s².

18. **A**—Average velocity is defined as displacement divided by time interval. Displacement is found from the area under a velocity-time graph. Here, the areas below and above the *t*-axis in the first 6 seconds cancel. The remaining area is the rectangle (4 s)(3 m/s) = 12 m. Divide by the time interval of 10 s to get 1.2 m/s.

19. **D**—The distance traveled by each car is found by taking the area under the graph. That's 8 m for Car A and 4 m for Car B. Car A's graph is above the horizontal axis, while car B's graph is below the horizontal axis; this means the cars move in different directions. Thus they end up 12 m apart.

20. **E**—The time we're talking about is ¼ of a period. The period of a pendulum equation has g in the denominator and under the square root. The gravitational field on Planet X is ½ that of Earth, so the period of the pendulum there is $1/(1/\sqrt{2})$ times the period on Earth; that's the same thing as $\sqrt{2}$ times the period on Earth.

21. **C**—The maximum speed comes from energy conservation: the gravitational energy at the top is equal to the kinetic energy at the bottom, $mgh = \frac{1}{2}mv^2$. Solve for v to get a maximum speed of $\sqrt{2gh}$. Here g is in the numerator and under the square root. Since the gravitational field on Planet X is half that of Earth, the max speed is $\sqrt{\dfrac{1}{2}}$ times the speed on Earth.

22. **D**—The period of a pendulum depends only on the length of the pendulum and the gravitational field. Choice I is, in fact, the period; so that and L can be used to solve for g. Choice II doesn't work because the speed as shown in the previous problem depends on the vertical height h from which the ball was released, not the string length; to find h we'd also need the angle from which the pendulum was released. And the mass is not in the period equation and cancels from the max-speed equation, so it is not useful.

23. B—Terminal velocity is when the ball falls at constant speed because the forces of gravity and air resistance balance. Before reaching terminal velocity, though, the ball had to speed up from rest to reach that speed—so velocity increased. And acceleration is the change in speed every second. Initially the ball was changing speed; once the ball hit terminal velocity, the speed was not changing. The acceleration was nonzero and then zero. So acceleration decreased.

24. C—After the collision, the dart-block system swings to the maximum height h. Use energy conservation: $(M_1+M_2)gh = \frac{1}{2}(M_1+M_2)v^2$. Solve for v, and the masses cancel.

25. C—Now use conservation of total momentum right before and after the collision: $M_2v + 0 = (M_1+M_2)\sqrt{2gh}$, using the result from the previous question for the speed of the blocks after collision. Solve for v to get choice C.

26. A—The mechanical energy of the object-Earth systems starts at mgh, and since no work is done by external forces on the objects, the mechanical energy is the same at the bottom as at the top. But that mechanical energy at the bottom consists of both rotational and translational kinetic energies. Since a hoop has mass distributed farther on average from the axis of rotation, the hoop must have a greater rotational inertia. Therefore, a greater proportion of its mechanical energy is rotational rather than translational, and the hoop moves slower, the disk faster.

27. D—No external torques act on the two-disk system (only the torque of disk 1 on disk 2 and vice versa). That's the very definition of when angular momentum is conserved. However, the collision is by definition inelastic because the disks stick together. In an inelastic collision, mechanical energy—including rotational kinetic energy—is not conserved.

28. C—The gravitational force is always attractive, so both forces act to the right. The formula is $F = Gm_1m_2/d^2$. This equation for F_B has a numerator that's twice as big as for F_C and a denominator $(2/3)^2 = 4/9$ as big. That makes F_B something like four times larger, as in choice C.

29. E—The expression for the force of sphere B on sphere A is $G(2m)(m)/(2x)^2$. The expression for the force of sphere C on sphere A is $G(m)(m)/(3x)^2$. Add the forces together because they act in the same direction; you get $(11/18)(Gm^2/x^2)$.

30. C—The time derivative of velocity is acceleration, and then net force is mass times acceleration. The time derivative of this function is $-6t$; multiply this by the 2 kg mass to get choice C.

31. E—The initial velocity is when time t is zero. That's just c in this expression, so +2 m/s. The positive means moving right. As time goes on, the second term becomes nonzero, which means we're subtracting something from the initial speed, so the object slows down.

32. A—Use the impulse-momentum theorem, $\Delta p = Ft$. Here the change in momentum is the satellite's mass times its change in speed, 5000 kg × 100 m/s. And the time interval is 60 s. So the force of the thruster is 500,000/60 = 8300 N.

33. E—Kepler's law says that the period of an orbit squared is proportional to the radius of the orbit cubed. Thus the expression for radius must have a cube root of T^2. Then when using Newton's second law by setting the gravitational force Gm_sm_e/r^2 equal to ma, the object undergoing acceleration is the satellite—so we use m_s in the right-hand-side expression, and the m_s cancels . . . leaving m_e as the only mass in the resulting expression.

34. A—Momentum is conserved when no external forces act on a system. The ball's momentum is not conserved here, because the external force of the wall acts on the ball. (The ball's direction changes, so even though the magnitude of the ball's momentum doesn't change, the ball's momentum vector does change.) Considering the ball-Earth system, though, no external forces act on that system—so momentum of the ball-Earth system is conserved.

35. C—Derive the orbital speed by setting the gravitational force GMm/r^2 equal to ma, where acceleration in a circle is v^2/r. Solving for v gives $v = \sqrt{\dfrac{GM}{r}}$, M being the mass of the central planet. With the r for satellite B being twice that for satellite A, that gives a ratio of $1:(1/\sqrt{2})$, which is the same thing as $\sqrt{2}:1$.

Physics C—Mechanics Practice Exam 3—Free-Response Solutions

1. (15 points)

   (a) The exponent must be unitless, so units of b must cancel the units of time.

   1 pt for the correct answer, 1/s or s^{-1}

   (b) Initial velocity is when $t = 0$. And e^0 is 1. So the initial velocity is 1.4 m/s.

   1 pt for the correct answer

   (c) Positive—when $t = 0$, the e^{-bt} term becomes 1, and the remaining expression is positive.

   1 pt for the correct answer
   1 pt for justification

   (d) As t increases, the e^{-bt} term gets smaller. So the whole expression gets smaller, and the speed decreases.

   1 pt for the correct answer
   1 pt for justification

   (e) The acceleration is the time derivative of the velocity. For this function, that's $-1.4be^{-bt}$. Again, the e^{-bt} term gets smaller as time goes on. That makes the absolute value of the whole expression get smaller. The magnitude of the acceleration decreases.

   1 pt for the correct answer
   1 pt for justification

   (f)

   1 pt for a graph never above the horizontal axis
   1 pt for an exponential graph decreasing in magnitude, even if in the wrong quadrant
   1 pt for labeling the y-intercept as "2.8b," whether positive or negative—the net force is ma, and m is 2 kg, so the intercept is $(2)(1.4b) = 2.8b$.

   (g)

   1 pt for setting up an integral of velocity with respect to time *with correct limits of 0 to infinity*
   1 pt for the correct answer of (positive) 1.4/b

$$\int_0^\infty 1.4e^{-bt}\, dt = \left. \frac{-1.4e^{-bt}}{b} \right|_0^\infty = 0 - \left(\frac{-1.4}{b} \right) = \frac{1.4}{b}$$

(h) The total energy dissipated is the change in kinetic energy. The initial kinetic energy is $\frac{1}{2}mv^2$, where m is 2 kg and v is $1.4b$. The final kinetic energy is zero. Total energy dissipated is $\frac{1}{2}(2)(1.4b)^2 = (1.4b)^2$ or $2.0b^2$.

1 pt for attempting to calculate a change in kinetic energy
1 pt for the the correct answer

2. (15 points)

(a)

1 pt for using a gravitational force expression in Newton's second law
1 pt for setting acceleration equal to v^2/r
1 pt for the correct expression for v

$$\frac{Gm_A M}{(2R)^2} = \frac{m_A V^2}{2R} \qquad \text{solve for } v, \; v = \sqrt{\frac{GM}{2R}}$$

(b)

1 pt for recognizing that the ratio can be calculated
1 pt for using any appropriate method to get the correct answer, such as recognizing that the orbital radius is under a square root in the denominator of the speed expression and all other quantities are unchanging, so doubling the radius multiplies the speed by $\frac{1}{\sqrt{2}}$.

(c)

1 pt for attempting to subtract the potential energies of satellite A at each orbital radius
1 pt for the correct answer

$$U_B - U_A = \frac{-GMm_A}{(4R)} - \frac{-GMm_A}{(2R)} = \frac{+GMm_A}{4R}$$

(d) Kepler's third law says period is proportional to the 3/2 power of orbital radius. Since satellite B has twice the orbital radius, its period is $2^{3/2}$ times larger. The ratio can be expressed as $2^{3/2}$, $\sqrt{8}$, $2\sqrt{2}$, 2.8, or any equivalent.

1 pt for citing Kepler's third law (or alternatively, expanding on the derivation in (a) by writing v as orbital circumference divided by period)
1 pt for the correct answer

(e)

1 pt for summing kinetic and potential energies to get total mechanical energy (or using the fact that in an orbit, the total mechanical energy is half the potential energy)
1 pt for an expression for gravitational potential energy, including the negative sign: $U = -GMm/r$
1 pt for the correct comparison—with a larger orbital radius, the mechanical energy for satellite B is less negative, and thus greater

(f)

1 pt for setting the total mechanical energy ($K + U$) to zero (because gravitational potential energy is defined as zero a long way away from the central planet, so the minimum mechanical energy a long way away will be zero)
1 pt for the correct expressions for kinetic and potential energies at the current location.
1 pt for the correct answer

$$O = \frac{1}{2}m_A v_{min}^2 + \frac{-GMm_A}{2R} \qquad \text{solve for } v_{min}, \; v_{min} = \sqrt{\frac{GM}{R}}$$

3. (15 points)

(a)

1 pt for an energy expression that includes rotational and linear kinetic energies
1 pt for using correct expressions for gravitational, rotational kinetic, and linear kinetic energies
1 pt for the relationship between h and d, $h = d \sin\theta$. 1 for using the relation $\omega = v/R$ to cancel the R term

$$U = K + K_{\text{rot}}$$

$$mgh = \frac{1}{2}mv^2 + \frac{1}{2}I\omega^2$$

$$\cancel{m}g\underbrace{(\cancel{h})}_{d\sin\theta} = \frac{1}{2}\cancel{m}v^2 + \frac{1}{2}\left(\frac{2}{3}\cancel{m}\cancel{R^2}\left(\frac{v^2}{\cancel{R^2}}\right)\right) \qquad \text{solve for } v$$

$$h \quad h = d\sin\theta$$

$$v = \sqrt{\frac{6}{5}gd\sin\theta}$$

(b)

1 pt for using a kinematic equation relating distance and time
1 pt for using a kinematic equation to relate acceleration to the speed from part (a)

with zero initial speed, $v^2 = 2ad$

so $\boxed{a = \dfrac{v^2}{2d}}$

$$d = \frac{1}{2}at^2$$

$$d = \frac{1}{2}\left(\frac{v^2}{2d}\right)t^2 \qquad \text{plug in } v \text{ from part (a)}$$

$$d = \frac{1}{2}\left(\frac{\frac{6}{5}g\cancel{d}\sin\theta}{2\cancel{d}}\right)t^2.$$

(c)

1 pt For any combination that would create a straight line graph. I've used d and t^2. It's also legit to use t and $\sqrt{d}$. Or graphing d and $(3/10)gt^2$ would give a slope that straight-up represents $\sin\theta$.

(d) If the chosen axes don't create a linear graph, only the first two of these points can be awarded.

1 pt for data plotted correctly
1 pt for linear scales on each axis that allow the data to take up about half of the grid area
1 pt for correct units on both axes
1 pt for a reasonable best-fit line

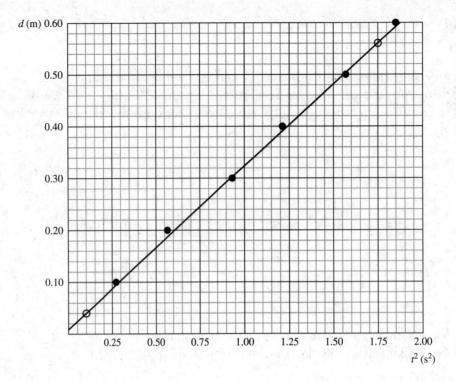

(e)

1 pt for correctly calculating the slope of the graph, using points on the line, not data points

1 pt for relating the slope to its physical meaning—in the example, the slope is shown to be equal to $(3/10)g \sin \theta$

1 pt for using the physical meaning of the slope in an attempt to determine θ

1 pt for a value of θ between 4 and 8 degrees

$$\text{slope} = \frac{\text{rise}}{\text{run}} = \frac{(0.56 - 0.04)\,\text{m}}{(1.75 - 0.10)\,\text{s}^2} = 0.32\,\frac{\text{m}}{\text{s}^2}$$

$$y = mx + b$$
$$d = \left(\frac{3}{10}\,g \sin \theta\right) t^2$$

$$\text{slope} = \frac{3}{10}\,g \sin \theta$$

$$\text{so} \quad \sin \theta = \frac{10}{3g}(\text{slope})$$

$$\boxed{\theta = 6.2°}$$

AP Physics C—Mechanics
Full Exam Scoring

Multiple-Choice: Number Correct_____(35 max)

Free-Response: Question 1_____(15 max)
              Question 2_____(15 max)
              Question 3_____(15 max)

Total Free-Response_____(45 max)

$1.286 \times$ Multiple-Choice + Free-Response = Raw Score_____(90 max)

59–90	5
45–58	4
35–44	3
23–34	2
0–22	1

Physics C—Electricity and Magnetism Practice Exam 3— Multiple-Choice Solutions

1. **A**—First, reduce the circuit to its simplest form. The parallel capacitors add algebraically to get an equivalent capacitance of 12 nF. Then the series capacitors add inversely by $1/C_{eq} = 1/C_1 + 1/C_2$. Add $1/12$ and $1/6$ to get $1/4$ . . . that means the equivalent capacitance of the circuit is 4 nF. Now by $Q = CV$, the whole circuit stores (4 nF) × (24 V) = 96 nC. Series capacitors each take the same charge as each other; that is ALSO equal to the total charge across the combination. So the 6 nF capacitor takes all 96 nC.

2. **D**—The parallel capacitors take the same voltage as each other. Their equivalent capacitance is 12 nF. Both the voltage across this 12 nF equivalent capacitance and the voltage across the 6 nF capacitor must add to 24 V by Kirchhoff's loop rule. And series capacitors take the same charge in $Q = CV$. Solving for voltage, the voltage across each capacitor is Q/C, where Q is the same for each. Even if you got the total charge wrong in question 1, you'll still see that the bigger capacitor takes the smaller voltage, and by a factor of 2 here since 12 nF is twice 6 nF. The 12 nF equivalent capacitor takes 8 V across it (96 nC/12 nF). This means both of the parallel capacitors also take 8 V.

3. **C**—The magnetic field due to a long straight wire is $\mu_0 I/2\pi r$, where r is the distance from the wire to the point being considered. So for the right-hand wire, $r = d$, and for the left-hand wire, $r = 2d$. The direction of the magnetic field is given by the second right-hand rule: point the thumb with the current, curl the fingers to show the field direction. That's down the page due to the right-hand wire, up the page due to the left-hand wire. So the magnitudes of the two magnetic fields subtract to the total: $\mu_0 I/2\pi d - \mu_0 I/2\pi(2d)$ gives choice C.

4. **B**—Use the second right-hand rule: point the thumb with the current, and the fingers show the magnetic field direction. The left-hand wire produces a field down and to the right. The right-hand wire produces a field up and to the left. These fields are of equal magnitude, because the currents are the same and the distances from the wires are the same. So the magnetic fields subtract to a net of zero.

5. **C**—Apply net$F = ma$ in circular motion. Here the net force on the object is qvB, and the acceleration in a circular path is v^2/r. Solve for r to get $r = mv/qB$. The electron and proton experience the same magnetic field B, the same speed v, and have the same amount of charge q. The difference is, the mass of a proton is something like 2000 times that of the electron. So the radius of the proton's circular motion will be 2000 times bigger. The only position close to showing an orbital radius 2000 times smaller for the electron is C.

6. **B**—The direction of a magnetic force is always perpendicular to the velocity vector. This means that the magnetic force causes circular motion, but not a change in speed, for an object in the field. The magnetic field won't change the speed of "any" particle.

7. **B**—Kirchoff's loop rule indicates that since this a closed circuit loop, the voltage across each must be the same. Capacitance is a property of a capacitor, so the capacitances can be different regardless of what circuit they're hooked up to. Then by $Q = CV$ the charge can be different if the capacitances are different, even with the same voltages.

8. **C**—Capacitance is a property of a capacitor. It's the same capacitor in both diagrams, so it has the same capacitance. Charge is free to flow between capacitors in diagram 3, so the charge on C_1 will change. And while the voltage across each capacitor in diagram 3 must be the same for each, that doesn't have to be 12 V and probably will not be.

9. **A**—The voltage across the middle branch of the circuit is $IR = $ (2 A)(50 Ω) = 100 V. That's the same as the voltage across R_2, because parallel resistors take the same voltage as each other. The current through R_2 is 3 A by Kirchoff's junction rule (5 A enters the junction, 2 A goes down the

middle, so the remaining 3 A goes through R_2). Set 100 V = (3 A)(R_2) and solve for R_2 = 33 Ω.

10. A—Use Kirchoff's loop rule. The battery provides 300 V. So the voltage drop across R_1 and the 50 Ω resistor must also be 300 V. The voltage across the 50 Ω resistor is (2 A)(50 Ω) = 100 V. So the remaining 200 V must be across R_1, which is what the voltmeter measures.

11. C—The capacitance of a parallel plate capacitor is $\varepsilon_0 A/d$, where A is the plate area and d is the distance between plates. Here that means the capacitance is proportional to d^2/x. Evaluating each capacitor according to d^2/x, capacitor C has largest capacitance of $(2d)^2/x = 4(d^2/x)$. Capacitor D works out to $2(d^2/x)$, capacitor A to $1(d^2/x)$, and capacitor B to $(1/2)(d^2/x)$.

12. A—The standard expression for energy stored on a capacitor is $\frac{1}{2}CV^2$. But the fundamental equation for capacitors says that $Q = CV$. So, substitute $V = Q/C$ into the standard expression. You're left with $\frac{1}{2}Q^2/C$.

13. A—The force on the charge is qE and thus is uniform within each region. A uniform force produces a uniform acceleration, and thus a uniform slope on a velocity-time graph. The graph must be straight in each region. In region 1, E is larger, so the force, the acceleration, and the slope of the velocity-time graph will be larger as well.

14. C—The symmetry is appropriate for Ampere's law. Never evaluate the integral in Ampere's law—it always simplifies to $BL = \mu_0 I_{enclosed}$. Here L is the circumference of an amperian loop, $2\pi r$. The current enclosed by this loop is a fraction of the total current. What fraction? A fraction equal to the area enclosed by the amperian loop over the total cross-sectional area of the wire. That's πr^2 over the total area of the wire. Point is, Ampere's law looks like $B(2\pi r) = \mu_0(\pi r^2/\text{total area})(\text{total } I)$. Solving for B, you're left with an expression with r by itself in the numerator. So the magnetic field is proportional to r. (You've memorized the equation $B = \mu_0 I/2\pi r$, but that's for the magnetic field *outside* a long straight wire. This question is asking about B inside the wire.)

15. B—Gauss's law says that for a closed surface, $\int E \cdot dA$ is proportional to the charge enclosed by the surface. While the mathematics of Gauss's law becomes difficult when the charge distribution and the surface are asymmetric, the law still holds. Since zero charge is enclosed, the integral becomes zero as well.

16. B—The force on the object is uniform and equal to qE = (0.001 C)(400 N/C) = 0.40 N. The work done by a uniform force is equal to force times distance, where that distance must be parallel (or antiparallel) to the direction of the force. The electric force is to the right; the force on a positive charge is likewise to the right. So the necessary distance is horizontal only . . . that's (3 m)(cos 45°) = 2.1 m. The work done is (0.40 N) × (2.1 m) = 0.84 J. That work is positive because the electric force is parallel, not antiparallel, to the component of displacement along the direction of force.

17. E—For the magnetic field, think of the moving charges as current-carrying wires. Use the second right-hand rule. The left charge carries a current—a flow of positive charge—up the page. Point the thumb with the current and curl the fingers. The fingers point into the page at point P. Similarly, the right charge can be thought of as a flow of negative charge up the page, and so is equivalent to a flow of positive charge down the page. The magnetic field at point P due to the right charge is also into the page. So the net magnetic field is into the page. Then the electric field due to a charge points away from a positive, toward a negative charge. At point P that's to the right due to the left-hand charge, and also to the right due to the right-hand charge, making the net electric field to the right.

18. E—The magnitude of the electric force is given by $F = kqq/d^2$. The magnitude of a force is just an amount—the + or – sign is not plugged into the equation. (The signs of the charges indicate directions of force—like charge signs repel, opposite charge signs repel.) So with the same amount of charge in each arrangement, the force will depend on the distance between charges—larger distance, smaller force.

19. **B**—Voltage—that is, potential difference—is provided by a battery. Since the battery remains connected, the potential difference across the plates does not change. Electric field between two parallel plates is equal to V/d, the potential difference the plates divided by the distance between the plates. Neither V nor d changes, so electric field doesn't change. A dielectric material changes the capacitance of the capacitor (the formula for the capacitance of a parallel-plate capacitor is $C = \kappa \varepsilon_0 A/d$—the effect of the dielectric slab is to increase the κ term). By $Q = CV$, a bigger C with an unchanged V gives larger charge Q.

20. **D**—Initially, the negative rod attracts positive charges in the conducting sphere and repels negative charges from the sphere into the ground. This makes the sphere have a net positive charge when the wire is cut. When the rod is moved far away, nothing is nearby to cause polarization. So the positive charges will distribute uniformly on the surface of the conductor, as in choice D.

21. **B**—The EMF is given by the time derivative of the magnetic flux, which is B times the area of the loop. The area of the loop is πr^2, so the expression for flux is $3\pi r^2 t^2$. The time derivative of this expression is $6\pi r^2 t$.

22. **A**—The kinetic energy gained by the proton is equal to the potential energy lost from A to B. The potential energy lost by the proton is $q\Delta V$, where the change in electric potential ΔV is Ed (derived from the equation for a uniform electric field, $E = \Delta V/\Delta x$). The charge q here is the charge of a proton; the distance d is the distance from point A to point P, 0.08 m. Not the distance between plates, but the distance the proton moves! So the change in potential energy is $(1.6 \times 10^{-19}$ C$)(80$ N/C$)(0.08$ m$) = 1.0 \times 10^{-18}$ J.

23. **D**—Induced current in the loop is, by Ohm's law, the induced voltage (EMF) divided by the constant resistance of the loop. So whether induced current is constant depends on the EMF. Induced EMF is dB/dt. The magnetic field produced by a current-carrying wire depends linearly on I. The time derivative of I is a constant value. Thus, the EMF is constant, and so is the induced current. Now, the direction of the magnetic field inside the wire is into the page by the second right-hand rule—point the thumb left with the current producing the field, the fingers curl into the page. This magnetic field is increasing because the current is increasing. So by Lenz's law, increasing flux is into the page, making decreasing flux out of the page . . . and the induced current is found by pointing the right thumb with decreasing flux and curling the fingers. That'd be counterclockwise.

24. **C**—The electric field inside a conductor is zero everywhere—and these two spheres are a single conductor, so they have electric field zero everywhere. The equation $E = -dV/dx$ indicates that electric field tells how electric potential changes. Since electric field is zero, that means electric potential can't change within the two spheres. But that potential isn't zero! The electric potential is considered zero a long way away from any charges. Since these spheres have positive charge, they create positive potential outside of the spheres, and so they must have a uniform but positive potential everywhere inside.

25. **D**—The positive charge initially on the conducting spheres must redistribute at the surface (because no charge can remain inside a conductor). We know the electric potential is the same everywhere in and on each sphere. And electric potential at the surface is given by kQ/r. The sphere with the bigger radius must likewise hold the bigger charge.

26. **A**—First, consider the whole circuit: the battery is the same, so the total voltage is unchanged. The equivalent resistance increases because we removed a parallel branch. By $V = IR$, the total current must decrease. Now apply Ohm's law to resistor X only: The reduced total current all runs through resistor X, but resistor X can't change its own resistance. So by $V = IR$, the voltage across bulb X is smaller than before. Kirchoff's loop rule says that the voltage across X and Y must sum to V . . . so with smaller voltage across X, there must be greater voltage across Y. Now apply Ohm's law to bulb Y: greater voltage with unchanged resistance means greater current, too.

27. **C**—The electric field inside a conductor is zero; charge can only sit on the surface of a conductor. Consider a Gaussian surface drawn inside the outer shell, going through point C. Since the

shell is conducting, there must be zero electric field inside. Therefore, this Gaussian surface must enclose zero total charge. The inner shell contains charge $-2Q$, so the inner surface of the outer shell—the part inside this Gaussian surface—contains $+2Q$ to make the total charge inside the Gaussian surface zero. Then the remaining $+1Q$ of charge on the outer shell must be on the outer surface.

28. **E**—The electric field inside a conductor is zero, so C is the smallest. A Gaussian sphere through A encloses no charge, so the electric field at A is also zero. A Gaussian sphere at position B encloses $-2Q$; a Gaussian sphere at position D encloses $+Q$. So the sphere at D encloses a smaller magnitude of charge AND has a larger distance from the center, meaning D has a smaller electric field than B.

29. **D**—Magnetic flux is BA, where A is the area of the loop that is directly penetrated by the magnetic field. Here the magnetic field is penetrating the loop at an angle, so we need to look at the component of the magnetic field that penetrates directly, that is, at a 90° angle to the plane of the loop. That's $B\sin 60°$, or $B\frac{\sqrt{3}}{2}$. (Not cosine of 60 degrees . . . if you're not sure, note that the magnetic field is closer to straight-through the loop than to along the loop, so we want the bigger component, and $\sin 60°$ is bigger than $\cos 60°$.) And the area of the loop is xy.

30. **E**—When the current is 0.43 A, the voltage across the resistor is $(70\ \Omega)(0.43\ \text{A}) = 30\ \text{V}$. That means the voltage across the capacitor is 20 V by Kirchoff's loop rule, to add to the total 50 V in the battery. For a capacitor, the charge stored is given by $Q = CV$. Here that's $(0.50\ \mu\text{F})(20\ \text{V}) = 10\ \mu\text{C}$.

31. **C**—Inductors resist changes in current. Since the current has been flowing for a long time and thus is steady, the inductor has no effect on the circuit. It just acts as a bare wire. So the two resistors are both in parallel with the battery, taking the voltage of the battery. The current through R_1 is $12\ \text{V} / 12\ \Omega = 1.0\ \text{A}$.

32. **D**—Inductors resist changes in current. So the current through the inductor now is the same as the current through the inductor before the switch was closed. The inductor was in series with the 24 Ω resistor, which carried $12\ \text{V}/24\ \Omega = 0.5\ \text{A}$ of current. With the battery removed, the resistor R_1 is in series with R_2, so it must carry the 0.5 A of current.

33. **E**—The magnetic field produced by a current-carrying wire is given by the second right-hand rule: Point the thumb to the right and curl. The fingers point out of the page above the wire, so that's the direction of the magnetic field. Now the force on the electron is given by the first right-hand rule: Point with the velocity, curl the fingers out of the page with the magnetic field, and the thumb gives the upward force on a positive charge. An electron has a negative charge, though, so the force is downward. Because the magnetic force is perpendicular to the velocity, the path is initially circular. But because the magnetic field isn't uniform (it drops off the farther you get from the current-carrying wire), the magnetic force isn't always of the same magnitude, and so the path becomes not circular.

34. **E**—Each charge contributes a potential of kQ/d to the total potential at the origin. That's $(9 \times 10^9\ \text{N/m}^2/\text{C}^2)(-2 \times 10^{-6}\ \text{C})/(0.04\ \text{m}) = -450{,}000\ \text{V}$ per charge. Both charges are negative and so produce negative electric potentials, and electric potentials add as scalars, making the total potential $-900{,}000\ \text{V}$.

35. **D**—By $E = kQ/d^2$, each charge creates an electric field of the same magnitude (because both are of the same amount of charge, located the same distance from the origin). A negative charge produces an electric field toward that charge. So the fields produced by each charge are pointed in opposite directions. Electric fields add as vectors; equal magnitude vectors pointing in opposite directions subtract to zero.

Physics C—Electricity and Magnetism Practice Exam 3— Free-Response Solutions

1. (15 points)

(a)

    i. Use Gauss's law with a cylindrical Gaussian surface. Because the length of the rod is big now compared to d, the electric field will always point straight away from the rod—so straight through the surface. Then Gauss's law says $EA = Q/\varepsilon_0$. Here the area A of the cylindrical Gaussian surface A is $2\pi r L$; we're looking for the electric field a distance d from the rod, so replace r with d. The charge Q enclosed by the surface is λL. Solve for E to get $E = \lambda/(2\pi d \varepsilon_0)$.

1 pt   for attempting to use Gauss's law reasonably
1 pt   for the correct area term
1 pt   for the correct expression for the charge enclosed
1 pt   for the correct answer

    ii.

1 pt   for an arrow straight up the page

    iii. The electric field expression is inversely related to the first power of r, the distance from the rod. That means doubling r cuts the electric field in half. (If you stated an incorrect expression in part (i) that has a clear r dependence, then award credit here for an answer and justification consistent with that incorrect equation.)

1 pt   for the answer
1 pt   for a correct justification

    iv.

1 pt   for substituting an electric field expression from part (i) into $V = -\int E\,dr$.
1 pt   for correct limits and an attempt to evaluate the integral with respect to r
1 pt   for the correct answer in any form that has correctly evaluated the correct integral

$$-\int_{d}^{2d} \frac{\lambda}{2\pi r t_0}\,dr = \frac{-\lambda}{2\pi t_0}\int_{d}^{2d}\frac{1}{4r}\,dr = \frac{-\lambda}{2\pi t_0}[\ln(2d)-\ln(d)]$$

$$= \frac{-\lambda}{2\pi t_0}\log 2$$

(b)

   i.

1 pt for using (not just writing) the expression $E = \int \frac{k\,dq}{r^2}$

1 pt for substituting $dq = \lambda dx$

1 pt for using geometry to write r, the distance from a position on the rod to point A, in terms of x and d as shown in the diagram below

1 pt for correct limits

$$r^2 = x^2 + d^2 \qquad E = \int\limits_{-L/2}^{+L/2} \frac{k\lambda}{(x^2 + d^2)}\,dx$$

   ii.

1 pt for an upward pointing arrow

2. (15 points)

   (a)

   i.

1 pt for zero current between ℓ and D

1 pt for a horizontal line between 0 and ℓ

1 pt for a horizontal line on the opposite side of the axis between D and $D + \ell$

1 pt for a graph entirely below the horizontal axis between 0 and ℓ

   ii.

1 pt For explaining that in general equation $\varepsilon = B\ell v$, here each term is unchanging, so the EMF and hence the current isn't changing either

   ii.

1 pt for the correct answer, Bsv. (Not $B\ell v$, because s is the side of the rectangle that is not changing how much is inside the field.)

   (b)

1 pt for recognizing that the magnetic flux or the induced EMF is doubled

1 pt for recognizing that the coil's resistance is also doubled

1 pt for using Ohm's law ($I = $ EMF/resistance) to determine that the induced current is unchanged

(c)

      i. Answer is $\varepsilon = Bs\sqrt{2ax}$.

1 pt for using the definition of induced EMF, $\varepsilon = d\Phi/dt$ or $\varepsilon = Bsv$ (full credit whether or not negative sign is included)

1 pt for substituting $v = \sqrt{2ax}$

     ii.

1 pt for the first segment starting at zero and concave toward the horizontal axis (This point is awarded if the shape is correct, even if drawn above the axis.)

1 pt for a curved segment between D and $D + \ell$

1 pt for this last segment starting at a greater vertical value than the first segment ended

1 pt for this last segment being concave toward the horizontal axis (Based on the answer to part (i), the square root function indicates the concave-down shape of the graph. The faster the coil moves, the more induced EMF/current by $\varepsilon = Bsv$. And the coil moves faster farther along the track because of the acceleration.)

3. (15 points)

Parts (a), (b), and (c) are graded all together. As long as the elements that earn points are there somewhere, award credit.

(a) Connect the inductor to a charged capacitor. Use a digital voltmeter to measure the voltage across the inductor as a function of time. Determine the period of the oscillating voltage from the voltmeter's output.

This example uses a circuit with a capacitor and inductor; something similar can be done with a resistor-inductor circuit and its time constant, or with other circuits.

1 pt for a conceptually plausible plan to collect data that could lead to a calculation of L

1 pt for a well-specified procedure that indicates correct use of appropriate equipment to measure the required quantities

1 pt for using more than a single measurement, that is, a graph or multiple trials to reduce error

(b) An example consistent with the method above:

Charged
capacitor

V   Inductor

Voltmeter

1 pt for drawing a diagram of a circuit that would function, that is, a complete circuit
1 pt for correctly placing an ammeter or voltmeter (an ammeter must be connected in series, a voltmeter in parallel)
1 pt for correct placement of all other equipment specified in part (a)

(c) An example continued from above:

The reading on the voltmeter will oscillate with a period given by $T = 2\pi\sqrt{LC}$. On the voltmeter output, look at the time from one maximum voltage to the next—that's the period. Plug in that period and the capacitance C, and you can solve for the inductance L.

1 pt for recognizing the existence of a period for an LC circuit, or a time constant for an LR circuit
1 pt for correctly relating the period/time constant to other circuit properties
1 pt for explaining how to find the period or time constant from the collected data

    i. The battery has been connected for a long time, so the inductor acts as a bare wire. The resistance of the active branch is 100 Ω, the battery is 15 V, so the current is $I = V/R = 15$ V/100 Ω = 0.15 A.

1 pt for the correct answer
1 pt for a correct verbal justification

    ii. The inductor resists changes in current. Since the current was 0.15 A right before the switch was closed, the initial current after the switch is closed is also 0.15 A.

1 pt for the correct answer
1 pt for a correct verbal justification

    iii. After a long time, the current again reaches a steady state with the inductor acting as a bare wire. The total resistance this time is 150 Ω, so the current is 15 V/150 Ω = 0.10 A.

1 pt for the correct answer
1 pt for a correct verbal justification

AP Physics C—Electricity and Magnetism
Full Exam Scoring

Multiple-Choice: Number Correct_____(35 max)

Free-Response: Question 1_____(15 max)
                Question 2_____(15 max)
                Question 3_____(15 max)

Total Free-Response_____(45 max)

$1.286 \times$ Multiple-Choice + Free-Response = Raw Score_____(90 max)

56–90	5
44–55	4
32–43	3
23–34	2
0–22	1

5 Minutes to a 5

120 Daily Questions and Activities in

5 Minutes a Day

INTRODUCTION

If you're signed up to take the calculus-based AP Physics C exams, you're probably pretty danged good at math. And you've learned in your calculus class how to take derivatives and evaluate integrals. I've found that once Physics C students set up a problem correctly, they get to the correct answer virtually every time.

The trick is, though, to set up the problem correctly. That's not easy at all, even for very good students.

In reviewing for the exam, I know that students' first instinct is to practice with problems that are mathematically intense, but that's not usually the best approach to improving skills. Rather, it's best to practice responding to questions that require difficult or tricky use of physics *concepts*. What facts of physics apply? How do you apply those facts to specific situations?

So, take a look at these five-minute exercises. They're definitely NOT mathematically intense. They often seem to have simple answers (*increase or decrease? Twice as much or four times as much?*). If you can answer these types of conceptual questions with clear and correct reasoning, then you'll likely set up your AP exam problems correctly, too.

See, good physics students don't know answers. They *figure out* answers. The trick is to start with a fundamental fact or equation related to the topic area. Then, to apply that fact or equation to the particular situation stated in the problem. That will lead you to the answer.

In order to prepare appropriately for the exam, you must look beyond whether you got the final answer right: Did you start with the correct physics principle? Does your reasoning match the solution's? If so, you're doing things right.

But . . . even if you got the final answer right for reasons far removed from the solution, then you've got some work to do. Figure out why your physics principles and/or reasoning are wrong. Understand how you could have known which principles or equations to start with. Try another problem within the same topic area. Look past the mathematics. A strong AP Physics C student doesn't just know how to do math; they also can figure out what math to do. These five-minute items will help you do just that.

Check off each activity as it is completed.

1. ❑	31. ❑	61. ❑	91. ❑
2. ❑	32. ❑	62. ❑	92. ❑
3. ❑	33. ❑	63. ❑	93. ❑
4. ❑	34. ❑	64. ❑	94. ❑
5. ❑	35. ❑	65. ❑	95. ❑
6. ❑	36. ❑	66. ❑	96. ❑
7. ❑	37. ❑	67. ❑	97. ❑
8. ❑	38. ❑	68. ❑	98. ❑
9. ❑	39. ❑	69. ❑	99. ❑
10. ❑	40. ❑	70. ❑	100. ❑
11. ❑	41. ❑	71. ❑	101. ❑
12. ❑	42. ❑	72. ❑	102. ❑
13. ❑	43. ❑	73. ❑	103. ❑
14. ❑	44. ❑	74. ❑	104. ❑
15. ❑	45. ❑	75. ❑	105. ❑
16. ❑	46. ❑	76. ❑	106. ❑
17. ❑	47. ❑	77. ❑	107. ❑
18. ❑	48. ❑	78. ❑	108. ❑
19. ❑	49. ❑	79. ❑	109. ❑
20. ❑	50. ❑	80. ❑	110. ❑
21. ❑	51. ❑	81. ❑	111. ❑
22. ❑	52. ❑	82. ❑	112. ❑
23. ❑	53. ❑	83. ❑	113. ❑
24. ❑	54. ❑	84. ❑	114. ❑
25. ❑	55. ❑	85. ❑	115. ❑
26. ❑	56. ❑	86. ❑	116. ❑
27. ❑	57. ❑	87. ❑	117. ❑
28. ❑	58. ❑	88. ❑	118. ❑
29. ❑	59. ❑	89. ❑	119. ❑
30. ❑	60. ❑	90. ❑	120. ❑

NEWTON'S LAWS

Scale

m_2

m_1

While doing an experiment with an Atwood's machine, two students hang the apparatus from a scale as shown. The hanging object m_2 has a larger mass than the hanging object m_1. The students are surprised to notice that when the objects are released from rest, the reading on the scale changes.

Explain why the scale reading changes. As part of your explanation, indicate whether the scale reading increases or decreases.

A hole is drilled in a board through which a string is run. On the board is object 1 of mass m_1. Hanging below the board is object 2 of larger mass m_2.

In the first experiment, object 1 is set into circular motion in such a way that the radius R of the circular motion does not change. In the second experiment, object 2 is placed on the board with the less massive object 1 hanging beneath.

How will the linear velocity v of object 2 in the second experiment compare to the linear velocity of object 1 in the first experiment?

Two ropes support a 30-kg stoplight, as shown. A student is asked to find the tension in each rope. Note that this problem does NOT ask for a complete solution to the problem.

1. On the dot above that represents the traffic light, draw and label the forces (not components) that act on the stoplight.

2. Derive two equations that together can be solved for the tension in each rope. If you need to draw anything other than what you have shown in Part (1) to assist in your solution, use the space below. Do NOT add anything to the figure in Part (1).

3. In your derived equations, circle the variables that represent unknown quantities; place a checkmark beside the variables that represent given variables or fundamental constants.

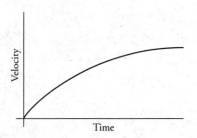

A lab cart moves according to the velocity-time graph shown above. The positive direction is to the right.

In a clear, coherent, paragraph-length response, describe how the cart moves and how the graph indicates the motion you describe. Include reference to the direction of motion and whether the cart is speeding up or slowing down.

In an experiment, two baseballs are dropped from the top of a tall building. When the first baseball is dropped, a timer is started. After 1.0 second, the second baseball is dropped. Air resistance can be neglected.

As the baseballs fall, what happens to the difference between the two baseballs' speeds?

_____ It increases.

_____ It decreases.

_____ It remains the same.

Justify your answer.

As the baseballs fall, what happens to the distance between them?

_____ It increases.

_____ It decreases.

_____ It remains the same.

Justify your answer.

In the graph above, the speed of a small object as it moves along a horizontal straight line is plotted against time. Which of the following methods is correct for determining the average speed between 0 and 4 s? Choose one, and justify your answer.

(A) Read the vertical axis at $t = 4$ s.

(B) Read the vertical axis at the average time, which is $t = 2$ s.

(C) Read the vertical axis to see the object starts at 0 m/s and finishes at 12 m/s, so add these speeds and divide by 2.

(D) Divide the area under the graph from 0–4 s by 4 s.

An alien visits Earth and discovers that she is able to jump incredibly high. The alien speculates that the free-fall acceleration g on Earth is different from that of her home planet. Her home planet is twice the diameter of Earth but made of material with the same density.

In terms of g, what is the free-fall acceleration on the alien's home planet?

A satellite is in circular orbit around an unknown planet. The satellite has a speed of 64 km/s, and the radius of its orbit (measured from the center of the planet) is 2,100 km. A second, identical satellite also has a circular orbit around this same planet, of radius 8,400 km.

Two students are discussing how the speed of the second satellite might be calculated:

Luis says, "The speed of the second satellite cannot be determined. We need to know the mass of the satellites and the unknown planet."

Marsha says, "But the mass of the unknown planet can be calculated using Newton's law of universal gravitation with the speed and radius of the first satellite. We have to do that first, but then we can calculate the speed of the second satellite."

Evaluate the arguments of Luis and Marsha. Indicate which statements they make are correct and incorrect.

A cart is released from rest from the top of a frictionless track, as shown above. The cart goes around the vertical loop, never leaving the track.

At which of the two labeled positions, if either, is the normal force of the track on the cart greater?

____ The normal force is greater at point A.

____ The normal force is greater at point B.

____ The normal force is the same at both locations.

Justify your answer.

5 Minutes to a 5

A lab cart moves according to the velocity-time graph shown above. The positive direction is to the right.

During the motion represented, is the magnitude of the object's acceleration increasing, decreasing, or remaining constant? Justify your answer.

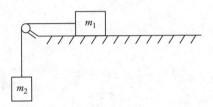

A cart of mass $m_1 = 0.50$ kg on a frictionless surface is connected by a string to a hanging object of mass $m_2 = 0.10$ kg.

In Experiment A, the system is released from rest. In Experiment B, a student gives the cart an initial push to the right to set it in motion.

(a) In which experiment, if either, is the magnitude of the cart's acceleration greater? Explain briefly.

(b) Is the direction of the cart's acceleration the same or different in each experiment? Explain briefly.

An object moves according to the position-time graph shown above. For each of the following, indicate and justify your answer with specific reference to the graph.

(a) Is the object's velocity

_____ positive

_____ negative

_____ zero

Justification:

(b) Is the object

_____ speeding up

_____ slowing down

_____ not changing speed

Justification:

(c) Is the object's acceleration

_____ positive

_____ negative

_____ zero

Justification:

Day 13

In the laboratory, students drop tennis balls from rest at various heights h above the ground. They measure the time t necessary for the balls to hit the ground.

The students are asked to plot a linear graph of their data whose slope can be used to determine g.

(a) What should be graphed on each axis such that the graph is linear?

(b) How can the slope of the best-fit line be used to determine g?

Justify your answer to each question.

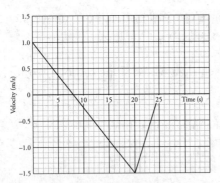

A lab cart moves according to the velocity-time graph shown above. A student is asked to determine the cart's displacement in the first 20 s of the cart's motion. His response—which is partially incorrect—is shown below.

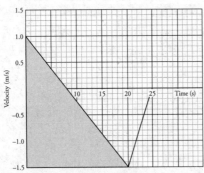

The cart's displacement is the area under the velocity-time graph from time $t = 0$ to $t = 20$ s. That area is shaded above in gray. The area of a triangle is ½(base)(height)—for this triangle, that's ½(20 s)(2.5 m/s) = **25 m**.

(a) Explain the error(s) in the student's solution.

(b) Does this student overestimate or underestimate the cart's displacement in the first 20 s of its motion? Explain your answer.

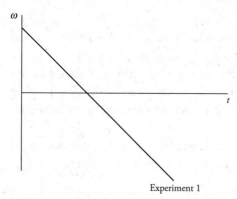

Two hanging objects are connected with light string passing over a pulley of mass 100 g, as shown above. The pulley consists of a massive ring with very light spokes.

In experiment 1, the pulley is given an initial clockwise angular velocity. The resulting angular velocity versus time graph is shown below.

Experiment 1

In experiment 2, the same hanging objects are instead connected over a different pulley, which has the same mass and radius but is shaped like a uniform disk. The pulley is given the same initial angular velocity.

On the same axes, sketch what the angular velocity versus time graph should look like for experiment 2. Justify your answer.

The diagram above shows a laboratory device for which the angular acceleration can be measured directly. A light string passes over a light pulley, attaching on one end to a hanging object of mass m_1. The other end of the string winds around the base of the device at radius r_1 from the center of the supporting pole's rotation. As the hanging object drops, the supporting pole and the attached objects of mass m_2 begin to rotate.

Describe two simple modifications to the device that would *increase* the device's angular acceleration. For each, explain why the angular acceleration would increase.

A 500-g cart sits on a frictionless track.

In experiment 1, a student pulls the cart to the right via a string attached to a spring scale. The student pulls such that the reading on the spring scale remains constant at 1.0 N.

Note: Figure not drawn to scale.

In experiment 2, an object of weight 1.0 N is attached to the same string. The string is passed over a light pulley, as shown.

In which experiment, if either, is the cart's acceleration greater? Justify your answer.

Day 18

For each prompt below, give a brief but specific description. Use normal, everyday language, without technical terms. In particular, do not use the words *positive* or *negative*.

(a) Describe an object that has zero velocity and zero acceleration.

(b) Describe an object that has nonzero velocity and zero acceleration.

(c) Describe an object that has zero velocity and nonzero acceleration.

(d) Describe an object that has nonzero velocity and nonzero acceleration.

A student designs an experiment to determine the linear relationship between acceleration and net force. The student sets up a cart on a frictionless horizontal surface, attached to a string that passes over a pulley, from which mass may be hung. The student varies the net force accelerating the cart by hanging additional mass from the string; the student measures the cart's acceleration with a motion detector placed behind the cart. The student plots the weight of the hanging objects versus the block's acceleration.

Describe at least one error in the student's lab design.

A box is moving up a frictionless incline with an initial velocity of v_0 as shown above. On the axes below, sketch position-time, velocity-time, and acceleration-time graphs for the period that the block slides up and back down the incline, reaching its highest point at time t_0. On the same graphs, create a second sketch of the position-, velocity-, and acceleration-time graphs if the experiment is repeated with friction present for the period that the block slides up and back down the incline, reaching its highest point at time t_0'. Explicitly label any intercepts, asymptotes, maxima or minima with algebraic expressions, given values, or fundamental constants as appropriate. Use a coordinate system with the origin at the base of the ramp, and the direction up the ramp considered positive.

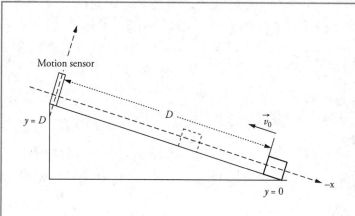

A box is moving up a frictionless incline with an initial velocity of v_0 as shown above. On the axes below, sketch position-time, velocity-time, and acceleration-time graphs. On the same graphs, create a second sketch of the position-, velocity-, and acceleration-time graphs for the same box if the angle of the incline to the horizontal is increased. Explicitly label any intercepts, asymptotes, maxima or minima with algebraic expressions, given values, or fundamental constants as appropriate.

A student is asked to determine the weight of a lab cart with a spring scale. However, when he hangs the cart directly from the spring scale as shown, the scale doesn't work, because it reaches its maximum reading.

Describe how the student could use this spring scale—and other lab equipment, but no other scales—to measure the weight of the lab cart.

A car traveling at highway speed collides with a bug, which was initially at rest. The bug sticks to the car after the collision.

Does the bug or the car experience a larger magnitude of acceleration during the collision? Justify your answer.

An automobile speeds up due to a constant force. The tires do not slip on the road. On the axes below, plot graphs of the linear distance traveled versus the angular displacement of one of the wheels, and the linear velocity of the car versus the angular velocity of one of the wheels.

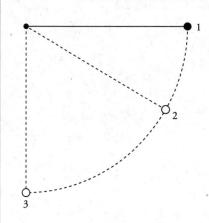

A pendulum is released from a horizontal position and swings through an arced path as shown above. On the diagram above, sketch a single vector to indicate the direction of the net force acting on the bob at locations 2 and 3. If there is zero net force at either location, clearly label as such by stating NONE.

Five equal forces are applied to either the corners or edges of a square as shown in the diagram above. Rank the forces, from greatest to least, in terms of the greatest magnitude of torque about point P.

A weightlifter is lifting a barbell over his head while standing on a scale. As the barbell is moving upward at a constant speed, the scale reading equals the weight of the barbell and weightlifter combined. During the time interval when the barbell slows to a stop, will the reading on the scale increase, decrease, or remain the same? Justify your answer.

Situation 1:

Two blocks on a frictionless surface are connected by a cord, as shown above. The block on the right is twice the mass of the block on the left. A second cord accelerates the system to the right. The two blocks then change position as shown below.

Situation 2:

Describe any changes in the tensions of each cord if the masses change locations, as shown, but the system is to have the same acceleration.

A student observes that a bicycle wheel take 20 seconds to reach a top speed by a motor providing a constant torque. A second wheel that is the same size, but of greater mass, is placed on the same axle and brought to the same initial speed by the motor. Predict how the time it takes for the second wheel to reach top speed compares to that of the first. Justify your answer.

Day 30

An object that weighs 20 N is attached to a string that is wrapped around a heavy, fixed pulley, as shown above, causing the pulley to accelerate. If the 20-N object is replaced by a rope pulling with a constant force of 20 N, predict how the angular acceleration of the pulley will change, if at all.

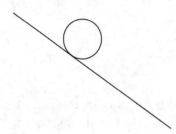

An iron hoop rolls without slipping down an incline.

(a) On the diagram above, indicate the forces (not force components) that act on the iron hoop. The tail of the arrow representing each force should begin at the point of that force's application.

(b) Which of the force(s) you drew will cause the hoop to have an angular acceleration about its center of mass? Justify your answer.

CONSERVATION

Day 32

A 0.5-kg object hanging from a 25-N/m spring is pulled 5 cm from its equilibrium position and released from rest. Two students are asked to calculate the maximum speed of the object.

- Student 1 says: "Elastic potential energy is converted entirely into kinetic energy.

  $\frac{1}{2}kx^2 = \frac{1}{2}mv^2$
  Plug in $k = 25$ N/m, $x = 0.05$ m, $m = 0.5$ kg; solve for v.
  Answer is 0.35 m/s."

- Student 2 says: "Acceleration is F/m, which is kx/m, where $k = 25$ N/m, $x = 0.05$ m, and $m = 0.5$ kg. That gives 2.5 m/s/s.

  Then use the kinematics equation $v^2 = v_0^2 + 2ax$, where $v_0 = 0$ and $x = 0.05$ m. Solve for v.

  Answer is 0.50 m/s."

Which student, if either, do you agree with?

Two balls of equal mass are dropped onto a hard surface from the same height above the surface. Both balls are in contact with the surface for about the same amount of time in their respective collisions. After its collision, ball A rebounds from the surface with approximately the same speed it had right before contact; ball B nearly sticks to the surface, rebounding with hardly any speed at all.

Which ball experiences a greater force during its collision? Justify your answer.

A 50-kg suitcase rolls down a chute and lands in a cart. Immediately before impact, the suitcase moves with a speed of 120 cm/s at an angle of 20° below the horizontal, as shown, while the cart moves to the right with a speed of 50 cm/s. Immediately after the collision, the suitcase is stuck inside the cart.

(a) Is the mechanical energy of the suitcase-cart system conserved during the collision? Justify your answer.

(b) Is the momentum of the suitcase-cart system in the vertical direction conserved during the collision? Justify your answer.

(c) Is the momentum of the suitcase-cart system in the horizontal direction conserved during the collision? Justify your answer.

Mother   Son

A mother and her son are initially at rest next to each other on an ice rink on which friction is negligible. The mother's mass is twice the son's mass. They push off of each other, causing them to glide apart.

Two students are discussing the quantities conserved in this collision. Each of the following statements is partially correct and partially incorrect. Identify the correct and incorrect parts, and explain why the incorrect parts are incorrect.

(a) Curtis says, "Linear momentum is conserved in this case. Even though the mother pushes with twice as much force as the son does, she will have only half of his speed after the collision, and by $p = mv$ they will have the same momentum as each other after the collision."

(b) Gregg says, "Kinetic energy is conserved in this case. The mother-son system begins with no speed and thus no kinetic energy. After the push, both have equal kinetic energy but in opposite directions; thus the system kinetic energy is zero, matching the system kinetic energy before collision."

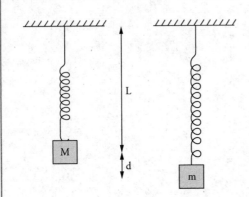

A cylinder of mass m is attached to a spring of spring constant k and length L. The cylinder initially hangs at rest. Next, the cylinder is pulled downward a distance of d from its resting position and released.

(a) Explain briefly how you know this cylinder's acceleration is not constant.

(b) Derive an expression in terms of given variables and fundamental constants for the maximum speed of the cylinder.

A block of known mass M moves from position 1 to position 2, as shown. The speeds of the block at positions 1 and 2 are known, as are the distances indicated in the figure.

Describe, as to another student at your level of physics, how you could show evidence for whether there is measurable friction between the surface and the block.

A child is standing in the center of a rotating platform and then walks toward the outside edge. Describe the change in the child-platform system, if any, of each of the following quantities. Justify your answers.

- Angular momentum
- Rotational inertia
- Angular velocity
- Rotational kinetic energy

An object attached to a spring oscillates horizontally in simple harmonic motion. Which of the following quantities is unchanged when the amplitude of the object's harmonic motion is doubled? Justify your answer.

(a) The period of oscillation

(b) The mass's maximum velocity

(c) The maximum potential energy stored in the spring-object system

Can a normal force ever do work on an object? If so, describe such a situation. If not, explain why not.

A skier of mass m starts from rest at the top of a hill that is inclined at an angle to the horizontal, as shown above. The hillside has a length D, and the coefficient of kinetic friction between snow and skis is μ.

For each of the following, choose one and justify your answer briefly.

1. Relative to the base of the hill, which of the following expressions gives the potential energy of the skier-Earth system?

   (A) $\dfrac{mgD}{\cos \theta}$

   (B) $\dfrac{mgD}{\sin \theta}$

   (C) $mgD \cos \theta$

   (D) $mgD \sin \theta$

   (E) mgD

2. Which of the following expressions gives the magnitude of the friction force on the skier while he moves down the incline?

   (A) $mg \sin \theta$
   (B) μmg
   (C) $\mu mg \cos \theta$
   (D) $\mu mg \sin \theta$
   (E) $mg \cos \theta$

3. Define the kinetic friction force on the skier as he slides down the incline as f. Which of the following expressions gives the work done on the skier by kinetic friction while the skier is on the incline?

(A) $-\dfrac{fD}{\cos\theta}$

(B) $-fD\sin\theta$

(C) $-fD$

(D) $-fD\cos\theta$

(E) $-\dfrac{fD}{\sin\theta}$

Day 42

A dart is shot with an initial speed of 15 m/s at an angle of 30° from the horizontal. The dart, when at the top of its trajectory, strikes and sticks to a pendulum bob, swinging the pendulum to an angle θ.

The experiment is repeated with the projectile shot at the same speed and the angle increased to 60°. The pendulum height is changed such that the dart again strikes and sticks to the pendulum bob when the dart is at the top of its trajectory. Will the maximum amplitude of the pendulum swing be greater than θ, equal to θ, or less than θ? Justify your answer.

Day 43

An object is compressed against a horizontal spring to location D and then released, as shown in the diagram below.

The block leaves the spring at position A. After sliding to position B, the block collides with an identical spring and stops at position C. There is friction between the block and the track between positions A and B, and no friction on any other portions of the track.

On the graphs below, sketch the total, kinetic, and potential energies as a function of location. You do not need to calculate values for the vertical axis, but the same vertical scale should be used for both quantities.

A rod—20 cm long, 0.060 kg in mass—slides across a low-friction air table. The rod rotates as it slides, as shown above.

You take high-speed video of the rod moving on the table. The video shows 1,000 frames per second and can be paused at any frame. A meterstick is clearly visible in the background for length measurements. The rotational inertia of a rod rotating about its center of mass in this manner is $\left(\frac{1}{12}\right)ML^2$, where M is the rod's mass and L is the rod's length.

Explain how to use the video to determine the angular momentum of the rod about point P (which is shown above). You need not actually make the determination, but you should state clearly what information you obtain from the video, how you obtain it, and how it will be used in a calculation to determine angular momentum.

Two identical pucks, each of mass M, move with equal speeds v on a horizontal, frictionless surface. The direction of their velocities is illustrated in the figure above. The pucks collide and stick together.

1. In terms of given variables and fundamental constants, determine the magnitude of the linear momentum of the two-puck system before the collision. Explain how you made this determination.

2. After the collision, the magnitude of the linear momentum of the two-puck system is

   (A) Greater than the answer to (1)

   (B) Less than the answer to (1)

   (C) Equal to the answer to (1)

Choose one, and justify your choice.

Two identical pucks, each of mass M, move with equal speeds v on a horizontal, frictionless surface. The direction of their velocities is illustrated in the figure above. The pucks collide and stick together.

1. In terms of given variables and fundamental constants, determine the kinetic energy of the two-puck system before the collision. Explain how you made this determination.

2. After the collision, the kinetic energy of the two-puck system is

   (A) Greater than the answer to (1)

   (B) Less than the answer to (1)

   (C) Equal to the answer to (1)

   Choose one, and justify your choice.

The dwarf planet Pluto goes around the sun in an elliptical orbit. Consider Pluto only. Is its angular momentum about the sun conserved? Justify your answer.

A 75-kg student is standing in a 25-kg boat at rest in still water. The student then walks to the right at a speed v relative to the shore. Describe the subsequent motion of the boat in terms of v. Justify your answer.

A ball moving to the right as shown strikes a second identical ball at rest. The vectors shown are the velocity of the first ball before and after the collision. Draw a vector that represents the velocity of the second ball after the collision on the diagram below.

Justify your answer.

Top view   Throw direction

Throw direction

Side view

A man stands on the edge of a heavy disk made of ice, such that it can slide along the ground without friction. From the location indicated in the diagram, the man throws a ball at an angle above the horizontal.

From immediately before the throw to immediately after the throw, is the angular momentum of the disk-man-ball system about its center of mass conserved? Justify your answer.

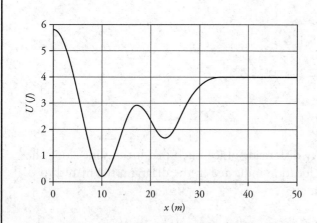

A particle's potential energy function is given in the graph above. The particle is moving to the left with 1 J of kinetic energy at the 40-m mark. Describe the subsequent motion of the particle.

Day 52

A pendulum is oscillating in an elevator with a regular period T. Predict changes to the period of the pendulum when the elevator moves with a downward acceleration. Justify your answer.

Diagram not to scale

Three identical balls are thrown from the top of a cliff, all with the same initial speed. The balls take three different trajectories: (a) one at an angle above the horizontal, (b) one thrown horizontally, and (c) one thrown at an angle below the horizontal.

Rank the three trajectories in terms of speed when they reach the ground.

_____   _____   _____

Fastest   Slowest

Justify your answer.

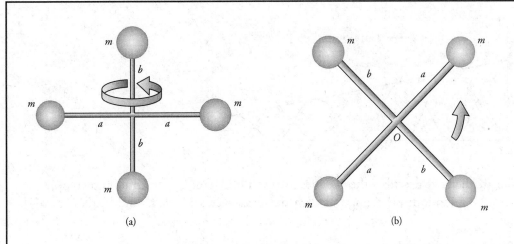

(a)   (b)

A mobile consists of four spheres of mass *m* attached to the end of rods of length *L,* as shown above. The mobile is set to rotate about two different axes. In the first instance, the mobile is rotated about an axis that passes through the rods. In the second instance, the mobile is rotated about an axis perpendicular to the plane that connects the two rods, passing through the page at point O in the diagram on the right. Two students make predictions about the kinetic energy of the mobile in each configuration when they are rotating at equal speeds.

- Student 1: "The mobile has different kinetic energies in each case. The rotational inertia is greater in the first case, with the axis through the rod, than in the second case, thereby increasing the rotational kinetic energy."
- Student 2: "The rotational kinetic energies are equal in each case. The axis of rotation passes through the center of the mobile, and the masses are at an equal distance from the axis, making the rotational inertias equal."

What, if anything, do you agree with in each student's statement?

The graph above describes the energies involved in the motion of an unknown object. Describe a motion, providing as much detail as necessary, that would produce this graph.

A train car filled with oil is moving at a constant speed on a level track. After a period of time, a leak develops in the bottom of the train car, slowly releasing oil onto the ground directly beneath the car. Predict any changes to the motion of the train car. Justify your answer.

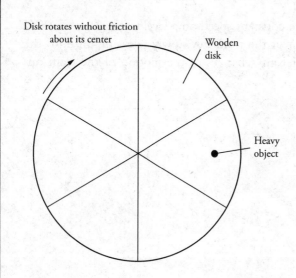

Disk rotates without friction
about its center

Wooden
disk

Heavy
object

In the laboratory, a wooden disk of known mass M and radius R is initially rotating at an approximately constant angular speed. A heavy object is then dropped onto the wooden disk, sticking to the wooden disk where it was dropped. The experiment—both before and after the collision—is recorded on video at 100 frames per second. The sketch above shows the disk and the heavy object; notice that the size of the heavy object is much smaller than the disk's radius. The rotational inertia of the disk is $\frac{1}{2}MR^2$.

By collecting data from the video, the mass of the heavy object can be determined. Explain how to make that determination, including what information must be obtained from the video and how that information should be used.

A 6-kg bowling ball rolls, starting from rest, down an incline and reaches a speed v at the bottom. A 12-kg bowling ball is then rolled from rest down the incline. Predict any changes in the speed of the 12-kg bowling ball as compared to the 6-kg bowling ball when it reaches the bottom. Justify your answer.

A bowling ball slides down a bowling lane with an initial speed v_0 without rotating. There is friction between the ball and the lane. Sometime later, the ball is rolling without slipping down the lane. Describe the changes in the translational and rotational energies of the ball between these two conditions, including the source of energy changes.

Two experiments are performed with an incline, an ideal spring, and two masses m and M, where the masses are such that $M > m$.

In experiment 1, mass m slides from rest and sticks to mass M, which is at rest in an equilibrium position on a spring. The blocks compress the spring and come to rest when the spring is compressed to a distance x.

In experiment 2, mass M slides from rest and sticks to mass m, which is at rest in an equilibrium position on the spring. The blocks compress the spring and come to rest when the spring is compressed to a distance x'.

Is x greater than, equal to, or less than x'?

Justify your answer.

Day 61

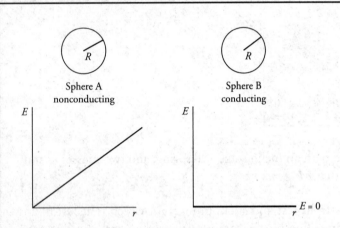

Sphere A
nonconducting

Sphere B
conducting

Sphere A is nonconducting, with uniform charge density. Sphere B is conducting. Both spheres carry the same total charge. The axes include sketches of the electric field as a function of the distance r from the center of each sphere for $r = 0$ to $r = R$. Justify the shape of each graph.

Sphere A
nonconducting

Sphere B
conducting

Sphere A is nonconducting with uniform charge density. Sphere B is conducting. Both spheres carry the same total charge. The axes include sketches of the electric field as a function of the distance r from the center of each sphere for $r = R$ to $r = 5R$. Justify the shape of each graph.

5 Minutes to a 5

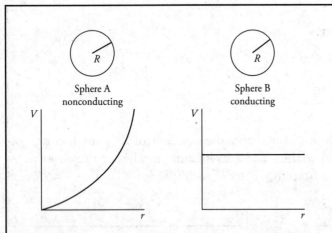

Sphere A is nonconducting with uniform charge density. Sphere B is conducting. Both spheres carry the same total charge. The axes include sketches of the electric potential as a function of the distance r from the center of each sphere for $r = 0$ to $r = R$. Justify the shape of each graph.

Sphere: charge +Q
Shell: charge −3Q

A nonconducting sphere of total charge $+Q$ has radius a. It is surrounded by a thin conducting shell of radius b. The shell holds a total charge of $-3Q$. Determine the charge residing on the outer and inner surfaces of the shell. Justify your answer.

In the circuit shown, the circuit has reached a steady state with switch A closed and switch B open. At time $t = 0$, switch A is opened, and switch B is simultaneously closed. Write a differential equation that could be used to solve for the charge stored on the capacitor as a function of time t. Explain the rationale for each term in the equation.

In the circuit shown, the capacitor is initially uncharged. Switch A is closed, causing the capacitor to charge; then, switch A is opened and switch B is closed, causing the capacitor to discharge. The two equations below represent the charge Q on the capacitor as a function of time t after charging or discharging begins. The variable R in each equation does not include a subscript. Indicate which subscript goes with R in each equation. Justify your answer.

(A) $Q = CV_1\, e^{-\frac{t}{RC}}$ (B) $Q = CV_1\, (1 - e^{-\frac{t}{RC}})$

A student is asked to calculate the magnetic flux through the rectangular wire loop shown in the diagram. They say:

"Magnetic flux is given by BA. Here A is 5 cm × 2 cm = 10 cm². The magnetic field B is due to the long straight current and is given by $\mu_0 I/2\pi r$. Here I is 2A, and r is the 2 cm distance from the current to the midpoint of the loop. This gives a magnetic flux of $(\mu_0/2\pi)(2A)(10 \text{ cm})/(2 \text{ m})$."

Explain the error in this student's reasoning.

5 cm

2 cm

1 cm

$I = 2A$

The current I is increasing. Explain why a clockwise current is induced in the loop.

$R_1 = 100 \; \Omega$

$100 \; V$

$R_2 = 200 \; \Omega$

C $100 \; \mu F$

The capacitor in the circuit shown is initially uncharged. Explain why the voltage across the 100 Ω resistor goes from 100 V just after the switch is closed to 33 V after the switch has been closed for a long time.

The switch in the circuit shown has been closed for a long time. Is the charge on each capacitor 33 μC, 67 μC, 17 μC, or 140 μC? Explain your choice.

The rectangular loop of wire in the diagram is moved at a constant speed to the right, entering and then leaving the magnetic field without changing speed. Consider the graph. Is the vertical axis magnetic flux or current in the wire loop? Justify your answer and the shape of the graph.

The single rectangular loop of wire in the diagram is moved at a constant speed v to the right, entering and then leaving the magnetic field without changing speed. Next, a rectangular wire of the same dimensions is moved into and out of the magnetic field at constant speed v, but this wire wraps around the loop twice, creating two rectangular coils. Explain why the induced current in the new double-loop is identical to the induced current in the original single loop.

In the circuit diagram, at the initial time $t = 0$, the switch is open with the capacitor uncharged. The switch is then closed at time $t = t_1$. Graphs of voltage V vs. t are shown below, one graph for each circuit element R_1, R_2, and C. Indicate which graph corresponds to which circuit element and label the vertical axis values for the asymptotes. Justify your answer.

Magnetic field

A thin conducting ring sits in a uniform rightward magnetic field that points to the right, as shown above. The ring begins to rotate with constant angular frequency ω about an axis pointing into the page.

(a) Explain why this is the graph of magnetic flux Φ vs. time t:

(b) Explain why this is the graph of EMF ε vs. time t:

A thin conducting ring sits in a uniform rightward magnetic field that points to the right, as shown. The ring begins to rotate about an axis pointing into the page, as in Day 74; but this time, the angular frequency is halved to $\omega/2$. Explain why the graphs of magnetic flux Φ and emf ε vs. time t are shaped like this:

A long, thin, nonconducting cylinder holds positive charge density λ. Position P_1 is a distance a from the cylinder, where $a \ll x_1$. Explain how to use Gauss's law to determine the electric field at position P_1.

A long, thin, nonconducting cylinder holds positive charge density λ. Position P_1 is a distance a from the cylinder, where $a \ll x_1$. Explain why Gauss's law is NOT useful to determine the electric field at point P_2.

A long, thin, nonconducting cylinder holds positive charge density λ. Position P_2 is a vertical distance a from the cylinder. The correct integral for finding the vertical component of the electric field at point P_2 is:

$$|E_y| = k\lambda \int_{-x_1}^{0} \frac{a\,dx}{[(x_2 - x)^2 + a^2]^{3/2}}$$

(a) Explain why the integral is taken over dx rather than dy.

(b) Explain where the $\dfrac{a}{[(x_2 - x)^2 + a^2]^{3/2}}$ term comes from.

The circuits above have both been connected for a long time. Explain why the current through resistor R_2 is nonzero in circuit A, but zero in circuit B.

The circuits above have both been connected a very short time ago and have not reached steady state. The capacitor was initially uncharged. Explain why the current through R_2 is zero in circuit A, but nonzero in circuit B.

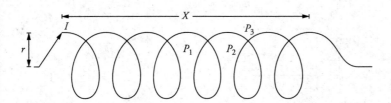

The solenoid shown carries a constant current I, contains N coils of radius r, and is of length X. Explain how Ampere's law can be used to derive the magnetic field at point P_1 to be $B = \mu_0 NI/X$.

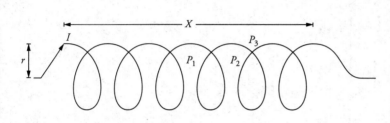

(a) Explain using Ampere's law why the magnetic field at position P_2 is equal to the magnetic field at position P_1.

In the diagram, the solenoid contains n turns per unit length. The current I in the solenoid is uniformly increased from zero to I_{max} over time t. The current induced in the resistor R is $\dfrac{\mu_0 n I_{max} \pi r_1^2}{tR}$.

(a) Explain how the expression for current is derived.

(b) Explain why r_1 rather than r_2 appears in the current formula.

In the diagram, the solenoid contains n turns per unit length. The current I in the solenoid is uniformly increased from zero to I_{max} over time t. In which direction is current induced in the resistor: back to front or front to back? Explain your response.

A nonconducting cylinder holds a negative charge. The cylinder is placed between two charged metal plates; the top plates holds positive charge while the bottom plate holds an equal negative charge. The electric field could be zero at point P_1, but not at point P_2 or P_3. Explain why.

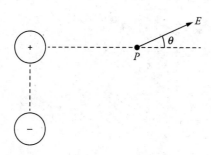

The two isolated point charges in the diagram produce an electric field E at point P (directed as shown), where the angle θ is *less than* 45°. Explain the direction of the electric field.

The two configurations of point charges shown above are isolated from one another. Explain why the magnitude of the electric field at point P_1 is greater than at point P_2.

Day 88

I (+)   II   (−) III

The two isolated small spherical objects shown hold equal magnitudes of charge, though the left one is positively charged and the right one is negatively charged. Explain why the electric potential could be zero somewhere in region II, but not in regions I or III.

I   II   III

The two isolated small spherical objects in the diagram above hold charges +3Q and +Q, as shown. Explain why the electric field produced by these charges could be zero somewhere in region II, but not in regions I or III.

5 Minutes to a 5

I $(+ 3Q)$ II $(- Q)$ III

The two isolated small spherical objects in the diagram above hold charges $+3Q$ and $-Q$, as shown. Explain why the electric field produced by these charges could be zero somewhere in region III, but not in regions I or II.

The capacitor in the circuit above is initially uncharged. The switch is closed for a long time, charging the capacitor. Then the switch is opened, allowing the capacitor to discharge. Explain why the time to charge the capacitor to 63% of its maximum charge is shorter than the time necessary to discharge 63% of the capacitor's maximum charge.

The capacitor in the circuit above is initially uncharged. The switch is closed for a long time, charging the capacitor. At a time 1 μs after the switch is closed, is the current through the 15 Ω resistor increasing, decreasing, or remaining constant? Justify your answer.

An ideal solenoid has N turns for wire length L. The current I is measured in the wire, as is the magnetic field B inside the solenoid. Describe a linear experimental graph that could be created with this data and how the best-fit line could be used to determine μ_0.

A parallel plate capacitor includes dielectric material of constant κ between the plates. Each plate is square-shaped, with side length s. The variable distance d between the plates is measured, as is the resulting capacitance C. Describe a linear experimental graph that could be created with this data and how the best-fit line could be used to determine ε_0.

A capacitor of capacitance C discharges through a single resistor of resistance R. At time $t = 0$, the capacitor is fully charged. The voltage V across the capacitor is measured as a function of t, where the initial voltage is V_0. An experimental graph is made with $[\ln (V/V_0)]$ on the vertical axis, and t on the horizontal axis. What is the physical meaning of the slope of this linear graph?

The two long wires shown carry currents $3I_1$ and I_1 to the right. Explain why the magnetic field produced by these wires could be zero in region II, but not in regions I or III.

Explain how it is possible for the electric field at a position to be zero, but the electric potential at that same position will NOT to be zero.

A student incorrectly claims, "a negative charge moves in a direction opposite the electric field." Explain what is incorrect about this claim.

Each of the three circuits above shows the same battery hooked to three identical resistors. Rank the current flowing from the battery, from greatest to least, in the circuits. If two or more circuits have the same current flowing from the battery, indicate so in your ranking.

Greatest current from the battery _____ _____ _____ Least current from the battery

Justify your ranking.

The circuit above shows three identical lightbulbs that obey Ohm's law, initially connected to a battery as shown. Then bulb C is removed.

(a) When bulb C is removed, does the potential difference provided by the battery change? Explain *briefly*.

(b) When bulb C is removed, does the potential difference across bulb B change? Explain *briefly*.

(c) When bulb C is removed, does the charge flowing through bulb B change every second? Explain *briefly*.

(d) When bulb C is removed, does the resistance of bulb B change? Explain *briefly*.

Three different resistors are connected to a battery of voltage V, as shown above.

Is it possible for R_1 to have smaller voltage across it than across R_2? If so, assign the resistors values that would cause R_1 to take smaller voltage across it than across R_2. If not, explain why not.

Three different resistors are connected to a battery of voltage V, as shown above.

Is it possible for R_1 to have smaller current through it than R_2? If so, assign the resistors values that would cause R_1 to take smaller current through it than through R_2. If not, explain why not.

A student is experimenting with static electricity. The student charges a comb by running the comb through her hair, then bringing the comb near small bits of paper. The student observes the paper move toward the comb, and then fly away after touching the comb. Explain the student's observations.

Two resistors and an ammeter are connected to a 30-V battery, as shown.

1. When the resistance of R_2 is increased, does the current through R_1 increase, decrease, or stay the same? Justify your answer.

2. When the resistance of R_2 is increased, does the reading in the ammeter increase, decrease, or stay the same? Justify your answer.

The circuit above consists of four identical ohmic lightbulbs connected to a battery. The switch S is initially open; then it is closed.

When the switch is closed, describe how, if at all, each of the following quantities changes. Justify your answer briefly.

(a) Voltage provided by the battery

(b) Current flowing from the battery

(c) Equivalent resistance of the circuit

(d) Power provided by the battery

The circuit above consists of three identical ohmic light bulbs connected to a battery. The switch *S* is initially open; then it is closed.

Lloyd is asked to explain what happens to the current through bulb 3 when the switch is closed. He says, "Closing the switch adds a parallel path, so now the total current must split between bulbs 2 and 3, decreasing bulb 3's current."

Explain what is correct and incorrect about Lloyd's statement.

The circuit above consists of four identical ohmic lightbulbs connected to a battery. The switch *S* is initially open; then it is closed.

When the switch is closed, describe how, if at all, each of the following quantities changes. Justify your answer.

(a) The current through bulb 3

(b) The brightness of bulb 3

Design an experiment to determine whether or not a given light bulb's resistance is constant. Describe what data should be collected and what equipment should be used to collect that data. Explain how that data should be analyzed to answer the question.

The circuit above shows three identical ohmic lightbulbs, connected to a battery as shown. The power dissipated by bulb A is 27 W. The power dissipated by bulb B is 7 W. The power dissipated by bulb C is 7 W.

What is the total power dissipated by the battery? Explain how you made this determination.

Two batteries each provide the same EMF. However, battery A has a larger internal resistance than battery B. Which battery, if either, provides a larger terminal voltage to an identical external circuit? Justify your answer.

A set of three ohmic lightbulbs are each rated at 60 W, 120 V. They are connected in series with each other and a 120-V outlet.

Is the power dissipated by each bulb individually greater than, less than, or equal to 60 W? Justify your answer.

A proton and an electron are both placed an equal distance from a fixed positive charge. A student makes the following statement about the motion of the electron and the proton: "The electron and proton experience the same magnitude of force, but in opposite directions. The proton will be pulled toward the positive charge, while the electron will be pushed away from the positive charge and have the same acceleration."

What, if anything, is incorrect with the student's statement?

$$\times \quad \times \quad \times \quad \times \quad \times \quad \times$$

$$\times \quad \times \quad \times \quad \times \quad \times \quad \times$$

$\times \quad \times \quad \times \quad \times \quad \times \quad \times \qquad \longleftarrow \; ^{-O}\; e^{-}$
V

$$\times \quad \times \quad \times \quad \times \quad \times \quad \times$$

Describe the path this electron will take in the uniform magnetic field shown. In your description, explain why the path will be circular rather than parabolic.

A battery with an internal resistance R_3 powers a circuit with two resistors as shown above. The R_1 is the largest resistance, while R_3 is the smallest, with no two resistors having equal value. Rank the magnitudes of the currents shown in the diagram from greatest to least. Justify your answer.

(a) Use Kirchhoff's loop rule to write an equation for the current i in the circuit shown above.

(b) Determine the magnitude and direction of the current i. Justify your choice of the current's direction.

(a) The current in the circuit above is 76 mA. On the axes below, sketch a graph of electric potential as a function of position in the circuit. Take the electric potential at position *A* to be zero.

(b) What would be the reading in a voltmeter placed between positions B and D as shown in the diagram? Justify your answer briefly.

A circuit consists of four identical lightbulbs. The bulbs are arranged in such a way that at least one bulb does not shine as brightly as the others. When that bulb is unscrewed, the remaining three bulbs are then equally bright. Describe a possible arrangement of the three lit bulbs.

Five charge arrangements are produced as shown above with two charges, either positive or negative, of varying magnitude. The arrangements are isolated from one another. Rank the five arrangements from greatest to least magnitude of the net force on the charge on the right. Justify your answer.

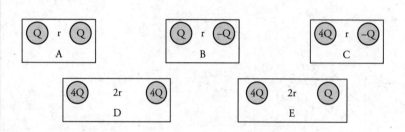

Five charge arrangements are produced as shown above with two charges of equal mass, either positive or negative, of varying magnitude. The arrangements are isolated from one another. Rank the five arrangements from greatest to least magnitude of the acceleration of the right-hand charge *at the instant the charges are released.*

An electron moves as shown, toward two charged metal plates. Describe the path this electron will take when it enters the region between the plates. In your description, explain why the path will be parabolic rather than circular.

Answers

Newton's Laws

Day 1

The center of mass of the two-object system will be located closer to the falling, more massive object. As the more massive object falls, the center of mass of the system drops. As the center of mass was initially not moving, the center of mass therefore has a downward acceleration, and there must be a net downward force on the system. Therefore, the system's weight (the downward force of Earth on the objects) is greater than the upward force of the spring scale on the objects; so the scale reading drops when the objects are released.

Day 2

The centripetal force is produced by the hanging object. In the second experiment, there is less mass hanging, thus less centripetal force. The centripetal force can also be found by the product of the table mass (m_2 in the second experiment) and the centripetal acceleration. Given that there is more mass accelerating in the second experiment, the centripetal acceleration must then be less than in the first experiment. With the same radius of a circle, to have less centripetal acceleration there must be less velocity by $a = \dfrac{v^2}{r}$.

Day 3

The stoplight is in equilibrium. Call the tension in the left rope T_1 and in the right rope T_2. Break these forces into components so that, for example, the horizontal component of T_1 is $T_1 \cos 37°$ and the vertical component of T_1 is $T_1 \sin 37°$. Set left forces equal to right forces and up forces equal to down forces to get the following.

$$T_1 \cos 37° = T_2 \cos 53°$$
$$T_1 \sin 37° + T_2 \sin 53° = mg$$

The variable m represents the 30-kg mass of the stoplight.

Day 4

The speed of a cart is indicated by the vertical axis of a velocity-time graph. Since the graph starts at a vertical axis value of zero, the cart begins at rest. Throughout the motion, the vertical axis value increases, so the cart speeds up the whole way, nearly reaching a constant speed at the end. The cart always moves to the right, because the vertical axis values are always positive.

Day 5

The speed difference between the two baseballs doesn't change. Both are in free fall, so both gain 10 m/s each second. When the second ball is dropped, the first ball is moving 10 m/s, and so the difference between their speeds is 10 m/s. Both get faster by the same amount each second and so maintain the same difference between their speeds.

The distance between them, however, increases. The first ball is always moving faster than the second ball; thus the first ball always goes a larger distance in 1 second than does the second ball. The second ball can never close the gap, because the second ball will never move faster than the first ball.

Day 6

Average speed is distance traveled divided by the time it takes to travel that distance. To get the distance traveled from a velocity-time graph, look at the area under the graph.

(Not that the problem asked, but the average speed calculated correctly is 30 m/4 s = 7.5 m/s. Method (A) gives the instantaneous speed at $t = 4$ s, 12 m/s; method (B) overestimates the average speed, giving 8 m/s, because the object spent more than half its time at a higher than average speed; method (C) underestimates the average speed, giving 6 m/s, also because the object spent more than half its time at a higher than average speed.)

Day 7

The free-fall acceleration is proportional to the mass and inversely proportional to the square of the radius, by $g = GM/r^2$. But we don't know directly about the planet's mass, just its density. So, we need to express g in terms of the planet's density, which I'll call ρ. Density is mass divided by volume, and volume depends on radius cubed. So get an r^3 term in the expression: multiply numerator and denominator by the planet's radius r to get $g = G\left(\dfrac{M}{r^3}\right)r = G\rho r$

Now it's clear: With G and density ρ unchanged on the new planet, doubling the planet's radius r will also double the gravitational field: **2g**.

Day 8

Luis is incorrect, contradicted by Marsha's correct first statement. For the first satellite, set $G\dfrac{Mm}{r^2} = m\dfrac{v^2}{r}$, where M is the mass of the central planet and m is the mass of the satellite. The speed v and the radius r are given in the problem statement. The satellite mass is unknown, but it cancels out. Thus Marsha is right that the mass of the central planet can be determined.

However, she is wrong that we have to calculate the planet's mass first in order to determine the second satellite's speed. Solving for v, $v = \sqrt{\dfrac{GM}{r}}$. Even though we don't know the mass m, we know it's the same for both satellites. The second satellite orbits with four times the radius of the first; since r is in the denominator and under the square root, the speed v is half (square root of ¼) as much for the second satellite as the first. So the speed is 32 km/s.

Day 9

At point A, the normal force is up while the weight mg is down. Since acceleration is toward the center of the circle, start with the normal force to write $F_n - mg = ma$. The normal force is $ma + mg$.

At point B, both the normal force and the weight are down, since the track is in contact with the cart from above. So we write $F_n + mg = ma$. Here the normal force is $ma - mg$.

The speed at the bottom is larger than at the top (by conservation of energy), so the centripetal acceleration $a = v^2/r$ is also larger at the bottom. Thus, at point A, the normal force includes a larger term added to the weight of the cart; and at point B, the normal force expression has the weight subtracted from the term ma, which was smaller to begin with. The expression for F_n at point A must be bigger!

Day 10

The acceleration is the slope of the v-t graph. This slope begins steep, then gets shallow. So the acceleration starts off large and gets smaller. The acceleration decreases throughout the motion.

Day 11

(a) Once the student releases the cart after the push, the free-body diagram is the same in either experiment—the only net force on the two-object system is the weight of the hanging object. Net force has nothing to do with speed or with the direction of motion. By Newton's second law, $a = F_{net}/m$, since the net force on the system is the same in each experiment, the acceleration is also the same in each experiment.

(b) In experiment A, the cart's acceleration is left—the cart speeds up, so acceleration is in the direction of motion. In experiment B, since the cart is slowing down, its acceleration is opposite the direction of its motion, which is still to the left.

$\downarrow$

Answers

Day 12

(a) Velocity is determined by the slope of a position-time graph. The slope of the graph everywhere looks like a backslash (\) and so is negative. Thus the velocity is always negative.

(b) Speed is the amount of velocity, determined by the steepness of the position-time graph. This graph gets steeper from A to B, so the object gains speed.

When an object speeds up (as this one does—see (b)), its acceleration is the same as its direction of motion. The object speeds up, as shown in (b). So its acceleration is negative.

Day 13

The relevant equation relating h and t comes from the constant-acceleration kinematics equations, with no initial velocity and an acceleration of g: $h = \frac{1}{2}gt^2$.

The students measured h, and that shows up in the equation directly, so they can put h on the vertical axis. They also measured t, but t doesn't show up directly; it shows up as t^2. So plot t^2 on the horizontal axis.

Then identify the values in $y = mx + b$:

$$\underbrace{(h)}_{(y)} = \underbrace{\left(\frac{1}{2}g\right)}_{(m)}\underbrace{(t^2)}_{(x)} + b$$

The slope is $\frac{1}{2}g$. So take the slope, multiply by 2, and that's g.

Day 14

(a) The "area under a graph" refers to the area between the graph and the horizontal axis. In this graph, the horizontal axis is in the middle of the displayed portion of the graph, where velocity = 0. The student should be taking the area of *two* triangles—shown below—and then subtracting the two areas, because the top triangle indicates displacement in the positive direction, while the bottom triangle indicates displacement in the negative direction.

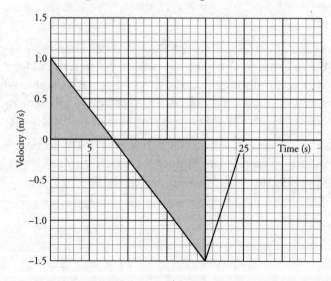

(b) The student is *overestimating* the cart's actual displacement. He's not accounting for the two different directions of motion—his calculation ends up giving the total distance traveled by the cart, not how far the cart ended up from its initial position.

Day 15

The net torque on the pulley does not change, since the weights of the hanging objects and the pulley's radius are unchanged. However, the rotational inertia of the pulley in experiment 2 is smaller—its identical mass is concentrated closer to the axis of rotation when shaped like a disk. In Newton's second law for rotation, $\tau = I\alpha$, constant net torque makes rotational inertia (I) and angular acceleration (α) inversely related. A smaller rotational inertia means the angular acceleration is larger.

Since angular acceleration is the slope of an angular velocity versus time graph, the slope should be steeper, as shown.

Day 16

The relevant equation is Newton's second law for rotation, $\tau = I\alpha$. To increase α, we must either decrease rotational inertia I or increase the net torque τ.

1. Increase the mass m_1 of the hanging object. This increases the force term in torque = force times lever arm, increasing the net torque on the device. (Another way to increase the net torque on the device would be to increase the radius r_1.)

2. Decrease the mass m_2 of the attached objects. This decreases the rotational inertia of the device, since now there's less mass to rotate. (Another way to decrease the rotational inertia of the device would be to shorten the distance r_2 from the attached objects to the pole.)

Day 17

In experiment 1, the tension in the string is measured to be 1.0 N; that's the only force on the 500-g (i.e., 0.5-kg) object, so we can apply Newton's second law to the cart: $a = (1.0\ N)/(0.5\ kg) = 2.0$ m/s/s.

In experiment 2, the tension in the string is *not* 1.0 N. Since the hanging object will speed up downward, it has a downward acceleration; thus the tension must be less than the hanging object's 1.0-N weight.

Answers

So consider the two-object system. The net force on this system is the weight of the hanging object, 1.0 N. The mass of this system is 0.5 kg plus the 0.1-kg mass of the hanging object. (On Earth, 1 kg weighs 10 N, so 0.1 kg weights 1.0 N.) By Newton's second law, $a = (1.0\ \text{N})/(0.6\ \text{kg}) = 1.7\ \text{m/s/s}$.

Since in experiment 2 more mass is accelerating due to the same net force, the denominator in $a = F_{net}/m$ is larger, making the acceleration smaller. The cart has a greater acceleration in **experiment 1**.

Day 18

(a) A boy sits still at his desk. (Zero velocity because he's not moving, zero acceleration because his velocity doesn't change.)

(b) A jet airplane cruises at steady speed. (Nonzero velocity because it movcs, zero acceleration because its velocity doesn't change.)

(c) A ball that was thrown straight upward, at the instant when it reaches the peak of its flight. (Zero velocity because at that instant, the ball briefly isn't moving; nonzero acceleration because the ball is in free fall. Its velocity is changing, going from upward to downward.)

(d) A car on a highway entrance ramp, speeding up. (Nonzero velocity because it is moving, nonzero acceleration because its velocity is changing.)

Day 19

The mass of the system is not constant. The system is the cart and hanging masses. When mass is added to increase the accelerating force, the mass of the system is no longer a constant, meaning that the graph proposed would not be linear.

Day 20

The thick lines indicate the behavior of the block without friction. Each graph is symmetric with respect to the time moving up and down the incline. The acceleration will be constant without friction and equal to $g \sin \theta$. The velocity function will then be linear due to the constant acceleration, beginning at the positive v_0 value. Constant accelerations will produce parabolic position paths.

With friction present, as indicated by the thinner lines, the acceleration will have a greater magnitude when the block is sliding up the incline than without friction. Friction will act against motion, which is down the incline while the block slides up.

The frictional force is independent of speed and is constant, thus just added to the gravitational acceleration. When the block slides downhill, friction will now be up the incline, making the net acceleration less than the magnitude of gravitational acceleration. Due to the greater acceleration while the block slides up the incline, the highest point will be reached sooner than without friction.

Velocity will exhibit linear behavior up and down the incline due to the constant acceleration in these regions. Due to the greater acceleration up the incline, the slope of the velocity graph is greater while moving up the incline than when moving down.

The velocity will follow parabolic-like paths due to the constant accelerations up and down the inclines, with an extended parabolic shape while moving down the incline.

Day 21

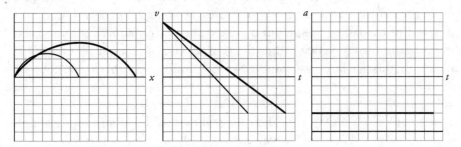

The acceleration is constant due to the constant slope of the incline, and is directed down the incline, and is thus negative. With the increased angle, the magnitude of acceleration will be greater. The velocity will have a slope equal to the magnitude of the acceleration, and with the steeper incline will reach the highest point and return to the base of the incline in less time. With constant accelerations, the position-time graphs will be parabolic, with the steeper inclined path returning to the base in less time.

Day 22

A multitude of solutions would work. (If you're not sure whether yours is correct, try it in the lab.) Here are a couple of ideas:

- Put the cart on an incline, and hold the scale parallel to the incline so that it measures the component of the cart's weight parallel to the incline. That component is the weight times the sine of the angle of the incline; solve to get the weight.
- Hang the cart from, say, four different ropes, spaced evenly along the cart. Attach three of these ropes to hooks on the ceiling; attach the other to the scale. The scale will read the tension in one rope. Multiply that by 4 to get the weight of the cart. (If the scale is still maxed out, add more ropes.)

Day 23

Two approaches:

- Acceleration is the change of speed per time. Both bug and car collide for the same amount of time. The car hardly changes its speed at all, while the bug goes from rest to near-highway speed. Thus the bug changes its speed by more in the same amount of time, meaning the bug has greater acceleration.

- Use Newton's second law, $F_{net} = ma$. Both bug and car experience the same force by Newton's third law. In this case, then, mass and acceleration are inversely related. The less massive bug experiences the larger acceleration.

Day 24

For rolling without slipping, rotational kinematic quantities are related to translational kinematic quantities by $x = r\theta$ and $v = r\omega$, no matter what the object's acceleration. As such, both graphs are linear with a positive slope equal to the radius of the tire.

Day 25

In each position, there are two forces acting, the weight of the bob and the tension from the string. In position 2, the net force will point to the left, but not necessarily horizontally. The net force will *not* point tangent to the arced path. There must be a component of the net force that is tangent to the arc at point 2, which will cause the increase in speed of the falling pendulum bob, and there must also be a component that points along the string, which causes the centripetal acceleration that results in a circular path. If the net force was tangent to the arced path, there would be no centripetal acceleration.

At point 3, the net force is NOT zero. There are still the two forces previously identified, tension and weight. These forces both act vertically, and the bob is still turning in the arced path, so the net force must point to the center of the circle, or straight up.

Day 26

Torque is the product of the applied force and the lever arm (the shortest distance from the axis to the line of the force). The diagram below illustrates this for force A.

Consequently, force A and force C will produce equal torques. Forces D and E will produce zero torque—since the line of these forces goes straight through point P, no lever arm exists. Force B will produce the greatest torque, as its lever arm is twice that of force A or C.

To summarize,

$B > A = C > D = E = 0$

Day 27

The system must be defined as the weightlifter and the barbell. On the system there are only two forces acting: the force of gravity, taken to be acting on the center of mass, and the normal force (which is directly measured by the scale). As the barbell is moving upward, the center of mass of the system is rising. If an acceleration is associated with the motion, then a net force must be acting on the system. Thus, as the barbell is moving at a constant speed, there is no acceleration on the system, making the scale reading equal to the weight of the system. As the barbell slows in the upward direction, there must be a net force down acting on the center of mass of the system. Since the gravitational force will remain constant, the scale reading must be less than the system weight, so the scale reading will decrease.

Day 28

Defining the system as both objects, to achieve the same acceleration in each instance, the same net force must be applied. The net force on the system is due to the cord on the right, thus T_2 will not change when the masses switch position. Following a similar argument, defining the system as the block on the left, in the second situation the net force on the system will be less, since a lesser mass is receiving the same acceleration. Thus T_1 will be less when the masses change position.

Day 29

The second wheel will take greater than 20 seconds to reach top speed. Each wheel is accelerated by an equal torque. Rotational inertia is proportional to the mass of the object, so the second wheel, with greater mass, will have a greater rotational inertia. By $\tau_{net} = I\alpha$, with the same torque applied to an object of larger rotational inertia, the angular acceleration will be less, therefore taking a greater time to reach top speed.

Day 30

In the first instance, if the pulley is accelerating, then the 20-N weight is also accelerating (down). The net force on the weight is therefore directed downward, making the tension in the string less than 20 N. The torque that therefore accelerates the pulley is produced by a force that is less than 20 N. In the second instance, the torque that accelerates the pulley is produced by a force of exactly 20 N. The torque in the second case is therefore larger, and the angular acceleration of the disk in the second instance is greater.

Day 31

(a)

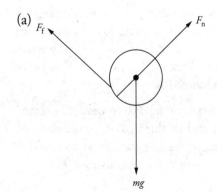

(b) An angular acceleration requires a net torque. A torque is applied by a force if the line of the force does not pass through the axis of rotation. Here, the normal force F_n and the weight mg both are applied directly through the center of the hoop. However, the friction force F_f is applied some distance from the center. So the friction force causes the angular acceleration.

Conservation

Day 32

Student 2's use of kinematics is valid only for constant acceleration. Here, the acceleration calculation using Newton's second law is correct, but only for the instant when the spring is stretched 5 cm. A moment later, when the spring is less stretched, the acceleration will be smaller. But the kinematics equation uses 2.5 m/s/s as the acceleration throughout, thus overestimating the final speed.

Student 1's approach is fully correct. Energy conservation applies whether or not acceleration is constant.

Day 33

Since it's a collision, it's likely that the impulse-momentum theorem is a good approach. That says $\Delta P = Ft$. In this case, the problem says the time of collision t is the same; so mathematically, whichever ball changes its momentum by more in the collision experiences more force. Both balls are dropped from the same height, so they hit the ground with the same speed; since they're of equal mass, they hit the ground with the same momentum.

Ball B loses all of that momentum upon hitting the ground. So does ball A. But ball A subsequently gains momentum in order to rebound. A's momentum thus changes by more than B's does, and A experiences more force in the collision.

Day 34

(a) Kinetic energy for this system is not conserved. Work is done by the cart on the suitcase when the two make contact; we know this because the suitcase changes its kinetic energy by slowing down. Mechanical energy would be conserved if this kinetic energy were stored in another form of mechanical energy such as a compressed spring. However, with no such storage mechanism, it becomes internal energy instead.

(b) Linear momentum in the vertical direction is not conserved. A net force external to the suitcase-cart system acts: that force is the normal force of the ground on the suitcase-cart system. (Alternatively: the system's center of mass initially has a downward component to its velocity, and after collision it has no vertical velocity at all. Thus the system's momentum vertically changed.)

(c) Linear momentum in the horizontal direction is conserved. No forces act horizontally except the force of the suitcase on the cart and its third law pair, the force of the cart on the suitcase. These forces are internal to the suitcase-cart system. With no net external force acting, the system's momentum must be conserved.

Day 35

(a) Curtis is correct that linear momentum is conserved, that the mother has half the son's speed after the collision, and that they will have the same (magnitude of) momentum as each other after the collision.

Curtis is incorrect that the mother pushes with twice as much force as the son—Newton's third law requires that both exert the same force on each other.

(The two statements above are sufficient. However, Curtis is also displaying a clear misconception of what conservation means—he doesn't compare the system momentum before and after the push; he compares the son's momentum to the mother's momentum, both after the push. To provide evidence for momentum conservation here, he must show that the total momentum is the same both before and after the push—which it is, because the momentums in opposite directions subtract to zero after the push, and there was no movement and thus no momentum before the push. Any reference to this issue is also correct.)

(b) Gregg is correct that initially the mother-son system has no initial kinetic energy and that both the mother and son have kinetic energy after the collision.

Gregg is incorrect in every other statement. Kinetic energy has no direction, so it cannot subtract to zero or to anything else. Thus kinetic energy is NOT conserved here—the system went from zero to not-zero kinetic energy.

(The two statements above are sufficient. It's also legitimate to point out that the mother and the son do not have the same kinetic energy as each other after the push. As shown in (a), the mother and son have the same amount of momentum. Since kinetic energy is $p^2/2m$, the larger-mass mother has less kinetic energy than the son after the push.)

Day 36

(a) The force of a spring is $F = kx$; the force depends on the distance the spring is stretched. So in this case, the net force on the cylinder is changing, so the acceleration is, too.

(b) Use the work-energy theorem on the cylinder-spring-earth system: $W_{ext} = \Delta KE + \Delta PE + \Delta U$

No work is done by external forces; no internal energy U is gained. The kinetic energy goes from 0 to $\frac{1}{2}mv^2$, where v is the speed we're looking for; the potential energy goes from $\frac{1}{2}kd^2$ to 0. The equation simplifies to

$$\frac{1}{2}kd^2 = \frac{1}{2}mv^2$$

And solving for v:

$$v = d\sqrt{\frac{k}{m}}$$

Day 37

Check whether the work-energy theorem requires a term for the work done by friction on the block. With no measurable friction, the kinetic energy of the block at position 1 ($\frac{1}{2}Mv^2$) should equal the sum of the kinetic energy of the block at position 2 plus the gravitational energy (Mgx_D) there. If the kinetic energy at position 1 is greater than the sum of the kinetic energy and gravitational energy at position 2, then friction was measurable.

Day 38

The angular momentum will remain constant. In the absence of a net external torque, angular momentum remains constant. Since the changes to the system are internal to the system, there is no change in angular momentum.

Rotational inertia will increase. As the child walks away from the axis of rotation, the rotational inertia of the system increases due to the movement of mass away from the axis of rotation.

The angular velocity will decrease. Since angular momentum remains constant and is the product of rotational inertia and angular velocity, with the increase in rotational inertia there must be a corresponding decrease in angular velocity by an equal factor.

The rotational kinetic energy will decrease. Rotational kinetic energy depends upon rotational inertia, which increases, and the square of angular velocity, which decreases. Rotational kinetic energy is more responsive to changes in velocity due to the velocity squared dependency. Since the velocity decreases by the same factor as the increase in rotational inertia, the kinetic energy will decrease due to the factor of velocity squared.

Day 39

(a) The period in simple harmonic motion depends only on mass and spring constant—not amplitude. So period is **unchanged**.

(b) To find maximum velocity, it's necessary to look at conservation of mechanical energy. Spring potential energy is converted to kinetic energy. Since the maximum potential energy increased, by conservation the maximum kinetic energy likewise increases. And velocity is related to kinetic energy, so maximum velocity increases, too.

(c) The potential energy of a spring is $\frac{1}{2}kx^2$. Here x represents the displacement of the spring from its equilibrium position. The amplitude is defined as the maximum displacement from equilibrium. So double A, double x in the formula, and maximum potential energy is changed.

Day 40

Work is done by a force on an object when that force and the object's direction of motion are in the same (or opposite) directions. A normal force, by definition, acts perpendicular to a surface. Thus if the object is moving along the surface, the normal force does no work—the normal force has no component in the direction of the object's motion.

However, consider an object on the floor of an elevator, which moves up. The normal force of the floor on the object is now in the same direction as the object moves. Thus the normal force does work on the object.

Day 41

1. Gravitational potential energy is generally defined as *mgh*, where *h* is the vertical distance above the reference position. Here, *h* is a component of the labeled distance *D*. Trigonometry shows this vertical distance to be *D sin θ*. Answer: (D)

2. The friction force is mF_n, where F_n is the normal force of the incline on the skier. The skier is in equilibrium in the direction perpendicular to the incline, so the normal force is equal to the component of the skier's weight perpendicular to the incline: *mg cos θ*. Answer: (C)

3. Work is force times the displacement parallel to that force. Here the force is given as *f*, and that friction force acts up the incline. The skier's displacement is *D* downward along the incline. Thus the friction force is directly opposite to the skier's displacement; no trig component is necessary, but the work done by the friction force will be negative. Answer: (C).

Day 42

The maximum amplitude will be less. When the dart is at the top of its trajectory, the vertical component of velocity will be zero; thus the impact velocity of the dart will equal the horizontal component of the velocity. With the increase in launch angle, the horizontal component of velocity at the 60° angle is less than the horizontal component of velocity at the 30° angle. The impact velocity at 60° is therefore less than that at 30°. Momentum is conserved in the collision with the dart and the pendulum bob. Since the momentum of the system is equal to the momentum of the dart, the momentum of the dart-bob system after the collision is equal to the initial momentum of the dart, and thus proportional to the speed of the dart. With the lesser speed at 60° upon collision, the speed of the dart-bob system after the collision is less at 60°. Energy is conserved in the system after the collision, as the only force on the system is the conservative gravitational force. The kinetic energy of the dart-bob system will then be entirely converted to gravitational potential energy. With less kinetic energy in the 60° system, the bob will swing to a lower height due to the lesser potential energy.

Day 43

The potential energy while the spring is relaxing between D and O will exhibit a parabolic shape as shown, because position is squared in the equation for potential energy of a spring. There is no potential energy while the block is sliding on the horizontal surface from A to B. The potential energy will increase parabolically as the spring is compressed from positions B to C, but to a lesser maximum value, as there was energy lost to friction between A and B.

The total mechanical energy remains constant at first, because no external force acts on the block-spring system. But when the block is experiencing a constant friction force from A to C, the total energy decreases. The formula for work is force times distance, so the total energy will decrease linearly.

Total mechanical energy is potential plus kinetic energy. So draw the kinetic energy graph at each position so that it adds with the potential graph to the total graph.

The maximum potential energy at position C should be less than at D by an amount equal to the kinetic energy lost by friction.

Day 44

The relevant formula for angular momentum is $L = I\omega$. The rotational inertia can be found from $(1/12)ML^2$. To find the angular speed, forward the video frame-by-frame until the rod has undergone a full rotation. Find how many frames that took; divide by 1,000 to get the number of seconds that took. Then divide 6.3 by that number of seconds to get the angular speed in radians per second. (Since the rod went one full rotation, that's 2π radians, or about 6.3 radians.)

Day 45

(a) $\sqrt{2}mv$. Each puck has momentum mv. Add the pucks' momentums as vectors. Since both pucks' momentums are perpendicular to one another, the magnitude of the resultant momentum is given by the Pythagorean theorem:
$$\sqrt{(mv)^2 + (mv)^2} = \sqrt{2}mv.$$

(b) Equal to $\sqrt{2}mv$. In a collision—when no net external forces act on a system—momentum is conserved. Here the only net force on either puck is the force of the other puck. The system's momentum cannot change due to the collision.

Day 46

(a) Each puck has kinetic energy $\frac{1}{2}mv^2$. Kinetic energy is scalar, so just add them together: total kinetic energy is $\frac{1}{2}mv^2 + \frac{1}{2}mv^2 = \boldsymbol{mv^2}$.

(b) Kinetic energy is conserved only in an elastic collision. This collision cannot be elastic, as the pucks stick together. Thus kinetic energy must be lost, making the total less than mv^2. Choice (**B**).

Day 47

Angular momentum is conserved when no net external torque acts on a system. There is a net external force on Pluto—the gravitational force of the sun on Pluto. The question is, does that force provide a torque? The direction of the gravitational force is directly toward the sun. Thus the line of force passes through the axis of rotation (the sun). The lever arm for this force is zero, and therefore the force of the sun provides no torque. Pluto's angular momentum is conserved.

(You must go through the net external torque analysis. It's not sufficient to say "Pluto speeds up when closer to the sun so that angular momentum, equal to mvr, remains constant. Unless you know offhand the speeds and distances to plug in to verify that mvr doesn't change, you need to explain how Pluto experiences no net torque.)

Day 48

There are no external forces acting on the boat along the direction of motion; as such momentum of the student-boat system must be conserved. Since the boat and student are initially at rest, the momentum of the system is zero. The student's momentum to the right ($75v$) must equal the boat's momentum to the left ($25v'$) to keep a system momentum of zero. Since the student's mass is three times the boat's mass, the boat must have three times the speed to have a momentum of equal magnitude, so the boat will move to the left with a speed of $3v$.

Day 49

The momentum of the system is conserved since the forces in the collision are internal to the system. Since the balls are identical, they have equal mass. The net momentum of the system can then be represented by the initial velocity vector, which is 3 units to the right. The total momentum in the horizontal direction after the collision must then also equal 3 net units to the right. Since the horizontal component of the recoil vector is 1 unit to the left, the second ball's velocity vector must act 4 units to the right. Additionally, there is no initial velocity (or momentum) along the y-axis, so there must be zero momentum after the collision along the y-axis. The first ball has a momentum component of 1 unit in the negative y direction, so the second ball must have a y-axis component of 1 unit in the positive y direction.

Day 50

Angular momentum is conserved if no net external torque acts on a system. The force of the man on the ball—and the force of the ball on the man—each produce a torque, because these forces are not directed through the system's center of mass. However, these torques are applied by and experienced by objects in the system—they do not contribute to external torques.

The only external forces acting are the downward gravitational force of Earth on the system and the upward normal force of the ground on the system. Each of these provides no torque. So with no external torques applied to the system at all, angular momentum is conserved.

Day 51

At the 40-m position, the object has a total of 4 J of potential energy, so the total energy is 5 J (4 J potential and 1 J kinetic). The particle will move to the left as long as the potential energy does not exceed the total energy. The potential energy does not reach 5 J until the $x = 5$ m mark. When the particle reaches that point, the particle is not in equilibrium and will begin to accelerate to the right and continue to move to the right until the potential energy equals the total energy of 5 J. Since there is no point to the right of $x = 5$ m where the potential energy equals 5 J, the particle will return to the original position with a kinetic energy of 1 J and continue to move to the right.

Day 52

The period of a pendulum depends upon the length and acceleration of gravity, as described by $T = 2\pi\sqrt{\dfrac{L}{g}}$, where g is the effective acceleration of gravity. In an elevator, the effective acceleration of gravity changes while the elevator accelerates. An easy way to analyze the situation is to take the acceleration to the extreme—if the elevator itself was accelerating downward at g. If the elevator is accelerating downward at g, then relative to the elevator, the pendulum would have zero acceleration. As such, a downward acceleration would decrease the effective g, or acceleration of the pendulum. A decrease in the effective g of the pendulum would lead to an increase in the period of the pendulum.

Day 53

Each ball will have the same speed when reaching the ground and be ranked equally. Given that each ball is thrown from the same height, the potential energy of each ball is equal, since the balls are identical and also have the same mass. It is given that they have the same initial velocity and thus the same initial kinetic energy. Since each ball has an identical potential energy and kinetic energy, the total energy of each ball is the same. Thus when striking the ground, the balls will have the same kinetic energy and therefore the same speed.

Day 54

Student 1 is correct to say that the kinetic energies differ. However, with the axis through one of the rods, the rotational inertia of the first rod is very small, while the rotational inertia of the second rod is appreciable due to the distance of the two spheres from the axis of rotation.

Student 2 is only correct with observations about the location of the masses and the axis.

Rotational kinetic energy depends on mass and distance from the axis of rotation. Since the two rotations involve two different axes, there are two different rotational inertias. With equal masses, the configuration that puts the mass farther from the rotating axis will have the greater rotational inertia and therefore greater rotational kinetic energy since the speeds are the same, by $KE = \frac{1}{2}I\omega^2$. The configuration that has the mass farther from the rotating axis is the second configuration; thus second rotation has a greater rotational kinetic energy.

Day 55

The motion described must involve an oscillatory motion, since kinetic energy and potential energy are continuously converted from one to the other, with a nonconservative force that is doing negative work on the object, reducing the total energy.

An example of an acceptable answer could be:

The graph is the energies of an object attached to the end of a horizontal spring on a surface with friction. The object begins at the equilibrium or unstretched position of the spring with kinetic energy. As the spring is either stretched or compressed, the system converts kinetic energy to potential energy, and then back again as the spring relaxes. While the oscillation occurs, there is friction between the mass and the surface, which does a net work on the system that reduces the total energy.

Day 56

The speed of the train car will remain constant. Defining the system as the car and oil, as the oil leaks from the car, the oil still has horizontal momentum. No forces have acted horizontally on the system; thus there is no change in the momentum of the system. Neither the oil nor the train will change the speed.

When the oil hits the ground and stops, the velocity of the center of mass of the oil-car system will decrease due to the friction between the oil and the ground, but this will not affect the speed of the car.

Day 57

Angular momentum for the disk-object system is conserved in this collision. Thus $I\omega = I'\omega'$—here I represents rotational inertia, ω represents angular speed, and the $'$ indicates quantities after collision. The rotational inertia of the disk is known; the angular speeds can be determined by counting how many frames the disk takes to make a full rotation, then dividing 6.3 radians (i.e., 2π radians) by the number of seconds it takes to make that full rotation.

So the rotational inertia I' of the system after collision can be calculated. Subtract that from the disk's rotational inertia to get the rotational inertia of just the heavy object. Since the heavy object can be treated as a point object—its radius is small compared to that of the disk—its rotational inertia is mr^2. Determine the radius r of its rotation by measuring on the video its distance from the disk's center. Then the object's mass m can be solved.

Day 58

The 12-kg bowling ball will have the same speed. In each case, energy is conserved. Gravitational potential energy will be converted to rotational kinetic energy and translational kinetic energy. Each of these energies is directly proportional to mass, making the final speed independent of the mass of the object, provided the bowling balls are the same structure with the same formula for rotational inertia (e.g., both are solid, as opposed to one being solid and one hollow).

Day 59

Examining the rotation of the ball: The friction between the ball and the lane as the ball slides produces a torque in the counterclockwise direction that starts the ball rotating. This torque does positive rotational work on the ball that increases the rotational kinetic energy.

Examining the translation of the ball: The friction force is in the opposite direction of motion. So friction does negative translational work, decreasing the translational kinetic energy of the ball.

Day 60

x' is greater than x. The moving block M in experiment 2 will have the same speed as block m in experiment 1, but a greater kinetic energy due to its greater mass. When the system comes to rest, the kinetic energy has been stored in the spring as elastic potential energy. With a greater kinetic energy in experiment 2, there will be more elastic potential energy stored in the spring, and therefore a greater spring compression.

Day 61

Draw a spherical Gaussian surface of radius r inside sphere A. The charge enclosed by this surface is $\dfrac{\frac{4}{3}\pi r^2}{\frac{4}{3}\pi R^3} Q$, where Q is the total charge on the sphere. Gauss's law says

$EA = Q_{\text{enclosed}}/\varepsilon_0$. Here A is the surface area of the Gaussian sphere, $4\pi r^2$. Solve for E.

You get $\dfrac{rQ}{R^3\varepsilon_0}$. Everything here is constant, except for r in the numerator to the first power. That's why sphere A's graph is linear.

Then, for sphere B, it's a fact that the electric field inside a conductor is zero. That's a good enough justification. (Okay, if you want something deeper . . . in a conductor, charge carriers always separate as far apart as possible, which means the charge resides only on the surface. So, draw a Gaussian sphere inside the conductor. It encloses no charge; so, by Gauss's law, $EA = Q_{enclosed}/\varepsilon_0$, a zero enclosed charge means a zero electric field.)

Day 62

Draw a spherical Gaussian surface outside sphere A. The charge enclosed by this surface is, well, all of it. We'll call it Q. Then, Gauss's law says $EA = Q_{enclosed}/\varepsilon_0$. Here, A is the surface area of the Gaussian sphere, $4\pi r^2$. Solve for E. You get $E = Q/4\pi r^2\varepsilon_0$. Everything here is constant except r, which is in the denominator; thus, you get the shape shown.

This time, the analysis is identical for sphere B. The charge on conducting sphere B resides on the surface, so it is still enclosed by the Gaussian surface.

Day 63

Gauss's law analysis shows that inside the nonconducting sphere, the electric field is proportional to r. (You can see the full analysis in the solution to Day 61.) The electric potential is the integral of the electric field with respect to r. Disregarding the constants, the integral of $r\,dr$ is proportional to r^2. Thus, the potential vs. r graph is parabolic.

For sphere B, the existence of an electric field means there must also be a change in electric potential; that's the physical meaning behind the equation $E = \Delta V/\Delta x$. Because there is no electric field inside conducting sphere B, the electric potential cannot change inside the sphere. That doesn't mean the potential must be zero, just that the potential cannot change, as shown in the graph.

Day 64

Consider a spherical Gaussian surface drawn *inside* the thin conducting shell. The electric field inside a conductor is zero; because Gauss's law says that the electric field at the position of the Gaussian surface depends on the charge enclosed by that surface, this surface must enclose a total charge of zero. The inner sphere has charge $+Q$, so the inner edge of the shell must have charge $-Q$. Thus, the Gaussian surface inside the shell encloses $(+Q) + (-Q)$ = zero charge.

Day 65

In the initial steady state, the capacitor stores charge and blocks current. Then with switch B closed and switch A open, the capacitor discharges. The voltage across the capacitor is Q/C. The voltage across the resistor is $-IR_1$ (negative because voltage *drops* across a resistor when tracing in the direction of current flow). Use Kirchoff's voltage rule for the loop including C and R_1, tracing in the direction of current flow, to get $Q/C - IR_1 = 0$. The definition of current I is dQ/dt. Putting it all together: $Q/C - R_1(dQ/dt) = 0$.

Day 66

For the equation on the left, when $t = 0$, the charge is CV_1, because e^0 is 1. Similarly, the right-hand equation gives a charge of zero at $t = 0$. So, equation (A) represents the capacitor charging (going from zero charge to nonzero charge), while equation (B) represents discharging (going from nonzero charge to zero charge). Charging happens when the capacitor is connected in a closed circuit with the battery; resistor R_2 is in that circuit, so the charging equation, equation (A), should include subscript R_2. Similarly, discharging occurs when the battery is not in the closed circuit, but rather the capacitor is in series with R_1. The discharging equation, equation (B), should include the subscript R_1.

Day 67

The value of r in the equation for the magnetic field due to the current is not simply the distance from the current to the loop's midpoint. In this equation, r does represent the distance from the current-carrying wire. Thus, the r value varies from 1 cm at the loop's bottom to 3 cm at the loop's top. To get the magnetic flux due to a magnetic field that varies, an integral is necessary, not just BA, but $\int BdA$.

Day 68

Lenz's law says an induced current causes a magnetic field in the direction of decreasing flux. Here, the magnetic flux through the loop is increasing, because the amount of the magnitude field produced by the current is increasing. The direction of the magnetic field produced by the current is out of the page, by the right-hand rule associated with $B = \mu_0 I/2\pi r$. So, with the direction of increasing flux out of the page, the direction of *decreasing* flux is into the page.

Day 69

Initially, an uncharged capacitor acts as a bare wire, like a zero-resistance path. So, the 200 Ω resistor might as well not be there, and the 100 Ω resistor might as well be connected directly across the poles of the battery, meaning 100 V across it.

After a long time, a steady-state capacitor stores charge and blocks current. So, the resistors are in series with each other and with the battery. The current through the circuit is the voltage of the battery divided by the equivalent resistance, 100 V/300 Ω = 0.33 A, all of which goes through the 100 Ω resistor. The voltage across the 100 Ω resistor is (.33 A)(100 Ω) = 33 V.

Day 70

After a long time, a steady-state capacitor stores charge and blocks current. So, the two resistors are in series with each other and with the battery. By the reasoning in the Day 69 solution, the voltage across the 100 Ω resistor is 33 V. Resistors in series take voltages that add to the total, so the voltage across the 200 Ω resistor is 67 V. With the switch closed, each capacitor is in parallel with the 200 Ω resistor. Things in parallel take the same voltage, so each capacitor takes 67 V across it. By $Q = CV$, the charge on each capacitor is 67 μC.

Day 71

Magnetic flux is BA, where A is the area of the loop penetrated by the magnetic field. That area increases linearly with time as the loop enters the field. Induced emf (voltage) is the time derivative of magnetic flux; with a linear flux, the time derivative is constant, meaning constant voltage in the loop as well as constant current in the loop. Then, while the loop is inside the field, the flux is constant and the time derivative of a constant function is zero—there is zero current in the loop for a while. Then, as the loop exits the field, the same reasoning as before applies to get a constant current: An induced current produces a magnetic field in the direction of decreasing flux. Because the flux decreases now rather than increasing, the direction of the current must switch.

Day 72

The induced emf (voltage) in each rectangular coil is given by the equation Blv. Each of these variables—magnetic field, length of the rectangle, and speed—remains unchanged. Now that the loop has two coils, the voltage induced in the loop is twice as much as in the original situation.

However, according to Ohm's law, current in the loop is voltage divided by resistance. While the voltage doubled, *so did the loop's resistance*. The resistance of a wire depends on length and cross-sectional area, by $R = \rho L/A$, and the total length L of the wire has doubled. Thus, doubling both voltage and resistance leaves the current unchanged.

Day 73

With the switch open, the circuit includes just two series resistors and a battery. In that case, the current in the circuit by Ohm's law is (100 V)/(300 Ω) = 0.33 A. This is the current through each resistor, so multiplying this current by each resistance gives voltages of 33 V across R_1 and 67 V across R_2. Initially, the capacitor is uncharged, so has no voltage across it by $Q = CV$. This identifies graph A with resistor R_2, graph B with resistor R_1, and graph C with the capacitor C.

After the switch is closed for a long time, the capacitor stores charge and blocks current. So, the resistors once again function as a simple series with the battery, recovering the initial voltages. That's why graphs A and B show an asymptote at the same vertical axis value as the initial voltages, 33 V and 67 V, respectively. The charged capacitor is in parallel with R_2, so takes on its 67 V value after a long time.

Day 74

(a) Magnetic flux is BA, where A is the area intersected by the magnetic field. Initially, that's the full area of the ring. After a quarter revolution, none of the magnetic field lines penetrate the ring, so A becomes zero and so does the magnetic flux. Then, after another quarter revolution, the magnetic flux becomes maximum again, but pointing through the ring in the opposite orientation. The flux goes back to zero and again to its initial maximum.

(b) EMF is the negative derivative of magnetic flux. Since the first graph looks like $y = \cos x$, the derivative should look like $y = \sin x$. (Or graphically, the negative slope of the first graph is what the second graph looks like.)

Day 75

As in Day 74's solution, the flux starts out maximum and becomes zero after a quarter turn. But with half the angular frequency, it takes twice as much time to make the quarter turn. So, the graphs have the same sinusoidal shape but their period is stretched out to twice as much.

Day 76

Because $a << x_1$, the cylinder can be considered essentially infinitely long. That means the "edge effects" of the cylinder's ends are ignorable, and the direction of the electric field is straight up. Consider a Gaussian cylinder of radius a going through P_1. Gauss's law says that $EA = q_{enclosed}/\varepsilon_0$. The A term here is the area of the Gaussian cylinder's surface that the electric field penetrates—not the endcaps of the cylinder, just the curved surface. The area of this cylindrical surface, from geometry class, is $2\pi aL$, where L is the length of the Gaussian cylinder.

Now, how much charge is enclosed? Charge is equal to the linear charge density times length. So, the cylinder encloses λL of charge. Put it all together: $E2\pi aL = \dfrac{\lambda L}{\varepsilon_0}$. The L cancels out. Solve for E to get $E = \dfrac{\lambda}{2\pi a\varepsilon_0}$.

Day 77

Gauss's law is only useful when the symmetry of the situation means the electric field is always either parallel to a Gaussian surface or penetrating the Gaussian surface at a $90°$ angle. That's true at point P_1, as long as a is less than the charged cylinder's length. But at P_2 (and all points nearby), the electric field will have a varying component both up and to the right. There's not a symmetric Gaussian surface—a sphere or cylinder—that will always have the electric field penetrating at a $90°$ angle. Thus, the integral $\int BdA$ in Gauss's law will not simplify to just EA, and Gauss's law will not be useful.

Day 78

(a) The meaning of this integral is the (vector) sum of the electric field produced by each teeny segment of the rod, from the left edge to right edge. The magnitude of the electric field due to each of these segments is $E = kQ/d^2$, where Q is the charge on the segment and d is the distance from the segment to position P_2. Each of these segments has a charge equal to the charge density λ times the length of the teeny segment. Since the cylinder's length is along the x axis, the teeny segments are also along the x axis, and each can be given a differential length, dx. We would only use dy if the cylinder were oriented along the y axis.

(b) This starts with the d^2 term in the denominator of the generic electric field equation. The horizontal distance between a teeny segment of the rod and position P_2 is $(x_2 - x)$. The minus sign is because the coordinate x has a negative value at each position on the rod, but the more negative the x coordinate, the *more* distance between the rod and P_2. The vertical distance from a teeny rod segment to P_2 is a. The Pythagorean theorem gives this total distance as $\text{root}(x_2 - x)^2 + a^2$, so the magnitude of the electric field produced at P_2 by a segment dx is $k\lambda$ (dx/distance).

But the question asks for the vertical component of this electric field! To take the vertical component, multiply the field by $\sin \theta$, What is $\sin \theta$? It's the opposite side divided by the hypotenuse of the triangle between the positions dx, P_2, and the horizontal axis (see below). The opposite leg of this triangle is a, the hypotenuse is $\text{root}(x_2 - x)^2 + a^2$, so $\sin \theta$ is $a/\text{root}(x_2 - x)^2 + a^2$. Multiply this by the electric field magnitude to get:

$$|E_y| = k\lambda \int_{-x_1}^{0} \frac{a\,dx}{[(x_2 - x)^2 + a^2]^{3/2}}$$

Day 79

In steady state, a capacitor stores charge and blocks current. The capacitor's branch in circuit A carries no current, leaving two resistors in series with a battery. According to Ohm's law, both series resistors carry a current.

But, an inductor in steady state acts as a zero-resistance wire. Parallel resistors take different currents, with the amount of current in each branch in proportion to the resistance of the branches. Since the inductor's branch is zero resistance, it takes not just a fraction of the current through R_2, but rather *all* the current through R_2, leaving none for the resistor.

Day 80

An uncharged capacitor in a circuit acts initially as a bare wire with zero resistance. Parallel resistors take different currents, with the amount of current in each branch in proportion to the resistance of the branches. Since the capacitor's branch initially has zero resistance, it takes not just a fraction of the current through R_2, but rather *all* the current through R_2, leaving none for the resistor.

But, an inductor resists a changing current. When the circuit is first connected, the inductor acts as a very large resistor because the current changes from zero to something nonzero. Virtually all of the current will initially take the parallel path through R_2.

Day 81

Ampere's law says the line integral of magnetic field along an Amperian loop equals μ_0 times the current enclosed by the Amperian loop. Here, draw a rectangle with one edge horizontally through point P_1, another horizontally through point P_3, and connected with sides covering all of the coils. This is a legitimate Amperian loop, because the magnetic field is always either uniform along the loop, perpendicular to the loop, or zero.

With this appropriate symmetry, the integral $\int B dl$ becomes just Bl, where l is the length of the rectangle's side that is parallel to the uniform magnetic field—that's the variable X in this situation. The current enclosed by this rectangle is the uniform current I times the number of coils that are inside the rectangle—that's N. Putting everything together, $BX = \mu_0 NI$, and solve for B.

Day 82

(a) Each coil of wire produces a magnetic field pointing to the left everywhere inside that coil. The multitude of coils produces magnetic fields whose resultant field is always uniform inside the coils. So, wherever you draw the rectangular Amperian loop—whether through point P_1 at the center of the coils or through point P_2 closer to the top of the coils—the magnetic field is still uniform and parallel to the bottom edge of the rectangle. Both rectangles enclose the same amount of current. So, the mathematics in Day 81's solution apply identically.

Day 83

(a) Induced emf (that is, voltage), is the change in magnetic flux divided by the time it takes for the flux to change. The magnetic flux is BA, where B is the magnetic field inside the solenoid ($\mu_0 n I_{max}$) and A is the area of the loop penetrated by the magnetic field, πr_1^2. The t in the denominator is the time it takes for the flux to change. Then, by Ohm's Law, current is equal to voltage divided by resistance, putting the R in the denominator.

(b) The A term in magnetic flux is not the area of the wire loop itself; rather, it's the area of the magnetic field that penetrates straight through the loop. The magnetic field produced by a solenoid only exists inside the solenoid and is zero elsewhere. So, the A term in BA is just the area of the solenoid itself (πr_1^2), not of the entire wire loop (πr_2^2).

Day 84

Lenz's law says an induced current causes a magnetic field in the direction of decreasing flux. The magnetic field in the solenoid points to the right according to the right-hand rule (i.e., curl the fingers of your right hand in the direction that the solenoid carries current, and your thumb points to the right). Because the current in the solenoid decreases, so does the magnetic field *and* the magnetic flux produced by the solenoid. So, the direction of decreasing flux is to the right. An induced current flowing back to front through the loop will produce a magnetic field to the right.

Day 85

The cylinder produces an electric field toward its negative charge. That's upward at P_1, downward at P_2, and zero in the middle of the cylinder at P_3 (because equal amounts of the negative charge are above and below P_3). The plates produce an electric field that is downward everywhere, away from its positive charge and toward its negative charge. At P_3, only the electric field due to the plates exists, which would not equal zero. At P_2, the fields due to the cylinder and the plates are both downward, so cannot cancel to zero. But at P_1, the upward and downward electric fields *could* cancel to zero, depending on the amount of charge on each object.

Day 86

Positive charges produce an electric field pointing away from the charge. The top charge produces a field directly right; the bottom charge produces a field up and right, at a 45° angle above horizontal. The field produced by the bottom charge is smaller than the field produced by the top charge, because the bottom charge is farther away from P. Adding the two individual electric field vectors tip to tail, you get a resultant that points below the 45° mark.

Day 87

Positive charges produce an electric field pointing away from the charge. The electric field at point P_1 is up and to the right, as shown in Day 86; the magnitude of the resultant field is greater than that due to only the top charge. At P_2, the top charge also produces a rightward electric field, yet the bottom charge produces a smaller electric field that points down and left, toward the negative charge. Adding the electric field vectors produced by both charges, the resultant points down and right, and the magnitude of the resultant field is *less than* that due to only the top charge.

Day 88

The electric potential due to a point charge is kQ/d. Negative charges produce negative potentials; and positive charges produce positive potentials. So, at all positions, the total electric potential is kQ/d due to the left charge minus kQ/d due to the right charge. In region II, the values of d (the distance from each charge to whatever location we're considering) are comparable, and the magnitude of the charge Q is identical. So, the kQ/d terms can subtract to zero. However, in region I, the distance d from the negative charge will always be larger than from the positive charge, so the positive potential term will always dominate. Similarly, in region III, the distance from the positive charge will always be larger, so the negative potential term will always dominate.

Day 89

Electric fields have direction: an electric field always points away from a positive charge. In region I, the electric field (due to each positive charge) points to the left; thus the electric field vectors add to produce an even larger leftward field at all positions. Similarly, in region III, the electric field due to each charge points right, and always adds to a rightward net field. But, in region II, the electric field from the left-hand charge points to the right, and the electric field due to the right-hand charge points to the left. These field vectors can cancel to zero at whichever position they have equal magnitude.

Day 90

Electric fields have direction: an electric field always points *away* from a positive charge, and *toward* a negative charge. In region II, the electric field (due to each charge) points to the right; thus, the electric field vectors add to produce an even larger rightward field at all positions. In regions I and III, the electric fields (due to each charge) point in different directions, and thus *could* cancel to zero if they were each of the same magnitude.

But in region I, the electric field due to the $+3Q$ charge will always be larger than the field due to the $-Q$ charge! The magnitude of the field is given by kQ/d^2. Everywhere in region I, the distance in the denominator from the $+3Q$ charge is smaller than the distance from the $-Q$ charge. And, the amount of charge in the numerator is larger for the $+3Q$ charge. The net electric field will always point to the left. In region III, though, there will be a place where the effect of the smaller denominator in the equation for the electric field produced by the $-Q$ charge will balance with the effect of the larger numerator in the equation for the electric field produced by the $+3Q$ charge, and the electric field vectors will cancel to zero.

Day 91

Consider Kirchhoff's loop rule applied with the switch closed to a loop including the 12 V battery, the 30 Ω resistor, and the 30 μF capacitor. You get the equation $0 = (12 \text{ V}) - (dQ/dt)(30 \text{ Ω}) - Q/(30 \text{ μF})$. The solution to this differential equation includes the term $e^{-t/RC}$, where RC is the time constant (the time for the capacitor to charge or discharge by 63%). In this equation, the only R that's included is the 30 Ω resistor. So, $RC = (30 \text{ Ω})(30 \text{ μF}) = 900$ microseconds.

Now, use Kirchhoff's loop rule while the capacitor discharges with the switch open. The circuit loop includes the capacitor and *both* resistors. Kirchhoff's rule gives $0 = Q/(30 \text{ μF}) - (dQ/dt)(30 \text{ Ω})(dQ/dt)(15 \text{ Ω})$. Now the RC term in the solution includes the resistance of both resistors together, 45 Ω. The time constant RC for discharging is $(45 \text{ Ω})(30 \text{ μF}) = 1350$ microseconds.

Day 92

With the switch closed, apply Kirchhoff's loop rule to the outside loop of the circuit containing only the 12 V battery and the 15 Ω resistor. You get $0 = (12 \text{ V}) - I(15 \text{ Ω})$ regardless of whether the capacitor is charged or not! So, the current is 0.80 A at all times after the switch is closed. The current through the 30 Ω resistor will start large and drop to zero, but that's irrelevant to the path including the 15 Ω resistor as long as the switch is closed.

Day 93

The relevant equation for the magnetic field of a solenoid is $B = \mu_0(N/L)I$. All of these variables are measured except for μ_0. So, one easy approach is to plot BL on the vertical axis and $(N/L)I$ on the horizontal axis. In this case, the graph would be linear with slope μ_0.

Other responses are possible. For example, you could plot B on the vertical axis, and I on the horizontal axis. The graph would be linear, but the slope would represent $\mu_0(N/L)$. To determine μ_0, then, divide the slope of the graph by (N/L).

Day 94

The relevant equation for the capacitance of a parallel plate capacitor is $C = \varepsilon_0 A/d$. All of these variables are measured except for ε_0. (Note that the area A of the plates wasn't measured directly; it is s^2.) So, one easy approach is to plot Cd on the vertical axis and s^2 on the horizontal axis. In this case, the graph would be linear with slope ε_0.

Other responses are possible. For example, you could plot C on the vertical axis and s^2 on the horizontal axis. The graph would be linear, but the slope would represent ε_0/d. To determine ε_0, then multiply the slope of the graph by d.

Day 95

The equation for the voltage V as a function of time t for the discharging capacitor can be derived from Kirchhoff's loop rule—or remembered to be $V = V_0 e^{-t/RC}$. Solving for V/V_0 and taking the natural log of both sides gives $[\ln(V/V_0)] = -t/RC$. So, the slope of the experimental graph is what is multiplying the t variable, or $\mathbf{-1/RC}$.

Day 96

The magnetic field due to a wire is $B = \dfrac{\mu_0 I}{2\pi r}$, and the direction of the magnetic field is given by the right-hand rule—point your thumb along the current and curl your fingers to find the direction of B. In region I, the magnetic field due to both wires points out of the page, and so cannot subtract to zero. In region III, both magnetic fields point into the page. Only in region II can the fields cancel—the field due to the top wire points into the page, while the field due to the bottom wire points out of the page.

Day 97

Consider a positive charge at the position. Positive charges are forced in the direction of an electric field, and from high to low potential. Because the electric field is zero, the charge experiences no force. Therefore, there must be no region of lower potential anywhere nearby—the electric potential at this position and all nearby positions must be the same. That does not mean the electric potential must be uniformly zero! If the electric potential were, say, 40 V everywhere near this charge, the charge would not be forced anywhere. Zero electric field means zero *change* in potential, not zero potential.

Day 98

It is true that a negative charge *is forced* in a direction opposite the electric field. But the direction of force does not have to be the same as the direction of motion! When an object's velocity vector is opposite the direction of the net force, then the object simply slows down. So, if the charge were moving already in the direction of the electric field, then the force on the charge is opposite the electric field, but the object continues to move *with* the field while slowing down.

Day 99

Since each battery is the same, the voltage in each circuit is the same. By Ohm's law ($V = IR$), the circuit with the smallest equivalent resistance provides the largest current. Resistors in parallel have an equivalent resistance less than that of any individual resistor by $1/R_1 + 1/R_2 = 1/R_{eq}$. Call each resistance R. Circuit A has the smallest equivalent resistance ($\frac{1}{3}R$) and the largest current. Circuit B has the largest equivalent resistance ($3R$) and the smallest current. Circuit C has two parallel resistors combined to be in series with one additional resistor; its equivalent resistance is $R + \frac{1}{2}R = 1.5R$ and so takes a current in between that of A and C. Ranking: **A > C > B**.

Day 100

(a) The potential difference provided by a battery is a property of a battery and does not depend on what kind of circuit it's connected to. **Unchanged.**

(b) Yes. By Kirchhoff's loop rule, the voltage drops twice—once after bulb A and once after bulb B. Once bulb C is removed, the equivalent resistance of the circuit changes, changing the current through A; this changes the voltage drop across A as well. Since the voltage drops across A and B must equal the voltage of the battery, B's voltage must also **change.**

(c) Yes. Change every second means current. B's voltage changed (as justified in (b)), so B's current must also change, since B's resistance is a property of an ohmic bulb and does not change.

(d) No. Resistance is a property of a resistor or any electronic device that obeys Ohm's law.

Day 101

For analysis, it's easier to redraw the circuit as two series resistors: R_1 and the equivalent resistance of the other two resistors—call it R_{23}. Since these two resistors are in series, they take the same current as each other. By $V = IR$, the larger resistor takes the larger voltage. So if R_{23} is greater than R_1, the two parallel resistors will take a greater voltage than R_1. Try 100 ohms for R_1, 500 ohms for R_2, and 600 ohms for R_3. The equivalent resistance R_{23} is 270 ohms, greater than R_1.

Day 102

Kirchhoff's junction rule applies, regardless of the values of the resistors. It says that the current entering a junction—the current through R_1—is equal to the current leaving the junction—the sum of the currents through R_2 and R_3. Since we always have to add something to R_2's current to get R_1's current, it's not possible for R_1 to take a smaller current than R_2.

Day 103

The paper is electrically neutral but can experience an attractive force by induction. When the paper touches the comb, some of the charge from the comb transfers to the paper. The paper and comb now have like charges and will repel.

Day 104

1. The battery's voltage does not change—voltage is a property of a battery. Resistor R_1 is connected directly across the battery terminals. Thus no matter what is in parallel with R_1, it will take the full voltage of the battery. Since the resistance if R_1 doesn't change, and the voltage across it doesn't change, by Ohm's law, the current through R_1 cannot change, either.

2. The ammeter reads the current in the entire circuit. Consider Ohm's law applied to the whole circuit. The voltage doesn't change, because it is provided by the unchanging battery. The circuit's equivalent resistance increases when R_2 increases, because in the parallel resistors equation, increasing one of the two resistors still increases the equivalent resistance. Then in Ohm's law with constant V, current and resistance are inversely related; current in the circuit decreases.

Day 105

(a) The voltage provided by a battery is a property of the battery; it does not change when the switch is closed.

(b) Closing the switch adds a resistor in parallel with bulb 3, meaning the resistance of that branch decreases. That decreases the overall resistance, too. By Ohm's law, with constant V, smaller resistance means bigger current. Current increases.

(c) As in (b), closing the switch adds a parallel path. The original circuit had three bulbs in series; the new circuit has two in series plus a parallel combination. Since the parallel combination has a smaller resistance than a single bulb, the overall resistance decreases.

(d) One expression for power is IV. Voltage of the battery doesn't change. Current from the battery increases (see (b)), so the power provided by the battery also increases.

Day 106

Lloyd is correct that closing the switch adds a parallel path. By Kirchhoff's junction rule, the total current must indeed now be split between bulbs 2 and 3.

He is incorrect, though, in relating the first part of his statement to a decrease in bulb 3's current. He is assuming that the total current to be split doesn't change. Not true: the total current increases, because the circuit's equivalent resistance decreases with a constant battery voltage.

We need to use Kirchhoff's loop rule to determine how the *voltage* across bulb 3 changes and thus how the current through that bulb changes. It is correct that bulb 3's current does increase, but Lloyd has incorrect reasoning leading to this conclusion.

Day 107

(a) For the whole circuit, the voltage of the battery is unchanged, but the equivalent resistance decreases. By Ohm's law, the total current increases.

Bulbs 1 and 3 take the whole battery current; thus their current increases while their individual resistances don't change (resistance is a property of an ohmic bulb). By Ohm's law, bulbs 1 and 3 take larger voltages. By Kirchhoff's loop rule, bulb 3 takes a smaller voltage.

Finally, consider Ohm's law for bulb 3 alone. Its resistance is unchanged, but its voltage decreases. Thus it takes a smaller current.

Note: It is *not* correct reasoning to say, "Closing the switch adds a parallel path, so now the current must split between bulbs 2 and 3, decreasing bulb 3's current." This reasoning assumes that the total current to be split doesn't change. Not true: the total current increases. We need to use Kirchhoff's loop rule to determine how the *voltage* across bulb 3 changes, and thus how the current through that bulb changes.

(b) Brightness is related to power. Power is I^2R. Bulb 3's resistance doesn't change; its current decreases, so its power decreases, making it less bright.

Day 108

Connect a variable voltage battery in series with this bulb and an ammeter (to read the current through the bulb). Connect a voltmeter across the bulb to read its voltage.

Plot the voltage readings on the vertical axis and the current readings on the horizontal axis. By $V = IR$, if the bulb's resistance is constant, then the slope on this graph will be the bulb's resistance. If the bulb's resistance changes, then the slope of the line will change.

Day 109

Power dissipated by a lightbulb means the energy converted (from electrical to light) every second. It makes no difference whether the bulbs are connected in series, parallel, or some combination—the amount of energy converted each second just adds together. The total power dissipated is thus $27\text{ W} + 7\text{ W} + 7\text{ W} = \textbf{41 W}$.

Day 110

Consider connecting each battery to a circuit containing a single resistor. The equivalent resistance of the circuit is the sum of the external and internal resistances. So the circuit with battery A in it has a larger equivalent resistance.

But both circuits have the same EMF; that is, total voltage. By Ohm's law, with the same voltage, a larger resistance means a smaller current. Thus battery A's circuit has a smaller current.

Consider the voltage drop across the external resistor, which is identical for each circuit. Battery B's circuit has more current, so it will have more voltage across the external resistor. That leaves less voltage for the internal resistor, by Kirchhoff's loop rule.

And finally, the terminal voltage of a battery is its EMF minus the voltage across its internal resistance. Regardless of the actual amount of current in the circuit, battery B will always have less voltage across its internal resistance than battery A. Thus **Battery B** will have the larger terminal voltage.

Day 111

The property of an ohmic bulb that remains unchanged regardless of what it's connected to is its resistance. The equation for power is $P = V^2/R$. Using the ratings of 60 W and 120 V, the resistance of each bulb is 240 Ω.

In series, the voltage across each bulb must add to the voltage of the battery—that's Kirchhoff's loop rule. In this circuit, then, the voltage across each bulb must then be *less* than 120 V. Since each bulb's resistance does not change, by $P = V^2/R$, a smaller voltage leads to a smaller power dissipated by each bulb.

Day 112

The student is incorrect about the direction of the force on each charge. Protons are positive and will thus be repelled by the positive charges, whereas electrons are negative and will thus be attracted to the positive charge. The student is also incorrect to say there are equal accelerations for each charge. The force will be the same magnitude, since the magnitudes of charge on an electron and a proton are equal. However, the electron has less mass than a proton, and will therefore have the greater acceleration with the equal applied force.

Day 113

The direction of the force on a charged particle in a magnetic field is given by the right-hand rule associated with $F = qvB$. Point your fingers left, along the velocity vector. Curl them into the page, toward the magnetic field vector. Your thumb points down . . . so, a positive charge would be forced downward. This negative charge is forced in the opposite direction, upward. So, the electron's path bends

upward, like this:

Once the electron enters the magnetic field, the magnetic force changes direction so that it is always perpendicular to the velocity vector. This is a definition of circular motion—the net force always points toward the circle's center, perpendicular to the object's velocity.

Day 114

$I_3 > I_2 > I_1$.

Current will be equal anywhere in a given path until a junction is reached where the current can split or join with other currents. I_3 is in series with the battery; therefore it carries the total current for the circuit and is the greatest. I_3 will split going to the resistors. By Kirchhoff's junction rule, $I_1 + I_2 = I_3$, and thus I_1 and I_2 must each be less than I_3. Less current will flow through R_1 than through R_2—by Kirchhoff's loop rule, both R_1 and R_2 take the same voltage. When voltage is the same, Ohm's law indicates that current and resistance are inversely related, putting the larger current through the smaller resistor.

Day 115

(a) Starting at the top left of the circuit, and tracing the circuit clockwise: the units in each term are volts. Each battery adds or subtracts its potential difference; each resistor causes a voltage drop of iR, meaning each voltage change across a resistor should come with a negative sign. And Kirchhoff's loop rule says the sum of the voltage changes around the entire loop will be zero. So:

$$0 = (8) + (-30i) + (-60i) + (-15i)$$

(b) Solve the above equation for i to get 0.076 A, or 76 mA. This current is clockwise—this is because the algebraic solution for i in the equation in (a) is a positive number. If i had turned out to be negative, then the direction of the circuit trace would have been opposite the direction of current flow.

Day 116

Each battery adds or subtracts a potential equal to the battery's voltage. Each resistor causes a loss of potential equal to iR, where i is the 76 mA of current. So:

(a) The voltage rises by 12 V after position A. The voltage drops by 4 V after position B. The 30-ohm resistor causes a voltage drop of 2.3 V, the 60-ohm resistor a 4.6-V drop, the 15-ohm resistor a 1.1-V drop. That brings the potential back down to zero.

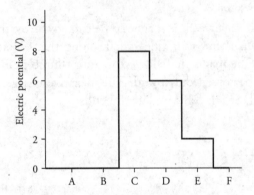

(b) That'd be the 8-V addition from the battery, minus the 2.3-V drop from the resistor: **5.7 V.**

Day 117

Brightness depends on power dissipated by a bulb. But since the bulbs are identical, they have the same resistance, and so by $P = V^2/R$ the voltage across each bulb is directly related to the power dissipated by that bulb. For the remaining bulbs to have equal brightness there must be an equal potential difference across each bulb. This is achieved if the three bulbs are either in series or in parallel. If the bulbs are in series, then the current through each bulb is the same, as there is nowhere for current to branch off, and the sum of the voltage drops across the bulbs equals the source voltage. With equal bulbs, the voltage drops across each bulb will be equal. In parallel, the current will branch equally through each bulb, since they are identical. With equal currents through equal resistances (bulbs), they will be equally bright.

Day 118

$D = C > A = B = E$

Each charge will experience a force according to Coulomb's law, $F = k\dfrac{q_1 q_x}{r^2}$. The magnitude of the force on the charge on the right (and the left, by Newton's third law) in arrangement A can then be described by $F = k\dfrac{q^2}{r^2}$.

The arrangement in B will have the same magnitude of force as A, due to the same charge magnitudes and separation distance.

Arrangement C will have four times the force, due to four times the charge magnitude on the left charge.

Arrangement D would tend to have a 16-times increase in force due to the four-times increase in each charge magnitude, but would also tend to have four times less force due to the doubling of the separation distance. Combining these factors, the change in force is 16/4 or a four-times increase in the magnitude of the force, making the magnitude the same as C.

Arrangement E will have four times more force due to the four-times increase in charge, but four times less force due to the doubling of separation distance, so it has the same magnitude of force as in arrangement A.

Day 119

$C = D > A = B = E$

Each charge will experience a force according to Coulomb's law, $F = k\dfrac{q_1 q_x}{r^2}$. The acceleration is directly proportional to the net force. Acceleration is inversely proportional to mass, but each charge has equal mass, so the contribution toward acceleration will be the same for each.

The magnitude of the force on the charge on the right (and the left, by Newton's third law) in arrangement A can then be described by $F = k\dfrac{q^2}{r^2}$. Since both charges are positive, the force is repulsive and the charge will accelerate to the right.

The arrangement in B will have the same magnitude of force as A, due to the same charge magnitudes and separation distance.

Arrangement C will have four times the force, due to four times the charge magnitude on the left charge, and thus four times the acceleration. The force is attractive, so the acceleration is negative (to the left).

Arrangement D would tend to have a 16-times increase in force due to the four-times increase in each charge magnitude, but would also tend to have four times less force due to the doubling of the separation distance. Combining these factors, the change in force is 16/4 or a four-times increase in the magnitude of the force and thereby the acceleration, making the magnitude the same as C (to the right since the force is repulsive).

Arrangement E will have four times more force due to the four-times increase in charge, but four times less force due to the doubling of separation distance, so it has the same magnitude of force and acceleration as in arrangement A and is repulsive.

Day 120

A negative charge is forced opposite an electric field. The electric field between the two parallel plates is uniform, and points from a positive to a negative plate—that's downward in this instance. So, the electron

is forced upward, bending the electron's path like this:

The force on the electron is always upward. So, the path is parabolic: The horizontal net force is zero, causing zero acceleration and a uniform speed; the vertical net force is uniform, producing uniform acceleration. Using the kinematics formula $x = \frac{1}{2}at^2$, uniform acceleration produces quadratically varying vertical position and a parabolic path.

Appendixes

Constants
Physics C Equations
Four-Minute Drill Prompts
Web Sites
Glossary
Bibliography
The Pantheon of Pizza

CONSTANTS

1 amu	u	1.7×10^{-27} kg
mass of proton	m_p	1.7×10^{-27} kg
mass of neutron	m_n	1.7×10^{-27} kg
mass of electron	m_e	9.1×10^{-31} kg
charge of proton	e	1.6×10^{-19} C
Avogadro's number	N	6.0×10^{-23} mol^{-1}
Universal gas constant	R	8.3 J/(mol·K)
Boltzmann's constant	k_B	1.4×10^{-23} J/K
Speed of light	c	3.0×10^{8} m/s
Planck's constant	h	6.6×10^{-34} J·s
	h	4.1×10^{-15} eV·s
Planck's constant · speed of light	hc	1.99×10^{-25} J·m
	hc	1.24×10^{3} eV·nm
Permittivity of free space	ε_o	8.9×10^{-12} C^2/N·m^2
Coulomb's law constant	k	9.0×10^{9} N·m^2/C^2
Permeability of free space	μ_o	$4\pi \times 10^{-7}$ T·m/A
Universal gravitation constant	G	6.7×10^{-11} N·m^2/kg^2
Earth's free fall acceleration	g	9.8 m/s^2
1 atmosphere of pressure	atm	1.0×10^{5} Pa
1 electron-volt	eV	1.6×10^{-19} J

PHYSICS C EQUATIONS

Read Chapter 6 about memorizing equations for more help with learning not only what the equations say, but also what they mean.

You'll notice that the C equation sheet often expresses relationships in calculus terms. Don't let that confuse you; for example, though impulse is expressed as an integral of force with respect to time, you should also interpret that as force times time if the force is constant, or as the area under a force vs. time graph.

Remember, your textbook might use slightly different symbols.

MECHANICS

$$v_f = v_o + at$$

$$x - x_o = v_o t + \tfrac{1}{2} a t^2$$

$$v_f^2 = v_0^2 + 2a(x - x_o)$$

$$F_{net} = ma$$

$$F = \frac{dp}{dt}$$

$$I = \Delta p = \int F \cdot dt$$

$$p = mv$$

$$F_f = \mu F_N$$

$$W = \int F \cdot dx$$

$$K = \tfrac{1}{2} m v^2$$

$$P = \frac{dW}{dt}$$

$$P = F \cdot v$$

$$U_g = mgh$$

$$a_c = \frac{v^2}{r} = \omega^2 r$$

$$\tau = F \cdot d$$

$$\tau_{net} = I\alpha$$

$$I = \int r^2 dm = \sum m_i r_i^2$$

$$M x_{cm} = \sum m_i x_i$$

$$v = r\omega$$

$$L = I\omega = mvr$$

$$K = \tfrac{1}{2} I \omega^2$$

$$\omega_f = \omega_0 + \alpha t$$

$$\Delta\theta = \omega_0 t + \tfrac{1}{2}\alpha t^2$$

$$F = -kx$$

$$U_s = \tfrac{1}{2} k x^2$$

$$T = \frac{2\pi}{\omega} = \frac{1}{f}$$

$$T = 2\pi \sqrt{\frac{m}{k}}$$

$$T = 2\pi \sqrt{\frac{L}{g}}$$

$$F_G = G\frac{m_1 m_2}{r^2}$$

$$U_G = -G\frac{m_1 m_2}{r}$$

ELECTRICITY AND MAGNETISM

$$F = \frac{1}{4\pi\varepsilon_o}\frac{q_1 q_2}{r^2}$$

$$F = qE$$

$$\oint E \cdot dA = \frac{Q_{enclosed}}{\varepsilon_0}$$

$$E = -\frac{dV}{dr}$$

$$U_E = qV = \frac{1}{4\pi\varepsilon_o}\frac{q_1 q_2}{r}$$

$$V = \frac{1}{4\pi\varepsilon_o}\sum\frac{q_i}{r_i}$$

$$Q = CV$$

$$C = \kappa\varepsilon_0\frac{A}{d}$$

$$C_p = \sum C_i$$

$$\frac{1}{C_s} = \sum\frac{1}{C_i}$$

$$I = \frac{dQ}{dt}$$

$$PE_C = \tfrac{1}{2}CV^2$$

$$R = \rho\frac{L}{A}$$

$$V = IR$$

$$R_s = \sum R_i$$

$$\frac{1}{R_p} = \sum\frac{1}{R_i}$$

$$P = IV$$

$$F = qvB\sin\theta$$

$$\oint B \cdot dl = \mu_0 I_c$$

$$F = ILB\sin\theta$$

$$B_s = \mu_o nl$$

$$\phi_m = \int B \cdot dA$$

$$\varepsilon = -\frac{d\phi_m}{dt}$$

$$\varepsilon = Blv$$

$$\varepsilon = -L\frac{dI}{dt}$$

$$PE_L = \frac{1}{2}LI^2$$

FOUR-MINUTE DRILL PROMPTS

The lists that follow are designed to help you study equations. Each prompt refers to a specific equation on the AP Equations sheet (we've listed the prompts in the same order in which the equations appear on the Equations sheet). So, for example, the prompt "Net force" refers to the equation, "$F_{net} = ma$."

There are several ways to use these prompts. First, you can use them as a self-test: For each prompt, write down the corresponding equation on a separate sheet of paper. Then check the equations you wrote down against the AP Equations sheet to see if you got any wrong. You can also use these prompts when you study with a friend: Have your friend read the prompts to you, and you respond by reciting the appropriate equation. Try to go through the list as fast as possible without making a mistake. Last, your physics teacher can use these prompts to lead your class through a four-minute drill, which is an activity we describe in Chapter 6.

Mechanics

1st kinematics equation
2nd kinematics equation
3rd kinematics equation
Net force
Force in terms of momentum
Impulse
Definition of momentum
Force of friction
Work
Kinetic energy
Power
Power—alternate expression
Gravitational potential energy near a planet
Centripetal acceleration
Torque
Newton's second law for rotation
Definition of rotational inertia
Position of the center of mass
Conversion between linear and angular velocity
Angular momentum
Rotational kinetic energy
1st rotational kinematics equation
2nd rotational kinematics equation

Force of a spring (The negative sign reminds you that the spring force is a restoring force, always acting toward the equilibrium point.)
Potential energy of a spring
Period in terms of angular frequency and standard frequency
Period of a mass on a spring
Period of a pendulum
Gravitational force between two massive objects
Gravitational potential energy between two massive objects (Don't use unless an object is far away from a planet's surface.)

Electricity and Magnetism

Electric force between two point charges
Definition of electric field
Gauss's law (Though you should never actually take an integral when using this.)
How to find electric field in terms of potential
Potential energy in terms of potential, and then potential energy between two point charges (This line on the equation sheet really has two different equations. $PE = qV$ is always valid, but $PE = kqq/r$ is only valid between two point charges.)
The electric potential at some point due to surrounding point charges
Definition of capacitance
Capacitance of a parallel-plate capacitor with a dielectric substance of constant κ added
How to add parallel capacitors
How to add series capacitors
Definition of current
Energy stored on a capacitor
Resistance of a wire
Ohm's law
How to add series resistors
How to add parallel resistors
Power in an electrical circuit
Magnetic force on a charge
Ampere's law
Magnetic force on a wire
Magnetic field of a solenoid
Magnetic flux
Induced EMF
Voltage across an inductor
Energy stored in an inductor

The Internet offers some great resources for preparing for the AP Physics exam.

Your textbook may have an associated Web site . . . if so, check it out! For example, Paul A. Tipler's Physics C-level text provides this Web site: http://www.whfreeman.com/tipler4e/

- Of course, the official site of the College Board, www.collegeboard.com, has administrative information and test-taking hints, as well as contact information for the organization that actually is in charge of the exam.
- Did you enjoy your first taste of physics? If so, you can try your hand at physics debating. The United States Association for Young Physicists Tournaments hosts a national tournament which consists of "physics fights," or debates, over experimental research projects. Check out www.usaypt.org for details.
- The author writes the country's leading physics teaching blog, available at jacobsphysics.blogspot.com. Students and teachers can obtain and share ideas at this site.
- Having trouble solving calculus problems associated with Physics C, especially differential equations? Don't spend a lot of time solving these. Use www.wolfranalpha.com to get the solution spit out for you. Sure, you can't use this on the exam, but it's worth using on homework to speed or check your solutions. Physics is generally more about setting up the problem correctly than carrying out the mathematics anyway.

acceleration—the change in an object's velocity divided by the time it took to make that change; equal to the derivative (slope) of an object's velocity–time function

amplitude—the maximum displacement from the equilibrium position during a cycle of periodic motion; also, the height of a wave

angular momentum—the amount of effort it would take to make a rotating object stop spinning

atom—the fundamental unit of matter; includes protons and neutrons in a small nucleus, surrounded by electrons

atomic mass unit (amu)—the mass of a proton; also the mass of a neutron

average speed—the distance an object travels divided by the time it took to travel that distance

capacitor—a charge-storage device, often used in circuits

centrifugal force—a made-up force; when discussing circular motion, only talk about "centripetal" forces

centripetal force—the force keeping an object in uniform circular motion

coefficient of friction—the ratio of the friction force to the normal force. The coefficient of static friction is used when an object has no velocity relative to the surface it is in contact with; the coefficient of kinetic friction is used for a moving object

concave lens—a translucent object that makes the light rays passing through it diverge

conservative force—a force that acts on an object without causing the dissipation of that object's energy in the form of heat

current—the flow of positive charge in a circuit; the amount of charge passing a given point per unit time

dipole—something, usually a set of charges, with two nonidentical ends

direction—the orientation of a vector

displacement—a vector quantity describing how far an object moved

elastic collision—a collision in which kinetic energy is conserved

electric field—a property of a region of space that affects charged objects in that particular region

electric flux—the amount of electric field that penetrates a certain area

electric potential—potential energy provided by an electric field per unit charge

electromagnetic induction—the production of a current by a changing magnetic field

electron—a subatomic particle that carries a negative charge

energy—the ability to do work

equilibrium—when the net force and net torque on an object equal zero

equipotential lines—lines that illustrate every point at which a charged particle would experience a given potential

field—a property of a region of space that can affect objects found in that particular region

free-body diagram—a picture that represents one or more objects, along with the forces acting on those objects

frequency—the number of cycles per second of periodic motion; also, the number of wavelengths of a wave passing a certain point per second

friction—a force acting parallel to two surfaces in contact; if an object moves, the friction force always acts opposite the direction of motion

fulcrum—the point about which an object rotates

g—free-fall acceleration near the Earth's surface, about 10 m/s^2

induced EMF—the potential difference created by a changing magnetic flux that causes a current to flow in a wire; EMF stands for "electro-motive force," but the units of EMF are *volts*.

inductance—the property of an inductor that describes how good it is at resisting changes in current in a circuit

inductor—a coil in a circuit that makes use of induced EMF to resist changes in current in the circuit

inelastic collision—a collision in which kinetic energy is not conserved, as opposed to an elastic collision, in which the total kinetic energy of all objects is the same before and after the collision

inertia—the tendency for a massive object to resist a change in its velocity

internal energy—the sum of the kinetic energies of each molecule of a substance

ion—an electrically charged atom or molecule

kinetic energy—energy of motion

Kirchoff's laws—in a circuit, 1) at any junction, the current entering equals the current leaving; 2) the sum of the voltages around a closed loop is zero

Lenz's law—the direction of the current induced by a changing magnetic flux creates a magnetic field that opposes the change in flux

magnetic field—a property of a region of space that causes magnets and moving charges to experience a force

magnetic flux—the amount of magnetic field that penetrates an area

magnitude—how much of a quantity is present; see "scalar" and "vector"

mass spectrometer—a device used to determine the mass of a particle

momentum—the amount of "oomph" an object has in a collision, equal to an object's mass multiplied by that object's velocity

net force—the vector sum of all the forces acting on an object

normal force—a force that acts perpendicular to the surface on which an object rests

nucleus—the small, dense core of an atom, made of protons and neutrons

oscillation—motion of an object that regularly repeats itself over the same path

parallel—the arrangement of elements in a circuit so that the charge that flows through one element does not flow through the others

perfectly inelastic collision—a collision in which the colliding objects stick together after impact

period—the time it takes for an object to pass through one cycle of periodic motion; also, the time for a wave to propagate by a distance of one wavelength

potential energy—energy of position

power—the amount of work done divided by the time it took to do that work; also, in a circuit, equal to the product of the current flowing through a resistor and the voltage drop across that resistor

resistance—a property of a circuit that resists the flow of current

resistor—something put in a circuit to increase its resistance

restoring force—a force that restores an oscillating object to its equilibrium position

rotational inertia—the rotational equivalent of mass

scalar—a quantity that has a magnitude but no direction

series—the arrangement of elements in a circuit so that they are connected in a line, one after the other

time constant—a value related to how long it takes to charge or discharge a capacitor, or for current to flow in an inductor

torque—the application of a force at some distance from a fulcrum; if the net torque on an object isn't zero, the object's rotational velocity will change

vector—a quantity that has both magnitude and direction

velocity—how fast an object's displacement changes; equal to the derivative (slope) of an object's position–time function

weight—the force due to gravity; equal to the mass of an object times g, the gravitational field

work—the product of the distance an object travels and the components of the force acting on that object directed parallel to the object's direction of motion

work-energy theorem—the net work done on an object equals that object's change in kinetic energy

BIBLIOGRAPHY

Your AP Physics textbook may have seemed difficult to read early in the year. But now that you have heard lectures, solved problems, and read our guide, try reading your text again—you'll be amazed at how much more clear the text has become.

If you'd like to look at another textbook, here is one that we recommend:

- Tipler, P. A., Mosca, G. (2007). *Physics for Scientists and Engineers* (6th ed.). New York: W. H. Freeman.

You might also find this book helpful:

- Hewitt, P. G. (2009). *Conceptual Physics* (11th ed.). San Francisco: Addison Wesley.

(Hewitt's is the classic text for readable, non-mathematical expositions of physics principles. If you are having trouble seeing the meaning behind the mathematics, check out this book.)

Just for fun, we also recommend these books . . . they might not help you too much for the AP exam, but they're great reads.

- Hawking, S. (1998). *A Brief History of Time.* New York: Bantam. (The canonical introduction to cosmology at a layperson's level.)
- Lederman, L. (1993). *The God Particle.* New York: Dell. (Written by a Nobel Prize–winning experimental physicist, this book not only discusses what kinds of strange subatomic particles exist, but goes through the amazing and interesting details of how these particles are discovered.)
- Walker, J. (2007). *The Flying Circus of Physics* (2nd ed.). New Jersey: Wiley. (This book provides numerous conceptual explanations of physics phenomena that you have observed. The classic "Physics of the world around you" book.)

THE PANTHEON OF PIZZA

Pizza is the traditional food of the physics study group. Why? Probably because it's widely available, relatively inexpensive, easily shareable, and doesn't cause arguments the way "let's order bean curd" might.

If you have not yet experienced the late-night physics group study session, you should. Physics is more fun with friends than alone, and you learn more productively with other people around. Ideally, you'll find a mix of people in which sometimes they are explaining things to you, but sometimes you are explaining things to them. Explaining physics to friends is the absolute best way to cement your own knowledge.

But if you don't already have a regular study group, how do you go about creating one? Use pizza as bait. "Hey, let's get together in my mom's basement to do the problem set" is like a party invitation from Bill Nye the Science Guy. But, "Hey, we're ordering seven large pizzas with extra cheese and a variety of toppings; why don't you come by and do your problem set with us?" sounds more like you're headed to *Encore* on the Vegas Strip.[1]

Over the years I've eaten enough pizza to fill several dozen dumpsters—and dumpsters have been an appropriate receptacle for much of that pizza. Given the choice between a five-star restaurant and a pizza place, I'd usually choose the five stars. Usually. I know of four—just four—pizza places I would prefer to anything recommended by Squilliam Fancyson.

These four make up the Pantheon of Pizza.

Please understand the rules of access to the Pantheon:

1. I must have eaten at a member restaurant at least twice. This unfortunately rules out the heavenly *Pepper's Pizza* in Chapel Hill, North Carolina.[2]
2. I must have such an affinity for their pepperoni-and-extra-cheese pizza that my mouth waters upon the mere mention of a potential visit to the restaurant.

That's it. It's my pantheon, so it's my choice who gets in.

That said, please do send your own corrections, additions, oversights, etc. You can contact me via Woodberry Forest School. If you make a good enough case for a particular pizza place possibly joining the Pantheon, I may attempt to make a pilgrimage.

The Pantheon

5. Homeslice, Kansas City, Missouri. Imagine you've been grading AP exams for eight hours in the heart of downtown Kansas City. Imagine you're hungry, on foot, and that you are not up for the two-mile hike to Gates Barbecue tonight. (I don't have to imagine. This is my life for several days each June.) Grab some friends and walk a few blocks toward the basketball arena, then turn right. The airy restaurant with the high tables and the Royals pregame on the TVs is Homeslice. Their defining pizza feature is fresh mozzarella, made each day in-house. One of the owners came out to earnestly tell our table the origin story of

---

[1] Sorry. I certainly do *not* intend to dis Bill Nye the Science Guy. He is demonstrably cool.
[2] Now, alas, I hear they've closed down for good. Sigh.

this fresh mozzarella, the recent genesis of their restaurant, and how AP readers are appreciated as customers, but can't top concert attendees of any genre. Nevertheless…the proof in the pizza is the eating of the same. The spices are just right; the large thin pepperoni slices taste excellent and add flavor to the entire pie. Bring whatever you don't finish back to the physics lounge in the basement of the Crowne Plaza hotel. Please.

4. Broadway Joe's Pizza, Riverdale, New York. This tiny shop below the #1 line train station in the North Bronx has everything you could ask for in a New York pizzeria—street noise, no air conditioning but instead a fan running all summer, the Yankees game on the television, and Broadway Joe himself behind the counter. Okay, I'm sure that there are hundreds of such places throughout New York City, all of which probably have tremendous pizza. But Broadway Joe's is the one I walk to every year during the AP Physics Teachers' Summer Institute that I run at Manhattan College. Bonus points to Mr. Joe for recognizing me each year: "Hey, you're the teacher who wants a small[3] pepperoni and extra cheese." Ten minutes later, out pops the classic New York–style pie with deciliters of cheese piled on top of a foldable crust. I can never finish the small by myself, but I so, so want to.

3. Thyme Market, Culpeper, Virginia. When I moved to central Virginia, I initially despaired at the food choices. But then we discovered Pizza Monday at Thyme Market. Even an unjuiced Alex Rodriguez[4] could knock a baseball across the length of Culpeper's Main Street, but it contains the heavenly brick oven from which its $5 pies spring forth each Monday, plus a lot of money for toppings, plus another $5 if you come on a day other than Monday. But it's well worth the cash and the trip. This is one of the few pizza places ever in which "extra cheese" provides a bit too much gooeyness. The pepperoni itself is the best of any in the Pantheon—just the right size, on top of the cheese, a bit of thickness to it, and baked until the edges begin to get crispy. While you're in the restaurant, try a bite of the "Culpeper Crack"–branded cheese spread that's always available to sample. The pizza may be only $5 per pie, but you'll spend an order of magnitude more than that after you buy up multiple tubs of the Crack to take home.

2. Big Ed's Pizza, Oak Ridge, Tennessee. I encountered Big Ed's in conjunction with the United States Invitational Young Physicists Tournament, which was held in Oak Ridge for several years due to the presence of Oak Ridge National Laboratory. My friend and fellow physics teacher Peggy insisted that it was worth waiting in the crowd outside the door for a table, and she was right. The pizza was, of course, fabulous: New York–style foldable crust, with plenty of cheese and a multitude thereof of pepperonis. What sold me on Big Ed's, more so than even the T-shirts with a cartoony drawing of Big Ed himself, was the Kneeling Bench. The kitchen is separated from the dining area by a high wooden façade. But in the middle of the façade are two holes, with benches underneath. I was instructed to kneel on a bench, cup my hands communion-style, and put them through the hole. Lo, a generous portion of shredded mozzarella was placed in my hands by unknown beneficiaries. I had to go through this ritual a second time—I probably had as much cheese from my trips to the Kneeling Bench as from the pizza itself.

1. Langel's Pizza, Highland, Indiana. Most people who sample Chicago-style deep-dish pizza go to the big chains that have sprouted up across the Chicagoland area. Burrito Girl[5] grew up in a small suburb in northwest Indiana, and so she is well aware of the famous fancy chains. Yet the first pizza place that Burrito Girl took me to consisted of

---

[3]Don't be deceived. A "small" pie at Broadway Joe's could last for three straight late nights of Minecraft. Just one extra-large could sustain the entire rat population along the banks of the East River.

[4]… if such a thing exists.

[5]My wife and sidekick, also known as the mild-mannered Shari.

about six booths sandwiched between an exotic reptiles store and a sports bar. I ordered, and I endured the requisite progression of helpfulness, skepticism, and then outright horror that waitresses in Chicago pizza places bestow upon me when I order extra cheese. Yes, I want extra cheese, even though the pizza is stuffed with seemingly an entire cow-day's worth of cheese already. Really. I've done this before, and lived to tell the tale. Please?

At Langel's, the extra cheese oozes and stretches beyond the mere constraints of slices. It takes a full 20 minutes before the cheese is congealed enough to hold the shape in which you cut it. But it's the sauce that makes Langel's the best pizza in the known universe. This deep-dish pizza does not come in layers, but rather mixed all about, which means that the sauce can be appreciated throughout every bite. The pepperoni is fine, but I actually recommend just getting a pure extra-cheese pie. You'll have enough for lunch right now, dinner tonight, and probably breakfast tomorrow. Too bad they don't deliver within a 1,200-km radius.

5 Steps to Teaching AP Physics C

TEACHER'S MANUAL

Greg Jacobs

AP Physics C Teacher at Woodberry Forest School in Virginia

Introduction to Teacher's Manual

Nowadays teachers have no shortage of resources for their physics class. No longer limited to just the teacher and the textbook, teachers and students can look at online simulations, apps, computer-based homework, video lectures, and so on. Even the College Board itself provides so much material related to the AP exam that the teachers can easily become overwhelmed by an excess of information.

This book explains in straightforward language what a student needs to know for the AP Physics C exams—nothing more, nothing less.

This teacher's manual will take you through what I would consider the five steps of teaching an AP Physics course. I'll talk through each of these steps, some in more detail than others. Most of the suggestions and ideas are things that I've done in my own class, but that doesn't mean they're uniquely *mine*—physics teachers, like baseball pitchers, do best when they hear new things, try new things, adapt new things, and eventually make new things their own.

This teacher's manual takes you through the five steps of teaching AP Physics C. These five steps are:

1. **Prepare a strategic plan for the course**

2. **Hold an interesting class every day**

3 **Evaluate your students' progress**

4. **Get students ready to take the AP exam**

5. **Become a better teacher every year**

I hope this teacher's manual inspires new ideas you can use in your own classroom. And feel free to write to me with your own thoughts. I'm always collecting and trying out new teaching ideas for myself, so I'd love to hear from readers. My physics teaching blog at jacobsphysics.blogspot.com regularly updates with new ideas, most of which are inspired by correspondence and discussion with other physics teachers.

What Is Your Audience for AP Physics C?

Before you can even begin the five steps of teaching AP Physics C, you need to know your audience. Here I list several different categories of Physics C courses. Any of them can be taught successfully!

AP Physics C—Mechanics   (as a first-time physics course)

I recommend just straight-up teaching AP Physics 1, with the only adjustment being pacing. Schedule to finish the first pass on all material by the end of February rather than the beginning of April. Use March to discuss how calculus applies to the core concepts you've already discussed in detail. A good AP Physics 1 student can already pass the AP Physics C—Mechanics exam with no further preparation! A student who knows concepts well can easily add on mathematical complexity, but being able to solve math problems has no intrinsic correlation to an ability to figure out physics concepts. Therefore, start with the concepts, as in AP Physics 1.

AP Physics C—Mechanics (as a second-year course)

If the prerequisite course was strong—especially if it was AP Physics 1—then this course can be relaxed, with as much lab work and enrichment as you can imagine. In fact, for students who did well in Physics 1, I don't recommend just doing Physics C—Mechanics by itself. Rather, do both Mechanics *and* Electricity and Magnetism (E&M). They'll handle it! Use the content sequencing described in Step 1 that follows. (If the prerequisite course was not an AP Physics 1 equivalent, or if it had a lot of math and not a lot of concepts, then I'd do the straight-up AP Physics 1 through February as recommended earlier.)

AP Physics C—E&M (as a second-year course for students who have had AP Physics 1 or AP Physics C—Mechanics)

You'll probably want to sequence the course starting with the algebra-based concepts covered in AP Physics 2, followed by a complete review of content with a more mathematical bent. This recommended sequencing is different from that in the Course and Exam Description (CED), but similar to that described in Step 1 that follows.

AP Physics C—Mechanics and E&M (as a second-year course for students who have taken AP Physics 1)

This is the AP Physics C course that I teach and the most common second-year course for those who have had AP Physics 1. Teaching this class is best done with a unique sequencing approach that differs from the one in the College Board's CED. I describe this in detail in Step 1 that follows.

Step 1: Prepare a Strategic Plan for the Course

By "strategic plan," I mean how your course is going to be structured from August to April. The obvious part of the strategic plan is which topics will be covered over what periods of time. While that is an important feature, there's much more to consider.

Use a creative approach to content sequencing for AP Physics C—Mechanics and E&M.[1]

Physics C seems at first glance like a difficult transition from the algebra-based AP course: Much of the mechanics portion of Physics C covers the very same concepts mastered in Physics 1, although there's a good bit of

calculus overlaid on those concepts. Such students have had zero exposure to electricity and magnetism. So it's important to sequence the Physics C course knowing your students' background.

September and October: Do algebra-based electricity and magnetism exactly as covered in AP Physics 2. Emphasize conceptual understanding.

November through mid-January: Go through the Physics C mechanics curriculum, paying primary attention to the calculus applications.

Mid-January through March: Start from scratch with the Physics C—Electricity and Magnetism curriculum, reviewing material from the fall in context, and adding calculus applications.

April: Put it all together.

---

[1]The advice in this section is taken from the *Jacobs Physics* blog post from September 2017.

Why this sequence? Electricity and magnetism are some of the most abstract concepts covered in introductory physics. They're quite a change from Physics 1, where virtually every problem can be set up quantitatively, at tabletop scale, in any high school laboratory. It's worth spending a significant amount of time just defining and using the concepts of electric field, electric potential, capacitors, magnetic field, and induced EMF. Using calculus while these ideas are introduced adds an unnecessary distraction. Don't start with integrals and derivatives, which are conceptually opaque even to some of the best-performing high school math students.

Start with the concept of the electric field and the relationship $F = qE$. Get students thoroughly comfortable with the direction of an electric force and field, with putting an electric force on a free-body diagram. Then deal with electric potential and $PE = qV$. Get students relating the existence and direction of an electric force to the difference in electric potential, and using electrical potential energy in energy bar charts. Introduce capacitors as devices that store charge (according to $Q = CV$) and block current. Consider electric fields and potentials produced by parallel plates and point charges.

Go on to magnetic fields and forces, first teaching $F = qvB$ and $F = ILB$ and their associated right-hand rule. Consider how a current can produce a magnetic field. Finally, explain induced EMF and how to find the magnitude and direction of an induced current in a wire.

This is all AP Physics 2 stuff. You can find a wealth of released exam questions on these topics, both free response and multiple choice, from both AP Physics 2 and the old AP Physics B courses. Use them.

In about November, you can move on to mechanics. You're at a significant advantage by waiting this long to start true Physics C material. A number of your students will be taking calculus concurrently. I used to have to teach them how to evaluate basic integrals, while my colleagues in the math department cringed and gnashed their teeth. It's likely, though,

that by November, calculus classes have begun teaching integration, at least conceptually. Physics can follow and reinforce calculus class, rather than the other way around. And since your students are so well versed in mechanics concepts from their Physics 1 experience, they can focus on how calculus serves as a language expressing those concepts.

Waiting until November to cover the mechanics section solves another problem. If you start with mechanics, you give the impression that Physics C will be nothing but boring review, more of the same stuff from the first-year course. Then when you bring on the electricity, you'll face a rather hostile audience that has already settled into a cozy senior year routine. Start with the tough new stuff while your seniors are fresh and motivated.

Finally, when you come back to electricity and magnetism, those concepts have had time to percolate in your students' brains. Physics isn't mastered the first time students see it; it's mastered after the same ideas are seen in multiple contexts. The full-on Physics C E&M unit doubly reinforces previous work: Students revisit the concepts of field, potential, and so on that you introduced in the fall, but they also revisit the calculus language that you introduced with the mechanics unit.

So much for content sequencing; now what about assignment and test sequencing?

Assign test dates in advance, and do not change them for anything less than the apocalypse.

I'll talk in Step 4 about the enormous utility of tests, how a test is the only event for which you can be guaranteed to have the class's universal attention. It's therefore important to schedule tests carefully. By scheduling them ahead of time in stone, you can avoid as many conflicts as possible. Don't schedule a test the Monday after the Super Bowl or the Friday before prom. But there's also no reason to postpone a test, other than the cancellation of school.

I discourage frequent "unit tests." Instead, I schedule a test once a month. Whatever you've covered from the first day of class up to the test date goes on the test. Students and parents will no doubt complain that such infrequent testing makes each test "high stakes." Good! That's kind of the point. The AP exam is a one-shot opportunity to earn college credit. By the time the AP exam happens, your students will have had experience with eight or so high-stakes practice tests, making the AP exam itself no big deal.

Don't expect students to do more than one or two problems each night.

If you assign too much homework, it won't be done right and therefore will be worse than useless to your students' progress. This doesn't mean you have to assign work due every class meeting, though. As long as students are accountable for doing thorough work, you can have problems due every other day or even once a week.

Let's say your overall plan involves 15 class days of work on kinematics. That means you can assign only 15 to 20 problems on kinematics. Better make 'em good!

So what makes a problem "good," anyway?

Homework problems should be similar in level and style to AP problems. Then when it's time for the real exam, everyone has the experience to know instinctively when they're overthinking or oversimplifying a question. Because you assign only one of these good problems per night, students can reasonably be expected to present a thorough, annotated solution rather than just "$3/2 = 1.5$ m/s/s."

You might be tempted to assign a bunch of straightforward plug-and-chug problems, such as "What is the acceleration of a 2 kg object experiencing a 3 N net force?" Perhaps you want students to gain experience solving new equations; perhaps you want your weaker students to build confidence. Nevertheless, assigning such problems is harmful, not helpful. Weak students develop a *false* sense

of confidence—since they can do the baby problems, they reason, they can do some physics, so there's no need to work too much on those other problems. And even worse, the good students develop an unhealthy antipathy toward homework problems. Plug-and-chug problems, to most students, fall into the category of "busywork," homework for the sake of giving homework rather than for serious practice. So the good students tune out *all* the homework, assuming everything to be busywork.

Conversely, you might be tempted to challenge your top students by assigning some really tough, involved problems that are beyond the level of the AP exam. Don't! It's easy to think that those top students will enjoy the challenge—because *you* like a good challenge—but more likely they'll resent the burden of the additional work. And for the rest of the class, even one problem beyond the level of the AP exam frustrates them, making them doubt their own skill. Their learned hopelessness means they are likely to assume that an AP exam problem is beyond them, even when it's not.

How do I know what's AP-level?

When you have a chance, read and solve some of the official College Board–released AP Physics C items. The Physics C courses have been essentially unchanged since the late 1970s! Use AP Classroom to get authentic items. Then read the practice problems and the practice tests in the *5 Steps* book. They should give you an idea of the style and level of descriptive response questions your students will need to be prepared for. (Multiple-choice problems are perfectly good in- and out-of-class assignments, as long as you demand that students justify their answer.)

Once the class starts, don't pull punches, especially to students who have reached a bit to be in the AP course. While I and the College Board encourage you to initially accept any student who is willing to do the work into your AP Physics C course, such an approach can turn into a disaster if students at the weaker end expect the class to slow down for them, or if they expect a route to high grades that doesn't involve performance on tests. The meaning of the AP grade—the 5, 4, 3, 2, 1 scale—is that it represents approximately an A, B, C, D, F in the equivalent college course. If someone is earning straight 1s on his tests, he should be getting D's or F's, not B's. Ideally, though, I recommend counseling such students into a lower-level physics course once it's clear that they have little possibility of passing.[2]

What should I assign as summer work?

Nothing. Summer work is a terrible idea. First of all, when does it get done? The night before class starts. What can be accomplished? Not much. You really want your students trying to learn about Gauss's law without your guidance?

_____

[2]On this point many people disagree with me. The College Board will tell you that a student who gets a 1 on the AP exam still has gained valuable experience that will be useful to them in college. I say, why would you allow an overmatched batter to hurt the team and his own confidence by hitting .100 all year, when you could have put him on JV where he would have hit .300 and been a star? I've had many, many students throughout the decades who couldn't handle AP Physics the first time they saw it, but did well in a general course and then subsequently performed brilliantly in AP or actual college physics.

The worst part of the summer assignment is that it sets you up for a worthless confrontation. In all their other AP courses your students have summer assignments, most of which are far more integral to the course than anything you can do for summer physics. Therefore, most will show up resentful at having to do your work on top of everything else, and some will show up without the work at all. Now you have to make a decision: do you ignore their failure, perhaps just giving them a slap on the wrist? That sends the message that you don't _really_ care whether your students do the assigned work, meaning you've got a huge fight on your hands to get the class to take their problem sets seriously. Or do you bring the hammer down on the lazy bums who didn't do the summer work, giving them a horrible grade out of the gate? That would present yourself in the most hostile way possible on the first day of class. Why not save that battle for the regularly scheduled problem sets, which are crucial to developing an understanding of the active course material?

AP PHYSICS C—MECHANICS OUTLINE FROM THE COLLEGE BOARD'S CED

TOPICS	APPROXIMATE PERCENTAGE OF EXAM QUESTIONS	_5 STEPS TO A 5_
Unit 1: Kinematics	16%	Chapter 9 pp. 81–93
Unit 2: Force	20%	Chapter 10 (pp. 94–105) and the portion of Chapter 13 on circular motion (pp. 125–134)
Unit 3: Work/Energy	15%	Chapter 12 pp. 114–124
Unit 4: Linear Momentum	15%	Chapter 11 pp. 106–113
Unit 5: Rotation	16%	Chapter 14 pp. 135–148
Unit 6: Oscillations	10%	Chapter 15 pp. 149–157
Unit 7: Gravitation	10%	Chapter 13 pp. 125–134

AP PHYSICS C—E&M OUTLINE FROM THE COLLEGE BOARD'S CED

TOPICS	APPROXIMATE PERCENTAGE OF EXAM QUESTIONS	*5 STEPS TO A 5*
Unit 1: Electrostatics	30%	Chapter 16 pp. 158–173
Unit 2: Capacitors and Connectors	15%	Chapter 17 pp. 174–194
Unit 3: Circuits	20%	Chapter 17 pp. 174–194
Unit 4: Magnetic Fields	20%	Chapter 18 pp. 195–212
Unit 5: Electromagnetism	16%	Chapter 18 pp. 195–212

The preceding charts correlate the College Board's CED units and exam percentage goals to the chapters in this book.

Step 2: Hold an Interesting Class Every Day

Most class days in an AP physics course include some mix of this broad categorization of activities:

▶ You presenting material to the class
▶ Lab work
▶ Independent/group work
▶ Quizzes
▶ Tests

There's no way to plan each class to the minute before the school year starts. But you certainly can decide how you want to distribute these activities over a typical week.

Give a short quiz every day.

While students don't listen to you—that's OK, they don't listen to me, either—they without question pay attention to quiz questions. Therefore, if there's a point you want to make about a common mistake on the homework, don't talk to the class about it; ask a pointed question about it on a daily quiz.

Quizzes can take any format you want. A colleague convinced me to use short-answer questions that can be either straight fact recall (The slope of a velocity-time graph is _____) or a bit more open-ended (On the homework problem for today,

why was the normal force greater than the cart's weight?). Multiple-choice questions have the advantage of quick and easy grading. A quiz could be word-for-word from a homework problem, thus ensuring that students didn't just copy their friend's or an online solution. Or better yet, you could change the situation from the homework slightly by making the cart heavier or doubling its initial speed.

However the daily quiz is structured, it's worth doing. It serves a multitude of purposes:

▶ Any issues of students arriving late will vanish after a few daily quizzes. Not in your seat when the bell rings? I'm not mad at you, you're not in trouble, you just don't get to take the quiz. Without confrontation or rancor I've bought five extra minutes per class period.

▶ The quiz provides a few quiet minutes for me to collect each student's homework individually from them at their seat. I can find out immediately if someone is unprepared, without interrupting the flow of the class. I can also deal with the unprepared student immediately. Everyone knows they can't hide missing homework.

▶ Going over the quiz as soon as it's over is as good a content review as you can find. Students care deeply about the answers, so they're willing to listen and engage in a way that wouldn't happen if you just said, "Let's go over homework problem 1."

▶ Try having students grade each other's quizzes. [3] Then each student is paying double attention to the answers—they're listening to see whether *they* got the answer right, *and* they're listening to see whether the paper they're grading should be marked right or wrong.

Sure, you might have to deal with some drama-mongering colleagues breathlessly wondering how you could be so cruel to your class as to give so many quizzes. Your response is to wonder in return, why must a quiz be considered cruel? Is the football coach cruel because he has the team play football during practice? Is the soccer coach cruel because she runs a 15-minute scrimmage at the end of each practice? So what's the problem with having students practice responding to physics questions every day? Isn't that exactly what we're *supposed* to be doing in a physics class? Keep giving your quizzes, and the complaints will become vanishing whispers in the wind.

It's fine to use "1960s equipment" for laboratory exercises.

While I recommend using whatever technology you can lay your hands on for demonstrations, for lab work I think it's perfectly reasonable to minimize technology.

The whole point of lab work is for students to get their hands dirty with experimental physics, to help them learn to be creative and rigorous in making direct measurements of physical quantities. If everything in lab is a preset app on a smartphone that automatically calculates whatever the students are measuring, much of that creativity is lost.

Perhaps you have enough motion detectors or magnetic field sensors to give one setup to each group. Perhaps you have a class set of iPads with video analysis software. That's awesome. But if you don't, that's fine, too. You can do all sorts of AP Physics C experiments using only equipment that was available in 1960: masses, carts, stopwatches, pulleys, compasses, batteries, resistors,

metersticks, spring scales, and so on. Just pick an equation from your text for which you can make direct measurements of two of the variables. Have the students measure and graph those variables, and you have created a laboratory exercise.

Are there other ways to do lab work? Sure. One different approach would be to pick one homework problem each week for which you have sufficient equipment for everyone to set it up live in class, just as you might set up a quantitative demonstration. Making the explicit link between problem solving and lab work is always a good idea if you can do it. Some teachers like to set up "stations," in which students are asked to make quick measurements of some quantity. After 20 minutes, students rotate to a new station, which uses similar equipment to ask for a different measurement. Any exercises that require your students to manipulate equipment with some degree of creativity work as AP Physics labs.

Make all graphs by hand. Never, ever use a graphical analysis program.

Many students will certainly kvetch about making graphs by hand. "That's what Excel is for," they'll say. "You're just making me do busywork." No, not the case. How many of your students have ever had to take a piece of graph paper, create their own scales for the axes, plot the points, draw a best-fit, and take the slope with no aid other than a ruler and calculator? Probably none. Yet the AP exam expects students to do just that process and to do it as just a small part of a 15-minute free-response problem.

Graphing by hand every week in lab not only gives your students practice to do well on the exam, it gives them visceral experience with analysis. For example, early on, students might try to record data from a voltmeter to four-figure precision. I don't object, I let them . . . because when they try to put that data on the graph, they realize for themselves that 4.318 volts looks exactly the same as 4.3 volts, but different from 4 volt. Or as they graph by hand, they see what looks like a linear pattern develop, but then they see for themselves that larger angles cause the graph to flatten. Later in the course, students will recognize for themselves how to collect data over

---

[3]This will work even if the quizzes themselves count minimally or not at all to the students' course grades.

an entire range of interest. But that recognition doesn't happen so easily if the computer just magically spits out a picture.

Dive into real physics from the first moment of the first day of class.

Within 10 minutes of arrival, I'm doing physics with both problem solving and experimentation. It's likely I'm introducing circuits and Ohm's law with measurements of current and voltage. Then by the second day, we've moved on to independent lab exercises setting up circuits with series and parallel resistors.

What about reading the syllabus, discussing grading policies, and describing class rules? I don't understand the thought behind even having "class rules." Your students may not be adults in the eyes of the law, but if you want a relaxed, cooperative atmosphere in class, you absolutely must treat your students like adults. When adults come together for, say, a business conference or a national meeting, the event doesn't start with an authority figure reading a list of things that the attendees can and can't do. How would *you* react to such a start to a conference? I know I'd be thinking right away about how I could passive-aggressively stick it to the person trying to tell me what to do.

You see what I mean. Your students are generally upperclassmen, and good-student upperclassmen at that. They have plenty of experience taking high school classes. They can read, so give them the syllabus with a brief summary of grading policies and tell 'em to read it. Going over the syllabus and rules begs for an argument and leaves the students trying to figure out how to game their grade based on the rules you laid out. But doing physics leaves the students saying, "Cool," and asking questions like "Wait, doesn't the block also apply a force to the table?"

If nothing else, you know darned well that virtually every other teacher at your school is using the first day of class to read the syllabus and discuss policies. You will have an especially enthusiastic audience if you're the only teacher doing something active and content-related on the first day of school.

Step 3: Evaluate Your Students' Progress

I'm a strong advocate of a "less is more" approach to teaching physics. You don't have to assign enormous amounts of work, you don't have to give tests every week, you don't have to assign any reading at all. One problem per night, a short quiz every day or two, and a test every month should be easily sufficient for your students to make appropriate progress. For one thing, such a small amount of assigned work will buy you a good bit of political capital, making students willing to work harder and without complaint. Even though the one problem each night requires a full page of presentation to answer three or four parts, students will compare their assignment favorably to math class's "do problems 1–51 odd." They will be pleased that your expectations seem to them reasonable in scope (i.e., 20–40 minutes per night rather than the hours expected in other AP classes) and productive in nature (i.e., not perceived as "busywork").

The more important reason to use a "less is more" philosophy is that by keeping the *amount* of work minimal, you can expect that work to be utterly brilliant.

Demand that homework problems be presented, not merely answered.

A homework problem in physics is far more similar to writing a paragraph for English class, or even to an assignment for AP Studio Art, than to solving a math problem. It's not good enough to get the right answer or even just to show your work; a well-presented problem should provide an annotated, reasoned solution. The explanation of the reasoning behind the answer is more important than the answer itself.

Imagine an English teacher assigns a paper: discuss, using textual evidence, the complexities of the relationship between Romeo and Juliet. Someone writes, as their entire paper, "He loved her." How well did this student meet their teacher's expectations? What grade is this student going to get? They'll complain, perhaps, that they don't deserve an F—because *their answer is exactly right.*

You may think I'm arguing *ab absurdum*, but have you not seen "solutions" to physics problems along these lines? A student whose answer to a physics problem is "$F = ma$, $30/6 = 5$ m/s/s" has in no way engaged with the problem, any more than "He loves her" has engaged with Shakespeare. You have every right, nay, every responsibility, to require more.

Another basic rule of teaching: Trust, but verify.

Grading practice problems doesn't have to be a detailed process. Scores of some sort on practice problems must exist; otherwise, "less is more" devolves into just "less." First, know that this feedback doesn't have to count as a significant part of the final course grade. I've had good success for a while putting a score on the problems, calling in the students who get less than about 50 percent of the points for a required extra help session to correct their mistakes. I'm transparent that homework or in-class work will not bring down the overall course grade unless either they don't do the problems to begin with or they don't show up to redo the problems the right way when asked.

Note that the score you write doesn't have to be the result of a long, careful, rigorous process. Ideally, you're grading student work every couple of days. Unless you have no life beyond school, you must find a way to grade a stack of problems quickly.

Start by recognizing that there's little point in writing more than a word or two on anyone's problem set. The students almost definitely won't read what you're writing, at least not carefully. Your time is valuable; don't use it in noble yet fruitless endeavors.

I recommend grading work holistically. That means, look at the solution as a whole. Did the student apply the correct physics principle? Did they explain the important or tricky parts of the solution? Is their answer right? Is a conceptual portion of the problem justified with a fact, equation, or calculation, and is that justification clear and correct? Does the solution include words, equations, diagrams, and numbers?

If you answered "yes" to all of these, give the assignment full credit. If you have doubts about some of these issues, give the problem partial credit—exactly how much doesn't really matter. And if pretty much none of the questions can be answered in the affirmative, don't give the problem much credit at all.

But won't the students argue about my grading? At the beginning of the year, probably they will. So what. *Don't engage* in a discussion about homework grades, especially during class. Answer any question about physics principles carefully and enthusiastically. But as soon as anyone asks about "points," stop talking and move on to something related to physics. Your students will quickly come to the realization that a point on one night's problem set, like a teensy drop of gasoline that didn't quite make it into the tank, is negligible and thus not worth worrying about. Especially once they realize that you won't even argue, they'll just drop the issue and move on.

Treat tests as the best teaching tool ever invented.

Because your students care so much about their test grades, milk the test for all it's worth to firm up students' physics ability. The test can be visited and revisited at least three times: once on the test itself, once when students do corrections on the problems they missed, and once more when you ask targeted quiz questions about issues with which the class struggled. The process of giving and debriefing a test can be compared to a football team's treatment of a regular-season game. Perform on game day; then, win or lose, deconstruct what went right or wrong so that the next game is even better.

Start with an authentic test. Ideally, a test is in identical style and format to the AP exam itself. That means students are given about one minute per multiple-choice item, and one minute per point on the free-response items. That means few if any questions that ask merely for a one-step calculation and certainly no questions at all like "Write the equation for net force in terms of acceleration."

Use the items released by the College Board (on AP classroom); use the questions in the *5 Steps* book's practice exam, and some of those at the end of the chapters. Be careful about other test question sources, though. While every test has a few hard questions and a few easy questions, be sure that your tests mix difficulty levels so that the overall test is consistent with what you see in official released exams.

Make the test as long and broad as time allows. I use my extended lab period for testing once a month. This allows me to give nearly a full-length mechanics or E&M exam (or a combination thereof). If you don't have that kind of time available, try giving the multiple-choice section on one day, with the free-response following on the next day. The longer the test, the better the students will do—they're more likely to find questions they can answer on a long test; one question that confuses a student will have a smaller impact on a longer test.

Make the test cumulative, covering *all* material you've covered this year. Otherwise, you give your class an excuse to forget or ignore old topics. Testing on only the current unit sends the message that the previous unit isn't important anymore, and then that attitude will bite your class when they prepare for the exam in April. When every test has several questions from previous topics as well as some free-response questions that integrate techniques from multiple topics, your students will spread their review time over the course of the year rather than trying to cram their review into an all-nighter on May 5.

Never, ever, allow students to ask questions on a test.

Every year when I grade AP exams I see students writing diatribes about how they don't understand the question, or that the question is unfair, or the sort of complaint that's generally accompanied by frustrated anger. Presumably these students have been in an AP class all year. So they can't answer one of the questions; why the hostility?

It's likely such students are not used to a testing situation without their teacher to rely on for guidance. Watch a colleague give a test in math or science class. How many times do you see students get stuck on a problem and *instantly* come to the teacher's desk to ask for help? Sure, a lot of the time the teacher might say something innocuous like "Why don't you read the question again?" which gets the student unstuck so they can make progress on the test. I agree that such

a teacher is not being unethical or dishonest in their testing. But that teacher *is* doing their students a tremendous disservice.[4]

When the AP exam presents a new and challenging situation, your students will not be able to ask you—or anyone—a question to point them in the right direction. They will be on their own. They need practice in figuring out problems on their own. If students haven't had such practice, if they've always had the teacher show them how to start difficult problems on their in-class tests, then it's no wonder they get upset when their training wheels are yanked away on the biggest test of the year. And even if you never truly gave useful hints, just the fact that they cannot come to a teacher's desk to ask for "clarification" of a question will throw your students for a loop.

Prepare your students ahead of time for your no-questions-on-tests policy. A day or two before the test, go over testing procedures with the students. Pass out the cover sheet on which is written the number of questions and the time for each section, and the AP table of information. Then explain: "Unless you are missing a page, you may not ask a question during the test. No exceptions."

But think why students ask questions. It's not true that most are desperately hoping you'll give them the answer. Most are genuinely confused, and when a smart student is confused, they quite reasonably assume that the issue is with the test question itself, not with her understanding. So the student comes to your desk to ask something like, "You didn't tell us the mass of the cart, shouldn't you do that, please?"

Well, as a physics teacher, you know that this student is missing something important. Either the mass isn't necessary to solve the problem, or perhaps the mass can be calculated or estimated through some indirect method. But no matter

[4]And the teacher who actually does help, who talks the student through the problem, has in my mind breached testing decorum. That's comparable to a referee helping a quarterback read the defense: "Now, son, you know they haven't covered your tight end the past three plays. You might want to throw to him." How would you feel about that referee?

what your response, by allowing that student to ask the question, you have defeated the point of the test question. Even saying "I think you can solve this problem" implies to the student—*and to the rest of the class*—that the mass isn't important. That's for the students to figure out for themselves, not for them to hear from you!

And it's an unfortunate fact that every other time she's challenged a test question in the past decade of school, her teacher's answer has been something like, "Oh, sorry, that question has a major typo."

So ahead of time, you must give your students a strategy for when they think a problem is misstated. "While you *may not* ask me a question during the test, you may write anything you like on the test. If you think you need more information to solve a problem, tell me so—make up the information and solve. If you think a multiple-choice item doesn't include the right answer or is ambiguous, write that down. When the test is over, I'll look at what you've written. Chances are, you're missing something; writing down your concern and moving on is the best approach to getting as much credit as possible. However, in the unlikely event that the question is poorly phrased, I will look at what you wrote and consider how to award credit fairly."

Proofread your tests rigorously. When you test, you're entering into a covenant with your students. They must, without help from you or their classmates, show you what they know so you can evaluate their physics knowledge. But in turn, *you* must write a test that fairly and clearly allows them to demonstrate that knowledge. If after every test you have to explain "Yeah, number 4 wasn't stated clearly, I meant find the speed of cart A but I said find the speed of cart B," then you'll lose your class's confidence.

Sure, mistakes happen. They've happened on the real AP exam; several released exams say "number 67 was not scored" or "since the problem as stated was not clear on this issue, either of two answers earned credit." If you screw up a question, be fair about it. Award credit for any reasonable approach, or just throw out a bad multiple-choice question. When you return the test, make sure your students know what happened and how you're dealing with it. But if you have to correct

a mistake more than once or twice in a year, you are not proofreading carefully enough.

Stick to your guns when they try to ask you questions anyway. I will bet my life savings[5] that no matter how well you prepare your students for your first test, one of them will get up and try to ask you a question. "I know I can't ask questions, but . . ." he'll say. *Cut him off.*

"Mr. Jones, are you missing a page? Did the copy machine mess up? Then what the heck are you doing up here, interrupting the rest of the class as they try to concentrate? Sit down, please, and consider apologizing to the class later for your disturbance."

It's worth fighting this battle. Once everyone realizes that they can't just go to you for hints, they will settle down and do great work. By the second test, you will be able to get enormous amounts of your own work done during a test. You can have colleagues or substitutes give tests on days you have to be gone. Most important, when it comes time for the real AP exam, your students will have the requisite confidence to deal with difficult and unusual problems, even though no help from the proctor is available.

How do I assign test grades?

I'm frequently asked how to "convert" an AP-style test to a standard high school grading scale. Generally, it takes about 65 percent of available points to get a 5, 50 percent to get a 4, 35 percent to get a 3, 25 percent to get a 2. But a typical school scale tells us that 90 percent is an A, 80 percent is a B.

I'll tell you how I make the conversion. However, my method is not gospel; you need to be creative within the parameters of your class, your school, your personality.

When students first get their tests back, they see a grading sheet exactly like the one on page 215 of the *5 Steps* book. You see the range of raw scores necessary to earn each AP score listed at the bottom. I circle the AP score of 5, 4, 3, 2, or 1. That's the first step toward building back confidence; everyone who thought they "failed"

---

5 $134.95